AF324608

ARTIFICIAL NEURAL NETWORKS - MODELS AND APPLICATIONS

Edited by **João Luís G. Rosa**

Artificial Neural Networks - Models and Applications

http://dx.doi.org/10.5772/61493
Edited by João Luís G. Rosa

Contributors

Hayrettin Okut, José Manuel Ortiz-Rodríguez, Luis Octavio Solís-Sánchez, Maria Del Rosario Martinéz-Blanco, Victor Hugo Castañeda-Miranda, Gerardo Ornelas-Vargas, Hector Alonso Guerrero-Osuna, Jose Maria Celaya-Padilla, Hector Rene Vega-Carrillo, Margarita Martinez-Fierro, Idalia Garza-Veloz, Rodrigo Castañeda-Miranda, Jorge Isaac Galvan-Tejada, Carlos Eric Galvan-Tejada, Celina Lizeth Castañeda-Miranda, Mohamad Mostafa, Giuseppe Oliveri, Werner Teich, Jürgen Lindner, Dongsheng Guo, Laicheng Yan, Yunong Zhang, Igor Loboda, Halil İbrahim Çelik, Lale Canan Dülger, Mehmet Topalbekiroğlu, Xiukai Ruan, Yanhua Tan, Xiaojing Shi, Qibo Cai, Guihua Cui, Chang Li, Yuxing Dai, Han Li, Liming Li, Dameng Dai, Waylon Gene Collins, Philippe Tissot, Daniel Dunea, Stefania Felicia Iordache, Oana Geman, Ovidiu-Andrei Schipor, Iuliana Chiuchisan, Mihai Covasa, Zbigniew Piotr Szadkowski, Dariusz Głas, Krzysztof Pytel, Emanuele Santi, Maosen Cao, Lixia Pan, Nizar Faisal Alkayem, Jie Zhang, Junliang Wang, Wei Qin, Luis Josue Ricalde Castellanos, Oscar May

CBS, Edition **2017**

Published by InTech

Janeza Trdine 9, 51000 Rijeka, Croatia

The moral rights of the editor(s) and the author(s) have been asserted.
All rights to the book as a whole are reserved by InTech. The book as a whole (compilation) cannot be reproduced, distributed or used for commercial or non-commercial purposes without InTech's written permission.
Enquiries concerning the use of the book should be directed to InTech's rights and permissions department (permissions@intechopen.com).
Violations are liable to prosecution under the governing Copyright Law.
© The Editor(s) and the Author(s) 2016

Individual chapters of this publication are distributed under the terms of the Creative Commons Attribution 3.0 Unported License which permits commercial use, distribution and reproduction of the individual chapters, provided the original author(s) and source publication are appropriately acknowledged. More details and guidelines concerning content reuse and adaptation can be found at http://www.intechopen.com/copyright-policy.html.

Notice

Statements and opinions expressed in the chapters are these of the individual contributors and not necessarily those of the editors or publisher. No responsibility is accepted for the accuracy of information contained in the published chapters. The publisher assumes no responsibility for any damage or injury to persons or property arising out of the use of any materials, instructions, methods or ideas contained in the book.

Publishing Process Manager Ana Simcic

Technical Editor SPi Global

Cover Designer InTech Design Team

Additional hard copies can be obtained from orders@intechopen.com

Artificial Neural Networks - Models and Applications, Edited by João Luís G. Rosa
p. cm.
Print ISBN 978-953-51-2704-8
Online ISBN 978-953-51-2705-5

Contents

Preface

The human brain is a natural model for building intelligent machines. An obvious idea for Artificial Intelligence is to simulate the brain into a computer. Learning in complex network representations is one of the most current topics in science, which promises great applications in computer science, neurobiology, psychology, and physics. A neural network is a computational model that shares some of the properties of the brain: it consists of many simple units working in parallel without any central control, connected by lines of communication. The connections between the units have numerical weights that can be modified by learning.

The neural network is a dynamic system, moving from one state to the next. As such, it has a mathematical rule that governs this movement. An infinite number of such rules is possible. However, we usually want to limit the models to influence the activation of a given node based only on the activation of the nodes connected to it and the weights of the connections to these nodes. Many criticisms of the connectionist model come from the fact that this approach is biologically impoverished. To enable the computer implementation, we simplify the model.

Neural networks are not explicitly programmed as conventional computers. In other words, they obey to laws, or rules, such as a physical system. You should program a conventional computer, but a neural network is simply conducted. The designers of neural networks see this as an advantage, since it provides a mechanism through which intelligence can arise from physical law.

Currently there has been a growing interest in the use of neural network models, also known as connectionist models. They are applicable to many complex problems.

This book presents some up-to-date models and several recent applications of artificial neural networks and brings to the reader chapters dealing with architectures or models of artificial neural networks, as well as various applications in various fields of knowledge. The researcher or student interested in this machine learning tool will certainly be excited about the presented models and applications, ranging from assisted speech therapy to gas turbine diagnosis, from thunderstorm prediction to urban contamination by air pollution. Enjoy your reading!

João Luís G. Rosa, Ph.D.
University of São Paulo
São Carlos, São Paulo, Brazil

Models

Chapter 1

Zhang Neural Networks for Online Solution of Time-Varying Linear Inequalities

Dongsheng Guo, Laicheng Yan and Yunong Zhang

Additional information is available at the end of the chapter

http://dx.doi.org/10.5772/62732

Abstract

In this chapter, a special type of recurrent neural networks termed "Zhang neural network" (ZNN) is presented and studied for online solution of time-varying linear (matrix-vector and matrix) inequalities. Specifically, focusing on solving the time-varying linear matrix-vector inequality (LMVI), we develop and investigate two different ZNN models based on two different Zhang functions (ZFs). Then, being an extension, by defining another two different ZFs, another two ZNN models are developed and investigated to solve the time-varying linear matrix inequality (LMI). For such ZNN models, theoretical results and analyses are presented as well to show their computational performances. Simulation results with two illustrative examples further substantiate the efficacy of the presented ZNN models for time-varying LMVI and LMI solving.

Keywords: Zhang neural network (ZNN), Zhang function (ZF), time-varying linear inequalities, design formulas, theoretical results

1. Introduction

In recent years, linear inequalities have played a more and more important role in numerous fields of science and engineering applications [1–9], such as obstacle avoidance of redundant robots [1, 2], robustness analysis of neural networks [3] and stability analysis of fuzzy control systems [5]. They, including linear matrix-vector inequality (LMVI) and linear matrix inequality (LMI), have now been considered as a powerful formulation and design technique

© 2016 The Author(s). Licensee InTech. This chapter is distributed under the terms of the Creative Commons Attribution License (http://creativecommons.org/licenses/by/3.0), which permits unrestricted use, distribution, and reproduction in any medium, provided the original work is properly cited.

for solving a variety of problems [7–11]. Due to their important roles, lots of numerical algorithms and neural networks have been presented and studied for online solution of linear inequalities [7–17]. For example, an iterative method was presented by Yang *et al.* for linear inequalities solving [12]. In [13], three continuous-time neural networks were developed by Cichocki and Bargiela to solve the system of linear inequalities. Besides, a gradient-based neural network and a simplified neural network were investigated respectively in [10] and [11] for solving a class of LMI problems (e.g., Lyapunov matrix inequalities and algebraic Riccati matrix inequalities).

It is worth pointing out that most of the reported approaches are designed intrinsically to solve the time-invariant (or say, static) linear inequalities. In view of the fact that many systems in science and engineering applications are time-varying, the resultant linear inequalities may be time-varying ones (i.e., the coefficients are time-varying). Generally speaking, to solve a time-varying problem, based on the assumption of the short-time invariance, such a time-varying problem can be treated as a time-invariant problem within a small time period [8]. The corresponding approaches (e.g., numerical algorithms and neural networks) are thus designed for solving the problem at each single time instant. Note that, as for this common way used to solve the time-varying problem, the time-derivative information (or say, the change trend) of the time-varying coefficients is not involved. Due to the lack of the consideration of such an important information, the aforementioned approaches may be less effective, when they are exploited directly to solve time-varying problems [7–9, 17–19].

Aiming at solving time-varying problems (e.g., time-varying matrix inversion and time-varying quadratic program), a special type of recurrent neural networks termed Zhang neural network (ZNN) has been formally proposed by Zhang *et al.* since March 2001 [7–9, 17–21]. According to Zhang *et al.*'s design method, the design of a ZNN is based on an indefinite Zhang function (ZF), with the word "indefinite" meaning that such a ZF can be positive, zero, negative or even lower-unbounded. By exploiting methodologically the time-derivative information of time-varying coefficients involved in the time-varying problems, the resultant ZNN models can thus solve the time-varying problems effectively and efficiently (in terms of avoiding the lagging errors generated by the conventional approaches) [18, 19]. For better understanding and to lay a basis for further investigation, the concepts of ZNN and ZF [18] are presented as follows.

Concept 1. Being a special type of recurrent neural networks, Zhang neural network (ZNN) has been developed and studied since 2001. It originates from the research of Hopfield-type neural networks and is a systematic approach for time-varying problems solving. Such a ZNN is different from the conventional gradient neural network(s) in terms of the problem to be solved, indefinite error function, exponent-type design formula, dynamic equation, and the utilization of time-derivative information.

Concept 2. Zhang function (ZF) is the design basis of ZNN. It differs from the common error/ energy functions in the study of conventional approaches. Specifically, compared with the conventional norm-based scalar-valued positive or at least lower-bounded energy function, ZF can be bounded, unbounded or even lower-unbounded (in a word, indefinite). Besides, corresponding to a vector- or matrix-valued problem to be solved, ZF can be vector- or matrix-valued to monitor the solving process fully.

In this chapter, focusing on time-varying linear (matrix-vector and matrix) inequalities solving, we present four different ZNN models based on four different ZFs. Specifically, by defining the first two different ZFs, the corresponding two ZNN models are developed and investigated for solving the time-varying LMVI. Then, being an extension, by defining another two different ZFs, another two ZNN models are developed and investigated to solve the time-varying LMI. For such ZNN models, theoretical results and analyses are also presented to show their computational performances. Simulation results with two illustrative examples further substantiate the efficacy of the presented ZNN models for time-varying LMVI and LMI solving.

2. Preliminaries

As mentioned in Concept 2, the ZF is the design basis for deriving ZNN models to solve time-varying LMVI and LMI. Thus, for presentation convenience, in this chapter, the ZF is denoted by $E(t)$ with $\dot{E}(t)$ being the time derivative of $E(t)$. Based on the ZF, the design procedure of a ZNN model for time-varying LMVI/LMI solving is presented as follows [18, 19].

1. Firstly, an indefinite ZF is defined as the error-monitoring function to monitor the solving process of time-varying LMVI/LMI.

2. Secondly, to force the ZF (i.e., $E(t)$) converge to zero, we choose its time derivative (i.e., $\dot{E}(t)$) via the ZNN design formula (including its variant).

3. Finally, by expanding the ZNN design formula, the dynamic equation of a ZNN model is thus established for time-varying LMVI/LMI solving.

In order to derive different ZNN models to solve time-varying LMVI and LMI, the following two design formulas (being an important part in the above ZNN design procedure) are exploited in this chapter [7–9, 17–21]:

$$\dot{E}(t) = -\gamma \mathcal{F}(E(t)), \tag{1}$$

$$\dot{E}(t) = -\gamma \mathrm{SGN}(E_0) \odot \mathcal{F}(E(t)), \tag{2}$$

where $\gamma > 0 \in R$, being the reciprocal of a capacitance parameter, is used to scale the convergence rate of the solution, and $\mathcal{F}(\cdot)$ denotes the activation-function array. Note that, in general, design parameter γ should be set as large as the hardware system would permit, or selected appropriately for simulation purposes [22]. In addition, function $f(\cdot)$, being a processing element of $\mathcal{F}(\cdot)$, can be any monotonically increasing odd activation function, e.g., the linear, power-sigmoid and hyperbolic-sine activation functions [19, 23]. Furthermore, $E_0 = E(t = 0)$

denotes the initial error, and the unipolar signum function $\text{sgn}(\cdot)$, being an element of $\text{SGN}(\cdot)$, is defined as

$$\text{sgn}(c) = \begin{cases} 1, & \text{if } c > 0, \\ 0, & \text{if } c \le 0. \end{cases}$$

Besides, the multiplication operator $\odot$ is the Hadamard product [24] and is defined as follows:

$$U \odot V = \begin{bmatrix} u_{11}v_{11} & u_{12}v_{12} & \cdots & u_{1n}v_{1n} \\ u_{21}v_{21} & u_{22}v_{22} & \cdots & u_{2n}v_{2n} \\ \vdots & \vdots & \ddots & \vdots \\ u_{m1}v_{m1} & u_{m2}w_{m2} & \cdots & u_{mn}v_{mn} \end{bmatrix} \in R^{m \times n}.$$

Note that, as for the presented design formulas (1) and (2), the former is the original ZNN design formula proposed by Zhang *et al.* to solve the time-varying Sylvester equation [20], while the latter is the variant of such a ZNN design formula constructed elaborately for time-varying linear inequalities solving [9]. Thus, for presentation convenience and better understanding, (1) is called the original design formula, while (2) is called the variant design formula for time-varying LMVI and LMI solving in this chapter.

Remark 1. For the variant design formula (2), when the initial error $E_0 > 0$, it reduces to $\dot{E}(t) = -\gamma \mathcal{F}(E(t))$, which is exactly the original design formula (1) for various time-varying problems solving [17–21]. In this case (i.e., $\dot{E}(t) = -\gamma \mathcal{F}(E(t))$), different convergence performances of $E(t)$ can be achieved by choosing different activation function arrays [17–21, 23]. For example, (2) reduces to $\dot{E}(t) = -\gamma E(t)$ with a linear activation function array used and with $E_0 > 0$. Evidently, its analytical solution is $E(t) = \exp(-\gamma t)E_0$, which means that $E(t)$ is globally and exponentially convergent to zero with rate γ. By following the previous successful researches [17–21, 23], superior convergence property of $E(t)$ can be achieved by exploiting nonlinear activation functions, e.g., the power-sigmoid and hyperbolic-sine activation functions [23]. In addition, the convergence property can be further improved by increasing the γ value. Therefore, in the case of $E_0 > 0$, the global and exponential convergence property is guaranteed for $E(t)$. Note that, in the case of $E_0 \le 0$, (2) reduces to $\dot{E}(t) = 0$, meaning that $E(t) = E_0$ as time t evolves. In this situation, there is no need to investigate the convergence performance of $E(t)$ with the different activation function arrays and different γ values used.

According to the presented design formulas (1) and (2), by defining different ZFs (i.e., $E(t)$ with different formulations), different ZNN models are thus developed and investigated for time-varying LMVI and LMI solving.

3. Time-varying linear matrix-vector inequality

In this section, we introduce two different ZFs and develop the resultant ZNN models for time-varying linear matrix-vector inequality (LMVI) solving. Then, theoretical results and analyses are provided to show the computational performances of such two ZNN models.

Specifically, the following problem of time-varying LMVI [7, 9] is considered in this chapter:

$$A(t)x(t) \leq b(t), \tag{3}$$

in which $A(t) \in R^{n \times n}$ and $b(t) \in R^{n}$ are smoothly time-varying matrix and vector, respectively. In addition, $x(t) \in R^{n}$ is the unknown time-varying vector to be obtained. The objective is to find a feasible solution $x(t)$ such that (3) holds true for any time instant $t \geq 0$. Note that, for further discussion, $A(t)$ is assumed to be nonsingular at any time instant $t \in [0, +\infty]$ in this chapter.

3.1. ZFs and ZNN models

In this subsection, by defining two different ZFs, two different ZNN models are developed and investigated for time-varying LMVI solving.

3.1.1. The first ZF and ZNN model

To monitor and control the process of solving the time-varying LMVI (3), the first ZF is defined as follows [7]:

$$E(t) = A(t)x(t) + \Lambda^{2}(t) - b(t) \in R^{n}, \tag{4}$$

where $\Lambda^{2}(t) = \Lambda(t) \odot \Lambda(t)$ with the time-varying vector $\Lambda(t)$ being $\Lambda(t) = [\lambda_{1}(t), \lambda_{2}(t), \cdots, \lambda_{n}(t)]^{T} \in R^{n}$. In view of the fact that $\Lambda^{2}(t) \geq 0$, when $E(t) = 0$, then we have

$$A(t)x(t) - b(t) = -\Lambda^{2}(t) \leq 0.$$

That is to say, time-varying LMVI (3) solving can be equivalent to solving the time-varying equation $A(t)x(t) + \Lambda^{2}(t) - b(t) = 0$. For further discussion, the following diagonal matrix $D(t)$ is defined:

$$D(t) = \begin{bmatrix} \lambda_1(t) & 0 & \cdots & 0 \\ 0 & \lambda_2(t) & \cdots & 0 \\ \vdots & \vdots & \ddots & \vdots \\ 0 & 0 & \cdots & \lambda_n(t) \end{bmatrix} \in R^{n \times n},$$

which yields

$$\Lambda^2(t) = D(t)\Lambda(t) \text{ and } \dot{\Lambda}^2(t) = \frac{d\Lambda^2(t)}{dt} = 2D(t)\dot{\Lambda}(t).$$

with $\dot{\Lambda}(t)$ being the time derivative of $\Lambda(t)$.

On the basis of ZF (4), by exploiting the original design formula (1), the dynamic equation of a ZNN model is established as follows:

$$A(t)\dot{x}(t) + 2D(t)\dot{\Lambda}(t) = -\dot{A}(t)x(t) + \dot{b}(t) - \gamma \mathcal{F}(A(t)x(t) + \Lambda^2(t) - b(t)), \tag{5}$$

where $\dot{x}(t)$, $\dot{A}(t)$ and $\dot{b}(t)$ are the time derivatives of $x(t)$, $A(t)$ and $b(t)$, respectively. As for (5), it is reformulated as

$$\begin{bmatrix} A(t) & 2D(t) \end{bmatrix} \begin{bmatrix} \dot{x}(t) \\ \dot{\Lambda}(t) \end{bmatrix} = \begin{bmatrix} -\dot{A}(t) & 0 \end{bmatrix} \begin{bmatrix} x(t) \\ \Lambda(t) \end{bmatrix} + \dot{b}(t) - \gamma \mathcal{F}\left(\begin{bmatrix} A(t) & D(t) \end{bmatrix} \begin{bmatrix} x(t) \\ \Lambda(t) \end{bmatrix} - b(t) \right). \tag{6}$$

By defining the augmented vector $y(t) = [x^{\mathrm{T}}(t), \Lambda^{\mathrm{T}}(t)]^{\mathrm{T}} \in R^{2n}$, (6) is further rewritten as follows:

$$C(t)\dot{y}(t) = P(t)y(t) + \dot{b}(t) - \gamma \mathcal{F}(Q(t)y(t) - b(t)), \tag{7}$$

with $\dot{y}(t)$ being the time derivative of $y(t)$, and the augmented matrices are being defined as below:

$$C(t) = \begin{bmatrix} A^{\mathrm{T}}(t) \\ 2D^{\mathrm{T}}(t) \end{bmatrix}^{\mathrm{T}} \in R^{n \times 2n}, P(t) = \begin{bmatrix} -\dot{A}^{\mathrm{T}}(t) \\ 0 \end{bmatrix}^{\mathrm{T}} \in R^{n \times 2n} \text{ and } Q(t) = \begin{bmatrix} A^{\mathrm{T}}(t) \\ D^{\mathrm{T}}(t) \end{bmatrix}^{\mathrm{T}} \in R^{n \times 2n}.$$

In order to make (7) more computable, we can reformulate (7) to the following explicit form:

$$\dot{y}(t) = C^{\dagger}(t)P(t)y(t) + C^{\dagger}(t)\dot{b}(t) - \gamma C^{\dagger}(t)\mathcal{F}(Q(t)y(t) - b(t)), \tag{8}$$

where $C^\dagger(t) = C^{\mathrm{T}}(t)(C(t)C^{\mathrm{T}}(t))^{-1} \in R^{2n \times n}$ denotes the right pseudoinverse of $C(t)$ and the MATLAB routine "pinv" is used to obtain $C^\dagger(t)$ at each time instant in the simulations. Therefore, based on ZF (4), ZNN model (8) is obtained for time-varying LMVI solving. Besides, for better understanding and potential hardware implementation, ZNN model (8) is expressed in the ith (with $i = 1,2,\cdots,2n$) neuron form as

$$y_i = \int \sum_{k=1}^{n} c_{ik} \left(\sum_{j=1}^{m} p_{kj} y_j + \dot{b}_k - \gamma f\left(\sum_{j=1}^{m} q_{kj} y_j - b_k \right) \right) \mathrm{d}t,$$

where y_i denotes the ith neuron of (8), $m = 2n$ and $f(\cdot)$ is a processing element of $\mathcal{F}(\cdot)$. In addition, time-varying weights c_{ik}, p_{kj} and q_{kj} denote the ikth element of $C^\dagger(t)$, the kjth element of $P(t)$ and kjth element of $Q(t)$, respectively. Moreover, time-varying thresholds $\dot{b}_k$ and b_k denote, respectively, the kth elements of $\dot{b}(t)$ and $b(t)$. Thus, the neural-network structure of (8) is shown in **Figure 1**.

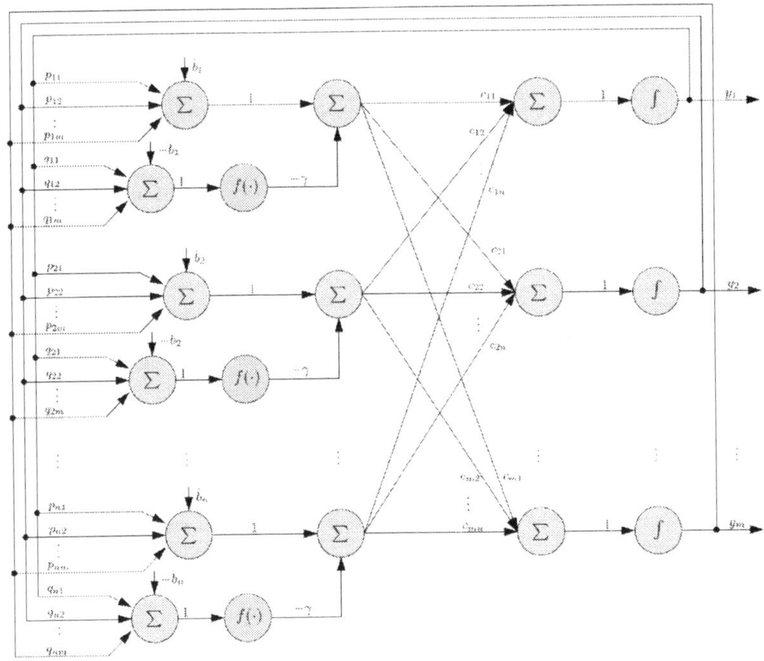

Figure 1. Structure of the neurons in ZNN model (8) for time-varying LMVI (3) solving.

3.1.2. The second ZF and ZNN model

Being different from the first ZF (4), the second ZF is defined as follows [9]:

$$E(t) = A(t)x(t) - b(t) \in R^n. \tag{9}$$

On the basis of such a ZF, by exploiting the variant design formula (2), another ZNN model is developed as follows:

$$A(t)\dot{x}(t) = -\dot{A}(t)x(t) + \dot{b}(t) - \gamma \mathrm{SGN}(E_0) \odot \mathcal{F}(A(t)x(t) - b(t)), \tag{10}$$

where the initial error $E_0 = E(t = 0) = A(0)x(0) - b(0)$. Therefore, based on ZF (9), ZNN model (10) is obtained for time-varying LMVI solving. Besides, for better understanding and potential hardware implementation, the block diagram of ZNN model (10) is shown in **Figure 2**, where $I \in R^{n \times n}$ denotes the identity matrix.

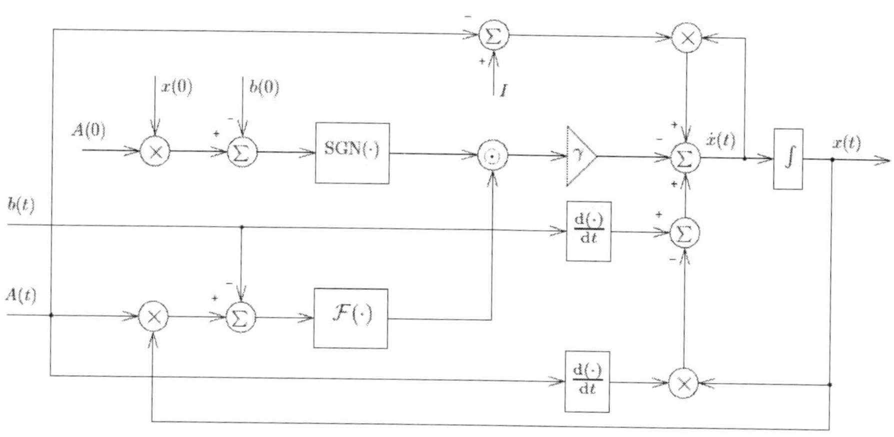

Figure 2. Block diagram of ZNN model (10) for time-varying LMVI (3) solving.

3.2. Theoretical results and analyses

In this subsection, theoretical results and analyses of the presented ZNN models (8) and (10) for solving the time-varying LMVI (3) are provided via the following theorems.

Theorem 1. Given a smoothly time-varying nonsingular coefficient matrix $A(t) \in R^{n \times n}$ and a smoothly time-varying coefficient vector $b(t) \in R^n$ in (3), if a monotonically increasing odd activation function array $\mathcal{F}(\cdot)$ is used, then ZNN model (8) generates an exact time-varying solution of the time-varying LMVI (3).

Proof: To lay a basis for discussion, we define $x^*(t)$ as a theoretical time-varying solution of (3), i.e., $A(t)x^*(t) \leq b(t)$. Then, a time-varying vector $\Lambda^*(t)$ would exist, which results in the time-varying matrix-vector equation as follows:

$$A(t)x^*(t) + \Lambda^{*2}(t) = b(t). \tag{11}$$

By differentiating (11) with respect to time t, we have

$$A(t)\dot{x}^*(t) + \dot{A}(t)x^*(t) + \dot{\Lambda}^{*2}(t) = \dot{b}(t), \tag{12}$$

with $\dot{x}^*(t)$ and $\dot{\Lambda}^{*2}(t)$ being respectively the time derivatives of $x^*(t)$ and $\Lambda^{*2}(t)$. Based on (7), (11) and (12), we further have

$$A(t)(\dot{x}(t) - \dot{x}^*(t)) + \dot{A}(t)(x(t) - x^*(t)) + \dot{\Lambda}^2(t) - \dot{\Lambda}^{*2}(t)$$
$$= -\gamma\mathcal{F}(A(t)(x(t) - x^*(t)) + \Lambda^2(t) - \Lambda^{*2}(t)),$$

which is rewritten as

$$\dot{\tilde{E}}(t) = -\gamma\mathcal{F}(\tilde{E}(t)), \tag{13}$$

where $\tilde{E}(t) = A(t)(x(t) - x^*(t)) + \Lambda^2(t) - \Lambda^{*2}(t) \in R^n$ with $\dot{\tilde{E}}(t)$ being the time derivative of $\tilde{E}(t)$.

As for (13), its compact form of a set of n decoupled differential equations is written as follows:

$$\dot{\tilde{e}}_i(t) = -\gamma f(\tilde{e}_i(t)), \tag{14}$$

where $i = 1, 2, \cdots, n$. To analyze (14), we define a Lyapunov function candidate $v_i(t) = \tilde{e}_i^2(t)/2 \geq 0$ with its time derivative being

$$\dot{v}_i(t) = \frac{\mathrm{d}v_i(t)}{\mathrm{d}t} = \tilde{e}_i(t)\dot{\tilde{e}}_i(t) = -\gamma\tilde{e}_i(t)f(\tilde{e}_i(t)).$$

Since $f(\cdot)$ is a monotonically increasing odd activation function, i.e., $f(-\tilde{e}_i(t)) = -f(\tilde{e}_i(t))$, then we have

$$\tilde{e}_i(t)f(\tilde{e}_i(t))\begin{cases} > 0, & \text{if } \tilde{e}_i(t) \neq 0, \\ = 0, & \text{if } \tilde{e}_i(t) = 0, \end{cases}$$

which guarantees the negative definiteness of $\dot{v}_i(t)$. That is to say, $\dot{v}_i(t) < 0$ for $\tilde{e}_i(t) \neq 0$, while $\dot{v}_i(t) = 0$ for $\tilde{e}_i(t) = 0$ only. By Lyapunov theory, $\tilde{e}_i(t)$ converges to zero for any $i \in \{1,2,\cdots,n\}$, thereby showing that $\tilde{E}(t)$ is convergent to zero as well.

Besides, based on (11), we have $A(t)x^*(t) + \Lambda^{*2}(t) = b(t)$. Then, $\tilde{E}(t)$ is rewritten as $\tilde{E}(t) = A(t)x(t) + \Lambda^2(t) - b(t)$, which is equivalent to $A(t)x(t) - b(t) = -\Lambda^2(t) + \tilde{E}(t)$. Note that, as analyzed previously, $\tilde{E}(t) \to 0$ with time $t \to +\infty$. Thus, as time evolves,

$$A(t)x(t) - b(t) = -\Lambda^2(t) + \tilde{E}(t) \to -\Lambda^2(t).$$

Since $-\Lambda^2(t) \leq 0$ (i.e., each element is less than or equal to zero), then we have $A(t)x(t) - b(t) \leq 0$. This implies that $x(t)$ (being the first n elements of $y(t)$ of (8)) would converge to a time-varying vector which satisfies the time-varying LMVI (3); i.e., $x(t) \to x^*(t)$ to make (3) hold true. In summary, the presented ZNN model (8) generates an exact time-varying solution of the time-varying LMVI (3). The proof is thus completed. □

Theorem 2. Given a smoothly time-varying nonsingular coefficient matrix $A(t) \in R^{n \times n}$ and a smoothly time-varying coefficient vector $b(t) \in R^n$ in (3), if a monotonically increasing odd activation function array $\mathcal{F}(\cdot)$ is used, then ZNN model (10) generates an exact time-varying solution of the time-varying LMVI (3).

Proof: Consider ZNN model (10), which is derived from the variant design formula (2). Thus, there are three cases as follows.

1. If the randomly generated initial state $x(0) \in R^n$ is outside the initial solution set $S(0)$ of (3), i.e., $E_0 > 0$ in (10), based on Remark 1 and the previous work [9], the global and exponential convergence of the error function $E(t)$ is achieved (or say, $E(t) = A(t)x(t) - b(t) \to 0$ globally and exponentially). This also means that the neural state $x(t)$ of ZNN model (10) is convergent to the theoretical time-varying solution of the matrix-vector equation $A(t)x(t) - b(t) = 0$. Note that $A(t)x(t) - b(t) = 0$ (i.e., $A(t)x(t) = b(t)$) is a special case of $A(t)x(t) \leq b(t)$. Therefore, ZNN model (10) is effective on solving the time-varying LMVI (3), in terms of $x(t)$ being convergent to the time-varying solution set $S(t)$ of (3).

2. If $x(0)$ is inside $S(0)$ of (3), i.e., $E_0 \leq 0$ in (10), based on Remark 1, the error function $E(t)$ would remain E_0 with $t \to +\infty$. That is, $E(t) = E_0 \leq 0$, no matter how time t evolves. In this situation, ZNN model (10) is still effective on solving the time-varying LMVI (3), in terms of its neural state $x(t)$ always being inside $S(t)$ of (3).

3. If some elements of $x(0)$ are inside $S(0)$ of (3) while the others are outside $S(0)$, i.e., some elements of E_0 are greater than zero while the rest elements of E_0 are less than or equal to zero, then, (i) for the elements of $E(t)$ that have positive initial values (i.e., their initial values are greater than zero), they can be convergent to zero globally and exponentially; and (ii) for the rest elements of $E(t)$, they can be always equal to their initial values that are less than or equal to zero. In view of the fact that, as time evolves, each element of $E(t) = A(t)x(t) - b(t)$ is less than or equal to zero, ZNN model (10) is thus effective on solving the time-varying LMVI (3).

By summarizing the above analyses, the time-varying LMVI (3) is solved effectively via ZNN model (10), in the sense that such a model can generate an exact time-varying solution of (3). The proof is thus completed. $\square$

Remark 2. On the basis of two different ZFs (i.e., (4) and (9)), two different ZNN models (i.e., (8) and (10)) are obtained for online solution of the time-varying LMVI (3). Note that the former aims at solving (3) aided with equality conversion (i.e., from inequality to equation) and the original design formula (1), while the latter focuses on solving (3) directly with the aid of the variant design formula (2). The resultant ZNN model (8) is depicted in an explicit dynamics (i.e., $\dot{y}(t) = \cdots$), and ZNN model (10) is depicted in an implicit dynamics (i.e., $A(t)\dot{x}(t) = \cdots$). As analyzed above and as demonstrated by the simulation results shown in Section 5, such two ZNN models are both effective on solving the time-varying LMVI (3). In summary, two different approaches for time-varying LMVI solving have been discovered and presented in this chapter; i.e., one is based on the variant of the original ZNN design formula, and the other is based on the conversion from inequality to equation. This can be viewed as an important breakthrough on (time-varying or static) inequalities solving [7–9].

4. Time-varying linear matrix inequality

In this section, being an extension, by defining another two different ZFs, another two ZNN models are developed and investigated for time-varying linear matrix inequality (LMI) solving.

Specifically, the following problem of time-varying LMI is considered [9]:

$$A(t)X(t) \le B(t), \tag{15}$$

where $A(t) \in R^{m \times m}$ and $B(t) \in R^{m \times n}$ are smoothly time-varying matrices, and $X(t) \in R^{m \times n}$ is the unknown matrix to be obtained. Note that (15) is a representative time-varying LMI problem which is studied here. The design approaches presented in this chapter (more specifically, summarized in Remark 2) can be directly extended to solve other types of time-varying LMIs [8, 10, 11].

4.1. The first ZF and ZNN model

In order to solve the time-varying LMI (15), the first ZF is defined as follows:

$$E(t) = A(t)X(t) + \Lambda^2(t) - B(t) \in R^{m \times n}, \tag{16}$$

where $\Lambda^2(t) = \Lambda(t) \odot \Lambda(t)$ with the time-varying vector $\Lambda(t)$ being

$$\Lambda(t) = \begin{bmatrix} \lambda_{11}(t) & \lambda_{12}(t) & \cdots & \lambda_{1n}(t) \\ \lambda_{21}(t) & \lambda_{22}(t) & \cdots & \lambda_{2n}(t) \\ \vdots & \vdots & \ddots & \vdots \\ \lambda_{m1}(t) & \lambda_{m2}(t) & \cdots & \lambda_{mn}(t) \end{bmatrix} \in R^{m \times n}.$$

In addition, for matrices $\Lambda(t)$ and $\Lambda^2(t)$, we have

$$\mathrm{vec}(\Lambda^2(t)) = D(t)\mathrm{vec}(\Lambda(t)),$$

where operator $\mathrm{vec}(\cdot) \in R^{mn}$ generates a column vector obtained by stacking all column vectors of a matrix together [8, 18, 19]. In addition, the diagonal matrix $D(t)$ is defined as follows:

$$D(t) = \begin{bmatrix} \tilde{\lambda}_1(t) & 0 & \cdots & 0 \\ 0 & \tilde{\lambda}_2(t) & \cdots & 0 \\ \vdots & \vdots & \ddots & \vdots \\ 0 & 0 & \cdots & \tilde{\lambda}_n(t) \end{bmatrix} \in R^{mn \times mn},$$

with the ith (with $i = 1,\cdots,n$) block matrix being

$$\tilde{\lambda}_i(t) = \begin{bmatrix} \lambda_{1i}(t) & 0 & \cdots & 0 \\ 0 & \lambda_{2i}(t) & \cdots & 0 \\ \vdots & \vdots & \ddots & \vdots \\ 0 & 0 & \cdots & \lambda_{mi}(t) \end{bmatrix} \in R^{m \times m}.$$

By defining $u(t) = \mathrm{vec}(X(t)) \in R^{mn}$, $v(t) = \mathrm{vec}(\Lambda(t)) \in R^{mn}$ and $w(t) = \mathrm{vec}(B(t)) \in R^{mn}$, ZF (16) is reformulated as $E(t) = M(t)u(t) - w(t) + D(t)v(t) \in R^{mn}$, where $M(t) = I \otimes A(t) \in R^{mn \times mn}$ with $I \in R^{n \times n}$ being the identity matrix and $\otimes$ denoting the

Kronecker product [18, 19]. Thus, on the basis of (16), by exploiting the original design formula (1), we have

$$C(t)\dot{y}(t) = P(t)y(t) + \dot{w}(t) - \gamma \mathcal{F}(Q(t)y(t) - w(t)),\tag{17}$$

where the augmented vector $y(t) = [u^{\mathrm{T}}(t), v^{\mathrm{T}}(t)]^{\mathrm{T}} \in R^{2mn}$, and $\dot{y}(t) \in R^{2mn}$ and $\dot{w}(t) \in R^{mn}$ are the time derivatives of $y(t)$ and $w(t)$, respectively. In addition, the augmented matrices are defined as

$$C(t) = \begin{bmatrix} M^{\mathrm{T}}(t) \\ 2D^{\mathrm{T}}(t) \end{bmatrix}^{\mathrm{T}} \in R^{mn \times 2mn}, P(t) = \begin{bmatrix} -N^{\mathrm{T}}(t) \\ 0 \end{bmatrix}^{\mathrm{T}} \in R^{mn \times 2mn}$$

$$\text{and } Q(t) = \begin{bmatrix} M^{\mathrm{T}}(t) \\ D^{\mathrm{T}}(t) \end{bmatrix}^{\mathrm{T}} \in R^{mn \times 2mn},$$

where $N(t) = \dot{M}(t) = I \otimes \dot{A}(t) \in R^{mn \times mn}$ with $\dot{A}(t)$ being the time derivative of $A(t)$.

Similarly, to make (17) more computable, we can reformulate (17) as the following explicit form:

$$\dot{y}(t) = C^{\dagger}(t)P(t)y(t) + C^{\dagger}(t)\dot{w}(t) - \gamma C^{\dagger}(t)\mathcal{F}(Q(t)y(t) - w(t)),\tag{18}$$

where $C^{\dagger}(t) = C^{\mathrm{T}}(t)(C(t)C^{\mathrm{T}}(t))^{-1} \in R^{2mn \times mn}$. Therefore, based on ZF (16), ZNN model (18) is obtained for time-varying LMI solving. Note that the neural-network structure of (18) is similar to the one shown in **Figure 1**, and is thus omitted here. Besides, as for ZNN model (18), we have the following theoretical result, with the related proof being generalized from the proof of Theorem 1 and being left to interested readers to complete as a topic of exercise.

Corollary 1. Given a smoothly time-varying nonsingular coefficient matrix $A(t) \in R^{m \times m}$ and a smoothly time-varying coefficient matrix $B(t) \in R^{m \times n}$ in (15), if a monotonically increasing odd activation function array $\mathcal{F}(\cdot)$ is used, then ZNN model (18) generates an exact time-varying solution of the time-varying LMI (15).

4.2. The second ZF and ZNN model

In this subsection, being different from the first ZF (16), the second ZF is defined as follows:

$$E(t) = A(t)X(t) - B(t) \in R^{m \times n}.\tag{19}$$

On the basis of such a ZF, by exploiting the variant design formula (2), the following ZNN model for time-varying LMI solving is developed:

$$A(t)\dot{X}(t) = -\dot{A}(t)X(t) + \dot{B}(t) - \gamma \mathrm{SGN}(E_0) \odot \mathcal{F}(A(t)X(t) - B(t)), \tag{20}$$

where the initial error $E_0 = E(t = 0) = A(0)X(0) - B(0)$. Note that, due to similarity to the block diagram of (10), the block diagram of ZNN model (20) is omitted. Besides, as for ZNN model (20), we have the following theoretical result, of which the proof is generalized from the proof of Theorem 2 (and is also left to interested readers to complete as a topic of exercise).

Corollary 2. Given a smoothly time-varying nonsingular coefficient matrix $A(t) \in R^{m \times m}$ and a smoothly time-varying coefficient matrix $B(t) \in R^{m \times n}$ in (15), if a monotonically increasing odd activation function array $\mathcal{F}(\cdot)$ is used, then ZNN model (20) generates an exact time-varying solution of the time-varying LMI (15).

5. Simulative verifications

In this section, one illustrative example is first simulated for demonstrating the efficacy of the presented ZNN models (8) and (10) for solving the time-varying LMVI (3). Then, another illustrative example is provided for substantiating the efficacy of the presented ZNN models (18) and (20) for solving the time-varying LMI (15).

Example 1 In the first example, the following smoothly time-varying coefficient matrix $A(t)$ and coefficient vector $b(t)$ of (3) are designed to test ZNN models (8) and (10):

$$A(t) = \begin{bmatrix} 3 + \sin(3t) & \cos(3t)/2 & \cos(3t) \\ \cos(3t)/2 & 3 + \sin(3t) & \cos(3t)/2 \\ \cos(3t) & \cos(3t)/2 & 3 + \sin(3t) \end{bmatrix} \in R^{3\times3}$$

$$\text{and } b(t) = \begin{bmatrix} \sin(3t) + 1 \\ \cos(3t) + 2 \\ \sin(3t) + \cos(3t) + 3 \end{bmatrix} \in R^3.$$

The corresponding simulation results are shown in **Figures 3** through **9**.

Specifically, **Figures 3** and **4** illustrate the state trajectories synthesized by ZNN model (8) using $\gamma = 1$ and the power-sigmoid activation function. As shown in **Figures 3** and **4**, starting from five randomly generated initial states, the $x(t)$ trajectories (being the first 3 elements of $y(t)$ in (8)) and the $\Lambda(t)$ trajectories (being the rest elements of $y(t)$) are time-varying. In addition, **Figure 5** presents the characteristics of residual error

$\| Q(t)y(t) - b(t) \|_2 = \| A(t)x(t) + \Lambda^2(t) - b(t) \|_2$ (with symbol $\| \cdot \|_2$ denoting the two norm of a vector), from which we can observe that the residual errors of ZNN model (8) (corresponding to **Figures 3** and **4**) are all convergent to zero. This means that the $x(t)$ and $\Lambda(t)$ solutions shown in **Figures 3** and **4** are the time-varying solutions of $A(t)x(t) + \Lambda^2(t) - b(t) = 0$. In view of $-\Lambda^2(t) \le 0$, such a solution of $x(t)$ is an exact solution of the time-varying LMVI (3), i.e., $A(t)x(t) \le b(t)$. For better understanding, the profiles of the testing error function $\varepsilon(t) = A(t)x(t) - b(t)$ (i.e., ZF (9)) are illustrated in **Figure 6**. As shown in the figure, all the elements of $\varepsilon(t)$ are less than or equal to zero, thereby meaning that the $x(t)$ solution satisfies $A(t)x(t) \le b(t)$ (being an exact time-varying solution of (3)). These simulation results substantiate the efficacy of ZNN model (8) for time-varying LMVI solving. Besides, **Figure 7** shows the simulation results synthesized by ZNN model (8) using different γ values (i.e., $\gamma = 1$ and $\gamma = 10$) and different activation functions (i.e., linear, hyperbolic-sine and power-sigmoid activation functions). As seen from **Figure 7**, the residual errors all converge to zero, which means that ZNN model (8) solves the time-varying LMVI (3) successfully. Note that, from **Figure 7**, we have a conclusion that superior computational performance of ZNN model (8) can be achieved by increasing the γ value and choosing a suitable activation function.

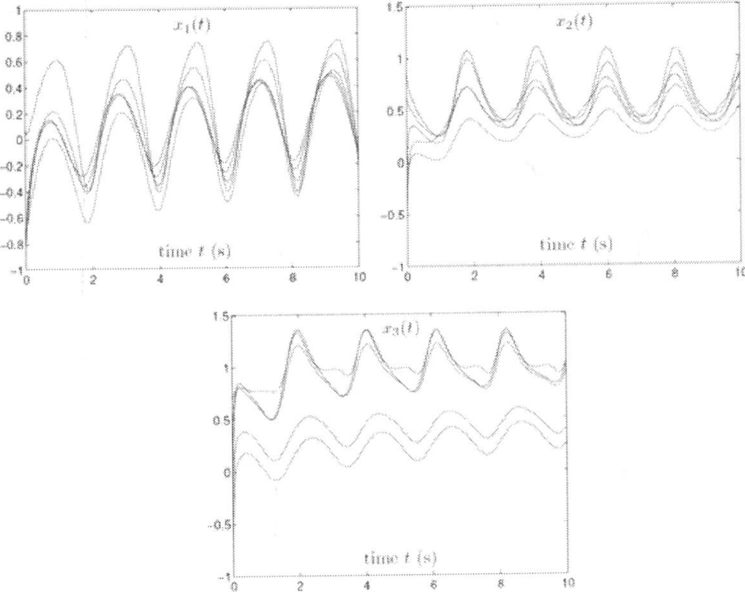

Figure 3. State trajectories of $x(t) \in R^3$ synthesized by ZNN model (8) with $\gamma = 1$ and the power-sigmoid activation function used for time-varying LMVI (3) solving.

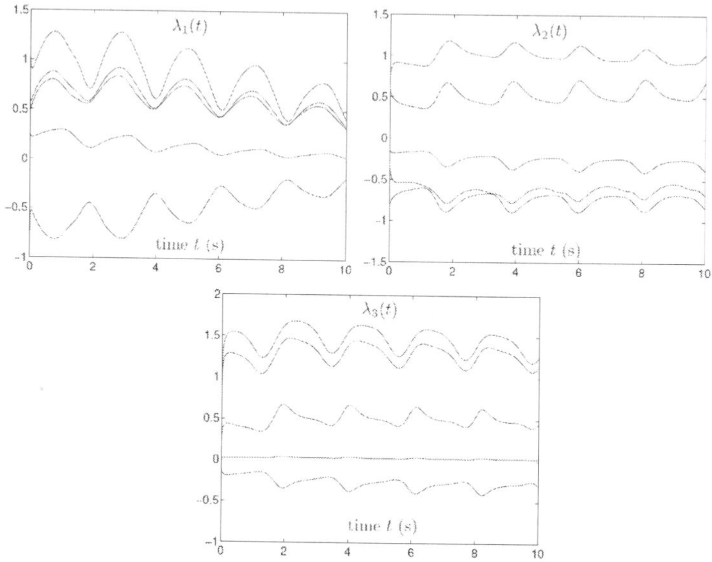

Figure 4. State trajectories of $\Lambda(t) \in R^3$ synthesized by ZNN model (8) with $\gamma = 1$ and the power-sigmoid activation function used for time-varying LMVI (3) solving.

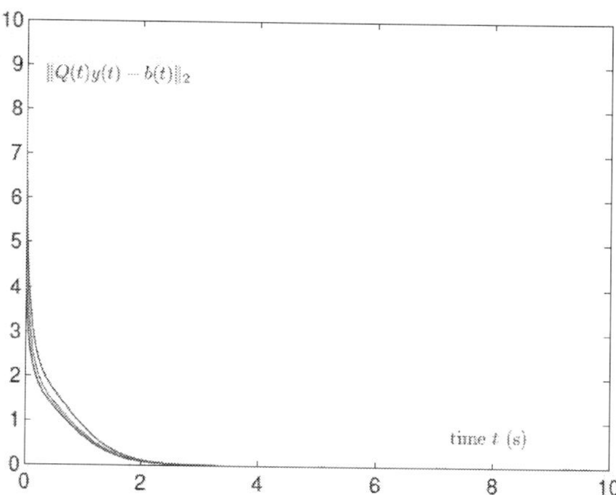

Figure 5. Residual errors $\| Q(t)y(t) - b(t) \|_2$ of ZNN model (8) for time-varying LMVI (3) solving.

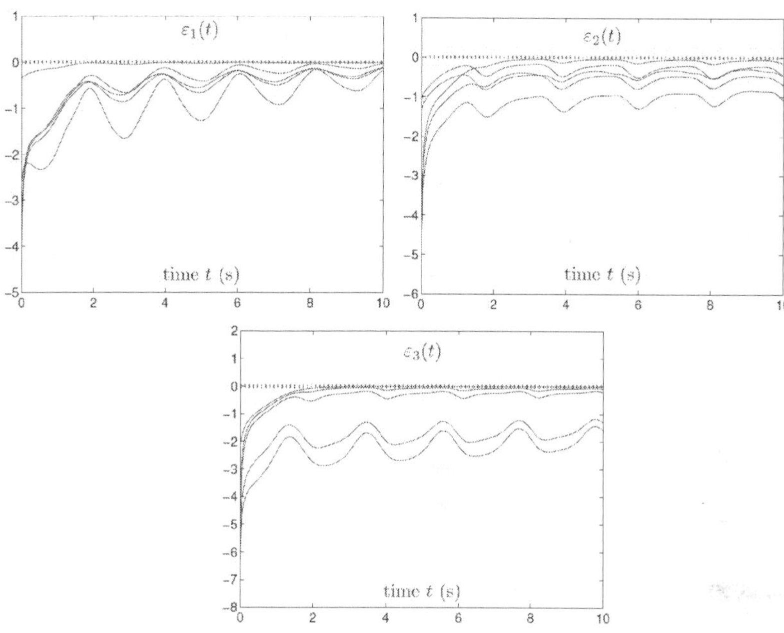

Figure 6. Profiles of $\varepsilon(t) = A(t)x(t) - b(t) \in R^3$ synthesized by ZNN model (8) with $\gamma = 1$ and the power-sigmoid activation function used for time-varying LMVI (3) solving.

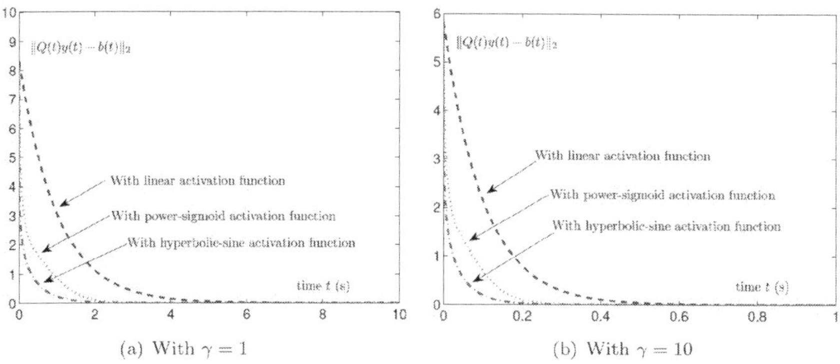

Figure 7. Residual errors $\parallel Q(t)y(t) - b(t) \parallel_2$ of ZNN model (8) with γ fixed and different activation functions used for time-varying LMVI (3) solving.

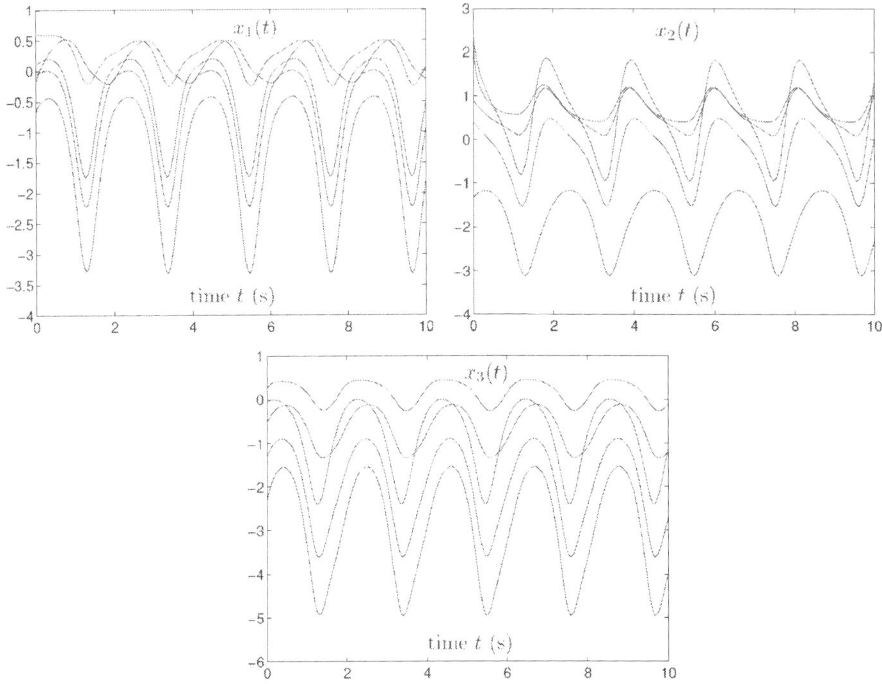

Figure 8. State trajectories of $x(t) \in R^3$ synthesized by ZNN model (10) with $\gamma = 1$ and the power-sigmoid activation function used for time-varying LMVI (3) solving.

It is worth pointing out here that, in general, it may be difficult to know whether the initial state $x(0)$ used for simulation/application is outside the initial solution set $S(0)$ of the time-varying LMVI (3) or not. Thus, as for ZNN model (10), we focus on investigating its computational performance when some elements of $x(0)$ are outside $S(0)$ while the others are inside $S(0)$. In this case, some elements of the initial error $E_0 = A(0)x(0) - b(0)$ are greater than zero, while the rest are less than or equal to zero. The corresponding simulation results synthesized by ZNN model (10) using $\gamma = 1$ and the power-sigmoid activation function are illustrated in **Figures 8** and **9**. As shown in **Figure 8**, starting from five randomly generated initial states, the $x(t)$ trajectories of ZNN model (10) are time-varying. Besides, from **Figure 9** which shows the profiles of the testing error function $\varepsilon(t) = A(t)x(t) \le b(t)$, we can observe that the elements of $\varepsilon(t)$ with positive initial values are convergent to zero, while the rest elements remain at their initial values. This result implies that the $x(t)$ solutions shown in **Figure 6** are the time-varying solutions of (3), i.e., $A(t)x(t) \le b(t)$, thereby showing the efficacy of ZNN model (10) for time-varying LMVI solving. That is, ZNN model (10) generates an exact time-varying solution of the time-varying LMVI (3). Note that the computational performance of ZNN model (10) can be improved by increasing the value of γ and choosing a suitable activation function (which is similar to that of ZNN model (8)). Being a topic of exercise, the corresponding simulative verifications of ZNN model (10) are left for interested readers.

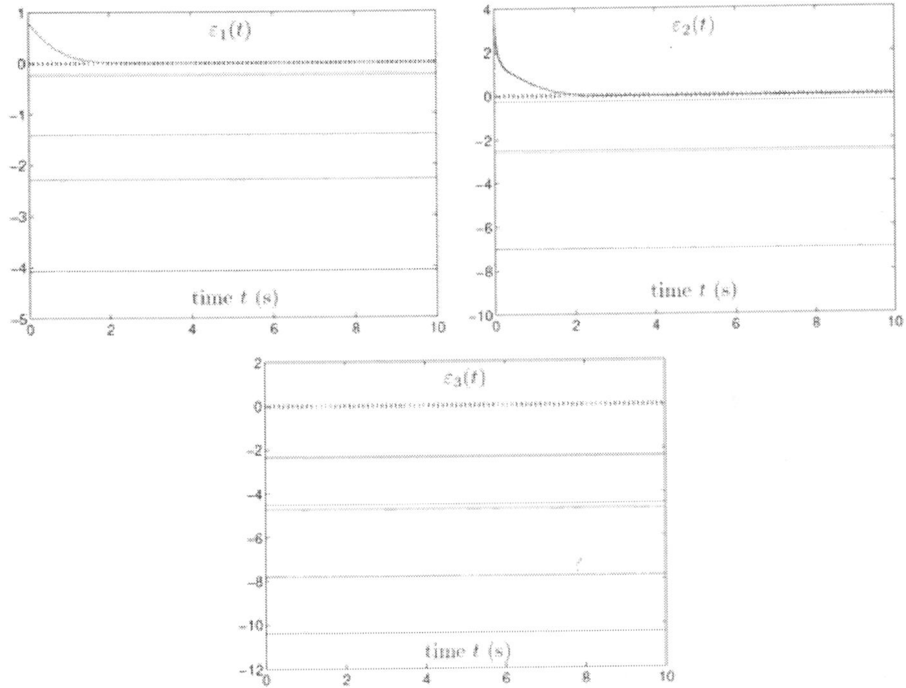

Figure 9. Profiles of $\varepsilon(t) = A(t)x(t) - b(t) \in R^3$ synthesized by ZNN model (10) with $\gamma = 1$ and the power-sigmoid activation function used for time-varying LMVI (3) solving.

In summary, the above simulation results (i.e., **Figures 3** through **9**) have substantiated that the presented ZNN models (8) and (10) are both effective on time-varying LMVI solving.

Example 2 In the second example, the following smoothly time-varying coefficient matrices $A(t)$ and $B(t)$ of (15) are designed to test ZNN models (18) and (20):

$$A(t) = \begin{bmatrix} \sin(10t) & \cos(10t) \\ -\cos(10t) & \sin(10t) \end{bmatrix} \in R^{2\times2} \text{ and}$$

$$B(t) = \begin{bmatrix} \cos(10t)+1 & \sin(10t)+1.5 \\ -\sin(10t)+1.5 & -\cos(10t)+1 \end{bmatrix} \in R^{2\times2}.$$

The corresponding simulation results are illustrated in **Figures 10** through **13**.

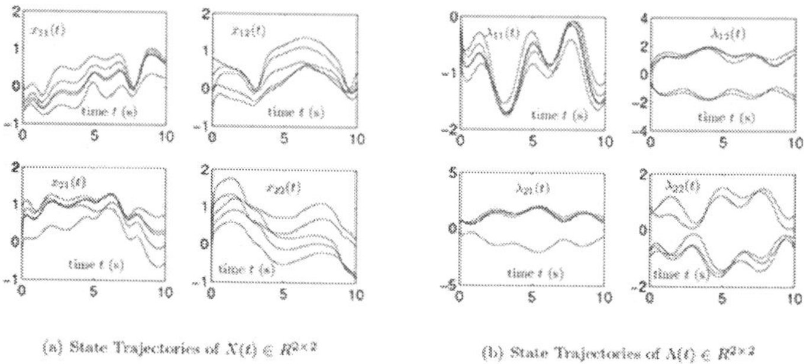

Figure 10. Neural states synthesized by ZNN model (18) with $\gamma = 1$ and the hyperbolic-sine activation function used for time-varying LMI (15) solving.

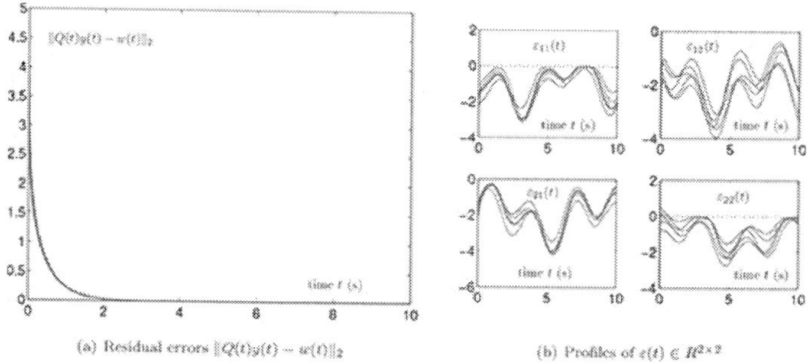

Figure 11. Profiles of residual errors $\| Q(t)y(t) - w(t) \|_2$ and $\varepsilon(t) = A(t)X(t) - B(t)$ synthesized by ZNN model (18) with $\gamma = 1$ and the hyperbolic-sine activation function used for time-varying LMI (15) solving.

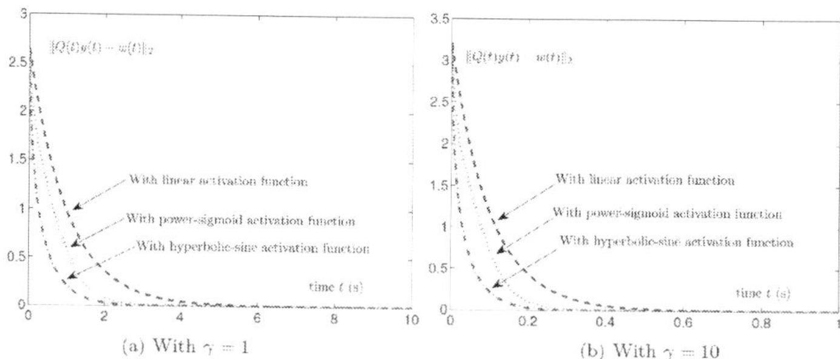

Figure 12. Residual errors $\| Q(t)y(t) - w(t) \|_2$ of ZNN model (18) with γ fixed and different activation functions used for time-varying LMI (15) solving.

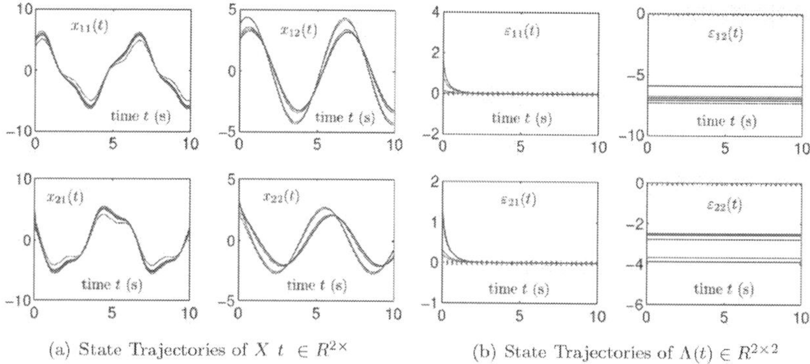

(a) State Trajectories of X $t \in R^{2\times}$ (b) State Trajectories of $\Lambda(t) \in R^{2\times 2}$

Figure 13. Simulation results synthesized by ZNN model (20) with $\gamma = 1$ and the hyperbolic-sine activation function used for time-varying LMI (15) solving.

On one hand, as synthesized by ZNN model (18) using $\gamma = 1$ and the hyperbolic-sine activation function, **Figure 10** shows the trajectories of $X(t)$ (being the first 4 elements of $y(t)$ in (18)) and $\Lambda(t)$ (being the rest elements of $y(t)$), which are time-varying. In addition, **Figure 11(a)** shows the characteristics of residual error $\| Q(t)y(t) - w(t) \|_2 = \| A(t)X(t) + \Lambda^2(t) - B(t) \|_F$ (with symbol $\| \cdot \|_F$ denoting the Frobenius norm of a matrix), from which we can observe that the residual errors of ZNN model (18) all converge to zero. This means that the solutions of $X(t)$ and $\Lambda(t)$ shown in **Figure 10** are the time-varying solutions of $A(t)X(t) + \Lambda^2(t) - B(t) = 0$. That is, $X(t)$ satisfies $A(t)X(t) = B(t) - \Lambda^2(t) \leq B(t)$, showing that such a solution is an exact time-varying solution of the time-varying LMI (15). For better understanding, **Figure 11(b)** shows the profiles of the testing error function $\varepsilon(t) = A(t)X(t) - B(t)$, from which we can observe that all the elements of $\varepsilon(t)$ are less than or equal to zero. These simulation results substantiate the efficacy of ZNN model (18) for time-varying LMI solving. Besides, **Figure 12** shows the simulation results synthesized by ZNN model (18) using different γ values and different activation functions. As seen from **Figure 12**, the residual errors all converge to zero, which means that the time-varying LMI (15) is solved successfully via ZNN model (18). Note that, as for ZNN model (18), its computational performance can be improved by increasing the γ value and choosing a suitable activation function (as shown in **Figure 12**).

On the other hand, as synthesized by ZNN model (20) using $\gamma = 1$ and the hyperbolic-sine activation function, **Figure 13** shows the related simulation results, where some elements of the initial state $X(0)$ are outside the initial solution set $S(0)$ of the time-varying LMI (15) while the others are inside $S(0)$. From **Figure 13(a)**, we can observe that the $X(t)$ trajectory of ZNN model (20) is time-varying. In addition, as shown in **Figure 13(b)**, the errors $\varepsilon_{11}(t)$ and $\varepsilon_{21}(t)$ (being the elements of the testing error function $\varepsilon(t) = A(t)X(t) - B(t)$) converge to zero, and the errors $\varepsilon_{12}(t)$ and $e_{22}(t)$ are always equal to $\varepsilon_{12}(0) < 0$ and $\varepsilon_{22}(0) < 0$. This means that the

$X(t)$ solution shown in **Figure 13(a)** is the time-varying solution of (15), i.e., $A(t)X(t) \leq B(t)$, thereby showing the efficacy of ZNN model (20). That is, ZNN model (20) generates an exact time-varying solution of the time-varying LMI (15). Besides, the investigations on the computational performance of (10) using different γ values and different activation functions are left to interested readers to complete as a topic of exercise.

In summary, the above simulation results (i.e., **Figures 10** through **13**) have substantiated that the presented ZNN models (18) and (20) are both effective on time-varying LMI solving.

6. Summary

In this chapter, by exploiting two design formulas (1) and (2), based on different ZFs (i.e., (4), (9), (16) and (19)), four different ZNN models (i.e., (8), (10), (18) and (20)) have been developed and investigated to solve the time-varying LMVI (3) and time-varying LMI (15). For such ZNN models, theoretical results and analyses have also been presented to show their computational performances. Simulation results with two illustrative examples have further substantiated the efficacy of the presented ZNN models for time-varying LMVI and LMI solving.

Acknowledgements

This work is supported by the National Natural Science Foundation of China (with number 61473323 and 61403149), and also by the Scientific Research Funds of Huaqiao University.

Author details

Dongsheng Guo[1*], Laicheng Yan[1] and Yunong Zhang[2]

*Address all correspondence to: gdongsh2008@126.com; gdongsh@hqu.edu.cn

1 College of Information Science and Engineering, Huaqiao University, Xiamen, China

2 School of Data and Computer Science, Sun Yat-sen University, Guangzhou, China

References

[1] Guo D, Zhang Y. Acceleration-level inequality-based MAN scheme for obstacle avoidance of redundant robot manipulators. IEEE Transactions on Industrial Electronics. 2014; 61:6903–6914. DOI: 10.1109/TIE.2014.2331036

[2] Guo D, Zhang Y. A new inequality-based obstacle-avoidance MVN scheme and its application to redundant robot manipulators. IEEE Transactions on Systems, Man, and Cybernetics, Part C. 2012; 42:1326–1340. DOI: 10.1109/TSMCC.2012.2183868

[3] Jing X. Robust adaptive learning of feedforward neural networks via LMI optimizations. Neural Networks. 2012; 31:33–45. DOI: 10.1016/j.neunet.2012.03.003

[4] Wang Z, Zhang H, Jiang B. LMI-based approach for global asymptotic stability analysis of recurrent neural networks with various delays and structures. IEEE Transactions on Neural Networks. 2011; 22:1032–1045. DOI: 10.1109/TNN.2011.2131679

[5] Kim E, Kang HJ, Park M. Numerical stability analysis of fuzzy control systems via quadratic programming and linear matrix inequalities. IEEE Transactions on Systems, Man, and Cybernetics, Part A. 1999; 29:333–346. DOI: 10.1109/3468.769752

[6] Xiao L, Zhang Y. Different Zhang functions resulting in different ZNN models demonstrated via time-varying linear matrix-vector inequalities solving. Neurocomputing. 2013; 121:140–149. DOI: 10.1016/j.neucom.2013.04.041

[7] Guo D, Zhang Y. ZNN for solving online time-varying linear matrix-vector inequality via equality conversion. Applied Mathematics and Computation. 2015; 259:327–338. DOI: 10.1016/j.amc.2015.02.060

[8] Guo D, Zhang Y. Zhang neural network for online solution of time-varying linear matrix inequality aided with an equality conversion. IEEE Transactions on Neural Networks and Learning Systems. 2014; 25:370–382. DOI: 10.1109/TNNLS.2013.2275011

[9] Guo D, Zhang Y. A new variant of the Zhang neural network for solving online time-varying linear inequalities. Proceedings of the Royal Society A. 2012; 468:2255–2271. DOI: 10.1098/rspa.2011.0668

[10] Lin C, Lai C, Huang T. A neural network for linear matrix inequality problems. IEEE Transactions on Neural Networks. 2000; 11:1078–1092. DOI: 10.1109/72.870041

[11] Cheng L, Hou ZG, Tan M, A simplified neural network for linear matrix inequality problems. Neural Processing Letters. 2009; 29:213–230. DOI: 10.1007/s11063-009-9105-5

[12] Yang K, Murty KG, Mangasarian OL. New iterative methods for linear inequalities. Journal of Optimization Theory and Applications. 1992; 72:163–185. DOI: 10.1007/BF00939954

[13] Cichocki A, Bargiela, A. Neural networks for solving linear inequality systems. Parallel Computing. 1997; 22:1455–1475. DOI: 10.1016/S0167-8191(96)00065-8

[14] Xia Y, Wang J, Hung DL. Recurrent neural networks for solving linear inequalities and equations. IEEE Transactions on Circuits and Systems - I. 1999; 46:452–462. DOI: 10.1109/81.754846

[15] Zhang Y. A set of nonlinear equations and inequalities arising in robotics and its online solution via a primal neural network. Neurocomputing. 2006; 70:513–524. DOI: 10.1016/j.neucom.2005.11.006

[16] Hu X. Dynamic system methods for solving mixed linear matrix inequalities and linear vector inequalities and equalities. Applied Mathematics and Computation. 2010; 216:1181–1193. DOI: 10.1016/j.amc.2010.02.010

[17] Xiao L, Zhang Y. Zhang neural network versus gradient neural network for solving time-varying linear inequalities. IEEE Transactions on Neural Networks. 2011; 22:1676–1684. DOI: 10.1109/TNN.2011.2163318

[18] Zhang Y, Guo D. Zhang Functions and Various Models. Heidelberg: Springer-Verlag; 2015. 236 p.

[19] Zhang Y, Yi C. Zhang Neural Networks and Neural-Dynamic Method. New York: Nova Science Publishers; 2011. 261 p.

[20] Zhang Y, Jiang D, Wang J. A recurrent neural network for solving Sylvester equation with time-varying coefficients. IEEE Transactions on Neural Networks. 2002; 13:1053–1063. DOI: 10.1109/TNN.2002.1031938

[21] Zhang Y, Ge SS. Design and analysis of a general recurrent neural network model for time-varying matrix inversion. IEEE Transactions on Neural Networks. 2005; 16:1477–1490. DOI: 10.1109/TNN.2005.857946

[22] Mead C. Analog VLSI and Neural Systems. Boston, USA: Addison-Wesley, Reading; 1989. 371 p.

[23] Li Z, Zhang Y. Improved Zhang neural network model and its solution of time-varying generalized linear matrix equations. Expert Systems with Applications. 2010; 37:7213–7218. DOI: 10.1016/j.eswa.2010.04.007

[24] Liu S, Trenkler G. Hadamard, Khatri-Rao, Kronecker and other matrix products. International Journal of Cooperative Information Systems. 2008; 4:160–177.

Chapter 2

Bayesian Regularized Neural Networks for Small *n* Big *p* Data

Hayrettin Okut

Additional information is available at the end of the chapter

http://dx.doi.org/10.5772/63256

Abstract

Artificial neural networks (ANN) mimic the function of the human brain and they have the capability to implement massively parallel computations for mapping, function approximation, classification, and pattern recognition processing. ANN can capture the highly nonlinear associations between inputs (predictors) and target (responses) variables and can adaptively learn the complex functional forms. Like other parametric and nonparametric methods, such as kernel regression and smoothing splines, ANNs can introduce overfitting (in particular with highly-dimensional data, such as genome wide association -GWAS-, microarray data etc.) and resulting predictions can be outside the range of the training data. Regularization (shrinkage) in ANN allows bias of parameter estimates towards what are considered to be probable. Most common techniques of regularizations techniques in ANN are the Bayesian regularization (BR) and the early stopping methods. Early stopping is effectively limiting the used weights in the network and thus imposes regularization, effectively lowering the Vapnik-Chervonenkis dimension. In Bayesian regularized ANN (BRANN), the regularization techniques involve imposing certain prior distributions on the model parameters and penalizes large weights in anticipation of achieving smoother mapping.

Keywords: artificial neural network, Bayesian regularization, shrinkage, $p \gg n$, prediction ability

1. Introduction

The issue of dimensionality of independent variables (i.e. when the number of observations is comparable to or larger than the sample size; small *n* big *p*; $p \gg n$) has garnered much attention

© 2016 The Author(s). Licensee InTech. This chapter is distributed under the terms of the Creative Commons Attribution License (http://creativecommons.org/licenses/by/3.0), which permits unrestricted use, distribution, and reproduction in any medium, provided the original work is properly cited.

over the last few years, primarily due to the fact that high-dimensional data are so common in up-to-date applications (e.g. microarray data, fMRI image processing, next generation sequencing, and many others assays of social and educational data). This issue is of particular interest in the field of human molecular genetics as the growing number of common single nucleotide polymorphisms (minor allele frequency > 0.01) available for assay in a single experiment, now close to 10 million (http://www.genome.gov/11511175), is quickly outpacing researchers' ability to increase sample sizes which typically number in the thousands to tens of thousands. Further, human studies of associations between molecular markers and any trait of interest include the possible presence of cryptic relationships between individuals that may not be tractable for use in traditional statistical models. These associations have been investigated primarily using a naïve single regression model for each molecular marker and linear regression models using Bayesian framework and some machine learning techniques typically ignoring interactions and non-linearity [1]. Soft computing techniques have also been used extensively to extract the necessary information from these types of data structures. As a universal approximator, Artificial Neural Networks (ANNs) are a powerful technique for extracting information from large data, in particular for $p>>n$ studies, and provide a computational approach with the ability to optimize the learning algorithm and make discoveries about functional forms in an adaptive approach [2, 3]. Moreover, ANNs offer several advantages, including requiring less formal statistical training, an ability to perfectly identify complex nonlinear relationships between dependent and independent variables, an ability to detect all possible interactions between input variables, and the availability of multiple training algorithms [4]. In general, the ANN architecture, or "model" in statistical jargon, is classified by the fashion in which neurons in a neural network are connected. Generally speaking, there are two different classes of ANN architecture (although each one has several subclasses). These are *feedforward* ANNs and *recurrent* ANNs. Only Bayesian regularized multilayer perceptron (MLP) *feedforward* ANNs will be discussed in this chapter.

This chapter begins with introducing of multilayer feedforward architectures. The regularization using other backpropagation algorithms to avoid overfitting will be explained briefly. Then Bayesian regularization (BR) for overfitting, Levenberg-Marquardt (LM) a training algorithm, BR, optimization of hyper parameters, inferring model parameters for given value of hyper parameters, pre-processing of data will be considered. Chapter will be ended with a MATLAB example for Bayesian Regularized feedforward multilayer artificial neural network (BRANN).

2. Multilayer perceptron feedforward neural networks

The MLP feedforward neural network considered herein is the most popular and most widely used ANN paradigm in many practical applications. The network is fully connected and divided into layers as depicted in **Figure 1**. In the left-most layer, there are input variables. The input layer consists of p_i (p=4 in **Figure 1** for illustration) independent variables and covariates. Then input layer is followed by a hidden layer, which consists of S number of neurons (S=3 in **Figure 1**), and there is a bias specific to each neuron. Algebraically, the process can be represented as follows. Let t_i (the target or dependent variable) be a trait (quantitative or qualitative) measured in individual i and let $p_i = \{p_{ij}\}$ be a vector of inputs (independent variables) or any other covariate measured for each individual. Suppose there are S neurons in the hidden layer. The input into neuron k (k=1, 2,…, S) prior to activation, as described in greater detail later in this chapter, is the linear function $w'_k\, p_i$, where $w'_k = \{w_{kj}\}$ is a vector of unknown connection strengths (slope in regression model) peculiar to neuron k, including a bias (e.g. the intercept in regression model). Each neuron in the hidden layer performs a weighted summation (n_i in **Figure 1**) of the inputs prior to activation which is then passed to a nonlinear activation function

$f_k\!\left(b_k^{(1)} + \sum_{j=1}^{P} w_{kj} p_j\right)$. Suppose the activation function chosen in the hidden layer is the

hyperbolic tangent transformation $f(x_i) = \dfrac{e^{x_i} - e^{-x_i}}{e^{x_i} + e^{-x_i}}$, where $f(x_i)$ is the neuron emission for

input variables [3]. Based on the illustration given in the **Figure 1**, the output of each neuron (shown as purple, orange, and green nodes) in the hidden layer (t_h) with hyperbolic tangent transformation are calculated as in equation (1).

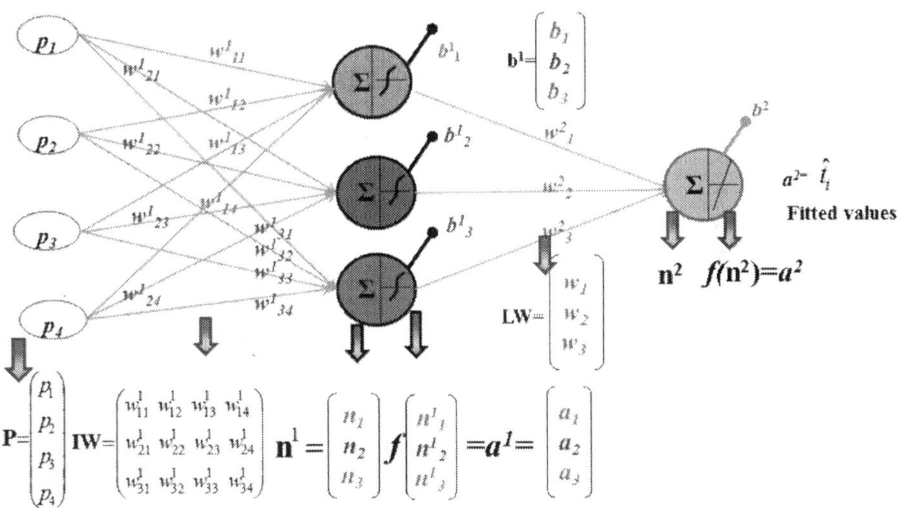

Figure 1. Artificial neural network design with 4 inputs (p_i). Each input is connected to up to 3 neurons via coefficients $w^{(l)}_{kj}$ (l denotes layer; j denotes neuron; k denotes input variable). Each hidden and output neuron has a bias parameter $b^{(l)}_j$. Here **P** = inputs, **IW** = weights from input to hidden layer (12 weights), **LW** = weights from hidden to output layer (3 weights), b^1 = Hidden layer biases (3 biases), b^2 = Output layer biases (1 bias), n^1 = **IWP** + b^1 is the weighted summation of the first layer, $a^1 = f(n^1)$ is output of hidden layer, n^2 = **LW**a^1 +b^2 is weighted summation of the second layer, and $\hat{t} = a^2 = f\!\left(n^2\right)$ is the predicted value of the network. The total number of parameters for this ANN is 12+3+3+1 =19.

$$t_{hidden} = \beta_0 + \beta_1 \left(\frac{\exp(b_1^1 + w_{11}^1 p_1 + w_{12}^1 p_2 + w_{13}^1 p_3 + w_{14}^1 p_4) - \exp(-b_1^1 - w_{11}^1 p_1 - w_{12}^1 p_2 - w_{13}^1 p_3 - w_{14}^1 p_4)}{\exp(b_1^1 + w_{11}^1 p_1 + w_{12}^1 p_2 + w_{13}^1 p_3 + w_{14}^1 p_4) + \exp(-b_1^1 - w_{11}^1 p_1 - w_{12}^1 p_2 - w_{13}^1 p_3 - w_{14}^1 p_4)} \right) \quad \text{ORANGE}$$

$$+ \beta_2 \left(\frac{\exp(b_2^1 + w_{21}^1 p_1 + w_{22}^1 p_2 + w_{23}^1 p_3 + w_{24}^1 p_4) - \exp(-b_2^1 - w_{21}^1 p_1 - w_{22}^1 p_2 - w_{23}^1 p_3 - w_{24}^1 p_4)}{\exp(b_2^1 + w_{21}^1 p_1 + w_{22}^1 p_2 + w_{23}^1 p_3 + w_{24}^1 p_4) + \exp(-b_2^1 - w_{21}^1 p_1 - w_{22}^1 p_2 - w_{23}^1 p_3 - w_{24}^1 p_4)} \right) \quad \text{PURPLE} \quad (1)$$

$$+ \beta_3 \left(\frac{\exp(b_3^1 + w_{31}^1 p_1 + w_{32}^1 p_2 + w_{33}^1 p_3 + w_{34}^1 p_4) - \exp(-b_3^1 - w_{31}^1 p_1 - w_{32}^1 p_2 - w_{33}^1 p_3 - w_{34}^1 p_4)}{\exp(b_3^1 + w_{31}^1 p_1 + w_{32}^1 p_2 + w_{33}^1 p_3 + w_{34}^1 p_4) + \exp(-b_3^1 - w_{31}^1 p_1 - w_{32}^1 p_2 - w_{33}^1 p_3 - w_{34}^1 p_4)} \right) \quad \text{GREEN}$$

The hidden layer outputs from neurons (orange, purple, and green) are the input of the next layer. After the activation function, the output from the hidden layer is then sent to the output layer again with weighted summation as $\sum_{k=1}^{S} w_k' f_k \left(b_k^{(1)} + \sum_{j=1}^{P} w_{kj} p_j \right) + b^{(2)}$, where w_k are weights specific to each neuron and $b^{(1)}$ and $b^{(2)}$ are bias parameters in the hidden and output layers, respectively. Finally, this quantity is again activated with the same or another activation function $g(.)$ as $g \left[\sum_{k=1}^{S} w_k' f_k(.) + b^{(2)} \right] = a^2 = \hat{t}$, which then becomes the predicted value $\hat{t}_i$ of the target variable in the training set. For instance, the predicted value $\hat{t}_i$ of the output layer based on details given in **Figure 1** and equation (1) can be calculated as,

$$\hat{t} = a^2 = g \left[\sum_{k=1}^{S} w_k' f_k(.) + b^{(2)} \right] = g \left[\begin{array}{l} \left(\frac{\exp(b_1^1 + w_{11}^1 p_1 + w_{12}^1 p_2 + w_{13}^1 p_3 + w_{14}^1 p_4) - \exp(-b_1^1 - w_{11}^1 p_1 - w_{12}^1 p_2 - w_{13}^1 p_3 - w_{14}^1 p_4)}{\exp(b_1^1 + w_{11}^1 p_1 + w_{12}^1 p_2 + w_{13}^1 p_3 + w_{14}^1 p_4) + \exp(-b_1^1 - w_{11}^1 p_1 - w_{12}^1 p_2 - w_{13}^1 p_3 - w_{14}^1 p_4)} \right) w_1^2 + \\[2mm] \left(\frac{\exp(b_2^1 + w_{21}^1 p_1 + w_{22}^1 p_2 + w_{23}^1 p_3 + w_{24}^1 p_4) - \exp(-b_2^1 - w_{21}^1 p_1 - w_{22}^1 p_2 - w_{23}^1 p_3 - w_{24}^1 p_4)}{\exp(b_2^1 + w_{21}^1 p_1 + w_{22}^1 p_2 + w_{23}^1 p_3 + w_{24}^1 p_4) + \exp(-b_2^1 - w_{21}^1 p_1 - w_{22}^1 p_2 - w_{23}^1 p_3 - w_{24}^1 p_4)} \right) w_2^2 + b^2 \\[2mm] \left(\frac{\exp(b_3^1 + w_{31}^1 p_1 + w_{32}^1 p_2 + w_{33}^1 p_3 + w_{34}^1 p_4) - \exp(-b_3^1 - w_{31}^1 p_1 - w_{32}^1 p_2 - w_{33}^1 p_3 - w_{34}^1 p_4)}{\exp(b_3^1 + w_{31}^1 p_1 + w_{32}^1 p_2 + w_{33}^1 p_3 + w_{34}^1 p_4) + \exp(-b_3^1 - w_{31}^1 p_1 - w_{32}^1 p_2 - w_{33}^1 p_3 - w_{34}^1 p_4)} \right) w_3^2 \end{array} \right] \quad (2)$$

This can be illustrated as,

$$\hat{t}_i = \textit{fitted value} = a^2 = g(n^2) = g\left[\Sigma \right] = g\left[w_1^2 \, \boxed{-f} + w_2^2 \, \boxed{-f} + w_3^2 \, \boxed{-f} + b^2 \right]$$

The activation function applied to the output layer depends on the type of target (dependent) variable and the values from the hidden units that are combined at the output units with additional (potentially different) activation functions applied. The activation functions most widely used are the hyperbolic tangent, which ranges from 1 to 1, in the hidden layer and linear in the output layer, as is the case in our example in **Figure 1** (the sigmoidal type activation function such as tangent hyperbolic and logit in the hidden layer are used for their convenient mathematical properties and these are usually chosen as a smooth step function). If the activation function at the output layer $g(.)$ is a linear or identity activation function, the model on the adaptive covariates $f_k(.)$ is also linear. Therefore, the regression model is entirely linear. The term "adaptive" denotes that the covariates in ANN are functions of unknown parameters (i.e. the $\{w_{kj}\}$ connection strengths), so the network can "learn" the association between independent (input) variables and target (output) variables, as is the case in standard regression models [1]. In this manner, this type of ANN architecture can also be regarded as a regression model. Of course, the level of non-linearity in ANNs is ultimately dictated by the type of activation functions used.

As depicted in **Figure 1**, a MLP feed forward architecture with one hidden layer can virtually predict any linear or non-linear model to any degree of accuracy, assuming that you have a suitable number of neurons in the hidden layer and an appropriate amount of data. But adding more neurons in hidden layers to the ANN architecture offers the model the flexibility of prediction of exceptionally complex nonlinear associations. This also holds true in function approximation, mapping, classification, and pattern recognition in approximating any nonlinear decision boundary with great precision. By adding additional neurons in the hidden layer to a MLP feedforward ANN is similar to adding additional polynomial terms to a regression model through the practice of generalization. Generalization is a method of indicating the appropriate complexity for the model in generating accurate prediction estimates based on data that is entirely separate from the training data that was used in fitting the model [5], commonly referred to as the test data set.

3. Overfitting and regularization

Like many other nonlinear estimation methods in supervised machine learning, such as kernel regression and smoothing splines, ANNs can suffer from either underfitting or overfitting. In particular, overfitting is more serious because it can easily lead to predictions that are far beyond the range of the training data [6–8]. Overfitting is unavoidable without practicing any regularization if the number of observations in the training data set is less than the number of parameters to be estimated. Before tackling the overfitting issue, let us first consider how the number of parameters in multilayer feedforward ANN is calculated. Suppose an ANN with **1000** inputs, **3** neurons in hidden and **1** neuron in output layer. The total number of parameters for this particular ANN is **3*1000** (number of weights from the input to the hidden layer) + **3** (number of biases in the hidden layer) + **3** (number of weights from the hidden to the output layer) + **1**(bias in output) = **3007**. The number of parameters for the entire network, for example, increases to **7015** when **7** neurons are assigned to the hidden layer. In these examples, either 3007 or 7015 parameters need to be estimated from 1000 observations. To wit, the number of neurons in the hidden layer controls the number of parameters (weights and biases) in the network. Determination of the optimal number of neurons to be retained in the hidden layer is an important step in the strategy of ANN. An ANN with less number of neurons may fails to capture the complex patterns between input and target variables. In contrast, an ANN with excess number of neurons in hidden layer will suffer from over-parameterization, leading to over-fitting and poor generalization ability [3]. Note that if the number of parameters in the network is much smaller than the total number of individuals in the training data set, then that is of no concern as there is little or no chance of overfitting for given ANN. If data assigned to the training set can be increased, then there is no need to worry about the following techniques to prevent overfitting. However, in most applications of ANN, data is typically partitioned to derive a finite training set. ANN algorithms train the model (architecture) based on this training data, and the performance and generalizability of the model is gauged on how well it predicts the observations in the training data set.

Overfitting occurs when a model fits the data in the training set well, while incurring larger generalization error. As depicted in **Figure 2**, the upper panel (**Figure 2a** and **b**) shows a model which has been fitted using too many free parameters. It seems that it does an excellent fitting of the data points, as the difference between outcome and predicted values (error) at the data points is almost zero. In reality, the data being studied often has some degree of error or random noise within it. Therefore, this does not mean our model (architecture) has good generalizability for given new values of the target variable t. It is said that the model has a bias-variance trade-off problem. In other words, the proposed model does not reproduce the structure which we expect to be present in any data set generated by function $f(.)$. **Figure 2c** shows that, while the network seems to get better and better (i.e., the error on the training set decreases; represented by the blue line in **Figure 2a**), at some point during training (epoch 2 in this example) it truly begins to get worse again (i.e. the error on test data set increases; represented by the

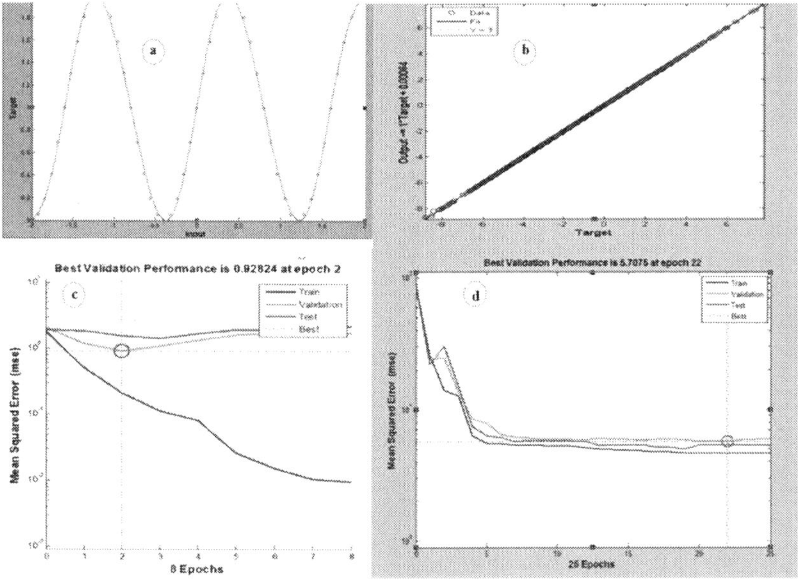

Figure 2. Function approximation of different regression models. Significant overfitting can be seen in (a)–(c).

red line in **Figure 2a**). The idealized expectation is that during training, the generalization error of the network progresses as shown in **Figure 2d**.

In general, there are two ways to deal with the overfitting problem in ANN (not considering ad hoc techniques such as pruning, greedy constructive learning, or weight sharing that reduces the number of parameters) [9]. These are **weight decay** and **early stopping**, both of which are known as *regularization* techniques. Regularization is the procedure of allowing parameter bias in the direction of what are considered to be more probable values, which reduces the variance of the estimates at the cost of introducing bias. Put in another way, regularization can be viewed as a way of compromising to minimize the objective function with regard to parameter (weights and bias) space. Next, we will briefly discuss **early stopping** before proceeding to the topic of weight decay (BR).

3.1. Early stopping

In the standard practice of backpropagation learning with early stopping, the data set is allocated into three sources: a training data set, a validation data set, and a testing data set. In most ANN practices, the biggest part of data is assigned to training data (by default a 60% of data is assigned for training in MATLAB). Each of these data sets have different task during the ANN prediction process. The training data set is used to estimate the neural network weights, while the validation data set is used to monitor the network and calculate the minimum error during the iterations till network is stopped. The last data set (test data set) is unseen data by network and task of the test data set is to decrease the bias and generate unbiased estimates for predicting future outcomes and generalizability. The test data set is used at the end of the iterative process for evaluating the performance of the model from an independently drawn sample [10]. With early stopping methods, a gradient descent algorithm is applied to the training and validation data sets. First, the training data set is used to calculate the weight and bias estimates, and then these parameter estimates are applied in the validation data set to calculate error values. The practice iterates substituting parameter estimates from the training data set into the validation data set to catch the likely smallest average error with respect to the prediction of the validation data set. Training ends when the error in the validation data set increases by certain epochs ("iterations" in statistical jargon) in order to avoid the problem of overfitting (the number of epoch is six by default in MATLAB) and then the weights at the minimum of the validation error are returned. The network parameter estimates with the best performance in the validation set are then used in analysis of the testing data to evaluate the predictive ability of the network [11].

Let the data set be $D = \{t, (p_i)_{i=1,\ldots,n}\}$, where p_i is a vector of inputs for individual i and t is a vector of target variables (input = independent and target = dependent variable in classical estimation terms in statistics). Once a set of weight values **w** is assigned to the connections in the networks, this defines a mapping from the input p_i to the output $\hat{t}_i$. Let M denote a specific network architecture (network architecture is the model in terms of numbers of neurons and choice of activation functions), then the typical objective function used for training a neural network using early stopping is the sum of squared estimation errors (E_D):

$$E_D\left(D \mid \mathbf{w}, M\right) = \sum_{i=1}^{n}\left(t_i - \hat{t}_i\right)^2 \tag{3}$$

for n input-target pairs defining D. Early stopping is effectively limiting the used weights in the network and thus imposes regularization, effectively lowering the Vapnik-Chervonenkis dimension. However, while early stopping often improves generalization, it does not do so in a mathematically well-defined way. It is crucial to realize that validation error is not a good estimate of generalization error. Early stopping regularization has a vital advantage over the usual regularized least square learning algorithm such as ridge regression (so-called penalized L_2) or Tikhonov regularization methods.

4. Bayesian regularization

The brief explanation given in the previous section described how early stopping works to deal with the overfitting issue in ANN. Another regularization procedure in ANN is BR, which is the linear combination of Bayesian methods and ANN to automatically determine the optimal regularization parameters (**Table 1**). In Bayesian regularized ANN (BRANN) models, regularization techniques involve imposing certain prior distributions on the model parameters. An extra term, E_w, is added by BRANN to the objective function of early stopping given in equation (3) which penalizes large weights in anticipation of reaching a better generalization and smoother mapping. As what happens in conventional backpropagation practices, a gradient-based optimization technique is then applied to minimize the function given in (4). This process is equal to a penalized log-likelihood,

$$F = \beta E_D(D \mid \mathbf{w}, M) + \alpha E_W(\mathbf{w} \mid M), \tag{4}$$

where $E_W(\mathbf{w} \mid M)$, is the sum of squares of architecture weights, M is the ANN architecture (model in statistical jargon), and α and β are objective function parameters (also referred to as regularization parameters or hyper-parameters and take the positive values) that need to be estimated adaptively [3]. The second term on the right hand side of equation (4), αE_W, is known as weight decay and α, the weight decay coefficient, favors small values of $\mathbf{w}$ and decreases the tendency of a model to overfit [12].

To add on a quadratic penalty function $E_W(\mathbf{w} \mid M)$, α yielding a version of nonlinear ridge regression with an estimate for $\mathbf{w}$ equivalent to the Bayesian maximum a prior (MAP) [1]. Therefore, the quadratic form (weight decay) favors small values of $\mathbf{w}$ and decreases the predisposition of a model to overfit the data. Here, in equation (4), training involves a tradeoff between model complexity and goodness of fit. If $\alpha \gg \beta$, highlighting is on reducing the extent of weights at the expense of goodness of fit, while producing a smoother network response [13]. If Bayes estimates of α are large, the posterior densities of the weights are highly concentrated around zero, so that the weights effectively disappear and the model discounts connections in the network [12, 14]. Therefore, α and β are adaptively predicted to deal with tradeoff model complexity and goodness of fit.

MATLAB Commend		Explanations
load myData		Loading data
net=newff(x,y,5,{'tansig', 'purelin'},'trainbr');		Creates a new network with a dialog box. The properties of architecture created here are: tangent sigmoid (tansig) and linear activation function (purelin) in hidden and output, respectively. The number of neuron in hidden layer is 5 and the number of neuron in output layer 1 (by default). The Bayesian regularized training algorithm (trainbr) takes play for training of data.
[net,tr]=train(net,x, y)		
randn('state',192736547)		Lets you seed the uniform random number generator.
y_t=sim(net, x)		Simulate net
net = init(net)		Reinitiate net to improve results
net = train(net,x,y)		Re-train net
net.trainParam.epochs	1000	Maximum number of epochs to train
net.trainParam.goal	0	Performance goal
net.trainParam.mu	0.005	Marquardt adjustment parameter
net.trainParam.mu_dec	0.1	Decrease factor for mu
net.trainParam.mu_inc	10	Increase factor for mu
net.trainParam.mu_max	1e10	Maximum value for mu
net.trainParam.min_grad	1e-7	Minimum performance gradient
net.trainParam.show	25	Epochs between displays (NaN for no displays)
net.trainParam. showCommandLine	False	Generate command-line output
net.trainParam. showWindow	True	Show training GUI

Table 1. Training occurs according to Bayesian regularization algorithms (trainbr) training parameters, shown here with their default values (commends given in bold face are required).

As stated in the early stopping regularization section of this chapter, the input and target data set is typically divided into three parts; the training data set, the validation data set, and the test data sets. In BRANNs, particularly when the input and target data set is small, it is not essential to divide the data into three subsets: training, validation, and testing sets. Conversely all available data set is devoted to model fitting and model comparison [15]. This implementation is important when training networks with small data sets as is thought that BR has better generalization ability than early stopping (http://www.faqs.org/faqs/ai-faq/neural-nets/part3/section-5.html).

The strength connections, **w**, of the network are considered random variables and have no meaning before training. After the data is taken, the density function for the weights can be updated according to Bayes' rule. The empirical Bayes approach in [12] is as follows. The posterior distribution of **w** given α, β, D, and M is

$$P(\mathbf{w} \mid D,\alpha,\beta,M) = \frac{P(D\big|\mathbf{w},\beta,M)P(\mathbf{w}\big|\alpha,M)}{P(D\mid\alpha,\beta,M)}, \qquad (5)$$

where D is the training data set and M is the specific functional form of the neural network architecture considered. The other terms in equation (5) are:

- $P(w\,|D,\,\alpha\,\beta,\,M)$ is the posterior probability of **w**,

- $P(D\,|\,w,\,\beta,\,M)$ is the likelihood function of **w**,

- $P(w\,|\,\alpha,\,M)$ is the prior distribution of weights under M, which is the probability of observing the data given **w** and

- $P(D\,|\,\alpha,\,\beta,\,M)$ is a normalization factor or evidence for hyperparameters α and β.

The normalization factor does not depend on **w** (Kumar, 2004). That is,

$$P(D\mid\alpha,\beta,M) = \int P(D\big|\mathbf{w},\beta,M)P(\mathbf{w}\big|\alpha,M)d\mathbf{w}.$$

The weights **w**, were assumed to be identically distributed, each following the Gaussian distribution $(\mathbf{w}\mid\alpha,\,M)\sim N(0,\,\alpha^{-1})$. Given this, the expression of joint prior density of **w** in equation (5) is

$$p\big(\mathbf{w} \mid a,M\big) \propto \prod_{l=1}^{m}\exp\left(-\frac{\alpha w_{kj}^2}{2}\right) = \exp\left[-\frac{\alpha E_W(\mathbf{w}\mid M)}{2}\right].$$

After normalization, the prior distribution is then [2]

$$p(\mathbf{w}\mid\alpha,M) = \frac{\exp\left[-\dfrac{\alpha E_W(\mathbf{w}\mid M)}{2}\right]}{\int\exp\left[-\dfrac{\alpha E_W(\mathbf{w}\mid M)}{2}\right]d\mathbf{w}} = \frac{\exp\left[-\dfrac{\alpha E_W(\mathbf{w}\mid M)}{2}\right]}{Z_w(\alpha)}, \qquad (6)$$

where $Z_W(\alpha) = \left(\dfrac{2\pi}{\alpha}\right)^{\frac{m}{2}}$.

As target variable t, is a function of input variables, $\mathbf{p}$, (the same association between dependent and independent variables in regression model) it is modeled as $t_i = f(\mathbf{p}_i) + e$, where $e \sim N(0, \beta^{-1})$ and $f(\mathbf{p}_i)$ is the function approximation to $E(t \mid \mathbf{p})$. Assuming Gaussian distribution, the joint density function of the target variables given the input variables, β and M is [2]:

$$P(\mathbf{t} \mid \mathbf{p}, \mathbf{w}, \beta, M) = \left(\frac{\beta}{2\pi}\right)^{\frac{N}{2}} \exp\left[-\frac{\beta}{2}\sum_{i=1}^{N}(t_i - f(\mathbf{p_i}))^2\right]$$

$$= \left(\frac{\beta}{2\pi}\right)^{\frac{N}{2}} \exp\left[-\frac{\beta}{2}E_D(D \mid \mathbf{w}, M)\right] \tag{7}$$

where $E_D(D \mid \mathbf{w}, M)$ is as given in equation (3) and (4). Letting $Z_D(\beta) = \int \exp\left[-\frac{\beta}{2}E_D(D \mid \mathbf{w}, M)\right] = \left(\frac{2\pi}{\beta}\right)^{\frac{N}{2}}$, the posterior density of $\mathbf{w}$ in equation (5) can be expressed as

$$P(\mathbf{w} \mid D, \alpha, \beta, M) = \frac{\dfrac{1}{Z_W(\alpha)Z_D(\beta)}\exp\left[-\dfrac{1}{2}(\beta E_D + \alpha E_W)\right]}{P(D \mid \alpha\,\beta\,M)},$$

$$= \frac{1}{Z_F(\alpha, \beta)}\exp\left[-\frac{F(w)}{2}\right] \tag{8}$$

where $Z_F(\alpha, \beta) = \left[Z_W(\alpha)Z_D(\beta)P(D \mid \alpha, \beta, M\right]$ and $F = \beta E_D + \alpha E_W$. In an empirical Bayesian framework, the "optimal" weights are those that maximize the posterior density $P(\mathbf{w} \mid D, \alpha, \beta, M)$. Maximizing the posterior density of $P(\mathbf{w} \mid D, \alpha, \beta, M)$ is equivalent to minimizing the regularized objective function F given in equation (4). Therefore, this indicates that values of α and β need to be predicted by architecture M, which will be further discussed in the next section.

While minimization of objective function F is identical to finding the (locally) maximum *a posteriori* estimates $\mathbf{w}^{MAP}$, minimization of E_D in F by any backpropagation training algorithm is identical to finding the maximum likelihood estimates $\mathbf{w}^{ML}$ [12]. Bayesian optimization of the regularization parameters require computation of the Hessian matrix of the objective function F evaluated at the optimum point $\mathbf{w}^{MAP}$ [3]. However, directly computing the Hessian matrix is not always required. As proposed by MacKay [12], the Gauss-Newton approximation to the Hessian matrix can be used if the LM optimization algorithm is employed to locate the minimum of F [16].

4.1. Brief discussion of Levenberg-Marquardt optimization

The LM algorithm is a robust numerical optimization technique for mapping as well as function approximation. The LM modification to Gauss-Newton is

38 Artificial Neural Networks - Models and Applications

$$(H + \mu I)\delta = -J'e \tag{9}$$

and the Hessian matrix can be approximated as:

$$H = J'J, \tag{10}$$

where J is the Jacobian matrix that contains first derivatives of the network errors with respect to network parameters (the weights and biases), μ is the Levenberg's damping factor, and δ is the parameter update vector. The δ indicates how much the magnitude of weights needs to be changed to attain better prediction ability. The way to calculate J matrix is given in equation (11). The gradient of the ANN is computed as $g = J'e$. The μ in equation (9) is adjustable in each iteration, and guides the optimization process during ANN learning with the training data set. If reductions of the cost function F are rapid, then the parameter μ is divided by a constant (c) to bring the algorithm closer to the Gauss-Newton, whereas if an iteration gives insufficient reduction in F, then μ is multiplied by the same constant giving a step closer to the gradient descent direction (http://crsouza-blog.azurewebsites.net/2009/11/neural-network-learning-by-the-levenberg-marquardt-algorithm-with-bayesian-regularization-part-1/#levenberg). Therefore, the LM algorithm can be considered a trust-region modification to Gauss-Newton designed to serve as an intermediate optimization algorithm between the Gauss-Newton method and the Gradient-Descent algorithm [17].

The Jacobian matrix is a matrix of all first-order partial derivatives of a vector-valued function. The dimensions of the matrix are formed by the number of observations in the training data and the total number of parameters (weights + biases) in the ANN being used. It can be created by taking the partial derivatives of each output with respect to each weight, and has the form:

$$J = \begin{bmatrix} \dfrac{\partial e_1(w)}{\partial w_1} & \dfrac{\partial e_1(w)}{\partial w_2} & \cdots & \dfrac{\partial e_1(w)}{\partial w_n} \\[2ex] \dfrac{\partial e_2(w)}{\partial w_1} & \dfrac{\partial e_2(w)}{\partial w_2} & \cdots & \dfrac{\partial e_2(w)}{\partial w_n} \\[2ex] \vdots & \vdots & \ddots & \vdots \\[2ex] \dfrac{\partial e_N(w)}{\partial w_1} & \dfrac{\partial e_N(w)}{\partial w_2} & \cdots & \dfrac{\partial e_N(w)}{\partial w_n} \end{bmatrix} \tag{11}$$

The parameters at l iteration are updated as in equation (12) when the Gauss-Newton approximation of the Hessian matrix by LM in Bayesian regularized neural network (BRANN) is used.

$$w^{l+1} = w^l - \left[\mathbf{J}^T \mathbf{J} + \mu \mathbf{I} \right]^{-1} \mathbf{J}^T \mathbf{e} \tag{12}$$

Therefore, this approach provides a numerical solution to the problem of minimizing a nonlinear function over the parameter space. In addition, this approach is a popular alternative to the Gauss-Newton method of finding the minimum of a function (http://crsouza-blog.azurewebsites.net/2009/11/neural-network-learning-by-the-levenberg-marquardt-algorithm-with-bayesian-regularization-part-1/#levenberg). Next, let's compare the equations for some common training algorithms and use this information to decipher how parameters are updated after each iteration (epoch) in ANN: Updating the strength connection in standard backpropagation training $w^{l+1} = w^l - \alpha \frac{\partial E_D}{w^l}$,

updating the strength connection in Quasi-Newton training $w^{l+1} = w^l - \mathbf{H}_l^{-1} \alpha \frac{\partial E}{w^l}$, and

updating the strength connection in LM training $w^{l+1} = w^l - \left[\mathbf{J}^T \mathbf{J} + \mu \mathbf{I} \right]^{-1} \mathbf{J}^T \mathbf{e}$.

Therefore, Quasi-Newton is necessary for actual calculation of the Hessian matrix $\mathbf{H}$ while LM is used to approximate $\mathbf{H}$. The α coefficient in the first two equations is referred to as the learning rate. The performance of the algorithm is very sensitive to proper setting of the learning rate. If the learning rate is set too high, the algorithm can oscillate and become unstable. On the other hand, too low learning rate makes the network learn very slowly and converging of ANN will take a while. In gradient descent learning, it is not practical to determine the optimal setting for the learning rate before training, and in fact, the optimal learning rate changes during the training process, as the algorithm moves across the performance surface [18].

5. Tuning parameters α and β

As discussed earlier, minimizing the regularized objective function $F = \beta E_D(D \mid w, M) + \alpha E_W(w \mid M)$ in equation (4) is equivalent to maximization of the posterior density $P(\mathbf{w} \mid D, \alpha, \beta, M)$. A typical procedure used in neural networks infers α and β by maximizing the marginal likelihood of the data in equation (5). The joint probability of α and β is

$$P(\alpha, \beta \mid D, M) = \frac{P(D \mid \alpha, \beta, M) P(\alpha, \beta \mid M)}{P(D \mid M)}. \tag{13}$$

Essentially, we need to maximize the posterior probability $P(\alpha\ \beta \mid D, M)$ with respect to hyperparameters α and β which is equivalent to maximization of $P(D \mid \alpha, \beta, M)$. $P(D \mid \alpha, \beta, M)$ is the normalization factor given for the posterior distribution of $\mathbf{w}$ in equation (5).

If we apply the unity activation function in equation (5), which is the analog of linear regression, then this equation will have a closed form. Otherwise, equation (5) does not have a closed form if we apply any sigmoidal activation function, such as logit or tangent hyperbolic in the hidden layer. Hence, the marginal likelihood is approximated using a Laplacian integration completed in the area of the current value $\mathbf{w}=\mathbf{w}^{MAP}$ [3]. The Laplacian approximation to the marginal density in equation (5) is expressed as

$$\log\left[p(D\mid\alpha,\beta,M)\right] \approx K + \frac{n}{2}\log(\beta) + \frac{m}{2}\log(\alpha) - \left|F(\alpha,\beta)\right|_{w=w_{(\alpha,\beta)}^{MAP}} - \frac{1}{2}\log\parallel\mathbf{H}\parallel_{w=w_{(\alpha,\beta)}^{MAP}} \tag{14}$$

where K is a constant and $\mathbf{H} = \dfrac{\partial^2}{\partial\mathbf{w}\,\partial\mathbf{w}'}F(\alpha,\beta)$ is the Hessian matrix as given in equation (10) and (11). A grid search can be used to locate the α, β maximizers of the marginal likelihood in the training set. An alternative approach [12, 14] involves iteration (updating is from right to left, with $\mathbf{w}^{MAP}$ evaluated at the "old" values of the tuning parameters)

$$\alpha_{new} = \frac{m}{2\left(\mathbf{w}^{MAP}{}'\mathbf{w}^{MAP} + tr\mathbf{H}_{MAP}^{-1}\right)}$$

and

$$\beta_{new} = \frac{n - m + 2\alpha_{MAP}tr\mathbf{H}_{MAP}^{-1}}{2\sum_{i=1}^{n}\left(t_i - b - \sum_{k=1}^{S}w_k g_k\left(b_k + \sum_{j=1}^{n}a_{ij}u_j^{\bullet\bullet[k]}\right)\right)^2_{w=w_{(\alpha,\beta)}^{MAP}}} \Rightarrow \beta_{new} = \frac{n - \gamma}{2E_D(\mathbf{w}^{MAP})} \tag{15}$$

The expression $\gamma = m - 2\alpha_{new}tr(\mathbf{H}^{MAP})^{-1}$ is referred to as the number of effective parameters in the neural network and its value ranges from 0 (or 1, if an overall intercept b is fitted) to m, the total number of connection strength coefficients, w, and bias, b, parameters in the network. The effective number of parameters indicates the number of effective weights being used by the network. Subsequently, the number of effective parameters is used to evaluate the model complexity and performance of BRANNs. If γ is close to m, over-fitting results, leading to poor generalization.

6. Steps in BRANN

A summary of steps in BRANN is given in **Figure 3**. Initialize α, β and the weights, w. After the first training step, the objective function parameters will recover from the initial setting.

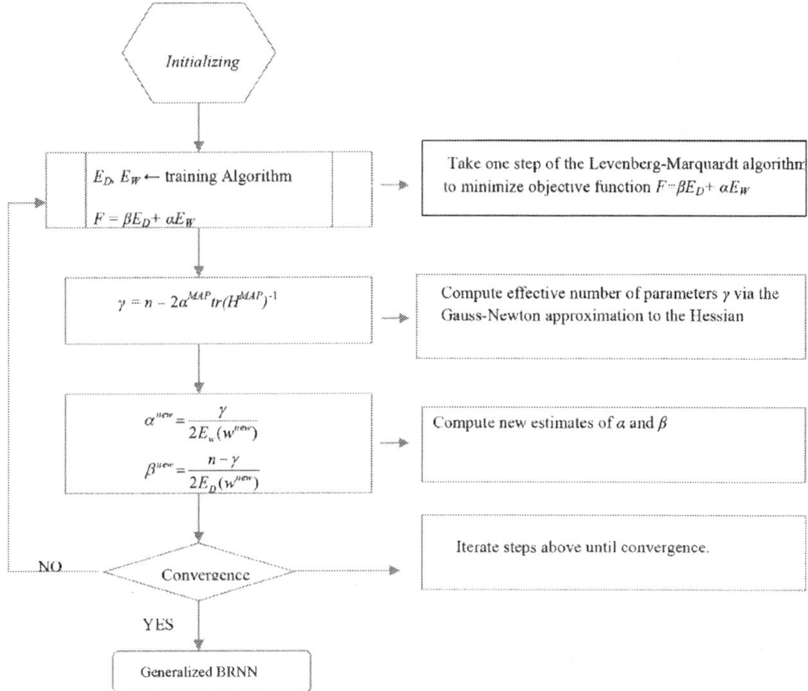

Figure 3. Flow chart for Bayesian optimization of regularization parameters α and β in the neural networks; MAP=maximum *a posteriori* [partially adapted from 16 and 2].

1. Take one step of the LM algorithm to minimize the objective function $F(\alpha,\beta)$ and find the current value of **w**.

    i.   Compute the Jacobian as given in equation (11).

    ii.   Compute the error gradient $g = J^T e$.

    iii. Approximate the Hessian matrix using $H = J^T J$.

          Calculate the objective function as given in equation (4).

          Solve the $J'J + \mu I)\delta = J'e$.

Update the network weights **w** using **δ**.

2. Compute the effective number of parameters $\gamma = N - 2a\,tr(\mathbf{H})^{-1}$ making use of the Gauss-Newton approximation to the Hessian matrix available from the LM training algorithm.

3. Compute updated α_{new} and β_{new} as

$$\alpha^{MAP} = \frac{\gamma}{2E_w(w^{MAP})} \quad and \quad \beta^{MAP} = \frac{m - \gamma}{2E_D(w^{MAP})} \quad ; and$$

4. Iterate steps 2-4 until convergence.

7. Practical considerations

In general, there are three steps between input and predicted values in ANN training. These are pre-processing, network object (training), and post-processing. These steps are important to make ANN more efficient as well as drive optimal knowledge from ANN. Some of these steps will be considered in the following sections.

7.1. Data cleaning

Before training, the data sets should be checked in terms of constant, corrupt, and incorrect values from the input and target data set. After checking for suspicious and improper data, the dimension of the input vector could be an important issue for efficient training. In some situations, the dimensions of the data vectors could be large, but the components in the data vectors can be highly correlated (redundant). Principal component analysis (PCA) is the most common technique for dimensionality reduction and orthogonalization.

7.2. Normalization

Normalization or scaling is not really a functional requirement for the neural networks to learn, but it significantly helps as it converts the input and target (independent and dependent variables in statistical jargon) into the data range that the sigmoid activation functions lie in (i.e. for logistic [0, 1] and tanh [−1, 1]. For example, in MLP, non-linear functions in hidden layers become saturated when the input is larger than six (exp(-6)~0.00247). Consequently, large inputs cause ill-conditioning by leading to very small weights. Further with large inputs, the gradient values become very small, and the network training will be very slow.

By default, before initiating the network processing, MATLAB Neural Network Toolbox® rescales both input and output variables such that they lie -1 to +1 range, to boost numerical stability. This task is done spontaneously in MATLAB Neural Network Toolbox® using the "mapminmax" function. To explain this, consider the simple data vector as x'=[8, 1, 5]. Here the $x_{min} = 1$ and $x_{max} = 8$. If values are to range between $A_{min} = -1$ and $A_{max} = +1$, one redefine the data vector temporarily as $x_{temp}' = [-1, 1, 5]$, so only $x_3 = 5$ needs to be rescaled to guarantee that all variables reside between -1 and +1. This is done by using the following formula:

$$x_{3,new} = A_{min} + \frac{x_3 - x_{min}}{x_{max} - x_{min}}(A_{max} - A_{min}) = -1 + \frac{5-1}{8-1}2 = -0.143.$$

When the input and target data is normalized, the network output always falls into a normalized range. The network output can then be reverse transformed into the units of the original target data when the network is put to use in the field [18].

7.3. Multiple runs

Each time a neural network is trained, the output obtained from each run can result in a different solution mainly due to: a) different initial weight and bias values, and b) different splitting of data into training, validation, and test sets (or into training and testing). As a result, function approximation using different neural network architectures trained on the same problem can produce different outputs for the same input fed into the ANN. For example, depending on the initial weights of the network, the algorithm may converge to local minima or not converge at all. To avoid local minima convergence and overtraining, improve the predictive ability of ANN, and eliminate spurious effects caused by random starting values. Several independent BRANNs, say 10, should be trained for each architecture. Results are then recorded as the average of several runs on each architecture.

7.4. Analyses and computing environment

Determination of the optimal number of neurons in the hidden layer is an essential task in ANN architectures. As stated earlier, network with only a few neurons in hidden layer may be incapable of capturing complex association between target and input variables. However, if too excessive neurons are assigned in hidden part of the network then it will follow the noise in the data due to overparameterization, leading to bad generalization and poor predictive ability of unseen data [3, 19]. Therefore, a different number of neurons in the hidden layer should be tried, and architecture performance should be assessed after each run with a certain number of neurons in the hidden layer. Because highly parameterized models are penalized in BRANN, the complexity of BRANN architectures using sum of squares weights as well as the degree of shrinkage attained by BRANN can be used to determine the optimal number of neurons. The number of parameters (weights and biases) is a function of the number of neurons. More neurons in the hidden layer imply that more parameters need to be estimated. Therefore, one criteria for model selection in complex BRANN concerns the number of weights. The more weights there are, relative to the number of training cases, the more overfitting amplifies noise in the target variables [1–3]. As demonstrated in **Figure 4**, BRANN also calculates the effective number of parameters to evaluate the degree of complexity in ANN architecture. BRANN uses the LM algorithm (based on linearization) for computing the posterior modes in BR. The penalized residual sum of squares is also used to determine the number of neurons in the hidden part of the network.

7.5. Stopping training of BRANN

In MATLAB applications, training of BRANN is stopped if:

1. The maximum number of epochs (number of iterations in statistical jargon) is reached

2. Performance of the network with the number of neurons and combinations of the activation functions has met a suitable level

3. The gradient ($\mathbf{J'e}$) was below a suitable target

4. The LM μ parameter exceeded a suitable maximum (training stopped when it became larger than 10^{10}).

Each of these targets and goals are set as the default values in MATLAB implementation. The maximum number of iterations (called epochs) in back-propagation was set to 1000, and iteration will stop earlier if the gradient of the objective function is below a suitable level, or when there are obvious problems with the algorithm [20].

8. Interpreting the results

8.1. Degree of complexity

This example illustrates the impact of shrinkage and how regularized neural networks deal with the "curse of dimensionality". The example given here has 500 inputs and the number of neurons in the hidden layer is 5, such that the total of nominal parameters (weights and biases) is 2511. However, the effective number of parameters is 316 (**Figure 4**). In other words, the model can be explained well with only with 316 parameters when BR is used for training the networks. In practice, different architectures (different activation functions and different numbers of neurons in the hidden layer) should be explored to decide which architecture best fits the data. Hence, incremental increasing of the number of neurons from one to several is the best practice to cope with the "curse of dimensionality".

8.2. Predictive performance

The predictive correlation is 0.87 (**Figure 4**) in the given example, which is quite high, implying that the predictive ability of the model used is sufficient. However, as stated earlier, to eliminate spurious effects caused by random starting values, several independent BRANNs should be trained for each architecture and the average value of multiple runs should be reported.

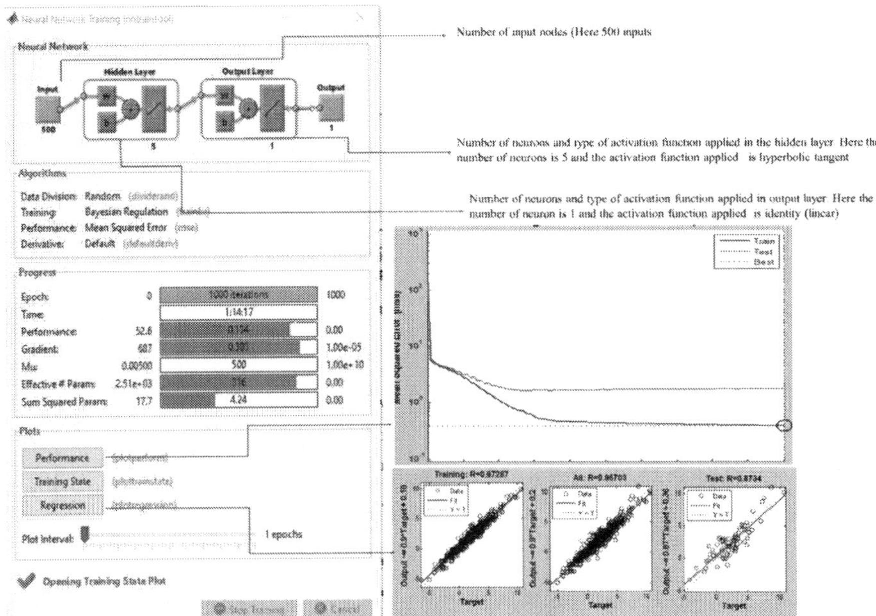

Figure 4. Output screens from MATLAB runs.

8.3. Shrinkage

The distribution of connection strengths (network parameters) in an ANN gives an evidence of the degree of regularization achieved by BRANNs. Conventionally, weight values are shrinkage with model complexity, in the same approach that estimates of network parameters become smaller in BR implementations. This is true when inputs p increase and training sample size remains constant. Moreover, the distribution of weights in any architecture is often associated with the predictive ability of network; small value weights tend to lead to better generalization for unseen data [1, 19]. **Figure 4** shows the distributions of weights for the nonlinear regularized networks with five neurons in the hidden layer. It is suggested that a linear activation function in the hidden and output layers, as well as a nonlinear activation function with different numbers of neurons in the hidden and a linear activation function in output layer should be tried. This provides a good opportunity to compare models for the extent of regularization attained. For example, the sum of squared weights for about 2500 parameters is only 4.24 in the given example (see **Figure 4**), indicating how Bayesian neural networks reduce the effective number of weights relative to what would be obtained without regularization. In other words, the method by which highly parameterized models are penalized in the Bayesian approach helps to prevent over-fitting.

9. Conclusion

Small *n and big p* (*p>>n*) is key issue for prediction of complex traits from big data sets, and ANNs provide efficient and functional approaches to deal with this problem. Because the competency of capturing highly nonlinear relationship between input and outcome variables, ANNs act as universal approximators to learn complex functional forms adaptively by using different type of nonlinear functions. Overfitting and over-parameterization are critical concerns when ANN is used for prediction in (*p>>n*). However, BRANN plays a fundamental role in attenuating these concerns. The objective function used in BRANN has an additional term that penalizes large weights to attain a smoother mapping and handle overfitting problem. Because of the shrinkage, the effective number of parameters attained by BRANN is less than the total number of parameters used in the model. Thus, the over-fitting is attenuated and generalization ability of the model is improved considerably.

Acknowledgements

Author would like to sincerely thank Jacob Keaton for his reduction, and comments.

Author details

Hayrettin Okut

Address all correspondence to: okut.hayrettin@gmail.com

Yüzüncü Yıl University, Faculty of Agriculture, Biometry and Genetic Branch, Van, Turkey

Wake Forest University, School of Medicine, Center for Diabetes Research, Center for Genomics and Personalized Medicine Research, Winston-Salem, NC, USA

References

[1] Gianola, D., Okut, H., Weigel, K., Rosa, J. G. Predicting complex quantitative traits with Bayesian neural networks: a case study with Jersey cows and wheat. BMC Genetics. 2011. 12:87.

[2] Okut, H., Gianola, D., Rosa, J. G., Weigel, K. Prediction of body mass index in mice using dense molecular markers and a regularized neural network. Genetics Research (Cambridge). 2011. 93:189–201

[3] Okut, H., Wu, X. L., Rosa, J. M. G., Bauck, S., Woodward, B., Schnabel, D. R., Taylor, F. J., Gianola, D. Predicting expected progeny difference for marbling score in Angus cattle using artificial neural networks and Bayesian regression models. Genetics Selection Evolution. 2014. 45:34. DOI: 10.1186/1297-9686-45-34.

[4] Lampinen, J., Vehtari, A. Bayesian approach for neural networks review and case studies. Neural Networks. 2001. 14:257–274.

[5] SAS® Enterprise Miner™ 14.1. Administration and Configuration Copyright©. Cary, NC: SAS Institute Inc.; 2015.

[6] Feng, N., Wang, F., Qiu, Y. Novel approach for promoting the generalization ability of neural networks. International Journal of Signal Processing. 2006. 2:131–135.

[7] Ping, G., Michael, R. L., Chen, C. L. P. Regularization parameter estimation for feed-forward neural networks. IEEE Transactions on Systems, Man, and Cybernetics—PART B: Cybernetics. 2003. 33:35–44.

[8] Wang, H. J., Ji, F., Leung, C. S., Sum, P. F. Regularization parameter selection for faulty neural networks. International Journal of Intelligent Systems and Technologies. 2009. 4:45–48.

[9] Marwala, T. Bayesian training of neural networks using genetic programming. Pattern Recognition Letters. 2007. 28:1452–1458.

[10] Matignon, R. Data Mining Using SAS Enterprise Miner. Chicago: Wiley; 2007. p. 584. ISBN: 978-0-470-14901-0. DOI: 10.1002/9780470171431

[11] Okut, H., Gianola, D., Rosa, J. G., Weigel, K. Evaluation of prediction ability of Cholesky factorization of genetic relationship matrix for additive and non-additive genetic effect using Bayesian regularized neural network. IORE Journal of Genetics. 2015. 1(1). 1–15

[12] MacKay, J. C. D. Information Theory, Inference and Learning Algorithms. Cambridge University Press, Cambridge-UK; 2008.

[13] Foresee, F. D., Hagan, M. T. Gauss-Newton approximation to Bayesian learning. Proceedings: IEEE International Conference on Neural Networks. 1997. Vol:3, 1930–1935.

[14] Titterington, D. M. Bayesian methods for neural networks and related models. Statistical Science. 2004. 19:128–139.

[15] Bishop, C. M., Tipping, M. E. A hierarchical latent variable model for data visualization. IEEE Transactions on Pattern Analysis and Machine Intelligence. 1998. 20(3):281–293.

[16] Shaneh, A., Butler, G. Bayesian learning for feedforward neural network with application to proteomic data: the glycosylation sites detection of the epidermal growth factor-

like proteins associated with cancer as a case study. In Canadian AI LNAI 4013, 2006 (ed. L. Lamontagne & M. Marchand). Berlin-Heiddelberg: Springer-Verleg; 2006. 110–121.

[17] Battiti, R. Using mutual information for selecting features in supervised neural net learning neural networks. IEEE Transactions on Neural Networks. 1994. 5(4):537–550.

[18] Demuth, H., Beale, M., Hagan, M. Neural Network ToolboxTM 6 User's Guide. Natick, MA: The MathWorks Inc.; 2010.

[19] Felipe, P.S. V., Okut, H., Gianola, D., Silva, A. M., Rosa, J. M. G. Effect of genotype imputation on genome-enabled prediction of complex traits: an empirical study with mice data. BMC Genetics. 2014. 15:149. DOI: 10.1186/s12863-014-0149-9

[20] Haykin, S. Neural Networks: Comprehensive Foundation. New York: Prentice-Hall; 2008.

Chapter 3

Generalized Regression Neural Networks with Application in Neutron Spectrometry

Ma. del Rosario Martinez-Blanco,

Víctor Hugo Castañeda-Miranda,

Gerardo Ornelas-Vargas,

Héctor Alonso Guerrero-Osuna,

Luis Octavio Solis-Sanchez,

Rodrigo Castañeda-Miranda,

José María Celaya-Padilla, Carlos Eric Galvan-Tejada,

Jorge Isaac Galvan-Tejada,

Héctor René Vega-Carrillo,

Margarita Martínez-Fierro, Idalia Garza-Veloz and

Jose Manuel Ortiz-Rodriguez

Additional information is available at the end of the chapter

http://dx.doi.org/10.5772/64047

Abstract

The aim of this research was to apply a generalized regression neural network (GRNN) to predict neutron spectrum using the rates count coming from a Bonner spheres system as the only piece of information. In the training and testing stages, a data set of 251 different types of neutron spectra, taken from the International Atomic Energy Agency compilation, were used. Fifty-one predicted spectra were analyzed at testing stage. Training and testing of GRNN were carried out in the MATLAB environment by means of a scientific and technological tool designed based on GRNN technology, which is capable of solving the neutron spectrometry problem with high performance and generalization capability. This computational tool automates the pre-processing of information, the training and testing stages, the statistical analysis, and the post-processing of the information. In this work, the performance of feed-forward backpropagation neural networks (FFBPNN) and GRNN was compared in the solution of the neutron spectrometry problem. From the results obtained, it can be observed that

© 2016 The Author(s). Licensee InTech. This chapter is distributed under the terms of the Creative Commons Attribution License (http://creativecommons.org/licenses/by/3.0), which permits unrestricted use, distribution, and reproduction in any medium, provided the original work is properly cited.

despite very similar results, GRNN performs better than FFBPNN because the former could be used as an alternative procedure in neutron spectrum unfolding methodologies with high performance and accuracy.

Keywords: artificial intelligence, statistical artificial neural networks, neutron spectrometry, unfolding codes, spectra unfolding

1. Introduction

Artificial Intelligence or AI is one of the newest fields of intellectual research that attempts to understand the intelligent entities [1]. Intelligence could be defined by the properties it exhibits: an ability to deal with new situations, to solve problems, to answer questions, to devise plans, and so on [2]. The phrase AI was coined by John McCarthy in the 1940s and to date evades a concise and formal definition [3]. A simple definition might be: AI is the study of systems that act in a way, that to any observer would appear to be intelligent, and involves using methods based on the intelligent behavior of humans and other animals to solve complex problems.

AI has been classified into three periods: the classical, the romantic, and the modern periods [1–4]. The major area of research covered under the classical period, in the 1950s, was intelligent search problems involved in game-playing and theorem proving. In the romantic period, from the mid-1960s until the mid-1970s, people were interested in making machines "understand," by which they usually meant the understanding of natural languages. The modern period started from the latter half of 1970s to the present day and includes research on both, theories and practical aspects of AI. This period is devoted to solving relatively simple or complex problems that are integral to more complex systems of practical interest.

The aim of the study of AI is to use algorithms, heuristics, and methodologies based on the ways in which the human brain solves problems. In the most recent decades, AI areas of particular importance include multi-agent systems; artificial life; computer vision; planning; playing games, chess in particular; and machine learning [5–6].

1.1. Machine learning and connectionism

Learning and intelligence are intimately related to each other. Learning is an inherent characteristic of human beings [3]. By virtue of this, people, while executing similar tasks, acquire the ability to improve their performance with the self-improvement of future behavior based on past experience. In most learning problems, the task is to learn to classify inputs according to a finite, or sometimes infinite, set of classifications [2]. Typically, a learning system is provided with a set of training data, which have been classified by hand. The system then attempts to learn from these training data how to classify the same data, usually a relative easy task, and also how to classify new data that are not seen [7].

The principles of learning can be applied to machines to improve their performance [8]. A system capable of learning is intelligent and is usually expected to be able to learn based on past experience. Such learning is usually referred to as "machine learning" (ML) which is an important part of AI and can be broadly classified into three categories: supervised, unsupervised, and reinforcement learning.

Supervised learning requires a trainer who supplies the input-output training instances. The learning system adapts its parameters using some algorithms to generate the desired output patterns from a given input pattern. In absence of trainers, the desired output of a given input instance is not known; consequently, the learner has to adapt its parameters autonomously. Such type of learning is termed unsupervised learning.

Reinforcement learning bridges the gap between the supervised and unsupervised categories. In reinforcement learning, the learner does not explicitly know the input-output instances, but it receives some form of feedback from its environment. The feedback signals help the learner to decide whether its action on the environment is rewarding or punishable. The learner thus adapts its parameters based on the states (rewarding/punishable) of its actions.

Recently, the connectionist approach for building intelligent machines with structured models like artificial neural networks (ANN) is receiving more attention [9]. Connectionist models are based on how computation occurs in biological neural networks. Connections play an essential role in connectionist models, hence the name *connectionism* [10]. The term connectionism was introduced by Donald Hebb in the 1940s, and it is a set of approaches in the fields of AI that models mental or behavioral phenomena as the emergent processes of interconnected networks of simple units [11]. The central connectionist principle is that mental phenomena can be described by interconnected networks of simple and uniform units.

Figure 1. The unit: the basic information processing structure of a connectionist model.

Units are to a connectionist model what neurons are to a biological neural network: the basic information processing structures. Since the flow of information in a network occurs through its connections, the link through which information flows from one member of the network to the next is known as synapses. Synapses are to neural networks what an Ethernet cable or telephone wire is to a computer network. Without synapses from other neurons, it would be impossible for a neuron to receive input and to send output from and to other neurons, respectively. Given the crucial role that connections play in a network of neurons, synapses in a biological neural network matter as much as the neurons themselves [12].

Most connectionist models are computer simulations executed on digital computers. In a connectionist computer model, units are usually represented by circles as shown in **Figure 1**. Because no unit by itself constitutes a network, connectionist models typically are composed of many units as illustrated in **Figure 2**. However, neural networks are organized in layers of neurons. For this reason, connectionist models are organized in layers of units as shown in **Figure 3**. **Figure 3** is still not a network because no group of objects qualifies as a network unless each member is connected to other members; it is the existence of connections that make a network, as illustrated in **Figure 4** [13].

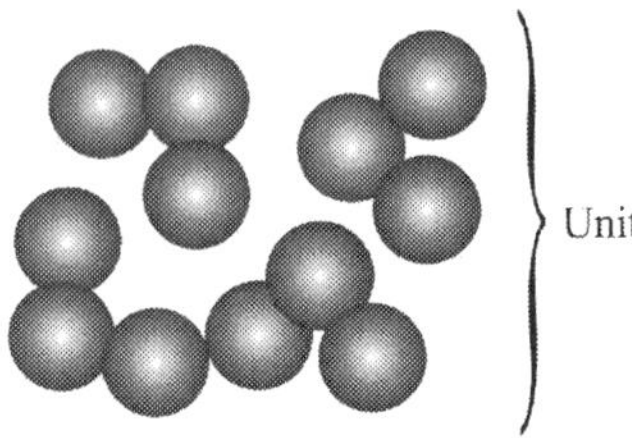

Figure 2. Connectionist model with 11 units.

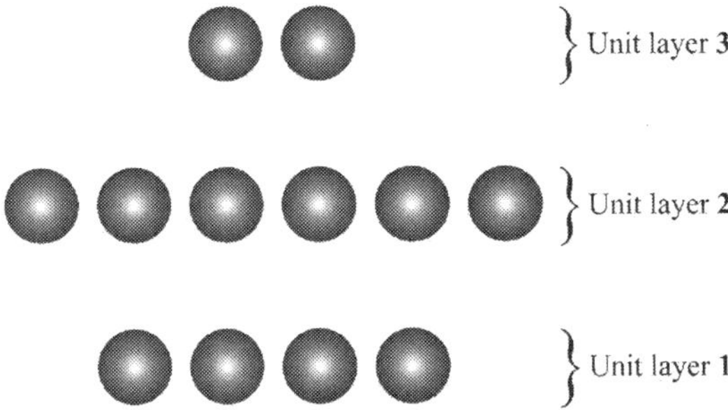

Figure 3. Connectionist model organized in layers.

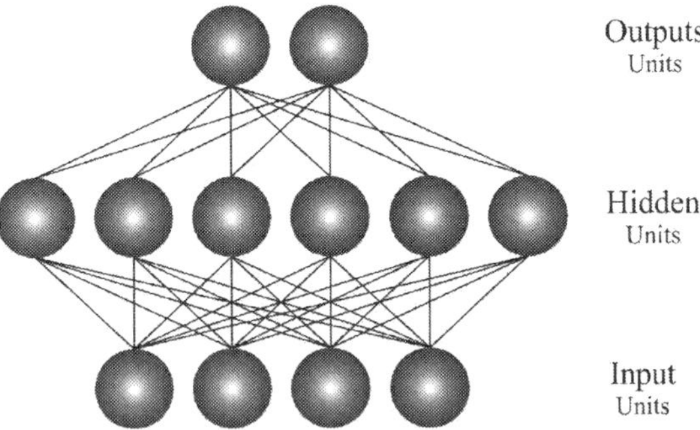

Figure 4. Network connectionist model.

In **Figure 4**, it can be seen that network connections are conduits through which information flows between the members of a network. In the absence of such connections, no group of objects qualifies as a network. There are two kinds of network connections: input and output. An input connection is a conduit through which a member of a network receives information. An output connection is a conduit through which a member of a network sends information. Although it is possible for a network connection to be both an input connection and an output connection, a unit does not qualify as a member of a network if it can neither receive information from other units nor send information to other units.

There are many forms of connectionism, but the most common forms use neural network models [14]. The form of the connections and the units can vary from model to model as shown in **Figures 5–9**, where it can be seen that any number of units may exist within each layer, and each unit of each layer is typically linked via a weighted connection to each node of the next layer. Data are supplied to the network through the input layer.

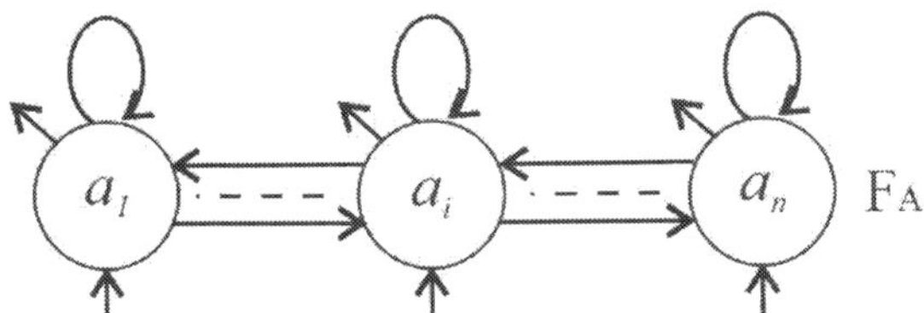

Figure 5. Single-layered recurrent net with lateral feedback structure.

Depending on the nature of the problems, neural network models are organized in different structural arrangements (architectures or topologies) [10]. The neural network architecture defines its structure including the number of hidden layers, number of hidden nodes, and number of nodes at the input and output layers. There are several types of ANN architectures. As illustrated in **Figures 5–9**, most of the widely used neural network models can be divided into two main categories: feed forward neural networks (FFNN) and feedback neural networks (FBNN) [10–14].

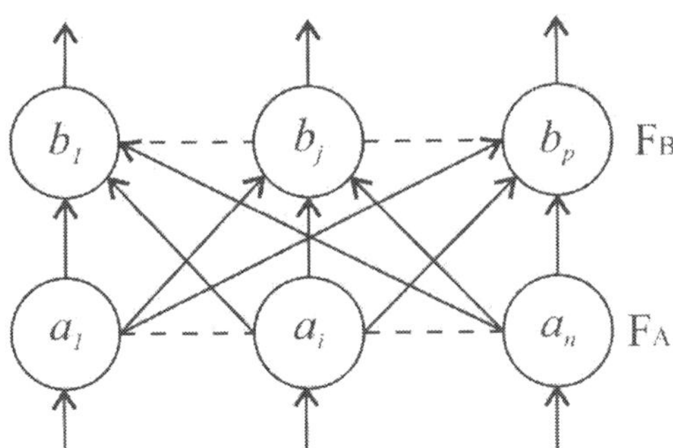

Figure 6. Two-layered feed-forward structure.

As shown in **Figures 6** and **8**, FFNNs allow signals to travel one way only; data enters the inputs and passes through the network, layer by layer, until it arrives at the output. There is no feedback or loops between layers. These networks are extensively used in pattern recognition and classification. FBNN can have signals traveling in both directions by introducing loops in the network as shown in **Figures 5, 7,** and **9**. FBNNs are dynamic; their state changes continuously until they reach an equilibrium point. They remain at the equilibrium point until the input changes and a new equilibrium needs to be found.

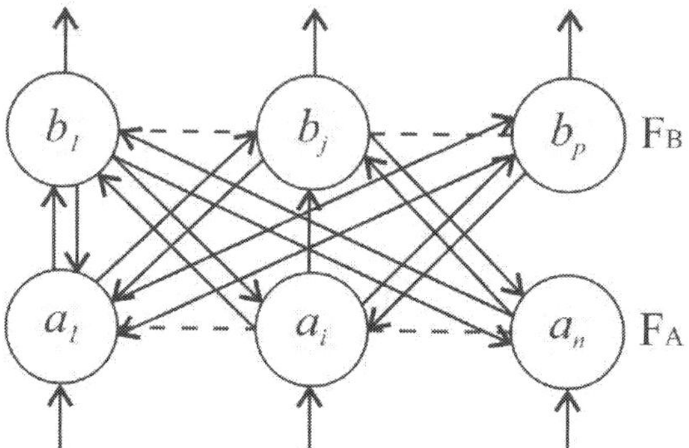

Figure 7. Two-layered feedback structure.

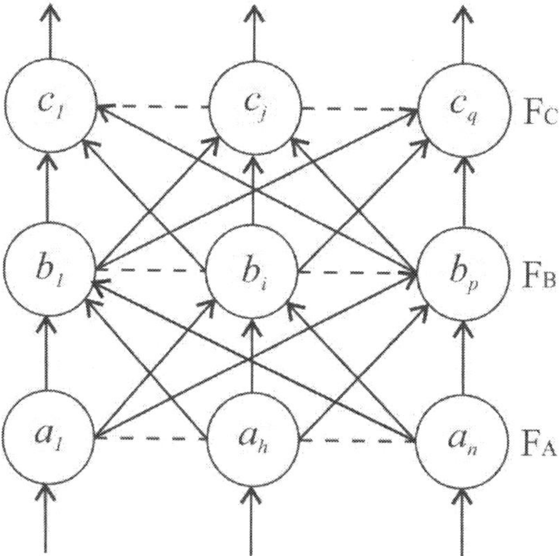

Figure 8. Three-layered feed-forward structure.

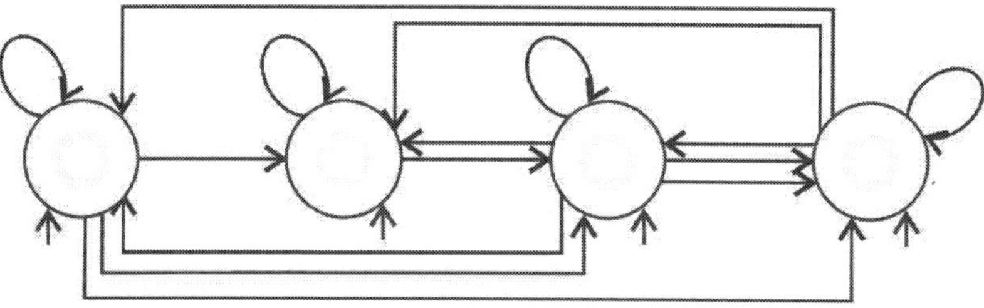

Figure 9. Single-layered recurrent structure.

In most connectionist models, units are organized into three layers: an input layer, one or more "hidden" layers, and an output layer [10–14]. **Figures 4** and **8** show a 3-layered FFNN consisting of 3 layers of units, where each unit is connected to each unit above it, and where information flows "forward" from the network's input units, through its "hidden" units, to its output units. The nodes of the hidden layer process input data they receive as the sum of the weighted outputs of the input layer. Nodes of the output layer process input data they receive as the sum of the weighted output of the units within the hidden layers, and supply the system output.

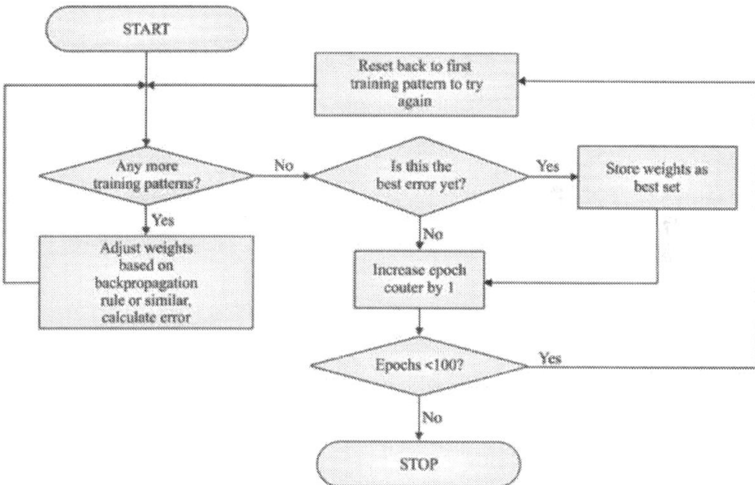

Figure 10. Supervised learning of ANN.

As mentioned earlier, the principles of learning can be applied to machines to improve their performance [15]. In FFNN, network learning is a very important process. The learning situation can be divided into two major categories: supervised and unsupervised. With supervised learning, the ANN must be trained before it becomes useful. Training consists of presenting input and output data to the network. **Figure 10** shows the distinguishing nature of supervised neural network, which incorporates an external trainer in which input and output are known, and its objective is to discover a relationship between the two. In this mode, the actual output of ANN is compared to the desired output.

An important issue concerning supervised learning is the problem of error convergence: the minimization of error between the desired and computed values. The performance of the network is evaluated based on the comparison between the computed (predicted) output and actual (desired) output value [10–15]. There are several types of measurements of prediction accuracy; the most common measurements used are as follows:

1. Coefficient of determination (R^2)

$$R^2 = \frac{\sum_{i=1}^{n}(\hat{Y}_i - \bar{Y})^2}{\sum_{i=1}^{n}(Y_i - \bar{Y})^2} \tag{1}$$

2. Mean Square Error (MSE)

$$MSE = \frac{1}{n}\sum_{i=0}^{n}(Y_i - \hat{Y}_i)^2 \tag{2}$$

3. Root Mean Square Error (RMSE)

$$RMSE = \left[\frac{1}{n}\sum_{i=0}^{n}(Y_i - \hat{Y}_i)^2\right]^{\frac{1}{2}} \tag{3}$$

4. Mean Absolute Percentage Error (MAPE)

$$MAPE\% = \frac{1}{n}\sum_{i=0}^{n}\left|\frac{Y_i - \hat{Y}_i}{Y_i}\right| \times 100 \tag{4}$$

where Y_i is the actual value of output, $\hat{Y}_i$ is the predicted value, and (n) is the number of observations.

Unlike supervised learning, unsupervised neural network uses no external feedback and it is based upon only local information. As can be seen from **Figure 11**, in unsupervised learning only the input is known and the goal is to uncover patterns in the features of the input data. It is also referred to as self-organization, in the sense that it self-organizes data presented to the network and detects their emergent collective properties. Unsupervised learning's goal is to have the computer learn how to do something that we do not tell it how to do. The common applications of unsupervised learning are classification, data mining, and self-organizing maps (SOM), also called Kohonen Neural Network (KNN).

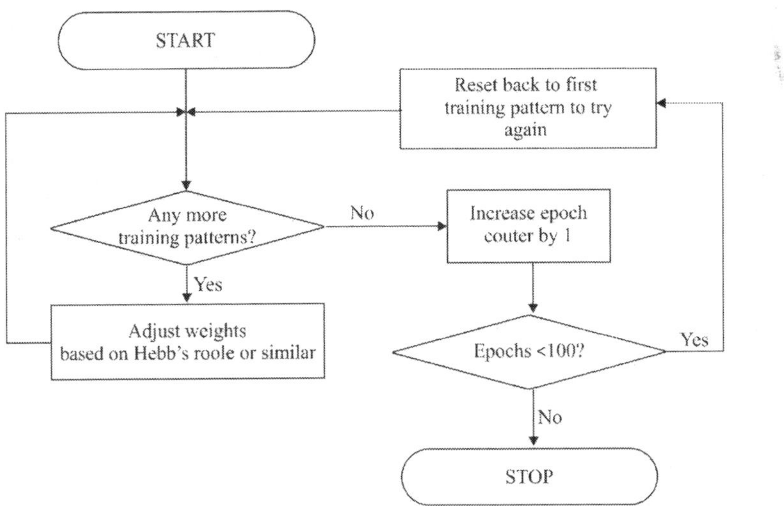

Figure 11. Unsupervised learning of ANN.

In FFNN with supervised training, two very different types of neural networks exist: FFNN trained with Backpropagation (BP) algorithm (FFBPNN) and Statistical Neural Networks (SNN) [10, 11, 14]. FFBPNNs use equations that are connected using weighting factors [11]. The selection of the weighting factors makes these neural nets very powerful. The multilayer perceptron (MLP) is the most common and successful neural network architecture with FFNN topologies, while the most common supervised learning technique used for training artificial neural networks is the multilayer backpropagation (BP) algorithm [10–15].

BP is a systematic method for training multilayer FFNN as shown in **Figure 8**. Since it is a supervised training algorithm, both the input and the target patterns are given (**Figure 10**). For a given input pattern, the output vector is estimated though a forward pass on the network. After the forward pass is over, the error vector at the output layer is estimated by taking the component-wise difference of the target pattern and the generated output vector. A function of errors of the output layered nodes is then propagated back through the network to each layer for adjustment of weights in that layer. The weight adaptation policy in BP algorithm is derived following the principle of steepest descent approach of finding minima of a multi-valued function.

BPFFNNs consist of neurons organized into one input layer and one output layer and several hidden layers of neurons as shown in **Figure 8**. Neurons perform some kind of calculation using inputs to compute an output that represents the system. The outputs are given on to the next neuron. An edge indicates to which neurons the output is given. These arcs carry weights.

Generally, BP learning consists of two passes: a forward pass and a backward pass. In the forward pass, an activity pattern is applied to the sensory nodes of the network. It is at last that a set of outputs is produced as the actual responses of the network. During this path, the synaptic weights are fixed. During backward pass, the synaptic weights are adjusted in accordance with an error correction rule.

BPFFNNs have the desirable characteristic of being very flexible. They can be used for pattern recognition as well as for decision-making problems. Another advantage is that like for every other neural network, the process is highly parallel and therefore the use of parallel processors is possible and cuts down the necessary time for calculations. However, BPNNs have negative characteristics. The training of the network can need a substantial amount of time [16]. The size of the training data for BPFFNN has to be very large. In some instances, it is almost impossible to provide enough training.

On the other hand, SNNs use statistical methods to select the equations within the structure and do not weigh these functions differently [17].

1.2. Statistical neural networks

SNNs are an important and very popular type of neural networks that mainly depend on statistical methods and probability theory [18]. Three of the most important types of these networks are Radial Basis Function Neural Network (RBFNNs), Probabilistic Neural Network (PNNs), and General Regression Neural Network (GRNNs) [19].

1.2.1. Radial basis function neural network

RBFNN was introduced by Broomhead and Lowe in 1988 and is a popular alternative to FFBPNN [20]. The behavior of the network depends on the weights and the activation of a transfer function F, specified for the units [21]. Activation functions are mathematical formulas that determine the output of a processing node [22]. The activation function maps the sum of weighted values passed to them by applying F into the output value, which is then "fired" on to the next layer.

There are several kinds of transfer or activation functions, typically falling into four common categories: Linear function (LF), Threshold function (TF), Sigmoid Function (SF), and Radial Basis Function (RBF) [23]. RBFs are a special class of activation functions which form a set of basis functions, one for each data set. The general form of RBF is:

$$G\left(\|X - \mu\|\right) \tag{5}$$

where G(.) is a positive nonlinear symmetric radial function (kernel); X is the input pattern and μ is the center of the function. Another important property of RBF is that its output is symmetric around the associated center μ. Thus, $f(X_i)$ can be taken to be a linear combination of the outputs of all the basis functions:

$$f(x) = \sum_{i=1}^{n} w_i G(X - \mu)$$

(6)

There are several common types of radial basis functions represented in **Table 1** [19–23]:

Function name	Mathematical form
Thin plate spline	$G(x) = (x - \mu)^2 \log(x - \mu)$
Multi-quadratic	$G(x) = \sqrt{(x - \mu)^2 + \sigma^2}$
Inverse multi-quadratic	$G(x) = \dfrac{1}{\sqrt{(x - \mu)^2 + \sigma^2}}$
Gaussian	$G(x) = exp\left(-\dfrac{(x - \mu)^2}{\sigma^2}\right)$

Table 1. Types of radial basis functions.

where these function parameters are the center (μ) and the radius (σ^2). A Gaussian function, also called "bell shaped curve" or normal distribution, is the most common applicable type of RBF. It is suitable not only in generalizing a global mapping but also in refining local features. The Gaussian function tends to be local in its response and is biologically more acceptable than other functions. RBF is unique, because unlike the others, it monotonically decreases with distance from the center, and forms the classic bell shaped curve which maps high values into low ones, and maps mid-range values into high ones. A plot of a Gaussian function is represented in **Figure 12**.

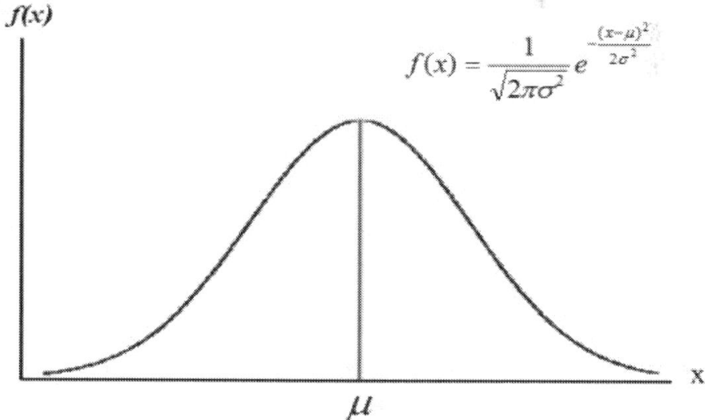

Figure 12. Plot representing a Gaussian function.

The mathematical form of this function for the case of a single variable is given by:

$$f(x) = \frac{1}{\sqrt{2\pi^2}}\, e^{\frac{(\chi-\mu)^2}{2\sigma^2}} \tag{7}$$

where

$$\mu = E(X) = \int_{-\infty}^{\infty} \chi.f(x)dx \tag{8}$$

$$\sigma^2 = E(X-\mu)^2 = \int_{-\infty}^{\infty} (\chi-\mu)^2.f(x)dx \tag{9}$$

μ: is the mean (center) of the distribution.

σ^2: is the variance (width or radius) of distribution.

Extending the formula (7) to multiple dimensions, we can get the general Gaussian probability density:

$$f(x) = \frac{1}{(2\pi)^{p/2}|\Sigma|^{p/2}} exp\left(-\frac{1}{2}(\underline{x}-\underline{\mu})^T \Sigma^{-1}(\underline{x}-\underline{\mu})\right) \tag{10}$$

where p is the number of dimensions, μ is the mean p-dimensional vector and Σ is the covariance p x p matrix.

RBFNNs are useful in solving problems where the input data are corrupted with additive noise and can be used for approximating functions and recognizing patterns [24]. As shown in **Figure 13**, the RBFNN has a feed forward architecture, and it is composed of many interconnected processing units or neurons organized in three successive layers. The first layer is the input layer. There is one neuron in the input layer for each predictor variable. The second layer is the hidden layer. This layer has a variable number of neurons. Each neuron consists of a RBF centered on a point with as many dimensions as there are predictor variables.

The standard euclidean distance is used to measure how far an input vector is located from the center. The value coming out from the neuron in the hidden layer is multiplied by a weight (W_i) associated with the neuron, also a bias value that is multiplied by a weight (W_o), is passed to the summation layer which adds up the weighted values and presents this sum as the network outputs.

The training of RBFNNs is radically different from the training of FFNNs [19–24]. RBFNN training may be done in two stages: First, calculating the RBF parameters, including centers and the scaling parameter. Various parameters, such as the number of neurons in the hidden layer, the coordinates of the center of each hidden layer function, the radius (width) of each function in each hidden unit, and the weights between the hidden and output units, are determined by the training process; second, estimating the weights between the hidden and output layers. Opposed to BPFFNN, in RBFNN training, there is no changing of the weights with the use of the gradient method for function minimization. In RBFNNs, training resolves itself into selecting the centers and calculating the weights of the output neuron.

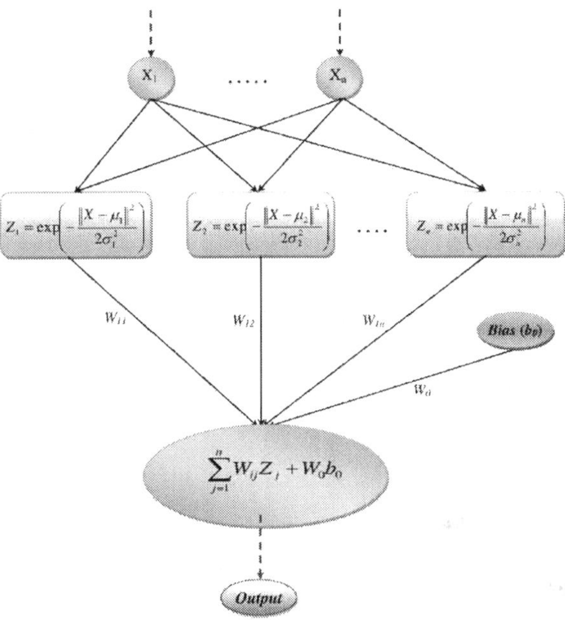

Figure 13. Network architecture of RBFNN.

The center (μ) and width radius (σ) of the radial function and final weights are the parameters of the model. Many algorithms have been designed to determine these parameters by minimizing the error between the target and actual output. Determination of centers is important for the success of the RBFNN and there are several methods to choose suitable centers for network, such as random selection from data set, randomly fixed, and clustering approach.

Determination of the width is very important for the success of the RBFNN. If the width values are large, the model will not be able to closely fit the function; on the other hand, a large width parameter would give better generalization but poorer output. A small width parameter gives good recall of the training patterns but poor generalization, and the model will over fit the data because each training point will have too much influence. There are several methods to determine the width. Two of the common methods for width selection are fixed method and distance averaging.

The number of hidden units is very important and plays a major role in RBFNN performance. It is very difficult to find a suitable number of hidden units. If the number of hidden units is too low, the network cannot reach a desired level of performance because of an insufficient number of hidden neurons. Many researchers assumed that the number of hidden units is fixed and is chose a priori.

There are several types of learning that can be used in RBFNNs, such as General Regression Neural Network (GRNN), Orthogonal Least Squares, K-Means Clustering, and P-Nearest Neighbour.

1.2.2. Probabilistic neural network

Specht first introduced the probabilistic neural network (PNN) in the 1990s. It closely related to "the Bayes Strategy for Pattern Classification" rule and Parzen nonparametric probability density function estimation theory. It performs classification where the target variable is categorical [19–24].

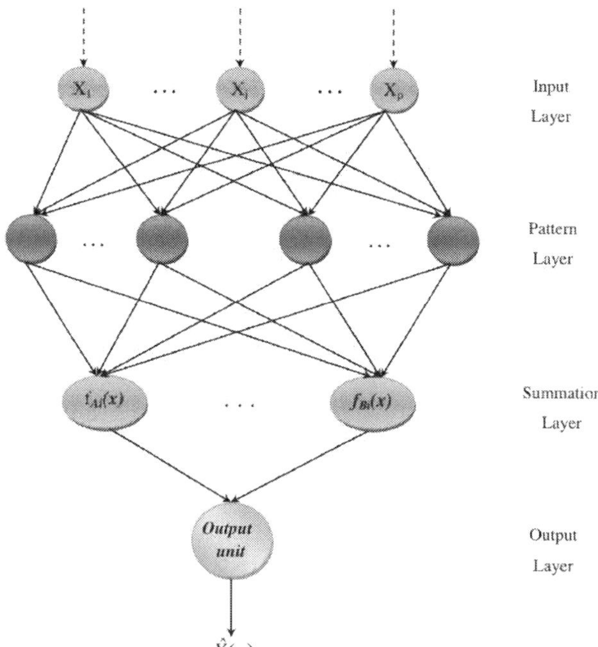

Figure 14. Block diagram of a probabilistic neural network (PNN).

PNNs are often more accurate than FFNNs and it is usually much faster to train PNNs than FFNNs. The greatest advantages of PNNs are the fact that the output is probabilistic which makes interpretation of output easy, and the training speed. Training a PNN is very fast because it requires that each pattern be presented to the network only once during training, unlike BPFFNNs, which require feedback of errors and adjusting weights and many presentations of training patterns. These PNNs, with variation can be used for mapping, classification, and associative memory. The greatest disadvantage is the network size since PNNs require more memory space to store the model.

The general structure of PNN, which is presented in **Figure 14**, consists of four layers. The first layer is the input layer. The input unit nodes do not perform any computation and simply distribute the input to the neurons in the first hidden layer (pattern layer). There is one neuron in the input layer for each predictor variable.

The second layer is the pattern layer. Each pattern unit represents information on one training sample. Each pattern unit calculates the probability of how well the input vector fits into the pattern unit. The neurons of the pattern layer are divided into K groups, one for each category. The i-th pattern neuron in the k-th group computes its output using a Gaussian kernel with the form:

$$f_{Ai}(X) = \frac{1}{(2\pi\sigma^2)^{p/2}} exp\left[-\frac{(X - X_{Ai})^T - (X - X_{Ai})}{2\sigma^2}\right]$$

(11)

where:

i: is the pattern number.

p: denotes the dimension of the pattern vector x.

σ: is the smoothing parameter of the Gaussian Kernel.

X_{Ai}: is the center of the kernel.

The third layer is the summation layer. In the summation layer, there is one pattern neuron for each category of the target variable. The neurons of this layer compute the approximation of the conditional class probability function through a combination of the previously computed densities as the following equation:

$$f_A(X) = \frac{1}{(2\pi\sigma^2)^{p/2}} \frac{1}{M} \sum_{i=1}^{M} exp\left[-\frac{(X - X_{Ai})^T - (X - X_{Ai})}{2\sigma^2}\right]$$

(12)

The fourth layer is the output layer (also called decision layer). At the output layer, we have a hard-limiting threshold: (+1) whenever an input pattern X belongs to category (A), and (-1) if it is from category (B).

The use of PNN is especially advantageous due to its ability to converge to the underlying function of the data with only few training samples available. The additional knowledge needed to get the fit in a satisfying way is relatively small and can be done without additional input by the user. GRNN falls into the category of PNN. This neural network, like other SNNs, needs only a fraction of the training samples a BPFFNN would need, mainly because the data available from measurements of an instance is generally never enough for a BPFFNN. This makes GRNN a very useful tool to perform predictions and comparisons of system performance in practice.

The invention of GRNN was a great turn in the history of neural networks. Researchers from many fields including medicine, engineering, commerce, physics, chemistry, geology, statistics, etc., benefited from this technique for their research.

1.2.3. Generalized regression neural network

GRNN is a type of supervised FFNN and is one of the most popular neural networks. Donald F. Specht first introduced it in 1991. Specht's GRNN is related to his probabilistic neural network (PNN) classifier. Like PNN networks, GRNNs are known for their ability to train quickly on sparse data sets. Rather than categorizing data like PNN, GRNN applications are able to produce continuous valued outputs. An important by-product of the GRNN network is Bayesian posterior probabilities. The training of GRNN networks is very fast because the data only needs to propagate forward once, unlike most other BPNNs, where data may be propagated forward and backward many times until an acceptable error is found [19–24].

GRNNs work well on interpolation problems. However, because they are function approximators, they tend to trade accuracy for speed. The GRNN is used for estimation of continuous variables, as in standard regression techniques. It uses a single common radial basis function kernel bandwidth (σ) that is tuned to achieve optimal learning.

The regression performed by GRNN is in fact the conditional expectation of Y, given X = x. In other words, it outputs the most probable scalar Y given specified input vector x. Let f(x, y) be the joint continuous probability density function of a vector random variable, X, and a scalar random variable, Y. Let x be a particular measured value of the random X. The regression of Y given x (also called conditional mean of Y given x) is given by:

$$E[Y\,/\,x] = \int_{-\infty}^{\infty} Y.f(Y\,/\,x)dy = \frac{\int_{-\infty}^{\infty} Y.f(x,\,Y)dy}{\int_{-\infty}^{\infty} (x,Y)dy} \tag{13}$$

If the relationship between independent (X) and dependent (Y) variables is expressed in a functional form with parameters, then the regression will be parametric. Without any real knowledge of the functional form between the x and y, nonparametric estimation method will be used. For a nonparametric estimate of f(x, y), we will use one of the consistent estimators that is a Gaussian function. This estimator is a good choice for estimating the probability density function, f, if it can be assumed that the underlying density is continuous and that the first partial derivatives of the function evaluated at any x are small. The good choice for probability estimator $\hat{f}(x, y)$ is based on sample values x_i and y_i of the random variables X and Y is given by:

$$\hat{f}(x,y) = \frac{1}{(2\pi)^{(p+1)/2} \cdot \sigma^{p+1}} \cdot \frac{1}{n} \sum_{i=1}^{n} \left\{ exp\left[-\frac{(X - X_i)^T (X - X_i)}{2\sigma^2} \right] exp\left[\frac{(Y - Y_i)^2}{2\sigma^2} \right] \right\} \tag{14}$$

p: is the dimension of the vector variable.

n: is the number of training pairs $(x_i \rightarrow y_i)$.

σ: is the single learning or smoothing parameter chosen during network training.

Y_i: is desired scalar output given the observed input x_i.

The topology of GRNN presented in **Figure 15** consists of four layers: The first layer is the input layer that is fully connected to the second layer. The input units are merely distribution units, which provide all of the (scaled) measurement variables X to all of the neurons on the second layer, the pattern units. The second layer is the first hidden layer (also called the pattern layer). This layer consists of N processing elements or nodes, where N is the number of sample within a training data set and each node represents the input vector, Xi, associated with the vector assigned with the jth sample in training data. In each node, each input vector is subtracted from the vector assigned to the node, Xj. This difference is then squared by the node. The result is fed into a nonlinear kernel, which is usually an exponential function. The pattern unit outputs are passed on to the summation units.

Note that the second hidden layer always has exactly one more node than the output layer. When you need a multidimensional (vector) output, the only change to the network is to add one additional node to the second hidden layer, plus an additional node in the output layer for each element of the output vector.

The third layer is the second hidden layer (Summation layer) which has two nodes. The input to the first node is the sum of the first hidden layer outputs, each weighted by the observed output yj corresponding to Xj. The input of the second node is the summation of the first hidden layer activations.

The fourth layer is the output layer. It receives the two outputs from the hidden layer and divides them to yield an estimate for y (or to provide the prediction result).

In the GRNN architecture, unlike other network architectures as in BP, there are no training parameters such as learning rate and momentum, but there is a smoothing factor (σ) that is applied after the network is trained. The choice of smoothing factor (parameter) of the kernel σ is very important. It has the effect of smoothing the training examples. Small values of σ tend to make each training point distinct, whereas large values force a greater degree of interpolation between the training observations. For GRNNs, the smoothing factor must be greater than 0 and can usually range from 0.01 to 1 with good results. We need to experiment in order to determine which smoothing factor is most appropriate for our data.

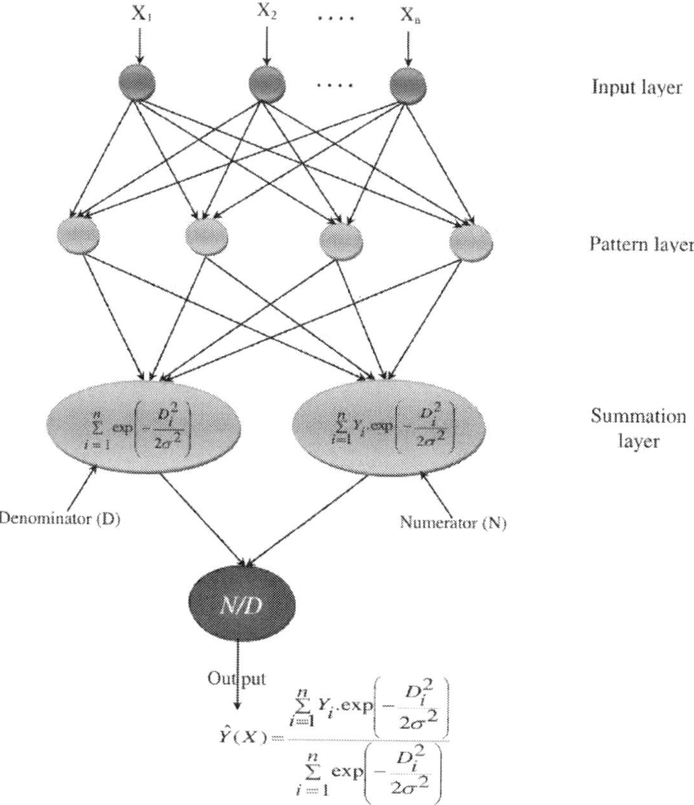

$$\hat{Y}(X) = \frac{\sum_{i=1}^{n} Y_i \cdot \exp\left(-\dfrac{D_i^2}{2\sigma^2}\right)}{\sum_{i=1}^{n} \exp\left(-\dfrac{D_i^2}{2\sigma^2}\right)}$$

Figure 15. The basic GRNN architecture.

A useful method of selecting an appropriate σ is the Holdout method. For a particular value of σ, the Holdout method consists in removing one sample at a time and constructing a network based on all of the other samples. The network is then used to estimate Y for the removed sample. By repeating this process for each sample and storing each estimate, the mean square error can be measured between the actual sample values Yi and the estimates. The value of σ giving the smallest error should be used in the final network.

Fortunately, in most applications there is a unique σ which produces the minimum MSE between the network output and the desired output for the testing set that can be found quickly by trial and error.

2. Neutron spectrometry by means of generalized regression neural networks

2.1. Neutron spectrometry

In general, neutrons are more difficult to detect than gamma rays because of their weak interaction with matter and their large dynamic range in energy [25]. Neutrons have mass but no electrical charge [26]. Because of this, they cannot directly produce ionization in a detector, and therefore cannot be directly detected. This means that neutron detectors must rely upon a conversion process where an incident neutron interacts with a nucleus to produce a secondary charged particle [27]. These charged particles are then directly detected and from them the presence of neutrons is deduced.

The derivation of the spectral information is not simple because the unknown is not given directly as a result of measurements [28]. The spectral information is derived through the discrete version of the Fredholm integral-differential equation of first type [29]. Normally, researchers solve a discrete version of this equation, which gives an ill-conditioned system of equations which have no explicit solution, may have no unique solution, and are referred to as ill-posed [30].

Since the 1960s, the Bonner Sphere Spectrometer (BSS) has been the most used method for radiological protection purposes [28]. The isotropy of the response, the wide energy range (from thermal to GeV neutrons), and the easy operation make these systems still applicable. BSS consists of a thermal neutron detector located at the center of several high-density polyethylene spheres of different diameters [29]. By measuring the count rates with each sphere individually, an unfolding process can, in principle, provide some information about the energy distribution of the incident neutrons.

The most delicate part of neutron spectrometry based on BSS is the unfolding process [30]. The unfolding spectrum of the neutrons measured consists of establishing the rate of energy distribution of fluency, known as response matrix, and the group of carried-out measures. Because the number of unknowns overcomes the number of equations, this ill-conditioned system has an infinite number of solutions. The process of selecting the solution that has meaning for the problem is part of the unfolding process.

To solve the system of equations for BSS unfolding, several approaches have been used [29]: iterative procedures, Monte Carlo, regularization, and maximum entropy methods. The drawbacks associated with these traditional unfolding procedures have motivated the need for complementary approaches. Novel methods based on AI have been suggested. In neutron spectrometry, the theory of ANN has offered a promising alternative to the classic calculations with traditional methods. Previous researches indicate that BPFFNNs perform well and have been the most popular networks used in neutron spectrometry [30–35].

BPFFNN have the characteristic of being very flexible; the process is highly parallel and can be used to solve diverse problems; however, this neural network topology has some drawbacks: the structural and learning parameters of the network are often determined using the trial-and-error technique [36]. This produces networks with poor performance and generalization capabilities which affect its application in real problems. Training can require a substantial amount of time to gradually approach good values of the weights. The size of the training data has to be very large and often it is almost impossible to provide enough training samples as in the case of the neutron spectrometry problem.

Another drawback is that adding new information requires retraining the network and this is computationally very expensive for BPFFNN, but not for GRNN which belongs to SNNs. GRNNs use a statistical approach in their prediction algorithm given the bases in the Bayes strategy for pattern recognition. To be able to use the Bayes strategy, it is necessary to estimate the probability density function accurately. The only available information to estimate the density functions is the training samples. These strategies can be applied to problems containing any number of categories as in the case of the neutron spectrometry problem.

2.2. Neutron spectrometry by means of generalized regression neural networks

A GRNN has certain differences compared to BPFFNN approach [24]. The learning of BPFFNN can be described as trial and error. This is no longer the case of the GRNNs because they use a statistical approach in their prediction algorithm which is capable of working with only few training samples. The experience is learned not by trial but by experience others made for the neural network. GRNNs are very flexible and new information can be added immediately with almost no retraining. The biggest advantage is the fact that the probabilistic approach of GRNN works with one-step-only learning.

A further big difference that exists between BPFFNN and GRNN is the difference in the process inside the neurons. A GRNN uses functions that are based on knowledge resulting from the Bayes strategy for pattern classification. The structure of the calculations for the probabilistic density function in GRNN has striking similarities to a BPFFNN. The strength of a GRNN lies in the function that is used inside the neuron.

It would be desirable to approach the parameters in one-step-only approach. The Bayes strategy for pattern classification extracts characteristics from the training samples to come to knowledge about underlying function.

In this work, both BPFFNN and GRNN architectures were trained in order to solve the neutron spectrometry problem using customized technological tools designed with this purpose. A comparison of the performance obtained using both architectures was performed. Results obtained show that the two architectures solve the neutron spectrometry problem well, with high performance and generalization capabilities; however, the results obtained with GRNN are better than those obtained with BPFFNN, mainly because GRNN does not produce negative values and oscillations around the target value.

As mentioned, a GRNN is a BPFFNN based on non-linear regression. It is suited to function approximation tasks such as system modeling and prediction. While the neurons in the first three layers are fully connected, each output neuron is connected only to some processing units in the summation layer. The function of the pattern layers of the GRNN is a Radial Basis Function (RBF), typically the Gaussian kernel function.

In this work, a neutron spectrum unfolding computer tool based on neural nets technology was designed to train a GRNN capable of solving the neutron spectrum unfolding problem with high performance and generalization capabilities. The code automates the pre-processing, training, testing, validation, and post-processing stages of the information regarded with GRNN. The code is capable of training, testing, and validating GRNN. After training and testing the neural net, the code analyzes, graphs, and stores the results obtained.

2.3. Methods

The use of GRNN to unfold the neutron spectra from the count rates measured with the BSS is a promising alternative procedure; however, one of the main drawbacks is the lack of scientific and technological tools based on this technology. In consequence, a scientific computational tool was designed to train, to test, to analyze, and to validate GRNN in this research domain.

Statistical methods tend to put more emphasis on the structure of the data. For neural network methods, the structure of the data is secondary. Therefore, the amount of data needed for statistical methods is a lot smaller than the amount of data needed for ANN approaches. GRNNs are frequently used to classify patterns based on learning from examples. PNNs base the algorithm on the Bayes strategy for pattern recognition.

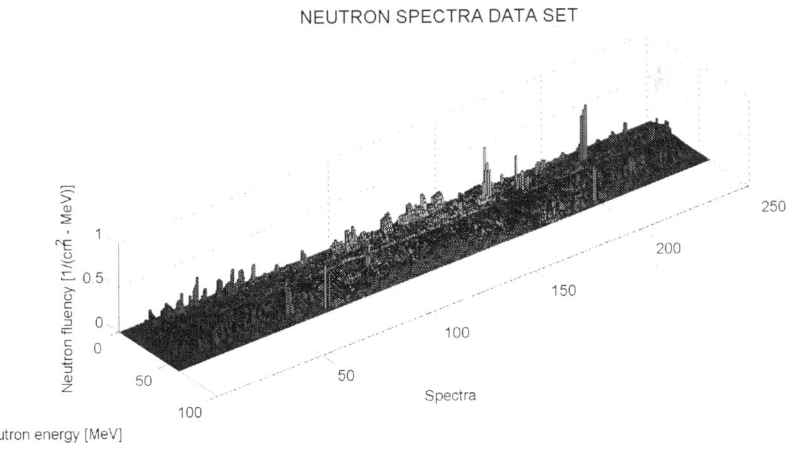

Figure 16. Neutron spectra data set expressed in energy units, used to train the GRNN.

In order to train both BPFFNNs and GRNNs, the only available information is a neutron spectra compilation of the International Atomic Energy Agency (IAEA) which contains a collection of 251 different neutron spectra [37]. This compendium was made with the aim to provide specific technical information that could be used by radiation protection specialists for proper selection of dosimeters and survey instruments, and for interpretation of data obtained with these detectors.

The developed code based on GRNNs technology utilizes these 251 neutron spectra and both, the response matrixes from IAEA's compilation and those that could be introduced by the user. The designed technological tool automates the following activities:

- Read the neutron spectra data set coming from IAEA's compendium, which are expressed in 60 energy bins.

- Read a response matrix used to train the neural network.

- Because the neutron spectra coming from IAEA's compendium are expressed in lethargy units, the code converts these spectra in energy units.

- The neutrons expressed in energy units are multiplied by the selected response matrix in order to calculate the count rates.

- To train the GRNN, the code uses the 251 calculated count rates as entrance data, and their corresponding neutron spectra are expressed in energy units as the output data as shown in **Figure 16**.

- The code randomly generates the training data set, 80% of the whole data, and the testing data set, remaining 20%, as shown in **Figure 17**.

- Using the earlier calculated information, the following stage is to determine the spread constant value. To calculate this value, the computer tool trains several neural networks varying this value from 0 in increments of 0.01 through 2 and compares the mean square error (MSE), which is used to determine the performance of the network. The minimum value obtained is selected as the spread constant value (**Figure 18**).

- After the developed code selects the spread constant value, a final GRNN is trained.

- After training, a testing stage is performed in order to analyze the performance and generalization capabilities of the trained network. In this stage only the input is proportionated to the network. Fifty neutron spectra are randomly selected by the code to test the performance and generalization capabilities of the trained network. In order to analyze the performance of the trained network, chi square and correlation tests are performed.

- Finally, the code plots and stores the generated information.

In this work, a comparison of the performance obtained in the solution of the neutron spectrometry problem using two different neural network architectures, BPFFNN and GRNN, is presented. Both BPFFNN and GRNN were trained and tested using the same information: 251 neutron spectra, extracted from IAEA's compilation. Eighty percent of the whole data set, randomly selected, was used at training stage and remaining 20% at testing stage. Fifty neutron spectra were used as testing data set.

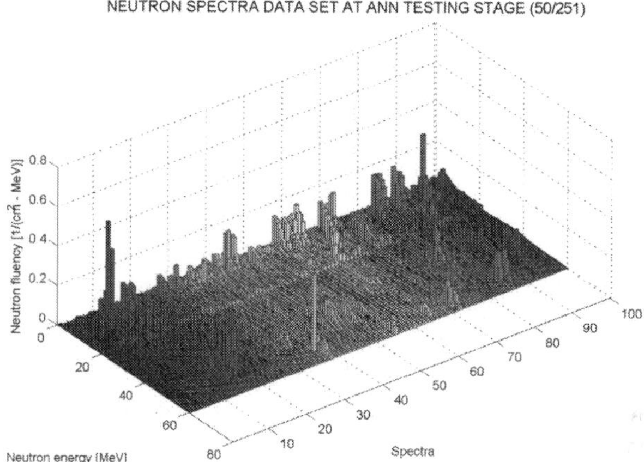

Figure 17. Neutron spectra data set used at testing stage, compared with target spectra.

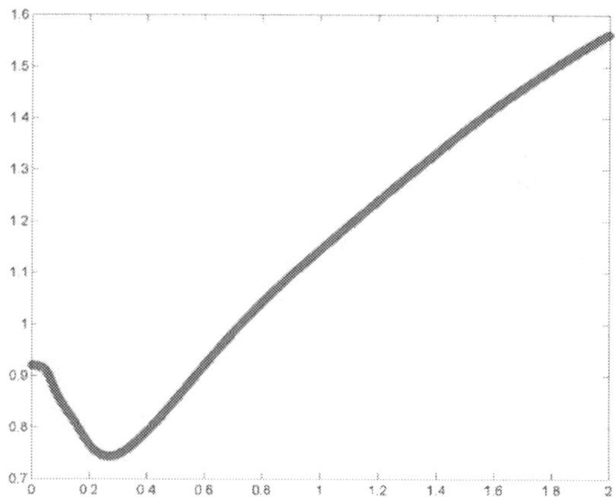

Figure 18. Optimum spread constant value, sigma, and determination.

The architectural and learning parameters of BPFFNN were optimized using a statistical methodology known as Robust Design of Artificial Neural Networks Methodology (RDANNM) [36]. In GRNN, the only parameter determined was the spread constant value, known as sigma. For both architectures, BPFFNN and GRNN, customized scientific computational tools were used for the training, testing, analysis, and storage of the information generated in the whole process of both network architectures. It can be observed from the results obtained that although the two network architectures present very similar performance and generalization capabilities, GRNN performs better than BPFFNN in the solution of the neutron spectrometry problem. BPFFNNs produce negative values and high oscillations around the target values, which makes this type of network unusable in the solution of the problem mentioned.

2.4. Results

In this work, by using two different technological tools, two different artificial neural networks architectures, BPFFNN and GRRN, were trained and tested using the same information. The performance of the networks was compared. From the results obtained, it can be observed that GRNN performs better than BPFFNN in the solution of the neutron spectrometry problem.

Network parameters	BPNN (trial and error)	BPNN (RDANNM)	GRNN
Networks tested before training	Undetermined	50 in 150 minutes	2000 in 154 seconds
Hidden layers	Undetermined	1	Fixed architecture
Neurons in hidden layer	Undetermined	10	According input
Training algorithm	Undetermined	Trainscg	Statistical methods
Learning rate	Undetermined	0.1	–
Momentum	Undetermined	0.01	–
Spread constant	–	–	0.2711
Performance (MSE)	Undetermined	2.12E-4	2.48E-4
Training time (seconds)	Several hours	170.40	0.058
Epochs	Often millions	50E3	1
Best chi-square test BPNN Statistical margin 34.7	–	2.3525	0.049
Best correlation test BPNN Statistical margin 1	–	0.9928	0.99571
Worst chi-square test BPNN	–	0.44704	0.3223
Worst correlation test BPNN	–	0.2926	0.46023

Table 2. Comparison between BPFFNN and GRNN values in neutron spectrometry.

By using the RDANNM, around 50 different network architectures were trained in 150 minutes average, before the selection of the near-optimum architecture. By testing different network architectures according to RDANNM, each network was trained in 50E3 epochs and 180 seconds average, stopping the training when the network reached the established mean square error (MSE) equal to 1E-4, the value used to measure the network performance. After selecting the near-optimum architectural and learning parameters of the BPFFNN, the network was trained and tested using the values shown in **Table 2**: one hidden layer with 10 neurons, a trainscg training algorithm, and a learning rate and momentum equal to 0.1 and 0.01, respectively.

As can be seen in **Table 2**, contrary to BPFFNN the spread constant or sigma was the only value determined in GRNN. Using the same training and testing data sets used for BPFFNN, around 2000 neural networks were trained in 154 seconds average in order to determine the spread constant equal to 0.2711. Each GRNN was trained in 0.058 seconds average in only one-step-only learning. Further, a final GRNN was trained and tested in 0.058 seconds average in only one epoch.

Table 2 shows the values obtained after training the two network architectures compared in this work. As can be seen, when the trial-and-error technique is used, it is very difficult to determine if the performance of the network is good or bad, mainly because a scientific and systematic methodology is not used for determining the near-optimum learning and architectural values as when RDANNM is used.

As can be appreciated in **Table 2**, after training both network architectures, BPFFNN was optimized using RDANNM and GRNN, the performance, MSE, reached by the two networks is very close to each other. In BPFFNNs, the MSE is a value optimized by the network designer using RDANNM; in GRNN network the value was automatically obtained by the network based on the training information used by the automated code. The anterior demonstrates the powerful RDANNM in the optimization of the near-optimum values of BPFFNN architectures.

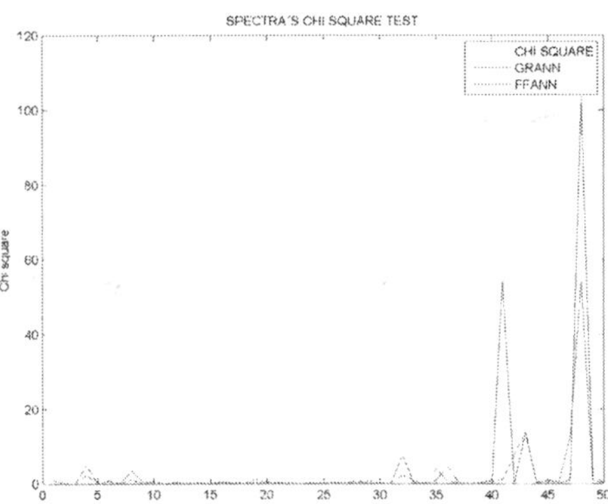

Figure 19. Chi-square test comparison for BPFFNN and GRNN.

Figures 19 and **20** show that at testing stage, the chi square and correlation tests are very close in both BPFFNN and GRNN network architectures. The same 50 neutron spectra were used for testing the two network architectures. At testing stage, only the count rates were proportionated to the trained networks. The output produced by the networks was compared with the expected neutron spectrum taken from IAEA's compilation by means of chi square and correlation tests. In the trained networks, two spectra are above the statistical margin of the chi-square test. In correlation tests, two values are below 0.5. This shows the high performance of the networks.

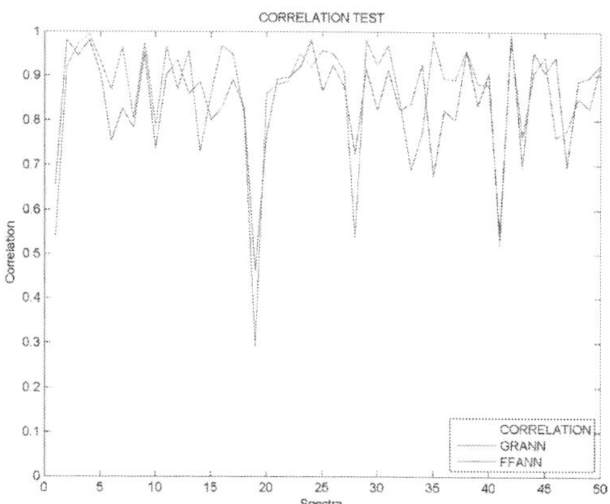

Figure 20. Correlation test comparison for BPFFNN and GRNN.

As can be seen from **Figures 19** and **20**, the 50 chi-square and correlation tests of trained networks are very similar. In both cases, the average value is around 0 and 0.8 respectively, which is near the optimum values equal to 0 and 1. This means that BPFFNN and GRNN have high performance and generalization capabilities and demonstrates the effectiveness of the RDANNM in the design of near-optimum architectures of BPFFNN.

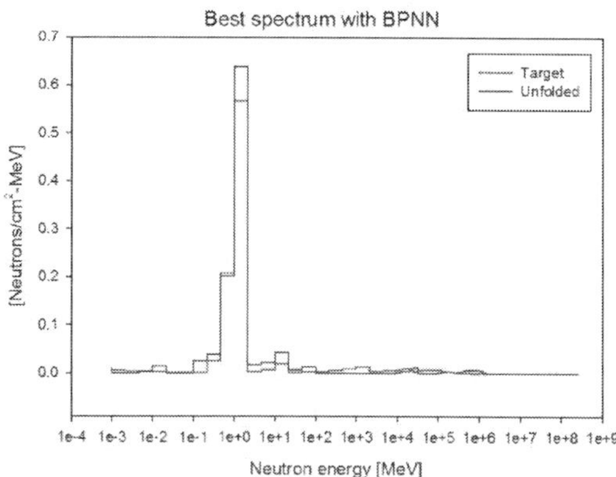

Figure 21. Best spectrum obtained with BPFFNN.

As mentioned earlier, 50 neutron spectra were randomly selected at the testing stage. The same training and testing data sets were used to train and to test the performance and generalization capability of the networks. The best and the worst cases for both BPFFNN and GRNN are showed in **Figures 21–28**. **Figures 21–22** and **23–24** show the best cases observed at testing stage for BPFFNN and GRNN, respectively. From these figures, it can be observed that the chi-square and correlations tests for both BPFFNN and GRNN are near 0 and 1, respectively, which means that the compared neutron spectra are very similar.

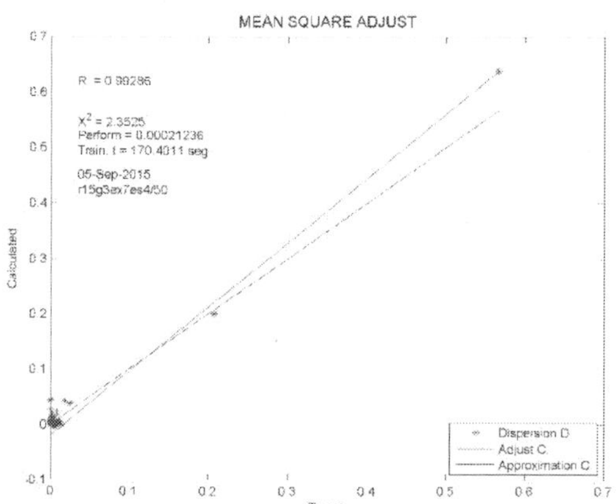

Figure 22. Best chi-square and correlation tests for spectrum obtained with BPNN.

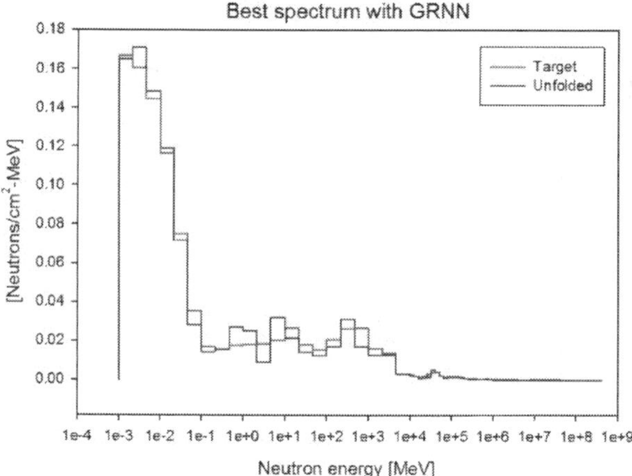

Figure 23. Best spectrum obtained with GRFFNN.

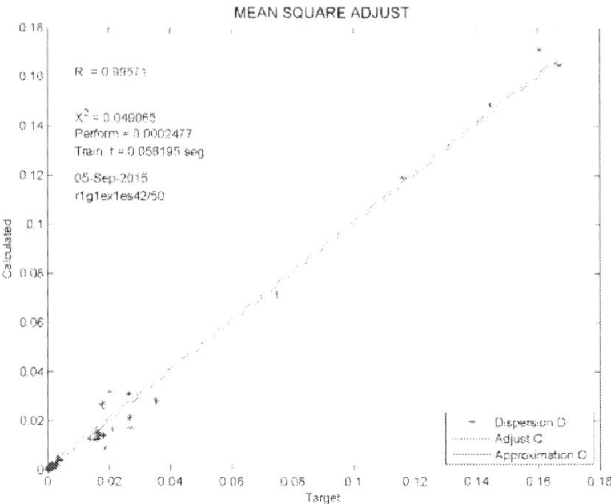

Figure 24. Best chi-square and correlation tests for spectrum obtained with GRNN.

As can be appreciated in **Figures 21–28**, despite the good results obtained with BPFFNN, one drawback is that the calculated neutron spectra produce negative values which have no meaning in real problems. These negative values are eliminated from the output produced by the network; however, when the BPFFNN is applied in real workplaces, because the training received, the network tends to produce negative values and oscillations around the target value. GRNN networks do not produce these negative values and oscillations and therefore the performance is better than BPFFNN in the solution of the neutron spectrometry problem.

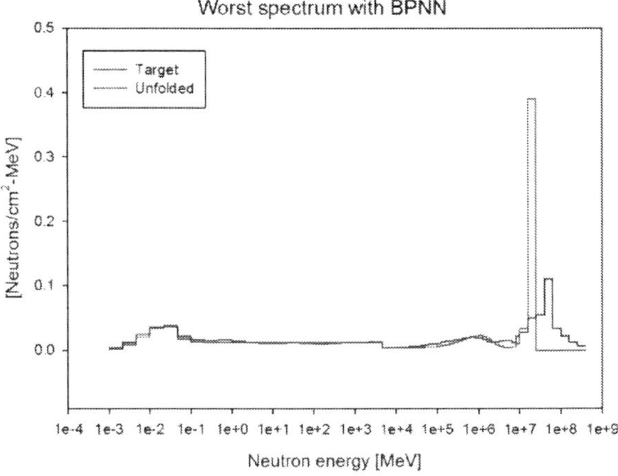

Figure 25. Worst spectrum obtained with BPFFNN.

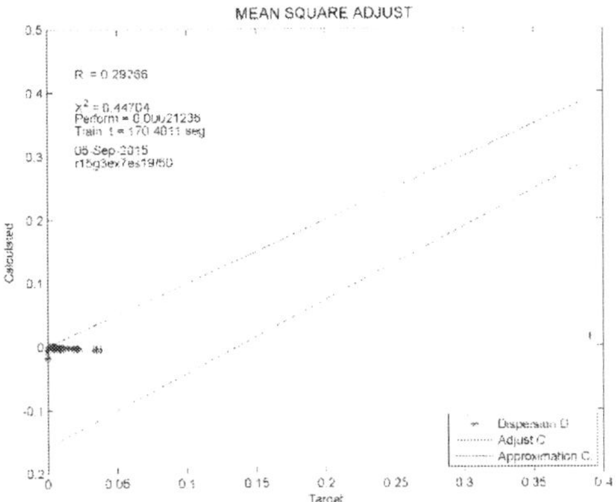

Figure 26. Worst chi-square and correlation tests for spectrum obtained with BPNN.

Figures 25–28 show the worst case observed at the testing stage for BPFFNN and GRNN networks, respectively. As can be seen from these figures, both BPFFNN and GRNN selected the same neutron spectra as the worst. This could be because of the 50 energy bins that the neural networks calculated; 49 values are very similar and only one value is far from the expected target value, which causes that the chi-square and correlation tests to produce low values. From **Figures 25–28**, it can be observed that in the GRNN architecture, the output is closer to the target values of the neutron spectra if compared with BPFFNN. This shows that in the worst case, GRNNs have better performance than BPFFNN.

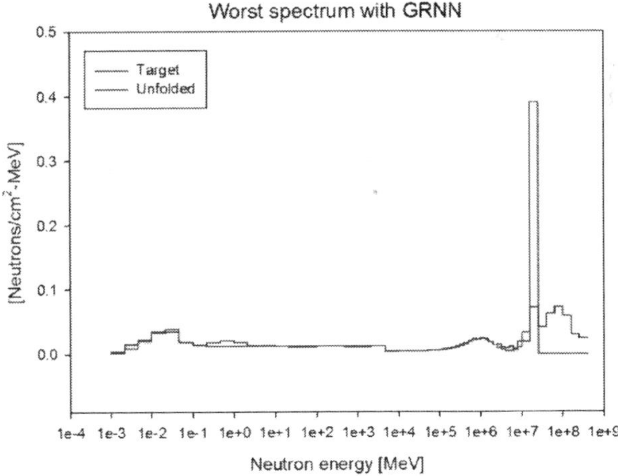

Figure 27. Worst spectrum obtained with BPFFNN.

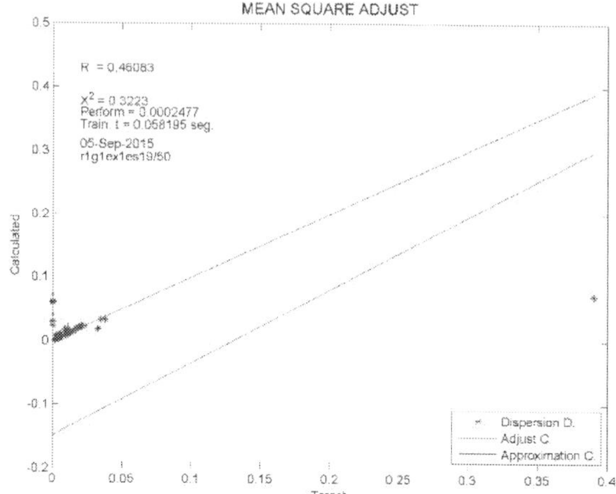

Figure 28. Worst chi-square and correlation tests for spectrum obtained with GRNN.

The results observed in this work indicate that GRNN is able to predict the unknown neutron spectrum presented to the network with good accuracy. As can be seen from **Figures 21–24**, due to proper selection of the spread constant value, the GRNN calculated values, each one of the 60 energy bins of the spectrum, are around the target value (the spectrum from IAEA's compendium). As opposed to BPFFNN, non-negative values and oscillations around the target value are generated when GRNNs are used.

Since there is only one parameter in GRNN, this type of ANN is also called a nonparametric model. It stores the training data as the parameter, rather than calculating and modifying the weights and bias in each hidden layer as the input data imported into the model. When the query comes, the model will calculate the value by summing the values of the other points weighted by the RBF function. Therefore, unlike parametric models such as BP, there are no weights and bias information produced to characterize the trained model.

3. Discussion and conclusions

Different approaches exist to model a system with available data. Each one of them has its own qualities and therefore advantages. GRNN falls into the category of PNN. This neural network, like other PNNs, needs only a fraction of the training samples a BPNN would need. The data available from measurements of an instance is generally never enough for a BPNN. Therefore, the use of GRNN is especially advantageous due to its ability to converge to the underlying function of the data with only few training samples available. The additional knowledge needed to get the fit in a satisfying way is relatively small and can be done without additional input by the user.

Statistical methods tend to put more emphasis on the structure of the data. For neural network methods, the structure of the data is secondary. Therefore, the amount of data needed for statistical methods is a lot smaller than the amount of data needed for ANN approaches.

Most methods are asymptotically good but most of them have severe drawbacks as well. BPNNs need a very large number of training samples and need a lot of time to gradually approach good values of the weights. Addition of new information requires retraining and this is computationally very expensive for BPNN but not for PNN. PNNs have the big advantage that the prediction algorithm works with only few training samples. Other big advantage is that they are very flexible and new information can be added immediately with almost no retraining.

PNNs use a statistical approach in their prediction algorithm. The bases for the statistical approach are given in the Bayes strategy for pattern recognition. These strategies can be applied to problems containing any number of categories as in the case of the neutron spectrometry problem. To be able to use the Bayes strategy, it is necessary to estimate the probability density function accurately. The only available information to estimate the density functions is the training samples.

The structure of the calculations for the probabilistic density function has striking similarities to a backpropagation feed-forward neural network. PNNs are frequently used to classify patterns based on learning from examples. PNNs base the algorithm on the Bayes strategy for pattern classification. Different rules determine patterns statistics from the training samples. BPNN uses methods that are not based on statistical methods and need a long time and many iterations and feedback until it gradually approaches the underlying function. It would be desirable to approach the parameters in one-step-only approach. The Bayes strategy for pattern classification extracts characteristics from the training samples to come to knowledge about underlying function.

In this work, two different artificial neural networks architectures, BPNN and GRRN, were trained and tested using the same information. The performance of the networks was compared. From the results obtained, it can be observed that GRNN performs better than BPNN in the solution of the neutron spectrometry problem.

PNNs have a very simple structure and are therefore very stable procedures. PNNs perform very well for only few available training samples and the quality increases as the number of training samples increases. This makes GRNN a very useful tool to perform predictions and comparisons of system performance in practice. GRNN is a promising technological tool that can be applied to solve with high efficiency the problems related to neutron spectrometry.

Acknowledgements

This work was partially supported by Fondo Sectorial de Investigación para la Eduación under contract 241771, Fondos Mixtos SEP-CONACYT under contract ZAC-C03-2015-26357-4, and PROSOFT under contract 201513723. The first and second authors want to thank the Doctorate scholarships, with scholarship holder numbers 23386 and 23385, respectively, received by Fondo Sectorial de Investigación para la Eduación under contract 241771. The third and fourth authors want to thank the Doctorate scholarships received by Fondos Mixtos SEP-CONACYT under contract ZAC-C03-2015-26357-4. The seventh author want to thank conacyt for the post-doctoral scholarship number 24296. The authors want to thank the active and determined participation and collaboration on several activities on this research project of the undergraduate students: Ana Isabel Ortiz Hernández, Miguel Ángel Acosta García, Fabian García Vázquez, Edgar Viveros Llamas, and Rogelio Osbaldo Reyes Vargas.

Author details

Ma. del Rosario Martinez-Blanco[1,3], Víctor Hugo Castañeda-Miranda[1,3],
Gerardo Ornelas-Vargas[1,3], Héctor Alonso Guerrero-Osuna[1,3], Luis Octavio Solis-Sanchez[1,3],
Rodrigo Castañeda-Miranda[1,3], José María Celaya-Padilla[1,3], Carlos Eric Galvan-Tejada[3],
Jorge Isaac Galvan-Tejada[3], Héctor René Vega-Carrillo[4], Margarita Martínez-Fierro[1,5],
Idalia Garza-Veloz[1,5] and Jose Manuel Ortiz-Rodriguez[1,3,2*]

*Address all correspondence to: morvymm@yahoo.com.mx

1 Centro de Investigación e Innovación Tecnológica Industrial (CIITI), Universidad Autónoma de Zacatecas, Zacatecas, México

2 Laboratorio de Innovación y Desarrollo Tecnológico en Inteligencia Artificial (LIDTIA), Universidad Autónoma de Zacatecas, Zacatecas, México

3 Unidad Académica de Ingeniería Eléctrica (UAIE), Universidad Autónoma de Zacatecas, Zacatecas, México

4 Unidad Académica de Estudios Nucleares (UAEN), Universidad Autónoma de Zacatecas, Zacatecas, México

5 Laboratorio de Medicina Molecular, Unidad académica de Medicina Humana y Ciencias de la Salud (UAMHCS), Universidad Autónoma de Zacatecas, Zacatecas, México

References

[1] Fritzsche P. Tools in artificial intelligence. Viena, Austria: InTech; 2008.

[2] Negnevitsky M. Artificial intelligence, a guide to intelligent systems. Reading, MA, USA: Addison Wesley; 2005.

[3] Coppin B. Artificial intelligence illuminated. Burlington, MA, USA: Jones and Barttlet Publishers; 2004.

[4] Russell S.J., Norvig P. Artificial intelligence a modern approach. Mexico: Prentice Hall; 2004.

[5] Luger G.F. Artificial intelligence structures and strategies for complex problem solving. Reading, MA, USA: Addison-Wesley; 2005.

[6] Baldi P., Brunak S. Bioinformatics, the machine learning approach. Cambridge, MA, USA: Mit Press; 2001.

[7] Yu W. Recent advances in intelligent control systems. London: Springer-Verlag; 2009.

[8] Munakata T. Fundamentals of the new artificial intelligence, neural, evolutionary, fuzzy and more. London: Springer; 2008.

[9] Chennakesava R.A. Fuzzy logic and neural networks, basic concepts and applications. New Delhi,India: New Age International Publishers; 2008.

[10] Arbib M.A. Brain theory and neural networks. Cambridge, MA, USA: The Mit Press; 2003.

[11] Haykin S. Neural networks: a comprehensive foundation. Mexico: Prentice Hall; 1999.

[12] Zupan J. Introduction to artificial neural network methods: what they are and how to use them. Acta Chimica Slovenica. 1994;41(3):327–352.

[13] Jain A.K., Mao J., Mohiuddin K.M. Artificial neural networks: a tutorial. IEEE: Computer. 1996;29(3):31–44.

[14] Lippmann R. An introduction to computing with neural nets. IEEE ASSP Magazine. 1987;4(2):4–22.

[15] Floreano F., Mattiussi C. Bio-inspired artificial intelligence, theories, methods and technologies. Cambridge, MA, USA: The MIT Press; 2008.

[16] Gupta M., Jin L., Homma N. Static and dynamic neural networks: from fundamentals to advanced theory. New Jersey, USA: John Wiley Sons; 2003.

[17] Huang D.S. Radial basis probabilistic neural networks: model and applications. International Journal of Pattern Recognition and Artificial Intelligence. 1999;13(7):1083–1101.

[18] Mao K., Tan K., Ser W. Probabilistic neural network structure determination for pattern classification. IEEE Transactions on Neural Networks. 2000;11(4):1009–1016.

[19] Spetch D.F. Probabilistic neural networks for classification, mapping or associative memory. IEEE International Conference on Neural Networks. 1998;1:525–532.

[20] Spetch D.F. Probabilistic neural networks. Neural Networks. 1990;3(1):109–118.

[21] Spetch D.F. Enhancements to probabilistic neural networks. International Joint Conference on Neural Networks. 1992;1:761–768.

[22] Taylor J.G. Mathematical approaches to neural networks. Holland: North-Holland Mathematical library; 1993.

[23] Spetch D.F., Romsdhal H. Experience with adaptive probabilistic neural networks and adaptive general regression neural networks. IEEE International Conference on Neural Networks. 1994;2:1203–1208.

[24] Spetch D.F., Shapiro P. Generalization accuracy of probabilistic neural networks compared with backpropagation networks. IJCNN-91-Seattle International Joint Conference on Neural Networks. 1991;1:887–892.

[25] Attix F.H. Introduction to radiological physics and radiation dosimetry. New Jersey, USA: Wiley-VCH; 2004.

[26] Lilley J. Nuclear physics, principles and applications. New Jersey, USA: John Wiley & Sons, Ltd.; 2001.

[27] Bromley D.A. Detectors in nuclear science. Nuclear Instruments and Methods. 1979;162:431–476.

[28] Bramblett R.L., Ewing R.I., Bonner T.W. A new type of neutron spectrometer. Nuclear Instruments and Methods. 1960;9:1–12.

[29] Thomas D.J. Neutron spectrometry for radiation protection. Radiation Protection Dosimetry. 2004;110(1–4):141–149.

[30] Matzke M. Unfolding procedures. Radiation Protection Dosimetry. 2003;107(1–3):155–174.

[31] Braga C.C., Dias M.S. Application of neural networks for unfolding neutron spectra measured by means of Bonner spheres. Nuclear Instruments and Methods in Physics Research Section A. 2002;476(1–2):252–255.

[32] Kardan M.R., Setayeshi S., Koohi-Fayegh R., Ghiassi-Nejad M. Neutron spectra unfolding in Bonner spheres spectrometry using neural networks. Radiation Protection Dosimetry. 2003;104(1):27–30.

[33] Kardan M.R., Koohi-Fayegh R., Setayeshi S., Ghiassi-Nejad M. Fast neutron spectra determination by threshold activation detectors using neural networks. Radiation Measurements. 2004;38:185–191.

[34] Vega-Carrillo H.R., et al. Neutron spectrometry using artificial neural networks. Radiation Measurements. 2006;41:425–431.

[35] Vega-Carrillo H.R., Martinez Blanco M.R., Hernandez Davila V.M., Ortiz Rodriguez J.M. Ann in spectroscopy and neutron dosimetry. Journal of Radioanalytical and Nuclear Chemistry. 2009;281(3):615–618.

[36] Ortiz-Rodriguez J.M., Martinez-Blanco H.R., Vega-Carrillo H.R. Robust design of artificial neural networks applying the Taguchi methodology and DoE. Proceedings of the Electronics, Robotics and Automotive Mechanics Conference (CERMA'06), IEEE Computer Society. 2006;1:1–6.

[37] IAEA. Compendium of neutron spectra and detector responses for radiation protection purposes. Technical Report 403; Vienna, Austria: International Atomic Energy Agency (IAEA); 2001.

Chapter 4

A Continuous-Time Recurrent Neural Network for Joint Equalization and Decoding – Analog Hardware Implementation Aspects

Mohamad Mostafa, Giuseppe Oliveri,
Werner G. Teich and Jürgen Lindner

Additional information is available at the end of the chapter

http://dx.doi.org/10.5772/63387

Abstract

Equalization and channel decoding are "traditionally" two cascade processes at the receiver side of a digital transmission. They aim to achieve a reliable and efficient transmission. For high data rates, the energy consumption of their corresponding algorithms is expected to become a limiting factor. For mobile devices with limited battery's size, the energy consumption, mirrored in the lifetime of the battery, becomes even more crucial. Therefore, an energy-efficient implementation of equalization and decoding algorithms is desirable. The prevailing way is by increasing the energy efficiency of the underlying digital circuits. However, we address here promising alternatives offered by mixed (analog/digital) circuits. We are concerned with modeling joint equalization and decoding *as a whole* in a continuous-time framework. In doing so, continuous-time recurrent neural networks play an essential role because of their nonlinear characteristic and special suitability for analog very-large-scale integration (VLSI). Based on the proposed model, we show that the superiority of joint equalization and decoding (a well-known fact from the discrete-time case) preserves in analog. Additionally, analog circuit design related aspects such as adaptivity, connectivity and accuracy are discussed and linked to theoretical aspects of recurrent neural networks such as Lyapunov stability and simulated annealing.

Keywords: continuous-time recurrent neural networks, analog hardware neural networks, belief propagation, vector equalization, joint equalization and decoding

1. Introduction

Energy efficiency has been increasingly attracting more interest due to economical and environmental reasons. Mobile communications sector has currently a share of 0.2% in global carbon emissions. This share is expected to double between 2007 and 2020 due to the ever-increasing

© 2016 The Author(s). Licensee InTech. This chapter is distributed under the terms of the Creative Commons Attribution License (http://creativecommons.org/licenses/by/3.0), which permits unrestricted use, distribution, and reproduction in any medium, provided the original work is properly cited.

demand for wireless devices [1, 2]. The sustained interest in higher data rate transmission is strengthening this impact. While major resources are being invested in increasing the energy efficiency of digital circuits, there is, on the other hand, a growing interest pointing at alternatives to the digital realization [3], including a mixed (analog/digital) approach. In such an approach, specific energy consuming (sub)tasks are implemented in analog instead of a "conventional" digital realization. The analog implementation possesses a high potential to significantly improve the energy efficiency [4] because of the inherent parallel processing of signals that are continuous in both time and amplitude. This has been shown in the field of error correction coding with a focus on decoding of low-density parity-check (LDPC) codes. Our ongoing research on equalization reveals similar results. We do not intend "analog" for linear signal processing with all its disadvantages like component inaccuracies and susceptibility to noise and temperature dependency [5] but for *nonlinear processing* instead. The work of Mead [6] and others on *Neuromorphic analog very-large-scale integration (VLSI)* has shown that *"analog signal processing systems can be built that share the robustness of digital systems but outperform digital systems by several orders of magnitude in terms of speed and/or power consumption"* [5].

The nonlinearity makes the analog implementation of an algorithm as robust as its digital counterpart [3, 5]. This profits from the match between the needed nonlinear operations for the algorithm and the physical properties of analog devices [7].

The capability of artificial neural networks (in the following neural networks) to successfully solve many scientific and engineering tasks has been shown oftentimes. Moreover, mapping algorithms to neural network structures can simplify the circuit design because of the regular (and repetitive) structure of neural networks and their limited number of *well-defined* arithmetic operations. Digital implementations can be considered precise (reproducibility of results under similar circumstances) but accurate (closeness of a result to the "true" value) *only* to the extent to which they have enough digits to represent [8]. This means, accuracy in digital implementations is achieved at the cost of efficiency (e.g., relatively larger chip area and more power consumption) [9]. An analog implementation is usually efficient in terms of chip area and processing speed [9], however, at the price of an inherent lack of the reproducibility of results [8] (because of a limited accuracy of the network components as an example [9]). However, by exploiting the distributed nature of neural structures the precision of the analog implementation can be improved despite inaccurate components and subsystems [8][1]. In other words, it is the distributed massively parallel nonlinear collective behavior of an analog implementation (of neural networks) which offers the possibility to make it as robust as its digital counterpart but more energy efficient[2] (additionally to smaller chip area). Particularly for *recurrent* neural networks (the class we focus on when considered as nonlinear dynamical systems), the robustness can be additionally achieved by exploiting "attracting" equilibrium points. In the light of this discussion, we map in this chapter a joint equalization and decoding algorithm into a novel *continuous-time* recurrent neural network structure. This class of neural networks has been attracting a lot of interest because of their widespread applications. They can be either trained for system identification [10], or they can be considered as dynamical

---

[1] For a clear distinction between *accuracy* and *precision* when used in hardware implementation context, we refer to [8].
[2] Energy efficiency is defined later as appropriate.

systems (dynamical solver). In the latter case, there is *no need* for a computationally complex and time-consuming training phase. This relies on the ability of these networks (under specific conditions) to be Lyapunov stable.

Equalization and channel decoding (together, in the following detection) are processes at the receiver side of a digital transmission. They aim to provide a reliable and efficient transmission. Equalization is needed to cope with the interference caused by multipath propagation, multiusers, multisubchannels, multiantennas and combinations thereof [11]. Channel (de)coding is applied for further improving the power efficiency. Equalization and decoding are nonlinear discrete optimization problems. The optimum solutions, in general, are computationally very demanding. Therefore, suboptimum solutions are applied, often soft-valued iterative schemes because of their good complexity-performance trade-off.

For high data rates, the energy consumption of equalization and decoding algorithms is expected to become a limiting factor. The need for floating-point computation and the nonlinear and iterative nature of (some of) these algorithms revive the option of an analog electronic implementation [12, 13], embedded in an essentially digital receiver. This option has been strengthened since the emergence of the "soft-valued" computation in this context [4] since soft-values are a natural property of analog signals. In contrast to analog decoding, analog equalization did not attract that amount of attention.

Furthermore, *joint* equalization and decoding (a technique where equalizer and decoder exchange their *local* available knowledge) further improves the efficiency of the transmission as an example in terms of lower bit error rates, however, at the cost of more computational complexity [14]. Most of the work related to joint equalization and decoding is limited to the discrete-time realization. One of the very few contributions focusing on continuous-time joint equalization and decoding is given in [13]. The consideration in [13] is not "neural networks-based". Stability and convergence are observed but not "deeply" considered.

We introduce in this chapter a novel continuous-time joint equalization and decoding structure. For this purpose, continuous-time single-layer recurrent neural networks play an essential role because of their nonlinear and recursive characteristic, special suitability for analog VLSI and since they serve as promising computational models for analog hardware implementation [15]. Both, equalizer and decoder are modeled as continuous-time recurrent neural networks. An additional proper feedback between equalizer and decoder is established for joint equalization and decoding. We also review individually, both continuous-time equalization and continuous-time decoding based on recurrent neural network structures. No training is needed since the recurrent neural network is serving as a dynamical solver or a computational model [15, 16]. This means, transmission properties are used to define the recurrent neural network (number of neurons, weight coefficients, activation functions, etc.) such that no training is needed. In addition, we highlight challenges emerging from the analog hardware implementation such as adaptivity, connectivity and accuracy. We also introduce our developed circuit for analog equalization based on continuous-time recurrent neural networks [3]. Characteristic properties of recurrent neural networks such as stability and convergence are addressed too. Based on the introduced model, we show by simulations that the superiority of joint equalization and decoding can be preserved in the analog "domain".

The main motivation for performing joint equalization and decoding in analog instead of using conventional digital circuits is to improve the energy efficiency and to minimize the area consumption in the VLSI chips [17]. The proposed continuous-time recurrent neural network serves as a promising computational model for analog hardware implementation.

The remainder of this chapter is organized as follows: In Section 2, we describe the block transmission model. Sections 3 and 4 are dedicated to the equalization process, the application of continuous-time recurrent neural networks and the analog circuit design and its corresponding performance and energy efficiency. Sections 5 and 6 are devoted to the channel decoding and the application of continuous-time recurrent neural networks for belief propagation (a decoding algorithm for LDPC codes). For both equalization and decoding cases, analog hardware design aspects and challenges and the behavior of the continuous-time recurrent neural network as a dynamical system are discussed. The continuous-time joint equalization and decoding based on recurrent neural networks is presented in Sections 7 and 8. Simulation results are shown in Section 9. We finish this chapter with a conclusion in Section 10.

Throughout this chapter, bold small and bold capital letters designate vectors (or finite discrete sets) and matrices, respectively.[3] All nonbold letters are scalars. $\text{diag}_m\{B\}$ returns the matrix B where the nondiagonal elements are set to zeros. $\text{diag}_v\{b\}$ returns a matrix where the vector b is put on the diagonal. $\mathbf{0}_N$ is the all-zero vector of length N. $\mathbf{0}, \mathbf{1}$ and I represent the all-zero, all-one and the identity matrix of suitable size, respectively. We consider column vectors. $(\cdot)^H$ represents the conjugate transpose of a vector or a matrix, whereas $(\cdot)^T$ represents the transpose. $z_r = \mathfrak{R}(z)$, $z_i = \mathfrak{I}(z)$ returns the real and imaginary part of the complex-valued argument $z = z_r + \iota z_i$, respectively. $\iota = \sqrt{-1}$. t and l are designated to the continuous-time variable and the discrete-time index, respectively.

2. Block transmission model

The block transmission model for linear modulation schemes is shown in **Figure 1**. For details, see [18]:

- **SRC** (**SNK**) represents the digital source (sink). **SRC** repeatedly generates successive streams of k bits, i.e., $q_1, q_2, \cdots, q_M$.

- $q\,(\hat{q}) \in \{0, 1\}^k$ is the vector of source (detected) bits of length k.

- $q_c \in \{0, 1\}^n$ is the vector of encoded source bits of length $n > k$. For an *uncoded* transmission $q_c = q$ (and thus $k = n$).

- COD performs a bijective map from q to q_c where $n > k$ (adding redundancy). We consider in this chapter binary LDPC codes. Only 2^k combinations of n bits out of overall 2^n

---

[3] Except for L, $\check{L}$ and L_{ch} which are vectors.

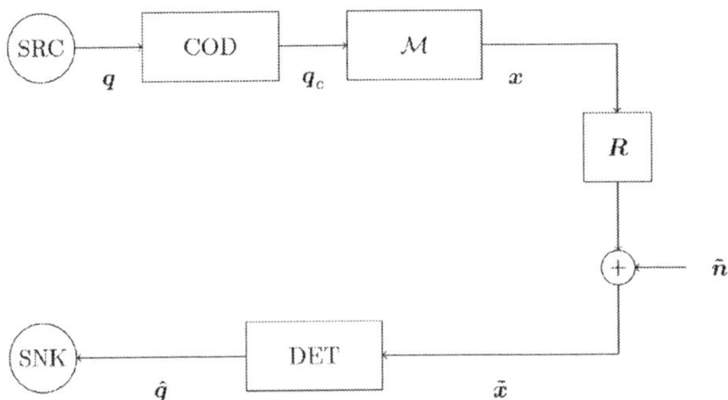

Figure 1. Block transmission model for linear modulation schemes. **SRC** (**SNK**) represents the digital source (sink). DET is the detector. COD performs the encoding process (adding redundancy). $\mathcal{M}$ maps encoded bits to complex-valued symbols. R is the block transmit matrix.

combinations are used. The set of the 2^k combinations represent the code book $\mathcal{C}$. $r_c = k/n$ is the code rate.

- $x \in \psi^N$ is the transmit vector of length N.

- N is the block size. Successive transmit vectors are separated by a guard time to avoid interference between different blocks. Thus, **Figure 1** describes the transmission for a single block and stays valid for the next block (possibly with a different R).

- $\psi = \{\psi_1, \psi_2, \ldots, \psi_{2^m}\}$, $m \in \mathbb{N}/\{0\}$ is the symbol alphabet. There exist $2^{m \cdot N}$ possible transmit vectors. The set of all possible transmit vectors is χ. The mapping from q_c to x is performed by $\mathcal{M}$. Each symbol ψ represents m bits. A special class of symbol alphabets are the so-called *separable* symbol alphabet $\psi^{(s)}$ [19, 20].

- $\tilde{x}$ is the receive vector of length N. In general $\tilde{x} \in \mathbb{C}^N$.

- We distinguish:

  - For an uncoded transmission $M \times k = m \times N$.

  - For a coded transmission and $N < n/m$: One codeword lasts over many transmit blocks.

  - For a coded transmission and $N = n/m$: One codeword lasts exactly over a single transmit block.

  - For a coded transmission and $N = M \times n/m$: M codewords are contained in a single transmit block.

- $R = \{r_{ij} : i, j \in \{1, 2, \cdots, N\}\}$ is the block transmit matrix of size $N \times N$. R is hermitian and positive semidefinite. The block transmit matrix R contains the whole knowledge about the transmission scheme (transmit and receive filters) and the physical propagation channel between transmitter(s) and receiver(s) [18].

- $\tilde{n}$ is a sample function of an additive Gaussian noise vector process of length N with zero mean and covariance matrix $\Phi_{\tilde{n}\tilde{n}} = \frac{N_0}{2} \cdot R$ where $\frac{N_0}{2}$ is the double-sided noise power spectral density.

- DET is the detector including equalization and decoding.

The model in **Figure 1** is a general model and fits to different transmission schemes like orthogonal frequency division multiplexing (OFDM), code division multiple access (CDMA), multicarrier CDMA (MC-CDMA) and multiple-input multiple-output (MIMO). The relation with the original continuous-time (physical) model can be found in [11, 18]. The model in **Figure 1** can be described mathematically as follows [11]:

$$\tilde{x} = R \cdot x + \tilde{n}. \tag{1}$$

By decomposing R into a diagonal part R_d = $\text{diag}_m\{R\}$ and a nondiagonal part $R_{\backslash d}$ = $R\text{–}R_d$, Eq. (1) can be rewritten as:

$$\tilde{x} = \underbrace{R_d \cdot x}_{\text{signal}} + \underbrace{R_{\backslash d} \cdot x}_{\text{interference}} + \underbrace{\tilde{n}}_{\text{additive noise}}. \tag{2}$$

For the j-th element of the receive vector $j \in \{1, 2, \cdots, N\}$ Eq. (2) can be expressed as

$$\tilde{x}_j = r_{jj} \cdot x_j + \sum_{\substack{m=1 \\ m \neq j}}^{N} r_{jm} \cdot x_m + \tilde{n}_j. \tag{3}$$

We notice from Eqs. (2), (3) that the nondiagonal elements of R describe the interference between the elements of the transmit vector at the receiver side. For interference-free transmission $R_{\backslash d}$ = 0. For an interference-free transmission over an additive white Gaussian noise (AWGN) channel $R = I$.

Figure 2 shows the channel matrix for a MIMO transmission scheme for different number of transmit/receive antennas. **Figure 3** shows the channel matrix for OFDM with/without spreading. **Figure 4** shows the channel matrix for MIMO-OFDM. In **Figures 2–4**, the darker the elements, the larger the absolute values of the entries of the corresponding matrix R, and hence larger the interference [21].

Remark 1. For a clear distinction between *channel matrix* and *block transmit matrix*, we refer to [11, 18]. Generally speaking, the block transmit matrix R is a block diagonal matrix of "many" channel matrices.

The detector DET in **Figure 1** has to deliver a vector $\hat{q}$ with a minimum bit error rate compared to q (conditional to the available computational power) given that COD, $\mathcal{M}$ and R are known at the receiver side. The optimum detection (maximum likelihood detection) for realistic cases is often infeasible. Therefore, suboptimum schemes are used, mainly based on separating the detection into an equalization EQ (to cope with interference caused by $R_{\backslash d}$) and a decoding DEC (to utilize the redundancy added by COD). In this case, we distinguish between separate

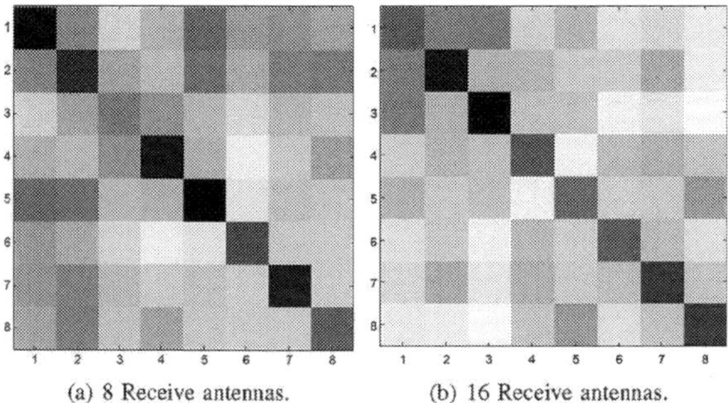

(a) 8 Receive antennas. (b) 16 Receive antennas.

Figure 2. Visualization of the channel matrix for a MIMO transmission scheme with eight transmit antennas and different receive antennas.

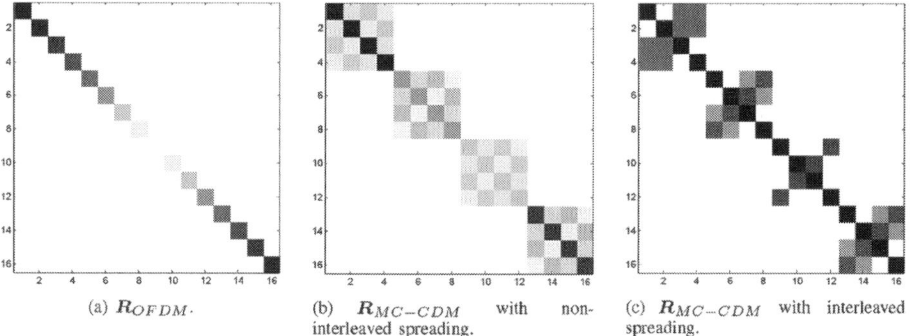

(a) R_{OFDM}. (b) R_{MC-CDM} with non-interleaved spreading. (c) R_{MC-CDM} with interleaved spreading.

Figure 3. Visualization of the channel matrix for OFDM with 16 subcarriers and spreading over four subcarriers with/ without interleaving.

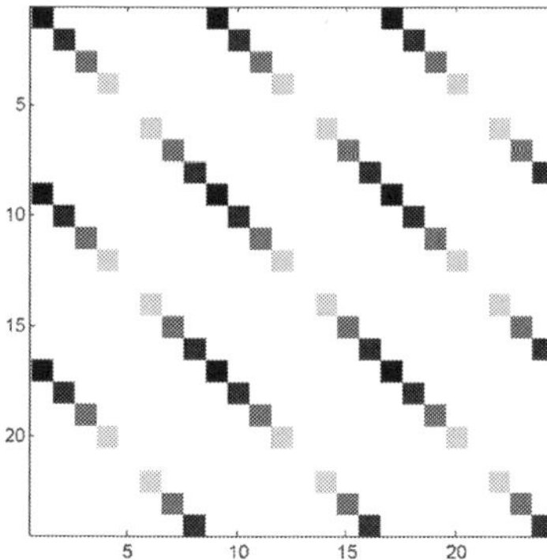

Figure 4. Visualization of the channel matrix for a MIMO-OFDM transmission scheme with eight subcarriers and three transmit antennas.

and joint equalization and decoding, cf. **Figure 5**. The superiority of the latter one is widely accepted: The separate equalization and decoding as in **Figure 5(a)** in general leads to a performance loss since the equalizer does not utilize the knowledge available at the decoder [14]. Each of the components DET, EQ and DEC can be seen as a pattern classifier. By separating the detection into equalization and decoding, an optimum detection in general cannot be achieved anymore (even if optimum equalization and optimum decoding are individually applied). Nevertheless, this is a common practice.

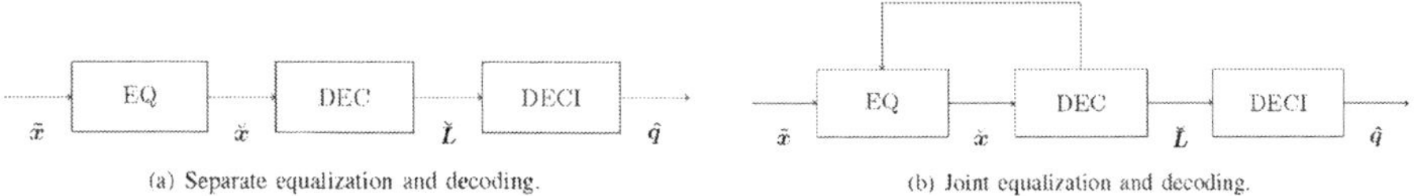

Figure 5. Detection: EQ is the equalizer, DEC is the decoder, DECI is a hard decision function. Notice the feedback from the decoder to the equalizer in (b), i.e., the turbo principle.

DECI in **Figure 5** is a hard decision function. For a coded transmission, DECI is a unit step function. For an uncoded transmission, COD and DEC are removed from **Figure 1** and **Figure 5**, respectively. DECI in this case is a stepwise function depending on the symbol alphabet ψ which maps the (in general complex-valued) elements of the equalized vector $\check{x}$ to the vector of detected symbols $\hat{x} \in \psi^N$ cf. **Figure 8**. The map from $\hat{x}$ to $\hat{q}$ is then straightforward. In summary

- For an uncoded transmission DECI: $\mathbb{C}^N \to \psi^N$.

- For a coded transmission DECI: $\mathbb{R}^k \to \{0,1\}^k$.

3. Vector equalization

For an uncoded transmission, the detection DET reduces to a vector equalization EQ as shown in **Figure 6**.

The optimum vector equalization rule (the maximum likelihood one) is based on the minimum Mahalanobis distance and is given as [21]

$$\hat{x}_{\mathrm{ML}} = \arg\min_{\xi \in \chi} \left\{ \frac{1}{2} \cdot \xi^H \cdot R \cdot \xi - \Re\{\xi^H \cdot \tilde{x}\} \right\}. \tag{4}$$

For each receive vector $\tilde{x}$, the optimum vector equalizer calculates the Mahalanobis distance Eq. (4) to *all* possible transmit vectors χ of cardinality $2^{m \cdot N}$ and decides in favor of that possible transmit vector $\hat{x}_{\mathrm{ML}}$ with the minimum Mahalanobis distance to the receive vector $\tilde{x}$, i.e., exhaustive search is required in general. This can be performed for small $2^{m \cdot N}$ which is usually

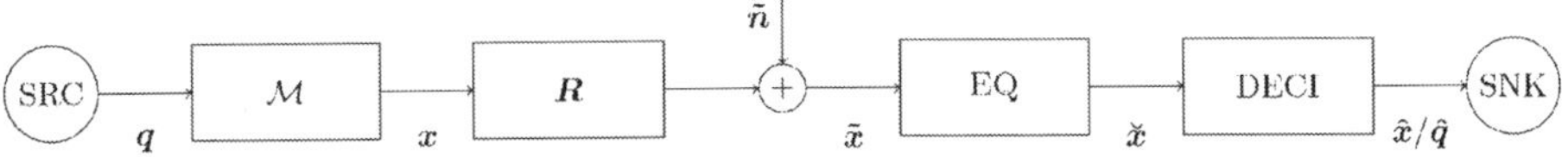

Figure 6. Uncoded block transmission model. Neither encoding at the transmitter nor decoding at the receiver. The detection reduces to a vector equalization EQ.

not the case in practice. Therefore, suboptimum equalization schemes are applied, which trade-off performance against complexity.

4. Continuous-time single-layer recurrent neural networks for vector equalization

The dynamical behavior of continuous-time single-layer recurrent neural networks of dimension N', abbreviated in the following by RNN[4], is given by the state-space equations [22]:

$$\Upsilon_e \cdot \frac{d\boldsymbol{u}(t)}{dt} = -\boldsymbol{u}(t) + \boldsymbol{W} \cdot \boldsymbol{v}(t) + \boldsymbol{W}_0 \cdot \boldsymbol{e},$$
$$\boldsymbol{v}(t) = \boldsymbol{\varphi}(\boldsymbol{u}(t)) = [\varphi_1(u_1(t)), \ \varphi_2(u_2(t)), \ \cdots, \ \varphi_{N'}(u_{N'}(t))]^T. \tag{5}$$

In Eq. (5), Υ_e is a diagonal and positive definite matrix of size $N' \times N'$. $\boldsymbol{v}(t)$ is the output, $\boldsymbol{u}(t)$ is the inner state, $\boldsymbol{e}$ is the external input. $\boldsymbol{v}, \boldsymbol{u}, \boldsymbol{e} \in \mathbb{C}^{N'}$. $\varphi_j(\cdot) : j \in \{1, 2, ..., N'\}$ is the j-th activation function. $\boldsymbol{W} = \{w_{jj'} : j, j' \in \{1, 2, \cdots, N'\}\} \in \mathbb{C}^{N' \times N'}$, $\boldsymbol{W}_0 = \mathrm{diag}_v\{[w_{10}, w_{20}, \cdots, w_{N'0}]^T\} \in \mathbb{R}^{N' \times N'}$ are the weight matrices. The real-valued RNN (all variables and functions in Eq. (5) are real-valued) is shown in **Figure 7**, which is known as "additive model" or "resistance-capacitance model" [23]. In this case, $w_{jj'} = \frac{R_j}{R_{jj'}}$ is the weight coefficient between the output of the j'-th neuron and the input of the j-th neuron, $w_{j0} = \frac{R_j}{R_{j0}}$ is the weight coefficient of the j-th external input. We also notice that the feedback $\boldsymbol{W} \cdot \boldsymbol{v}$ in Eq. (5) and **Figure 7** is a linear function of the output $\boldsymbol{v}$. Moreover, Υ_e can be given in this case as $\Upsilon_e = \mathrm{diag}_v\{[R_1 \cdot C_1, R_2 \cdot C_2, ..., R_{N'} \cdot C_{N'}]^T\}$.

As a nonlinear dynamical system, the stability of the RNN is of primary interest [16]. This has been proven under specific conditions by Lyapunov's stability theory in [24] for real-valued RNN and in [22, 25] for complex-valued ones, among others. The RNN in Eq. (5) represents a general purpose structure. Based on N', φ, $\boldsymbol{W}$, $\boldsymbol{W}_0$ a wide range of optimization problems can be solved. First and most well-investigated applications of the RNN include the content addressable memory [24, 26], analog-to-digital converter (ADC) [27] and the traveling salesman problem [28]. In all these cases, no training is needed since the RNN is acting as a dynamical solver. This feature is desirable in many engineering fields like signal processing, communications, automatic control, etc., and has first been exploited by Hopfield in his

---

[4] The abbreviation RNN in this chapter inherently includes the continuous-time and the single-layer properties.

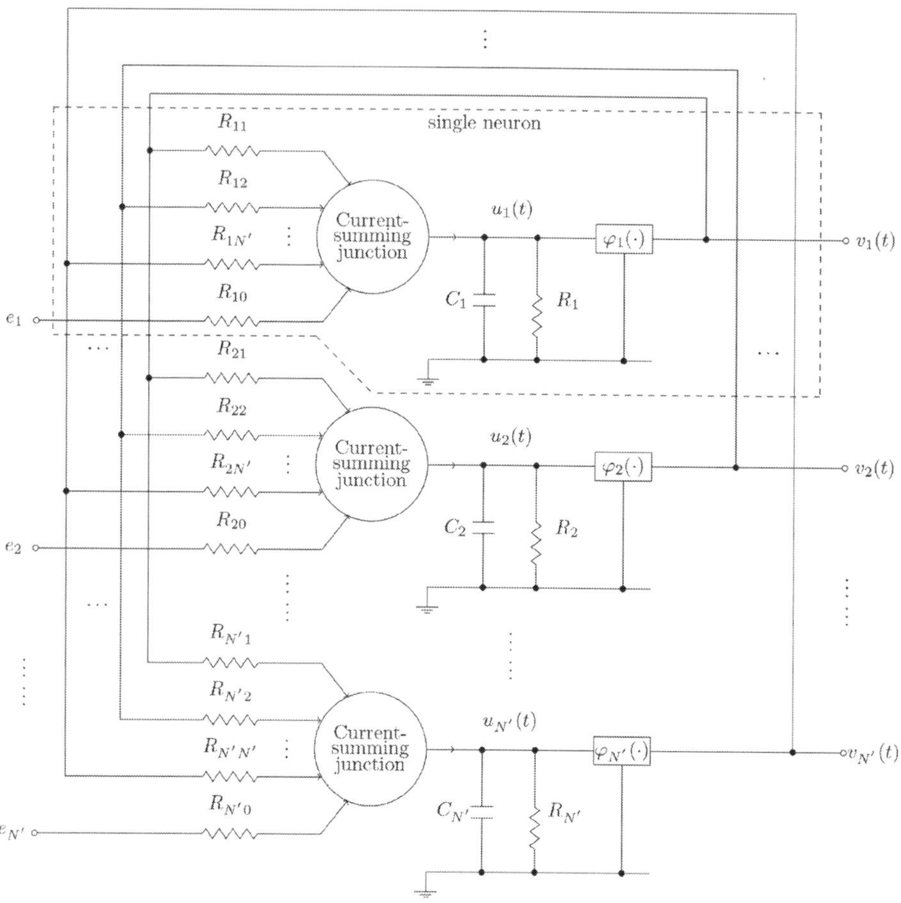

Figure 7. Continuous-time single-layer real-valued recurrent neural network. $v(t)$ is the output, $u(t)$ is the inner state, e is the external input and $\varphi(\cdot)$ is the activation function. This model is known as "additive model" or "resistance-capacitance model" [23].

pioneering work [24, 29], where information has been stored in a dynamically stable RNN. We focus in the following on the vector equalization.

Remark 2. The dimension of a real-valued RNN is the same as the number of neurons.

Remark 3. Two real-valued RNNs each of N' neurons are required to represent one complex-valued RNN (with dimension N'). This is possible by separating Eq. (5) into real and imaginary parts. However, this doubles in general the number of connections per neuron (and hence the number of multiplications) because of the required connections (represented by W_i) between the two real-valued RNNs as it can be seen from the following equation:

$$\Upsilon_e \cdot \frac{\mathrm{d}}{\mathrm{d}t} \begin{bmatrix} u_r(t) \\ u_i(t) \end{bmatrix} = - \begin{bmatrix} u_r(t) \\ u_i(t) \end{bmatrix} + \begin{bmatrix} W_r & -W_i \\ W_i & W_r \end{bmatrix} \cdot \begin{bmatrix} v_r(t) \\ v_i(t) \end{bmatrix} + \begin{bmatrix} W_0 & 0 \\ 0 & W_0 \end{bmatrix} \cdot \begin{bmatrix} e_r \\ e_i \end{bmatrix}. \tag{6}$$

Υ_e in this case is a diagonal positive definite matrix of size $2 \cdot N' \times 2 \cdot N'$ and

$$\begin{aligned} u(t) &= u_r(t) + \imath u_i(t) &, &\qquad e = e_r + \imath e_i \\ v(t) &= v_r(t) + \imath v_i(t) &, &\qquad W = W_r + \imath W_i. \end{aligned}$$

A. Vector equalization based on RNN

The usage of the RNN for vector equalization became known for multiuser interference cancellation in CDMA environments [30, 31]. However, this was limited to the binary phase-shift keying (BPSK) symbol alphabet $\psi = \{-1, +1\}$. This has been generalized to complex-valued symbol alphabets in [21] by combining the results of references [20, 22, 32][5]. Based thereon, it has been proven that the RNN ends in a *local* minimum of Eq. (4) if the following relations are fulfilled [21], cf. Eqs. (1), (2), (5) and **Figures 6** and **7**.

$$\begin{aligned} e &= \tilde{x} & v &= \check{x} & N' &= N \\ W_0 &= R_d^{-1} & W &= I - R_d^{-1} \cdot R & \varphi(\cdot) &= \theta^{(opt)}(\cdot) \end{aligned} \tag{7}$$

and therefore $\hat{x} = \mathrm{DECI}(v)$. **Figure 8** shows an example of an eight quadrature amplitude modulation (8 QAM) symbol alphabet and its corresponding DECI function. The relations in Eq. (7) are obtained by the comparison between the maximum likelihood function of the vector equalization and the Lyapunov function of the RNN.

The dynamical behavior of the vector equalization based on RNN can be given as, cf. Eqs. (1), (5), (7)

$$\begin{aligned} \Upsilon_e \cdot \frac{\mathrm{d}u(t)}{\mathrm{d}t} &= -u(t) + \check{x}(t) + R_d^{-1} \cdot R \cdot [x - \check{x}(t)] + R_d^{-1} \cdot \tilde{n}, \\ \check{x}(t) &= \theta^{(opt)}\left(u(t)\right) = [\theta_1^{(opt)}\left(u_1(t)\right), \theta_2^{(opt)}\left(u_2(t)\right), \cdots, \theta_N^{(opt)}\left(u_N(t)\right)]^T. \end{aligned} \tag{8}$$

The locally asymptotical stability of Eq. (8) based on Lyapunov functions has been proved in [21] (based on [22]) for separable symbol alphabets $\psi^{(s)}$. When Eq. (8) reaches an equilibrium point u_{ep}, i.e., $\frac{\mathrm{d}u(t)}{\mathrm{d}t} = 0_N \Rightarrow u = u_{ep}$, Eq. (8) can be rewritten as

$$u_{ep} = \check{x}_{ep} + R_d^{-1} \cdot R \cdot [x - \check{x}_{ep}] + R_d^{-1} \cdot \tilde{n}. \tag{9}$$

If additionally, a correct equalization is achieved, i.e., $\check{x}_{ep} = x$, the inner state is

---

[5] For *discrete-time* single-layer recurrent neural networks for vector equalization, we refer to references [19, 33].

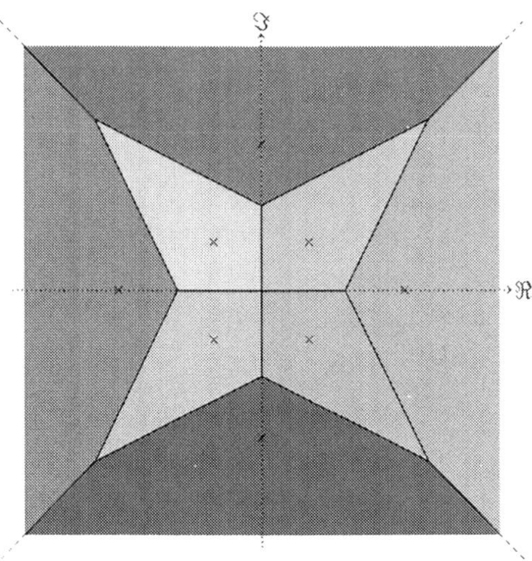

Figure 8. An example of an 8 QAM symbol alphabet and its corresponding DECI function. Each element of the symbol alphabet (marked with ×) has its own "decisions region" visualized by different colors. The function DECI delivers that element of the symbol alphabet, where the input argument lies in its corresponding decision region.

$$u_{ep} = x + R_d^{-1} \cdot \tilde{n} \; . \tag{10}$$

$$\underbrace{\qquad}_{n_e}$$

Thus, the RNN as vector equalizer, Eq. (8) acts as "analog dynamical solver" and there is no need for a training. The covariance matrix of n_e is $\Phi_{n_e n_e} = \frac{N_0}{2} \cdot R_d^{-1} \cdot R \cdot R_d^{-1}$. We define

$$\Sigma_{n_e} = \text{diag}_v\{[\sigma_1^2, \sigma_2^2, \cdots, \sigma_N^2]^T\} = \text{diag}_m\{\Phi_{n_e n_e}\} = \frac{N_0}{2} \cdot R_d^{-1} . \tag{11}$$

In Eq. (7), $\theta^{(opt)}\,(\cdot)$ is the optimum activation function and depends on the symbol alphabet ψ. For BPSK (a real-valued case)

$$\theta^{(opt)}(u) = \tanh\left(\frac{u}{\sigma^2}\right) . \tag{12}$$

where σ^2 is given in Eq. (11).

Remark 4. For separable symbol alphabets, $\psi = \psi^{(s)} \Rightarrow \theta^{(opt)}(u = u_r + \iota u_i) = \theta_r^{(opt)}(u_r) + \iota \theta_i^{(opt)}(u_i)$ [19].

B. Analog hardware implementation aspects: equalization

The analog signal processing as a matter of topical importance for modern receiver architectures was recognized in [34], where an analog vector equalizer—designed in BiCMOS technology—was considered as a promising application for the analog processing of baseband signals. The equalizer accepts sampled vector symbols in analog form with an advantage that the equalizer does not require an ADC at the input interface. At very high data rates, the exclusion of an ADC softens the trade-off between chip area requirement and overall power consumption. We discuss in the following section the main features/challenges of the analog implementation of the vector equalizer based on RNN.

Structure: An RNN of dimension N' (in general $2 \cdot N'$ neurons) is capable to act as a vector equalizer as long as the block size at the transmitter side N (over all possible symbol alphabets, coding schemes and block sizes) is as maximum as N', i.e., $N \leq N'$.

Activation function: The definition of the optimum activation function $\theta^{(opt)}(\cdot)$ is not general, but depends on the symbol alphabet under consideration. Different symbol alphabets need different activation functions. However, we have proven in [20] that for square QAM symbol alphabets—the most relevant ones in practice—$\theta^{(opt)}(\cdot)$ can be approximated as a sum of a limited number of shifted and weighted hyperbolic tangent functions. Square QAM symbol alphabets are separable ones, cf. Remark 4. The analog implementation of the hyperbolic tangent well befits the large-signal transfer function of transconductance stages based on bipolar differential amplifiers [3, 34].

Adaptivity: A vector equalizer must be capable to adapt to different and time-variant interference levels. The adaptivity is regulated by the measurement of the block transmit matrix R, a task performed by a "channel estimation unit" (CEU). The weight matrices W and W_0 are then computed as in Eq. (7) and forwarded to the RNN (**Figure 9**). Thus, the weight matrices W and W_0 are *not* the outcome of any training algorithm but related directly to R, cf. Eq. (7). This represents a typical example for the mixed-signal integrated circuit, where the weight coefficients are (obtained and) stored digitally, converted into analog values, later used as weight coefficients for the analog RNN [8].

For the j-th neuron in the additive model **Figure 7**, the ratio between two resistors R_j and $R_{jj'}$ (R_j and R_{j0}) is used to configure each weight coefficient $w_{jj'}$ (w_{j0}). According to the additive

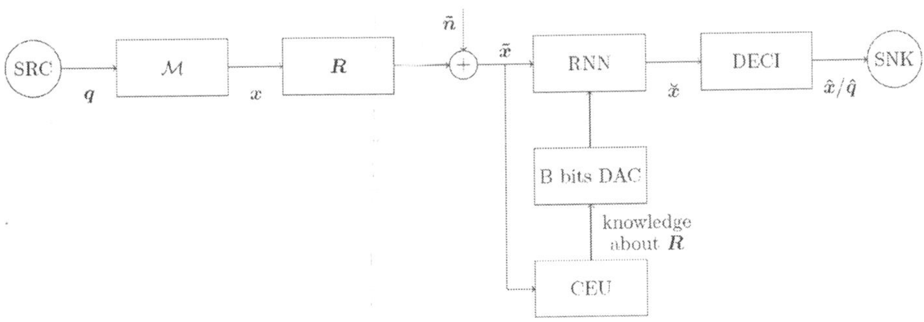

Figure 9. Uncoded block transmission model. The detection reduces to a vector equalization EQ. The channel estimation unit (CEU) estimates the block transmit matrix R.

model, $R_{jj'}$ and R_{j0} can assume both positive and negative values, and the absolute value theoretically extends from R_j to infinite (for $w_{jj'} \in [-1, +1]$). This puts serious limitations to the direct implementation of the model. In [3], we showed how this difficulty can be overcome by using a Gilbert cell as a four-quadrant analog multiplier. A Gilbert cell [35] is composed of two pairs of differential amplifiers with cross-coupled collectors, and is controlled by a differential voltage input G_{ji} applied at the base gate of the transistors. When biased with a differential tail current $I_{ji} = I_{ji}^{+} - I_{ji}^{-}$, the differential output current $I_{ji,w} = I_{ji,w}^{+} - I_{ji,w}^{-}$ is a fraction w of the tail current I_{ji}, as a function of the input voltage G_{ji}:

$$I_{ji,w} = I_{ji,w}^{+} - I_{ji,w}^{-} = f_{Gc}(I_{ji} = I_{ji}^{+} - I_{ji}^{-}, G_{ji}) = w \cdot I_{ji} \in [-I_{ji}, +I_{ji}]. \tag{13}$$

Accuracy: Locally asymptotical Lyapunov stability can be guaranteed for the RNN in Eqs. (5), (8) if, among others, the hermitian property is verified for the weight matrix W (the symmetric property in the real-valued case). Inaccuracies in the weights' representation may jeopardize the Lyapunov stability and impact the performance of the vector equalizer. The first cause of weights' inaccuracy may arise from the limited accuracy of the analog design in terms of components' parasitics, devices' mismatch, process variation, just to name a few. Those inaccuracies (if modest) are expected to slightly degrade the performance without causing a catastrophic failure, thanks to the high nonlinearity of the equalization algorithm. Moreover, it has been shown in [8, 36] that in some cases, they produce beneficial effects: These imperfections incorporate some kind of simulated annealing which enables escaping local minima by allowing occasionally "uphill steps" since the Lyapunov stable RNN is a gradient-like system. This feature is emulated in discrete-time by *stochastic* Hopfield networks [23]. Non-precision of the weights may also arise from an insufficient resolution of the digital-to-analog converter (DAC) (**Figure 9**). On the other hand, an overzealous DAC design increases the chip area, the power consumption and adds complexity to the interface between the analog vector equalizer and the digital CEU. In this case, a conservative approach suggests to use a DAC with enough resolution to match the precision used by the CEU.

Interneuron connectivity and reconfigurability: Scaling the architecture of an analog VLSI design is not straightforward. A vector equalizer based on recurrent neural networks is composed by the repetition of equal sub-systems, i.e., the neurons. Using a bottom-up approach, the first step to scale the system involves the redesign of the single neuron in order to handle more feedback inputs. In a successive step, the neurons are connected together and a system-level simulation is performed to check the functionality of the system. However, several design choices must be made during the process and it is not guaranteed that the optimum architecture for a certain number of neurons is still the best choice when the number of neurons changes. For large N, the block transmit matrix R, defining the weight matrix W, is usually sparse. If a maximum number of nonzero elements over the rows of R is assumed, the requirement for a full connectivity between the neurons in **Figure 7** can be relaxed, and only a maximum number of connections per neuron will be necessary. In this case, however, in addition to the "adaptivity", the RNN must be reconfigured according to the position of the nonzero elements in R. The hardware simplification given by the partial connectivity may be counterbalanced by the necessity of a further routing (e.g., multiplexing/demultiplexing) of the feedback. For special cases, where the block transmit matrix can be reordered around the diagonal, more independent RNNs can be simply used in parallel. In **Figures 3(b)** and **3(c)**, four independent RNNs, each of dimension four, can be used in parallel. Additionally, for specific transmission schemes such as MIMO-OFDM in **Figure 4**, the connectivity can be assumed limited (number of transmit antennas minus one) and fixed (crosstalk only between *same* subcarriers, when used simultaneously on different transmit antennas).

Example 1. In **Figure 4**, eight RNNs (number of subcarriers) each of dimension of three (number of transmit antennas) can be used in parallel. Each neuron has two feedback inputs.

C. Circuit design

We review here the main features of the analog circuit design of an RNN as vector equalizer working with the BPSK symbol alphabet and composed of four neurons. Detailed explanation can be found in reference [3]. The RNN is realized in IHP 0.25 μm SiGe BiCMOS technology (SG25H3). A simplified schematic of a neuron is shown in **Figure 10**. Schematics of gray boxes are presented in **Figure 11**.

The dynamical behavior of the circuit in **Figures 10** and **11** is described as [3]

$$
\begin{aligned}
\Upsilon \cdot \frac{\mathrm{d}u^{'}(t)}{\mathrm{d}t} &= -u^{'}(t) + W \cdot v^{'}(t) + W_0 \cdot e^{'}, \\
\frac{R \cdot I_t}{N-1} \cdot \tanh\left(\frac{u^{'}(t)}{2 \cdot V_t}\right) &= v^{'}(t), \\
\tau \cdot I &= \Upsilon.
\end{aligned}
\tag{14}
$$

which is equivalent to Eq. (5). $\tau = R \cdot C$ is the time constant of the circuit. R is shown in **Figure 10** and C is a fictitious capacitance between the nodes and u_j^+ and u_j^-. V_t is the thermal voltage and I_t is the tail current in **Figure 11**. The circuit is fully differential and the differential currents and voltages are denoted as, cf. **Figures 10** and **11**:

$$
\begin{aligned}
I_{ji} &= I_{ji}^+ - I_{ji}^- & I_j &= I_j^+ - I_j^- & I_o &= I_o^+ - I_o^-, \\
I_{ji,w} &= I_{ji,w}^+ - I_{ji,w}^- & u_j^{'} &= u_j^+ - u_j^- & e_j^{'} &= e_j^+ - e_j^-
\end{aligned}
\tag{15}
$$

(1) Performance: Simulation results based on the above described analog RNN are shown in **Figure 12**. The interference is described by the channel matrix R_{test}.

$$
R_{test} = \begin{bmatrix}
1 & 0.24 & -0.34 & -0.57 \\
0.24 & 1 & 0.32 & 0.29 \\
-0.34 & 0.32 & 1 & 0.25 \\
-0.57 & 0.29 & 0.25 & 1
\end{bmatrix}
$$

The black dashed line shows the bit error rate (BER) for a BPSK symbol alphabet in an AWGN channel (an interference-free channel). Performance achieved by the maximum likelihood

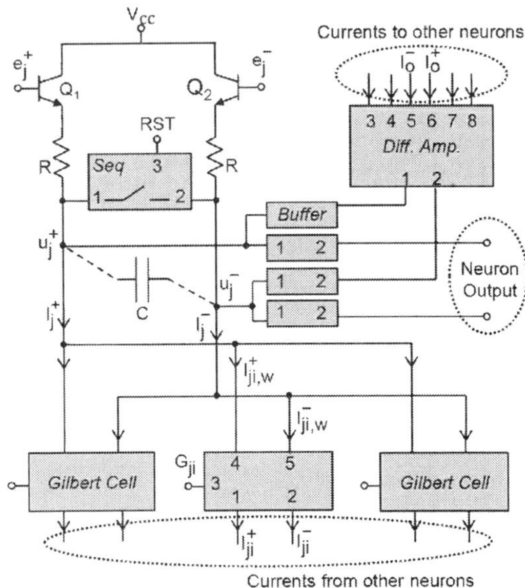

Figure 10. A simplified schematic of a single neuron as a part of a (four neurons) RNN analog vector equalizer. u'_j is the inner state, e'_j is the external input and G_{ji} is used for adapting the weight coefficient w_{ji} from the output of the i-th neuron to the input of the j-th neuron. The circuit is fully differential [3].

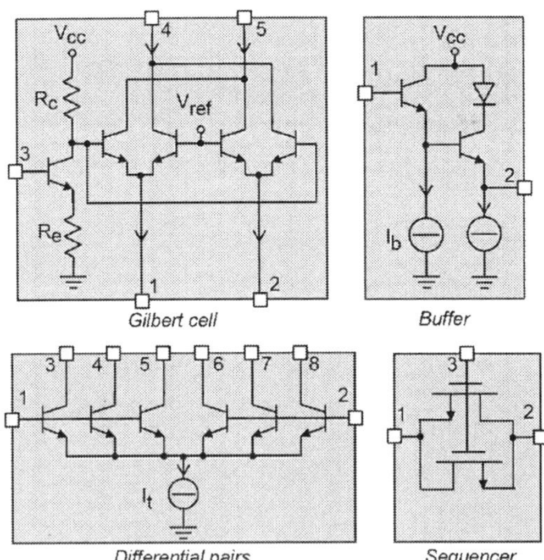

Figure 11. Details of the circuit building blocks. Gilbert cell used as a four-quadrant analog multiplier, buffer stages, BJT differential pairs for the generation of the hyperbolic tangent function and a metal-oxide-semiconductor field-effect transistor (MOSFET) switch used as a sequencer [3].

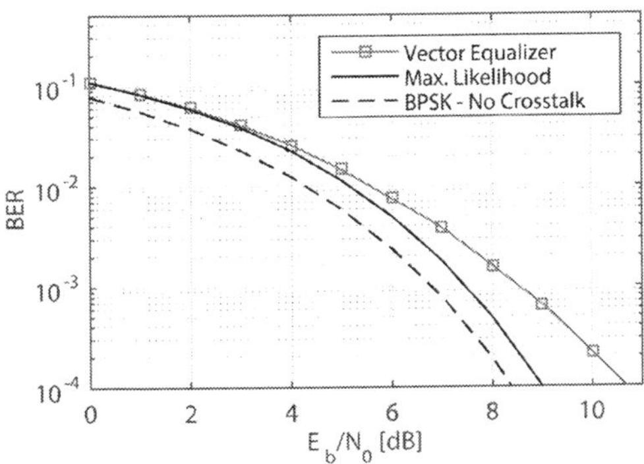

Figure 12. BER vs. E_b/N_0 for the analog RNN vector equalizer. Evolution time equals $10 \cdot \tau$. BPSK symbol alphabet and channel matrix R_{test}.

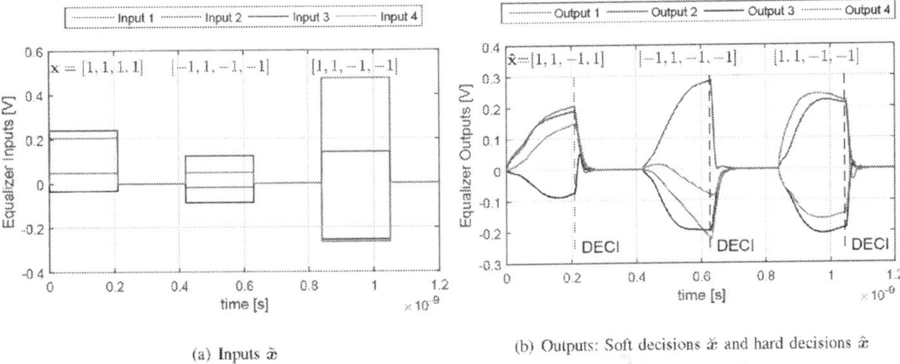

(a) Inputs $\tilde{x}$

(b) Outputs: Soft decisions $\tilde{x}$ and hard decisions $\hat{x}$

Figure 13. An example of a transient simulation for the analog RNN vector equalizer. (a) Inputs $\tilde{x}$ (b) Outputs: soft decisions $\tilde{x}$ and hard decisions $\hat{x}$.

algorithm in Eq. (4) is included as a solid black line. The performance of the analog RNN vector equalizer[6] is presented in a solid red line with square markers. Compared to the optimum algorithm, the signal-to-noise ratio (SNR) loss for the analog RNN vector equalizer can be quantified in approximately 1.7 dB at a BER of 10^{-4}. This loss in SNR emphasizes the suboptimality of the RNN as vector equalizer and depends on the channel matrix. **Figure 13** shows an example of a transient simulation for the analog RNN vector equalizer. The time constant is approximately $\tau = 40$ ps. The SNR ratio is set to 2 dB and a series of three receive vectors are equalized in sequence. Because of the channel matrix and noise, the sampled vectors at the input of the equalizer $\tilde{x}$ present different signs and values, compared to the sent

---

[6]Analog RNN vector equalizer refers to the described analog hardware-implemented RNN for vector equalization.

vectors x (shown in square brackets). The equalization of each receive vector lasts $10 \cdot \tau$. First half of this interval (evolution time) is used to reach a stable state, while the second half of the interval (reset time) is used to return to a predefined inner state (all-zero state) before the equalization of a new vector starts. At the end of the evolution time, a decision is made based on the sign of the output vector (the decision function DECI for BPSK is a sign function). In our example, a comparison between the sent and the recovered bits shows an error of one bit out of twelve, equivalent to a BER$\approx \frac{1}{12}$, a result in line with the BER shown in **Figure 12**.

Remark 5. The evolution and reset times are the two limiting factors for the maximum throughput of the analog RNN vector equalizer. However, they cannot be unlimitedly minimized since the RNN needs a minimum evolution time to reach an equilibrium point representing a local minimum of the Lyapunov function, i.e., a local minimum of Eq. (4).

(2) Energy efficiency: The energy efficiency of a hardware "architecture" is the ratio between the power requirement (Watt) of the architecture and its achievement in a given time period. In our case, the throughput of the equalizer represents the achievement. Combining the value of τ and the power consumption, the abovementioned analog vector equalizer is expected to win the competition versus common digital signal processing, thanks to three to four orders of magnitude better energy efficiency [3].

5. Channel coding

Channel coding (including encoding at the transmitter side COD and decoding at the receiver side DEC) aims to enable an error-free transmission over noisy channels with maximum possible transmit rate. This is done by adding redundancy (extra bits) at the transmitter side, i.e., the bijective map from q to q_c (**Figure 14,**) such that the codewords q_c are sufficiently distinguishable at the receiver side even if the noisy channel corrupts some bits during the transmission. **Figure 14** shows a coded transmission over an AWGN channel.

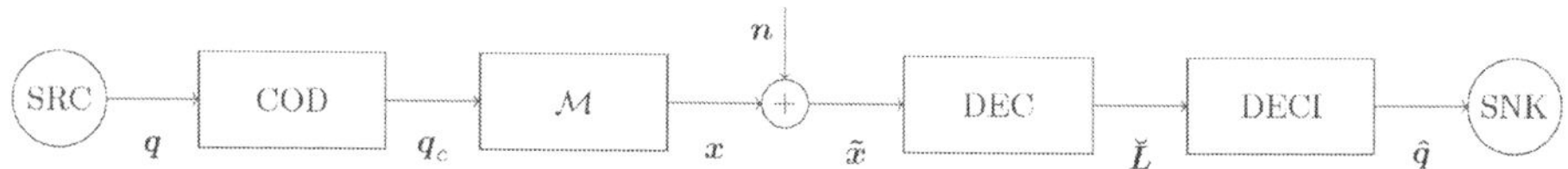

Figure 14. Coded transmission over an BER channel.

For every received codeword, the optimum decoding (the maximum likelihood one) needs to calculate the distance between the received codeword and all possible codewords C, which makes it infeasible for realistic cases (except for convolutional codes which are not considered here). We focus on binary LDPC codes and their corresponding suboptimum decoding algorithm: the *belief propagation* with BPSK symbol alphabet. LDPC codes [37] belong to the class of binary linear block codes and have been shown to achieve an error rate very close to the Shannon limit (a performance lower bound) for the AWGN channel and have been implemented in many practical systems such as the satellite digital video broadcast (DVB-S2)

[38]. A binary linear block code is characterized by a binary parity check matrix H of size $(n-k) \times n$ for $n > k$.

6. Continuous-time single-layer high-order recurrent neural networks for belief propagation

One of the largest drawbacks of RNNs is their quadratic Lyapunov function [39]. Optimization problems associated with cost functions of higher degree cannot be solved "satisfactorily" by RNNs. Increasing the order of the Lyapunov function leads to a nonlinear feedback in the network. In doing so, we obtain the single-layer high-order recurrent neural network, named differently in literature, depending on the nonlinear feedback [39–42].

Remark 6. High-order recurrent neural networks are in the literature exclusively real-valued.

Figure 15 shows the continuous-time single-layer high-order recurrent neural network, abbreviated in the following by HORNN[7].

The dynamical behavior is given by

$$
\begin{aligned}
\mathbf{\Upsilon}_d \cdot \frac{\mathrm{d}\breve{u}(t)}{\mathrm{d}t} &= -\breve{u}(t) + \breve{W} \cdot \breve{f}\left(\breve{v}(t)\right) + \breve{W}_0 \cdot \breve{e}, \\
\breve{v}(t) &= \breve{\varphi}\left(\breve{u}(t)\right) = \left[\breve{\varphi}_1\left(\breve{u}_1(t)\right), \breve{\varphi}_2\left(\breve{u}_2(t)\right), \cdots, \breve{\varphi}_{\breve{n}}\left(\breve{u}_{\breve{n}}(t)\right)\right]^T, \\
\mathbf{\Upsilon}_d &= \mathrm{diag}_v\left\{\left[\breve{R}_1 \cdot \breve{C}_1, \breve{R}_2 \cdot \breve{C}_2, \ldots, \breve{R}_{\breve{n}} \cdot \breve{C}_{\breve{n}}\right]^T\right\}.
\end{aligned}
\tag{16}
$$

The parameters in Eq. (16) can be linked to **Figure 15** in the same way as Eq. (5) linked to **Figure 7**. $\breve{f}(\breve{v})$ is a real-valued continuously differentiable vector function. In addition, $\breve{f}(\mathbf{0}_{\breve{n}}) = \mathbf{0}_{\breve{n}}$. It is worth mentioning that the term "high-order" in this case refers to the interconnections between the neurons rather than the degree of the differential equation describing the dynamics. As for RNNs, this is still of first order, cf. Eq. (16).

Remark 7. In the special case $\breve{f}(\breve{v}) = \breve{v}$, the HORNN reduces to the (real-valued) RNN.

In order to apply HORNNs to solve optimization tasks, their stability has to be investigated. A property without which the behavior of dynamical systems is often suspected [39]. This was the topic of many publications [39–42]. A common denominator of the locally asymptotical stability proof of the HORNN based on Lyapunov functions is

- $\breve{\varphi}(\cdot)$ is continuously differentiable and a strictly increasing function.

- The right side of the first line of Eq. (16) can be rewritten as a gradient of a scalar function.

---

[7]The abbreviation HORNN in this chapter inherently includes the continuous-time, single-layer and real-valued properties.

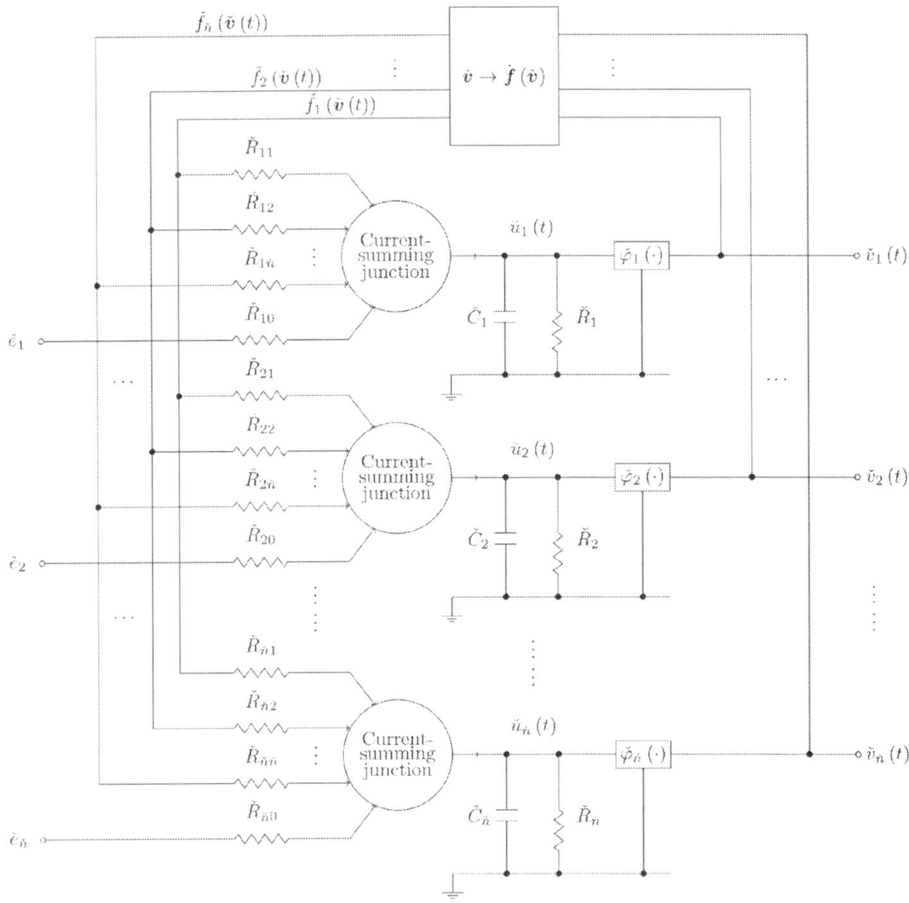

Figure 15. Continuous-time single-layer real-valued high-order recurrent neural network. $\check{v}(t)$ is the output, $\check{u}(t)$ is the inner state, $\check{e}$ is the external input and $\check{\varphi}(\cdot)$ is the activation function. $\check{f}(\check{v})$ is a real-valued continuously differentiable vector function with $\check{f}(\mathbf{0}_{\check{n}}) = \mathbf{0}_{\check{n}}$ [21].

A. Belief propagation based on HORNN

Originally proposed by Gallager [37], belief propagation is a suboptimum graph-based decoding algorithm for LDPC codes. The corresponding graph is bipartite (n parity nodes and $n - k$ check nodes) and known as Tanner graph [43]. This is shown in **Figure 16** for the Hamming code with the parity check matrix $\boldsymbol{H}_{\text{Hamming}}$ Eq. (17) where $n = 7$, $k = 4$. The belief propagation algorithm iteratively exchanges "messages" between parity and check nodes.

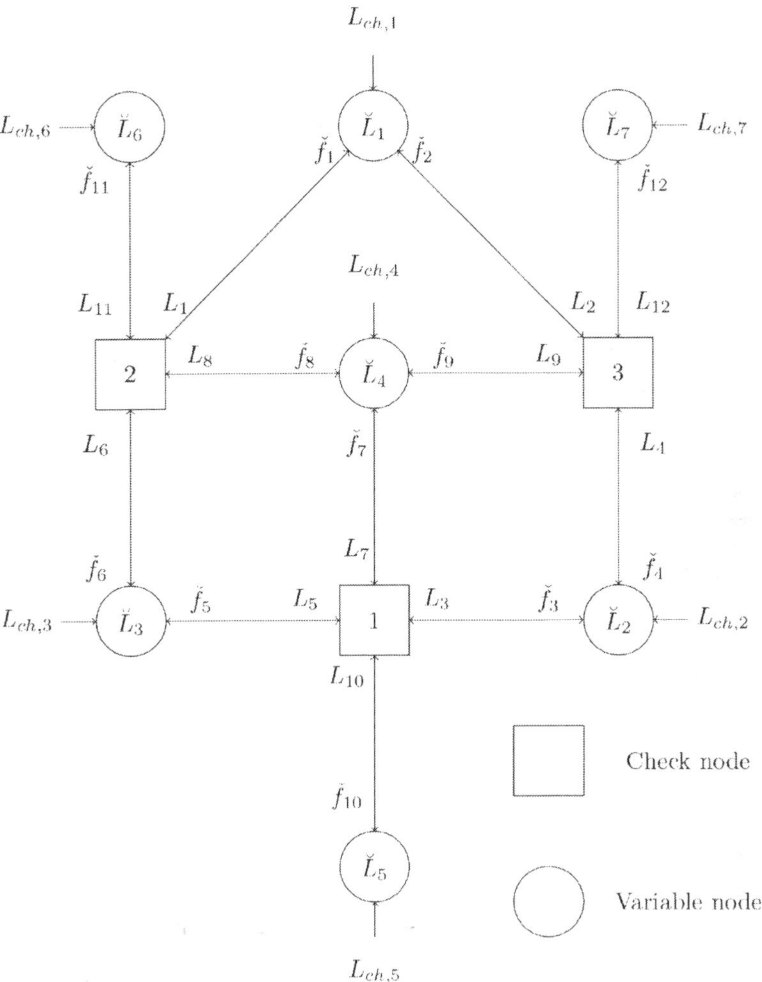

Figure 16. Tanner graph of the systematic Hamming code $n = 7$ and $k = 4$.

$$H_{\text{Hamming}} = \begin{bmatrix} 0 & 1 & 1 & 1 & 1 & 0 & 0 \\ 1 & 0 & 1 & 1 & 0 & 1 & 0 \\ 1 & 1 & 0 & 1 & 0 & 0 & 1 \end{bmatrix} \qquad (17)$$

For every binary linear block code characterized by the binary parity check matrix H of size ($n - k$) $\times$ n for $n > k$, three *binary* matrices $P_{n_h \times n_h}$, $S_{n_h \times n_h}$ and $B_{n_h \times n}$ can be uniquely defined [44, 45] such that Eq. (16) and **Figure 15** perform continuous-time belief propagation if the following relations are fulfilled:

$$\check{u} = L, \tag{18a}$$

$$\check{e} = B \cdot L_{ch}, \tag{18b}$$

$$\check{\varphi}(\cdot) = \tanh\left(\frac{\cdot}{2}\right), \tag{18c}$$

$$\check{v} = \check{\varphi}(L), \tag{18d}$$

$$\check{W} = P, \tag{18e}$$

$$\check{W}_0 = I_{n_h \times n_h}, \tag{18f}$$

$$\check{f}_j = 2 \cdot \operatorname{atanh}\left\{ \prod_{j' \in \text{pos}[S(j,:)=1]} \check{v}_{j'} \right\} \quad \text{for } j, j' \in \{1,\ 2,\ \dots, n_h\}, \tag{18g}$$

$$\check{n} = n_h. \tag{18h}$$

In Eq. (18)[8],

- k is the length of the information word (q in **Figures 1** and **14**).

- n is the length of the codeword (q_c in **Figures 1** and **14**).

- $n_h = \mathbf{1}^T_{\left(1 \times (n-k)\right)} \cdot H \cdot \mathbf{1}_{(n \times 1)} \in [k+1,\, n \cdot (n{-}k)]$ is the number of nonzero elements in H.

- $L_{ch,(n \times 1)}$ is the vector of intrinsic log-likelihood ratio (LLR), which depends on the transition probability of the channel. For $q_{c,j}$ (the j-th element of q_c for $j \in \{1, 2, \cdots, n\}$) it is given as

$$L_{ch,j} = \ln \frac{p(\dot{x}_j = \tilde{x}_j | q_{c,j} = 0)}{p(\dot{x}_j = \tilde{x}_j | q_{c,j} = 1)}. \tag{19}$$

In the last relation, $\dot{x}_j$ is the variable of the conditioned probability density function $p(\dot{x}_j | q_{c,j})$. $\ln(\cdot)$ is the natural logarithm. For an AWGN channel, $\mathcal{N}(0, \sigma_n^2)$: $L_{ch,j} = \frac{\tilde{x}_j}{2 \cdot \sigma_n^2}$.

- $L_{(n_h \times 1)}$ is the "message" sent from the variable nodes to the check nodes.

- $\check{f}_{(n_h \times 1)}$ is the "message" sent from check nodes to variable nodes.

- $I_{(n_h \times n_h)}$ is an identity matrix of size $n_h \times n_h$.

- $\text{pos}[S(j, :) = 1]$ delivers the positions of the nonzero elements in the j-th row of the matrix S.

---

[8] L, $\check{L}$ and L_{ch} are vectors.

The dynamical behavior of belief propagation can be described based on Eqs. (16), (18) and **Figures 14, 15,** and **16** [45]

$$
\begin{aligned}
\Upsilon_d \cdot \frac{\mathrm{d}L(t)}{\mathrm{d}t} &= -L(t) + P \cdot \check{f}\!\left(\check{v}(t)\right) + B \cdot L_{ch}, \\
\check{v}(t) &= \tanh\!\left(\frac{L(t)}{2}\right), \\
\check{L}(t) &= B^T \cdot \check{f}\!\left(\check{v}(t)\right) + L_{ch}.
\end{aligned}
\tag{20}
$$

$\check{L}(t)$ is the soft-output of the decoding algorithm, cf. **Figures 5** and **14**. The discrete-time description is given as [44]

$$
\begin{aligned}
L[l+1] &= P \cdot \check{f}(\check{v}[l]) + B \cdot L_{ch}, \\
\check{v}[l] &= \tanh\!\left(\frac{L[l]}{2}\right), \\
\check{L}[l] &= B^T \cdot \check{f}(\check{v}[l]) + L_{ch}.
\end{aligned}
\tag{21}
$$

B. Dynamical behavior of belief propagation

In a series of papers, Hemati *et. al.* [12, 17, 46–49] also modeled the dynamics of analog belief propagation as a set of first-order nonlinear differential equations Eq. (20). This was motivated from a circuit design aspect, where Υ_d (the same is valid for Υ_e) can be seen as a bandwidth limitation of the analog circuit, realized taking advantage of the low-pass filter behavior of transmission lines **Figure 17**. We have shown in [45] that the model in **Figure 17** also has important dynamical properties when compared with the discrete-time belief propagation Eq. (21) [44]. Particularly, the equilibrium points of the continuous-time belief propagation of Eq. (20) coincide with the fixed points of the discrete-time belief propagation of Eq. (21). This has been proved in [45]. In both cases

$$
L_{ep} = P \cdot \check{f}\!\left(\tanh\!\left(\frac{L_{ep}}{2}\right)\right) + B \cdot L_{ch}.
\tag{22}
$$

The absolute stability of belief propagation Eqs. (20), (21) was proven for repetition codes (one of the simplest binary linear block codes) in [44, 45]. In this case

$$
\check{L}_{ep} = \mathbf{1}_{(n \times n)} \cdot L_{ch}.
\tag{23}
$$

Far away from repetition codes, it has been noticed that iterative decoding algorithms (belief propagation is one of them) exhibit depending on the SNR a wide range of phenomena associated with nonlinear dynamical systems such as existence of multiple fixed points, oscillatory behavior, bifurcation, chaos and transit chaos [50]. Equilibrium points are reached at "relatively" high SNR. The analysis in reference [50] is limited to the discrete-time case.

Remark 8. The HORNN in **Figure 15**, Eqs. (18), (20) for belief propagation acts as a computational model.

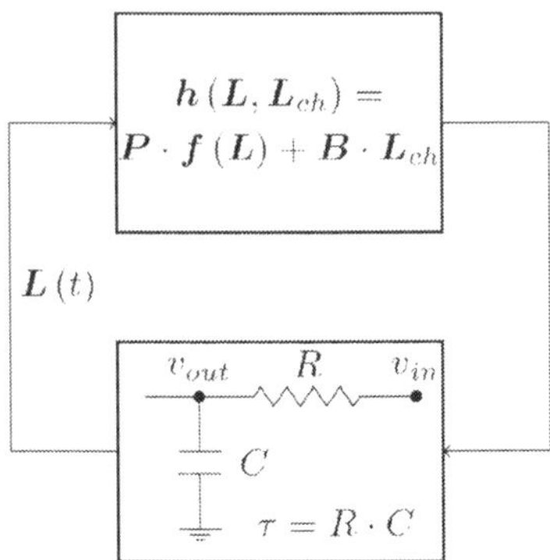

Figure 17. A simple model for analog decoding as presented in [46].

C. Analog hardware implementation aspects: decoding

Many analog hardware implementation aspects have been already mentioned in Section 4-B. We mention here only additional aspects exclusively related to the analog belief propagation based on HORNN.

Structure: In practice, different coding schemes (different parity check matrices H) with various (k, n) constellations are applied to modify the code rate $r_c = k/n$ depending on the channel state. The HORNN in **Figure 15** is capable to act as a continuous-time belief propagation (decoder) as long as the number of neurons $\check{n}$ in **Figure 15** equals (or is larger than) the maximum number of nonzero elements over all parity check matrices and all (k,n) constellations, i.e., $\check{n} \geq \max_H n_h$.

Adaptivity: No training is needed. $\check{W}_0$ and $\check{W}$ are directly related to the parity check matrix H. In contrast to the analog RNN vector equalizer, the weight coefficients are binary, i.e., the weight matrices $\check{W}_0$ and $\check{W}$ define a feedback to be either existent or not. In such a case for **Figure 15**, $\check{R}_{jj}$, $\check{R}_{j0} \in \{\check{R}_j, \infty\}$. Moreover, there is no need for high-resolution DAC for the weight coefficients.

Interneuron connectivity: No full connection is needed since the matrix P for LDPC codes is sparse. The number of connections per neuron must equal the maximum number of nonzero elements in P row-wise over all considered coding schemes and equals $\max_H P \cdot 1_{(n_h \times 1)}$. If this is fulfilled and if interneuron connectivity control is available, the structure in **Figure 15** becomes valid for all considered coding scheme.

Vector function connectivity: For different coding schemes, the number of the arguments $\check{v}'_j$ to evaluate the function $\check{f}_j$ changes, cf. Eq. (18g). The maximum number of the arguments depends on the number of the nonzero elements in S row-wise and equals $\max_H S \cdot 1_{(n_h \times 1)}$. Thus, implementing the function $\check{f}_j$ according to this maximum number enables evaluating the function $\check{f}_j$ for all considered coding schemes.

Remark 9. For a specific coding scheme, the interneuron connectivity can be made fixed. The resulted HORNN structure in this case is valid also for all codeword lengths resulted after performing a puncturing of the original code.

Remark 10. Both, the interneuron connectivity and the weight adaptation play a significant role, in the equalization as well as in the decoding. It can safely be said that they represent the major challenge of the circuit, since the analog circuit must be capable to perform equalization and decoding for a given number of possible combinations of block size, symbol alphabet, coding scheme, etc. Particularly for the decoding, the advantage of having a non-full connectivity is counterbalanced by a double (and very complex) (de)multiplexing of the signals (once for the vector function $\check{f}$ and once for the interneuron connectivity).

7. Joint equalization and decoding

Turbo equalization is a joint iterative equalization and decoding scheme. In this case, a symbol-by-symbol maximum aposteriori probability (s/s MAP) equalizer exchanges in an iterative way reliability values L with a (s/s MAP) decoder [51, 52]. This concept is inspired from the decoding concept of turbo codes, where two (s/s MAP) decoders exchange iteratively reliability values [53]. Despite its good performance, the main drawback of the turbo equalizer is the very high complexity of the s/s MAP-equalizer for multipath channels with long impulse response (compared with symbol duration) and/or symbol alphabets with large cardinality. Therefore, a suboptimum equalization (and a suboptimum decoding) usually replace the s/s-MAP ones (**Figure 18**).

One discrete-time joint equalization and decoding approach has been introduced in [52] and is shown in **Figure 19**. $\tilde{x}$, R_d and R are as in Eq. (2) and z^{-1} is a delay unit. We notice that there are two different (iteration) loops in **Figure 19**: the equalization loop (the blue one) on symbol basis (in the sense of ψ) and the decoding loop (the dashed one) on bit basis. $a = \{1, 2, 3, \cdots\}$, $\rho \in \mathbb{N}$, i.e., after each ρ equalization loops, one decoding loop is performed. The conversion between symbol basis and bit basis (u to L_{ch}) is performed by $\theta_{S/L}(\cdot)$, the way around ($\check{L}$ to $\check{x}$) by $\theta_{L/S}(\cdot)$. The expressions for $\theta_{L/S}(\cdot)$ and $\theta_{L/S}(\cdot)$ can be found in [52]. However, for BPSK, they are given as

$$
\begin{aligned}
\theta_{S/L}(u) &= \frac{2}{\sigma^2} \cdot u, \\
\theta_{L/S}(\check{L}) &= \tanh\left(\frac{\check{L}}{2}\right).
\end{aligned}
\tag{24}
$$

Figure 18. Two examples for joint equalization and decoding. Notice the feedback from the decoder to the equalizer, i.e., turbo principle.

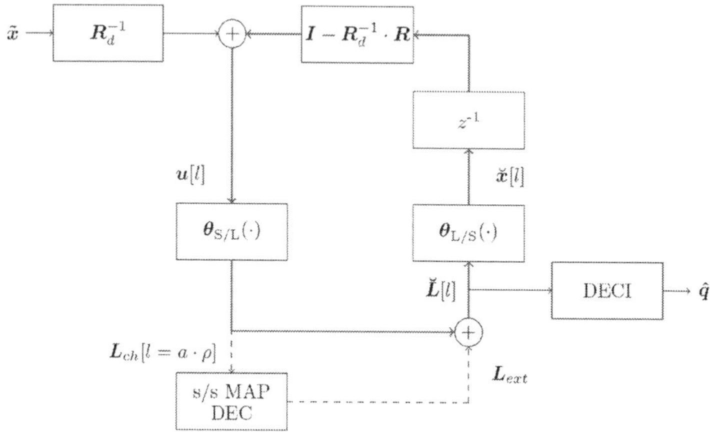

Figure 19. Joint equalization and decoding as described in [52]. L_{ext} represents the "knowledge" obtained by exploiting the redundancy of the code.

σ^2 is given in Eq. (11). If we consider *only* the equalization loop in **Figure 19**, we notice that it describes exactly the dynamical behavior of discrete-time recurrent neural networks [19, 25, 33, 54–56]

$$
\begin{aligned}
u[l+1] &= [I-R_d^{-1} \cdot R] \cdot \check{x}[l] + R_d^{-1} \cdot \tilde{x}, \\
\check{x}[l] &= \theta_{L/S}(\theta_{S/L}(u[l])).
\end{aligned}
\tag{25}
$$

Remark 11. If $\theta_{L/S}\big(\theta_{S/L}(u)\big) = \theta^{(opt)}(u)$, Eqs. (8), (25) share the same equilibrium/fixed points. For BPSK, it can be easily shown based on Eqs. (12), (24) that this is fulfilled.

8. Continuous-time joint equalization and decoding

Motivated by the expected improvement of the energy efficiency by analog implementation compared with the conventional digital one, we map in this section the joint equalization and decoding structure given in **Figure 19** to a continuous-time framework. s/s MAP DEC in **Figure 19** is replaced by a suboptimum decoding algorithm: the *belief propagation*. Moreover, equalization and decoding loops in **Figure 19** are replaced by RNN and HORNN as discussed previously in Sections 4-A and 6-A, respectively. The introduced structure serves as a computational model for an analog hardware implementation and does not need any training.

Figure 20 shows a novel continuous-time joint equalization and decoding based on recurrent neural network structures. The dynamical behavior of the whole system is described by the following differential equations:

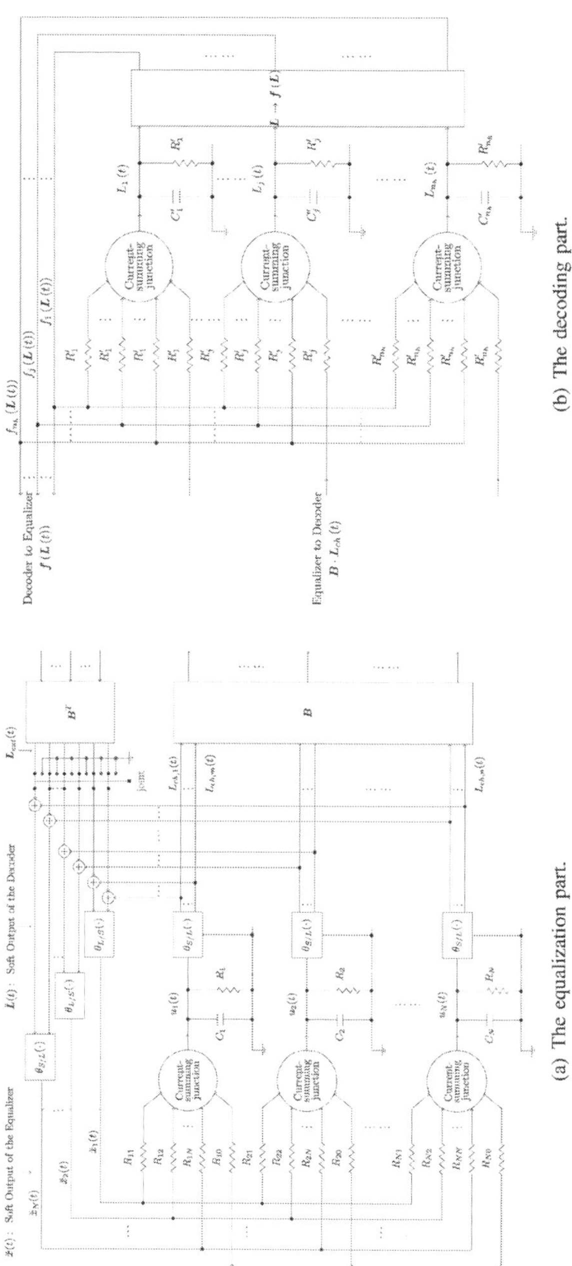

Figure 20. Continuous-time *joint* equalization and decoding based on a recurrent neural network structure for real-valued symbol alphabet (for complex-valued ones, cf. Remark 3). $\check{L}(t)$, $\check{x}(t)$ are the soft output of the decoder and the equalizer, respectively. (a) The equalization part. (b) The decoding part.

$$\Upsilon_e \cdot \frac{\mathrm{d}u(t)}{\mathrm{d}t} = -u(t) + W \cdot \check{x}(t) + W_0 \cdot \tilde{x}, \qquad (26a)$$

$$L_{ch}(t) = \theta_{\mathrm{S/L}}\Big(u(t)\Big), \qquad (26b)$$

$$\Upsilon_d \cdot \frac{\mathrm{d}L(t)}{\mathrm{d}t} = -L(t) + P \cdot f\Big(L(t)\Big) + B \cdot L_{ch}(t), \qquad (26c)$$

$$\check{L}(t) = \underbrace{B^T \cdot f\Big(L(t)\Big)}_{L_{ext}(t)} + L_{ch}(t), \qquad (26d)$$

$$\check{x}(t) = \theta_{\mathrm{L/S}}\Big(\check{L}(t)\Big), \qquad (26e)$$

$$f_j = 2 \cdot \mathrm{atanh}\left\{ \prod_{j \in \mathrm{pos}[S(j,:)=1]} \tanh\left(\frac{L_j}{2}\right) \right\}. \qquad (26f)$$

- Eq. (26a) and **Figure 20(a)** describe the continuous-time vector equalization, cf. Eqs. (1), (5), (7), (8).

- Eq. (26c) and **Figure 20(b)** describe the continuous-time belief propagation, cf. Eqs. (16), (18), (20).

Comparing **Figure 20** with **Figures 7** and **15**, we notice that

- The function $\varphi(\cdot)$ in **Figure 7** (the optimum activation function $\theta^{(opt)}(\cdot)$) has been split into two functions $\theta_{\mathrm{S/L}}(\cdot)$ and $\theta_{\mathrm{L/S}}(\cdot)$ in **Figure 20(a)**. For BPSK symbol alphabet and based on Eqs. (12), (24), it can be easily shown that $\theta^{(opt)}(u) = \theta_{\mathrm{L/S}}\Big(\theta_{\mathrm{S/L}}(u)\Big)$, cf. Remark 11.

- The functions $\check{\varphi}(\cdot)$ and $\check{f}(\cdot)$ in **Figure 15**, Eq. (18) have been merged to one function $f(\cdot)$ in **Figure 20(b)**, Eq. (26f) $f(L) = \check{f}\Big(\check{\varphi}(L)\Big)$. $\check{L}(t)$ and $\check{x}(t)$ are the soft output of the decoder and the equalizer, respectively.

A. Special cases

The novel structure in **Figure 20** is general and stays valid for the following cases:

- **Separate equalization and decoding**: In this case, **Figure 20(a)** is modified such that no feedback from decoder to equalizer is applied. This is shown in **Figure 21(a)**. *Only* at the end of the separate equalization and decoding process, the output is given as $\check{L} = L_{ext} + L_{ch}$. We distinguish between two cases

   1. Equalization and decoding take place separately *at the same time*.

   2. Successive equalization and decoding: *only* after the end of the equalization process, L_{ch} are forwarded to the decoder and the decoder starts the evolution. We focus on this case.

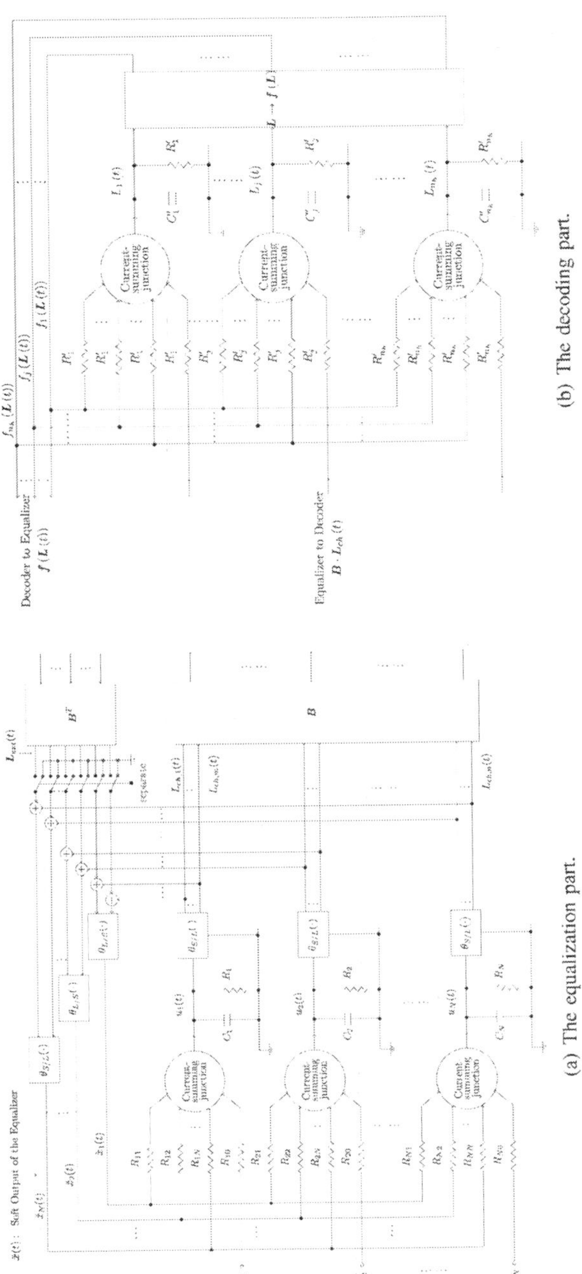

Figure 21. Continuous-time *separate* equalization and decoding based on a recurrent neural network structure for real-valued symbol alphabet (for complex-valued ones, cf. Remark 3). $\check{x}(t)$ is the soft output of the equalizer.

- **Coded transmission over an AWGN channel**: In this case, $R = I$ and hence based on Eq. (7) $W = 0$, $W_0 = I$. Under these conditions, Eq. (26a) becomes linear and can easily be solved $u(t) \rightarrow \tilde{x}$ and $L_{ch}(t)$ in Eq. (26b) becomes time independent L_{ch}. In this case, Eq. (26c) reduces to Eqs. (16), (18).

- **Uncoded transmission over an "interference-causing" channel**: In this case, $P = 0$, $B = 0$ and Eq. (26c) becomes $L = 0_{n_h}$. Under these conditions, Eq. (26a) reduces to Eqs. (5), (7), (8) (notice, however, Remark 11).

B. Throughput, asynchronicity and scheduling

The diagonal elements in Υ_d define the duration of the transient response the HORNN needs in order to converge eventually (in case of convergence). The larger they are, the longer is the transient response and consequently the less is the decoding throughput. The same is valid for Υ_e. The diagonal elements of Υ_e based on our analog RNN vector equalizer are in the range of a few tens of picoseconds.

Unequal diagonal elements in Υ_e (and Υ_d) represent some kind of continuous-time asynchronicity [46]. Asynchronicity in discrete-time RNNs is desirable since it provides the ability to avoid limit cycles, which can probably occur in synchronous discrete-time RNNs [54, 57].

Assuming $\Upsilon_d = \tau_d \cdot I$ and $\Upsilon_e = \tau_e \cdot I$, we notice that the ratio τ_e/τ_d is comparable to the scheduling problem in the discrete-time joint equalization and decoding case. More precisely, how many iterations ρ within the equalizer should be performed before a decoding process takes place, cf. **Figure 19**. This is optimized usually by simulations and is case dependent.

From a dynamical point of view, the case $\tau_e/\tau_d \ll 1$ (or $\tau_d/\tau_e \ll 1$) could be seen as a singular perturbation (in time). In this case, one part of **Figure 20** can be seen as "frozen" compared with the other part.

Remark 12. We notice that the parameters of the transmission model (block transmit matrix, symbol alphabet, block size, channel coding scheme) are utilized to define the parameters of the continuous-time recurrent neural network structure in **Figure 20** such that no training is needed. This represents in practice a big advantage especially for analog hardware. However, to enable different coding schemes and symbol alphabets, either a full connectivity or a vector and interneuron connectivity controls are needed. Both structures are challenging from a hardware implementation point of view.

Remark 13. For the ease of depiction, **Figures 20** and **21** assume that one transmitted block contains exactly one codeword. This is not necessarily the case in practice. As an example, if one transmitted block contains two codewords, one RNN and two parallel HORNNs will be needed. On the other hand, if one codeword lasts over two transmitted blocks, two parallel RNNs and one HORNN is needed.

9. Simulation results

We simulate the dynamical system as given in Eq. (26) and **Figure 20** based on the first Euler method [58]. We assume:

- BPSK modulation scheme (symbol alphabet $\psi = \{-1, +1\}$).

- Each transmitted block contains one codeword, cf. Remark 13.

- $\Upsilon_d = \Upsilon_e = \tau \cdot I$.

- Channel coding scheme: An LDPC code with $k = 204$, code rate 0.5 ($n = 408$) and column weight 3 taken from [59].

- Multipath channels [60]:

  –Proakis-a abbreviated in the following by its channel impulse response h_a leading to a small interference.

  –Proakis-b abbreviated in the following by its channel impulse response h_b leading to a moderate interference.

The impulse response of h_a and h_b are

$$h_a = [0.04 \quad -0.05 \quad 0.07 \quad -0.21 \quad -0.5 \quad 0.72 \quad 0.36 \quad 0 \quad 0.21 \quad 0.03 \quad 0.07],$$
$$h_b = [\quad 0.407 \quad 0.815 \quad 0.407 \quad].$$

The block transmission matrix R is a banded Toeplitz matrix of the autocorrelation function of the channel impulse response [61]. The following cases are considered:

- Uncoded transmission over AWGN channel. The bit error rate can be obtained analytically and is given as $\frac{1}{2} \cdot \text{erfc}\left\{\frac{E_b}{N_0}\right\}$ [62]. $\text{erfc}(\cdot)$ is the complementary error function and E_b is the energy per bit.

- Coded transmission over AWGN channel and continuous-time decoding at the receiver (HORNN-belief propagation).

- Uncoded transmission over (the abovementioned) multipath channels and continuous-time equalization at the receiver (RNN-equalization).

- Coded transmission over (the abovementioned) multipath channels. We distinguish between joint equalization and decoding (**Figure 20**) and separate equalization and decoding (**Figure 21**). In the latter case, equalization is performed firstly, and consequently the decoding.

The evolution time for the whole system in all cases is $20 \cdot \tau$, i.e., all simulated scenarios deliver the same throughput. For separate equalization and decoding, the evolution time of the equalization equals the evolution time of the decoding and equals $10\ \tau$. The simulation results are shown in **Figure 22**. We notice the following:

- Joint equalization and decoding outperforms the separate one, which is a fact we know from the discrete-time case. Our proposed model in **Figure 20** is capable of "transforming" this advantage to the continuous-time case.

- For the channel h_a, the BER (for continuous-time joint equalization and decoding) is close to the coded BER curve.

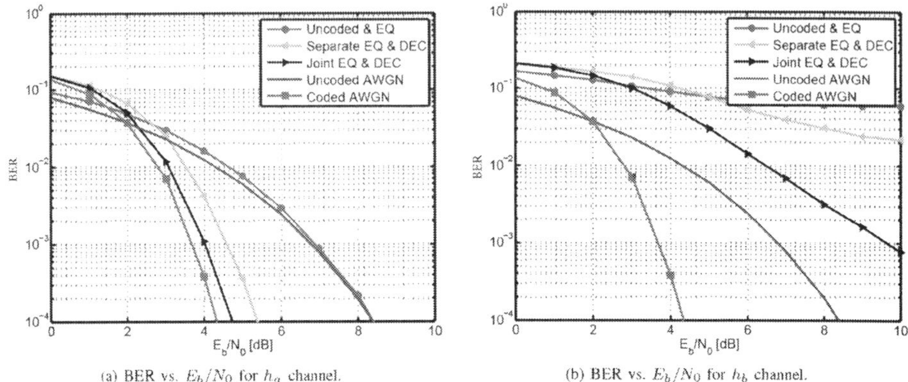

Figure 22. BER vs. E_b/N_0 for evolution time equals $20 \cdot \tau$. Continuous-time (joint) equalization and decoding. BPSK symbol alphabet.

- For the channel h_b, there exists a gap between the obtained results and the coded AWGN curve. This was expected, since h_b represents a more severe multipath channel compared with h_a.

- If only equalization performance is considered, we compare between "Uncoded & EQ" curves and "Uncoded BER" curves. In **Figure 22(a)**, the vector equalizer based on continuous-time recurrent neural networks is capable to remove already all interferences caused by the multipath channel h_a, whereas in **Figure 22(b)**, the "Uncoded & EQ" curve approaches an error floor.

Remark 14. Interleaving and antigray mapping often encountered in the context of iterative equalization and decoding can be easily integrated in the proposed model in **Figure 20**. Antigray mapping will influence the functions $\theta_{S/L}(\cdot)$ and $\theta_{L/S}(\cdot)$, whereas interleaving affects the matrix B.

10. Conclusion

Joint equalization and decoding is a detection technique which possesses the potential for improving the bit error rates of the transmission at the cost of additional computational complexity at the receiver. Joint equalization and decoding is being considered only for the discrete-time case. However, for high data rates, the energy consumption of a digital implementation becomes a limiting factor and shortens the lifetime of the battery. Improving the energy efficiency revives the analog implementation option for joint equalization and decoding algorithms, particularly taking advantage of the nonlinearity of the corresponding algorithms.

Continuous-time recurrent neural networks serve as promising computational models for analog hardware implementation and stand out due to their Lyapunov stability (the proved existence of attracting equilibrium points under specific conditions) and special suitability for analog VLSI. They have often been applied for solving optimization problems even without the need for a training. The drop of the training is particularly favorable for analog hardware implementation.

In this chapter, we introduced a novel continuous-time recurrent neural network structure, which is capable to perform continuous-time joint equalization and decoding. This structure is based on continuous-time recurrent neural networks for equalization and continuous-time high-order recurrent neural networks for belief propagation, a well-known decoding algorithm for low-density parity-check codes. In both cases, the behavior of the underlying dynamical system has been addressed, Lyapunov stability and simulated annealing are a few examples. The parameters of the transmission system (channel matrix, symbol alphabet, block size, channel coding scheme) are used to define the parameters of the proposed recurrent neural network such that *no training* is needed.

Simulation results showed that the superiority of joint equalization and decoding preserves, if this is done in analog according to our proposed model. Compared with the digital implementation, the analog one is expected to improve the energy efficiency and consume less chip area. We confirmed this for the analog hardware implementation of the equalization part. In this case, the analog vector equalization achieves an energy efficiency of a few picojoule per equalized bit, which is three to four orders of magnitude better than the digital counterparts. Additionally, analog hardware implementation aspects have been discussed. We showed as an example the importance of the interneuron connectivity, especially pointing out the challenges represented either by the hardware implementation of a massively distributed network, or by the routing of the signals using (de)multiplexers.

Author details

Mohamad Mostafa[1]*, Giuseppe Oliveri[2], Werner G. Teich[3] and Jürgen Lindner[3]

*Address all correspondence to: Mohamad.Mostafa@DLR.de

1 German Aerospace Center (DLR), Institute of Communications and Navigation, Wessling, Germany

2 Ulm University, Institute of Electron Devices and Circuits, Ulm, Germany

3 Ulm University, Institute of Communications Engineering, Ulm, Germany

References

[1] G. P. Fettweis, K.-C. Chen, and R. Tafazoli, "Green radio: Energy efficiency in wireless networks," *Journal of Communications and Networks*, vol. 12, no. 2, pp. 99–102, April 2010.

[2] C. A. Chan, A. F. Gygax, E. Wong, C. A. Leckie, A. Nirmalathas, and D. C. Kilper, "Methodologies for assessing the use-phase power consumption and greenhouse gas emissions of telecommunications network services," *Environmental Science & Technology*, vol. 47, no. 1, pp. 485–492, January 2013.

[3] G. Oliveri, M. Mostafa, W. G. Teich, J. Lindner, and H. Schumacher, "Advanced low power, high speed nonlinear analog signal processing: An analog VLSI example," in *Wireless Innovation Forum, European Conference on Communications Technologies and Software Defined Radio*, Erlangen, Germany, 5–9 October 2015.

[4] H.-A. Löliger, "Analog decoding and beyond," in *IEEE Information Theory Workshop*, 2–7 September 2001, pp. 126–127.

[5] H.-A. Löliger, F. Tarköy, F. Lustenberger, and M. Helfenstein, "Decoding in analog VLSI," *IEEE Communications Magazine*, vol. 37, no. 4, pp. 99–101, April 1999.

[6] C. Mead, *Analog VLSI and neural systems*, ser. Addison-Wesley VLSI system series. Addison-Wesley, 1989.

[7] E. A. Vittoz, "Analog VLSI signal processing: Why, where and how?" *Journal of VLSI Signal Processing Systems for Signal, Image and Video Technology*, vol. 8, no. 1, pp. 27–44, February 1994.

[8] S. Draghici, "Neural networks in analog hardware - Design and implementation issues," *International Journal of Neural Systems*, vol. 10, no. 1, pp. 19–42, February 2000.

[9] J. Misra and I. Saha, "Artificial neural networks in hardware: A survey of two decades of progress," *Neurocomputing*, vol. 74, no. 1-3, pp. 239–255, December 2010.

[10] S. L. Goh and D. P. Mandic, "A complex-valued RTRL algorithm for recurrent neural networks," *Neural Computation*, vol. 16, no. 12, pp. 2699–2713, December 2004.

[11] J. Lindner, "MC-CDMA in the context of general multiuser/multisubchannel transmission methods," *European Transactions on Telecommunications*, vol. 10, no. 4, pp. 351–367, July-August 1999.

[12] S. Hemati and A. H. Banihashemi, "Dynamics and performance analysis of analog iterative decoding for low-density parity-check LDPC codes," *IEEE Transactions on Communications*, vol. 54, no. 1, pp. 61–70, January 2006.

[13] J. Hagenauer, E. Offer, C. Méasson, and M. Mörz, "Decoding and equalization with analog non-linear networks," *European Transactions on Telecommunications*, vol. 10, no. 6, pp. 659–680, November-December 1999.

[14] M. Dangl, *Iterative estimation and detection for single carrier block transmission*. Der Andere Verlag, Dissertation, Ulm University, Institute of Information Technology, 2007.

[15] A. Cichocki and R. Unbehauen, *Neural networks for optimization and signal processing*. John Wiley & Sons Ltd. & B. G. Teubner, Stuttgart, 1993, ch. 2.

[16] H. Tang, K. C. Tan, and Z. Yi, "Various computational models and applications," in *Neural networks: Computational models and applications*, ser. Studies in computational intelligence, J. Kacprzyk, Ed. Springer-Verlag Berlin Heidelberg, 2007, vol. 53, ch. 5, pp. 57–79.

[17] S. Hemati and A. Yongacoglu, "Dynamics of analog decoders for different message representation domains," *IEEE Transactions on Communications*, vol. 58, no. 3, pp. 721–723, May 2010.

[18] W. G. Teich, M. A. Ibrahim, F. Waeckerle, and R. F. H. Fischer, "Equalization for fiber-optic transmission systems: Low-complexity iterative implementations," in *17th ITG-Fachtagung Photonische Netze*, Leipzig, Germany, May 2016.

[19] A. Engelhart, *Vector detection techniques with moderate complexity.* VDI Verlag GmbH, Dissertation, Ulm University, Institute of Information Technology, 2003.

[20] M. Mostafa, W. G. Teich, and J. Lindner, "Approximation of activation functions for vector equalization based on recurrent neural networks," in *6th International Symposium on Turbo Codes and Iterative Information Processing*, Bremen, Germany, 18-22 August 2014, pp. 52–56.

[21] M. Mostafa, *Equalization and decoding: A continuous-time dynamical approach.* Der Andre-Verlag, Dissertation, Ulm University, Institute of Communications Engineering, 2014, ch. 1 & 3.

[22] K. Kuroe, N. Hashimoto, and T. Mori, "On energy function for complex-valued neural networks and its applications," in *9th International Conference on Neural Information Processing*, vol. 3, 18-22 November 2002, pp. 1079–1083.

[23] S. Haykin, *Neural networks: A comprehensive foundation.* USA: Macmillan college publishing company, Inc., 1994.

[24] J. J. Hopfield, "Neurons with graded response have collective computational properties like those of two-state neurons," in *Proceedings of the National Academy of Sciences of the USA*, vol. 81, no. 10, pp. 3088–3092, May 1984.

[25] M. Yoshida and T. Mori, "Global stability analysis for complex-valued recurrent neural networks and its application to convex optimization problems," in *Complex-valued neural networks: Utilizing high-dimensional parameters*, T. Nitta, Ed. Information science reference, 2009, ch. 5, pp. 104–114.

[26] J. M. Zurada, I. Cloete, and W. van der Poel, "Generalized Hopfield networks for associative memories with multi-valued stable states," *Neurocomputing*, vol. 13, pp. 135–149, 1996.

[27] D. Tank and J. J. Hopfield, "Simple 'neural' optimization network: An A/D converter, signal decision circuit, and a linear programming circuit," *IEEE Transactions on Circuits and Systems*, vol. 33, no. 5, pp. 553–541, May 1986.

[28] J. J. Hopfield and D. W. Tank, "'Neural' computation of decisions in optimization problems," *Biological Cybernatics*, vol. 52, no. 3, pp. 141–152, 1985.

[29] J. J. Hopfield, "Neurons networks and physical systems with emergent collective computational abilities," in *Proceedings of the National Academy of Sciences of the USA*, vol. 79, no. 8, pp. 2554–2558, April 1982.

[30] G. I. Kechriotis and E. S. Manolakos, "Hopfield neural network implementation for optimum CDMA multiuser detector," *IEEE Transactions on Neural Networks*, vol. 7, no. 1, pp. 131–141, January 1996.

[31] T. Miyajima, T. Hasegawa, and M. Haneishi, "On the multiuser detection using a neural network in code-division multiple-access communications," *IEICE Transactions on Communications*, vol. E76-B, pp. 961–968, 1993.

[32] M. Mostafa, W. G. Teich, and J. Lindner, "Vector equalization based on continuous-time recurrent neural networks," in *6th IEEE International Conference on Signal Processing and Communication Systems*, Gold Coast, Australia, 12-14 December 2012, pp. 1–7.

[33] W. G. Teich and M. Seidl, "Code division multiple access communications: Multiuser detection based on a recurrent neural network structure," in *4th IEEE International Symposium on Spread Spectrum Techniques and Applications*, vol. 3, Mainz, Germany, 22-25 September 1996, pp. 979–984.

[34] H. Schumacher, A. C. Ulusoy, G. Liu, and G. Oliveri, "Si/SiGe ICs for ultra-broadband communications: The analog signal processing perspective," in *IEEE MTT-S International Microwave Symposium Digest (IMS)*, Seattle, WA, June 2013, pp. 1–4.

[35] B. Gilbert, "A precise four-quadrant multiplier with subnanosecond response," *IEEE Journal of Solid-State Circuits*, vol. 3, no. 4, pp. 365–373, December 1968.

[36] A. F. Murray and A. V. W. Smith, "Asynchronous arithmetic for VLSI neural systems," *Electronic Letters*, vol. 23, no. 12, pp. 642–643, June 1987.

[37] R. G. Gallager, "Low-density parity-check codes," *IRE Transactions on Information Theory*, vol. 8, no. 1, pp. 21–28, January 1962.

[38] "Digital video broadcasting (DVB), Second generation framing structure, channel coding and modulation systems for broadcasting, interactive services, news gathering and other broadband satellite applications; Part 1: DVB-S2," ETSI EN 302 307-1 V1.4.1, Tech. Rep., 11 2014. [Online]. Available: http://www.etsi.org/deliver/etsi_en/302300_302399/30230701/01.04.01_60/en_30230701v010401p.pdf

[39] A. Dembo, O. Farotimi, and T. Kailath, "High-order absolutely stable neural networks," *IEEE Transactions on Circuits and Systems*, vol. 38, no. 1, pp. 57–65, January 1991.

[40] M. Vidyasagar, "Minimum-seeking properties of analog neural networks with multilinear objective functions," *IEEE Transactions on Automatic Control*, vol. 40, no. 8, pp. 1359–1375, August 1995.

[41] E. B. Kosmatopoulos and M. A. Christodoulou, "Structural properties of gradient recurrent high-order neural networks," *IEEE Transactions on Circuits and Systems-II: Analog and Digital Signal Processing*, vol. 42, no. 9, pp. 592–603, September 1995.

[42] X. Xu, N. K. Huang, and W. T. Tsai, "A Generalized Neural Network Model," *Technical report*, Computer Science Department, Inst. of Technology, Univ. vol. 1, supplement 1, pp. 150, 1988.

[43] R. M. Tanner, "A recursive approach to low complexity codes," *IEEE Transactions on Information Theory*, vol. IT-27, no. 5, pp. 533–547, September 1981.

[44] B. S. Rüffer, C.-M. Kellett, P.-M. Dower, and S. R. Weller, "Belief propagation as a dynamical system: The linear case and open problems," *Control Theory & Applications, IET*, vol. 4, no. 7, pp. 1188–1200, July 2010.

[45] M. Mostafa, W. G. Teich, and J. Lindner, "Comparison of belief propagation and iterative threshold decoding based on dynamical systems," in *IEEE International Symposium on Information Theory*, Istanbul, Turkey, 7-12 July 2013, pp. 2995–2999.

[46] S. Hemati and A. H. Banihashemi, "Comparison between continuous-time asynchronous and discrete-time synchronous iterative decoding," in *IEEE Global Telecommunications Conference*, vol. 1, 29 November-3 December 2004, pp. 356–360.

[47] S. Hemati and A. H. Banihashemi, "Convergence speed and throughput of analog decoders," *IEEE Transactions on Communications*, vol. 55, no. 5, pp. 833–836, May 2007.

[48] S. Hemati and A. Yongacoglu, "On the dynamics of analog min-sum iterative decoders: An analytical approach," *IEEE Transactions on Communications*, vol. 58, no. 5, pp. 2225–2231, August 2010.

[49] S. Hemati, A. H. Banihashemi, and C. Plett, "A 0.18 μm CMOS analog min-sum iterative decoder for a (32,8) low-density paroty-check LDPC code," *IEEE Journal on Solid-State Circuits*, vol. 41, no. 11, pp. 2531–2540, November 2006.

[50] L. Kocarev, F. Lehman, G. M. Maggio, B. Scanavino, Z. Tasev, and A. Vardi, "Nonlinear dynamics of iterative decoding systems: Analysis and applications," *IEEE Transactions on Information Theory*, vol. 52, no. 4, pp. 1366–1384, April 2006.

[51] C. Douillard, M. Jézéquel, C. Berrou, A. Picart, P. Didier, and A. Glavieux, "Iterative correction of intersymbol interference: Turbo-equalization," *European Transactions on Telecommunications*, vol. 6, no. 5, pp. 507–511, 1995.

[52] C. Sgraja, A. Engelhart, W. G. Teich, and J. Lindner, "Combined equalization and decoding for BFDM packet transmission schemes," in *1st International OFDM-Workshop*, vol. 3, Hamburg, Germany, 21-22 September 1999, pp. 1–5.

[53] C. Berrou, A. Glavieux, and P. Thitimajshima, "Near shannon limit error-correcting coding and decoding: Turbo codes(1)," in *IEEE International Conference on Communications ICC*, vol. 2, Geneva, Switzerland, 1993, pp. 1064–1070.

[54] M. Mostafa, W. G. Teich, and J. Lindner, "Local stability analysis of discrete-time, continuous-state, complex-valued recurrent neural networks with inner state feedback," *IEEE Transactions on Neural Networks and Learning Systems*, vol. 25, no. 4, pp. 830–836, April 2014.

[55] A. Engelhart, W. G. Teich, J. Lindner, G. Jeney, S. Imre, and L. Pap, "A survey of multi-user/multisubchannel detection schemes based on recurrent neural networks," *Wireless Communications and Mobile Computing, Special Issue on Advances in 3G Wireless Networks*, vol. 2, no. 3, pp. 269–284, May 2002.

[56] E. Goles, E. Chacc, F. Fogelman-Soulié, and D. Pellegrin, "Decreasing energy functions as a tool for studying threshold functions," *Discrete Applied Mathematics*, vol. 12, no. 3, pp. 261–277, 1985.

[57] E. Goles, and S. Martinez, "A short proof on the cyclic behaviour of multithreshold symmetric automata," *Information and Control*, vol. 51, no. 2, pp. 95–97, November 1981.

[58] D. G. Zill, *A first course in differential equations with modeling applications*. Cengage Learning, Inc., 2009, ch. 9, pp. 340–345.

[59] T. J. C. MacKay. Encyclopedia of sparse graph codes. [Online]. Available: http://www.inference.phy.cam.ac.uk/mackay/codes/data.html

[60] J. G. Proakis, *Digital Communications*. McGraw-Hill, Inc, 1995.

[61] R. M. Gray, *Toeplitz and Circulant Matrices: A Review*, ser. Foundations and Trends in Technology. Now Publishers, 2006.

[62] J. Lindner, *Informations übertragung*. Springer-Verlag Berlin Heidelberg, 2005.

Chapter 5

Direct Signal Detection Without Data-Aided: A MIMO Functional Network Approach

Xiukai Ruan , Yanhua Tan , Yuxing Dai , Guihua Cui ,
Xiaojing Shi , Qibo Cai , Chang Li , Han Li ,
Yaoju Zhang and Dameng Dai

Additional information is available at the end of the chapter

http://dx.doi.org/10.5772/63213

Abstract

Functional network (FN) has been successfully applied in many fields, but so far no methods of direct signal detection (DSD) using FN have been published. In this chapter, a novel DSD approach using FN, which can be applied to cases with a plural source signal sequence, with short sequence, and even with the absence of a training sequence, is presented. Firstly, a multiple-input multiple-output FN (MIMOFN), in which the initial input vector is devised via QR decomposition of the receiving signal matrix, is constructed to solve the special issues of DSD. In the meantime, the design method for the neural function of this special MIMOFN is proposed. Then the learning rule for the parameters of neural functions is trained and updated by back-propagation (BP) algorithm. The correctness and effectiveness of the new approach are verified by simulation results, together with some special simulation phenomena of the algorithm. The proposed method can detect the source sequence directly from the observed output data by utilizing MIMOFN without a training sequence and estimating the channel impulse response.

Keywords: direct signal detection, MIMO, functional neural network, QAM, back propagation

1. Introduction

Signal detection has become an integral part of applications in many areas, including wireless communications, optical telecommunications, automatic control system, magnetic resonance

---

© 2016 The Author(s). Licensee InTech. This chapter is distributed under the terms of the Creative Commons Attribution License (http://creativecommons.org/licenses/by/3.0), which permits unrestricted use, distribution, and reproduction in any medium, provided the original work is properly cited.

imaging, underwater acoustics, and radio astronomy. Typical digital communication environments involve transmission of analog pulses over a dispersive medium, inevitably corrupting the received signal by inter-symbol interference (ISI). The present sequence estimation approaches, for example, maximum-likelihood sequence estimation (MLSE) [1] and 'Bussgang' [2–4], usually estimate first the communication channel impulse response and then the transmitted sequence by an optimum method. MLSE is a useful approach for equalization of ISI but requires knowledge of the possibly time-variant channel impulse response, and its complexity increases exponentially with the length of the channel delay spread. Consequently, adaptive channel estimation algorithms have to be employed [1]. "Bussgang" and its modified algorithms [2–4] are well-known channel estimation algorithms but are costly and indirect due to their necessity for a long block of data to achieve algorithm convergence since they exploit implicit (embedded) statistical knowledge. Direct signal detection (DSD) is a new emerging method in communication systems, which can directly estimate the input sequence without estimating the channel impulse response [5–7].

In this work, we propose a new method that merges the functional network (FN) [8–9] models into a DSD technique for removing ISI without the training sequence. FN is a very useful general framework for modeling a wide range of probabilistic, statistical, mathematical, and engineering problems [10]. For instance, Iglesias et al. [11] adopted FN to improve the results of a determined artificial neural networks (ANN) application for the estimation of fishing possibilities, Zhou et al. [12] employed FN to solve classification problem, Emad et al. [13] found that FN (separable and generalized associativity) architecture with polynomial basis was accurate, was reliable, and outperforms most of the existing predictive data mining modeling approaches for the issue of permeability prediction, and Alonso-Betanzos et al. [14] applied FN to predict the failure shear effort in concrete beams. As mentioned above, FN has been successfully applied in many fields, but so far methods of DSD using FN have not been reported.

The chapter is organized as follows. In Section 2, a system model is described. Then the network structure of MIMOFN to solve the special issues of DSD is constructed in Section 3. A multiple-input multiple-output FN (MIMOFN), in which the initial input vector is devised via QR decomposition of receiving signal matrix, is constructed to solve the special issues of DSD. The design method of the neural function of this special MIMOFN is proposed. Then the learning rule for the parameters of neural functions is trained and updated by back-propagation (BP) algorithm in Section 4. In Section 5, simulation results are shown to verify the new approach's correctness and effectiveness, and some special simulation phenomena of this algorithm are given out followed by Conclusion and Discussion in Section 6.

2. The system model and basic assumptions

This system model is a linear single-input multiple-output (SIMO) (see **Figure 1**) finite impulse response channel with N output [15]. The following basic assumptions are adopted [16].

A1: Channel order L_h is assumed to be known as a priori.

A2: The input signal $\mathbf{s}(t)$ is zero-mean and temporally independent and identically distributed (i.i.d).

A3: Additive noise is spatially and temporally white noise and is statistically independent of the source.

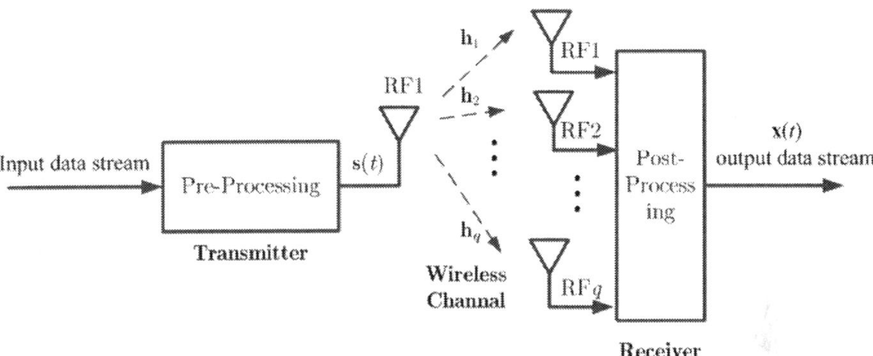

Figure 1. Example of SIMO channel.

For the simplification of the presentation of the proposed DSD without loss of generality, the i-th sub-channel output of an SIMO channel system in a noise-free environment is expressed as

$$x_i(t) = \sum_{\tau=0}^{L_h-1} h_i(\tau) s(t-\tau) \tag{1}$$

where $s(t)$ is the Quadrature Amplitude Modulation (QAM) input signal, and $h_i(\tau)$ is the i-th system impulse response of length L_h[5]. Clearly, the column vector $\mathbf{x}(t)$ can be expressed as

$$\left(\mathbf{x}(t)\right)_{q\times 1} = \left[\mathbf{h}_1, \mathbf{h}_2, \cdots, \mathbf{h}_q\right]^T_{q\times(L_h+1)} \cdot \left(\mathbf{s}(t)\right)_{(L_h+1)\times 1} \tag{2}$$

where q and L_h denote the over-sample factor and the order of channel impulse response, respectively, and superscript T denotes transpose of a matrix, and

$$\mathbf{h}_p = \left[h_p(0), h_p(1), \cdots, h_p(L_h)\right]^T_{1\times L_h}, p = 1, 2, \cdots, q \tag{3}$$

and

$$\mathbf{s}(t) = \left[s(t), s(t-1), \cdots, s(t-L_h) \right]^{\mathrm{T}}_{(L_h+1)\times 1} \tag{4}$$

Thus, the received data matrix can be formulated as

$$\left(\mathbf{X} \right)_{N\times(L_w+1)q} = \mathbf{S}\Gamma \tag{5}$$

where $(\mathbf{S})_{N\times(L_h+L_w+1)} = \left[\mathbf{s}_N(t), \mathbf{s}_N(t-1), \cdots, \mathbf{s}_N(t-L_h-L_w) \right]$,

and $\mathbf{s}_N(t) = [s(t), s(t-1), \cdots, s(t-N+1)]^T$ is the transmitted signal matrix, N and L_w are the source signal length and length of the equalizer, respectively, and Toeplitz matrix $\Gamma = \left[\mathbf{H}_1^T, \mathbf{H}_2^T, \cdots \mathbf{H}_q^T \right]$ with

$$\mathbf{H}_p = \begin{bmatrix} \mathbf{h}_p^T & 0 & \cdots & 0 & 0 \\ 0 & \mathbf{h}_p^T & 0 & \ddots & 0 \\ \vdots & \ddots & \ddots & \ddots & \vdots \\ 0 & \cdots & 0 & \mathbf{h}_p^T & 0 \end{bmatrix}, p = 1, 2, \cdots q \tag{6}$$

3. The FN structure for DSD

FN is a generalization of neural networks achieved by using multi-argument and learnable functions, that is, in these models, transfer functions, associated with neurons, are not fixed but learned from data. There is a need to include weights to ponder links among neurons since their effect is subsumed by the neural functions. **Figure 2** shows an example of a general FN topology, where the input layer consists of the units $G = (x, y, z)$; the first layer contains neurons P, G, N, Q; the second layer contains neurons J, K, F, L; and the output layer contains α, β, γ, θ. According to Castillo's approach, each neuron function, P, G, N, Q, J, K, F, L, is represented as a linear combination of the known functions of a given family such as polynomials, trigonometric functions, and Fourier expansions and is estimated during the learning process. Generally, instead of fixed functions, FNs extend the standard neural networks by allowing neuron functions P, G, N, Q, J, K, F, L to be not only true multi-argument and multivariate functions but also different and learnable. Two types of learning methods exist: structural learning and parametric learning. The latter estimates the activation functions with the consideration of the combination of "basis" functions such as the least square, steepest descent, and mini-max methods [13]. In this chapter, the least square method for estimating sequence is used.

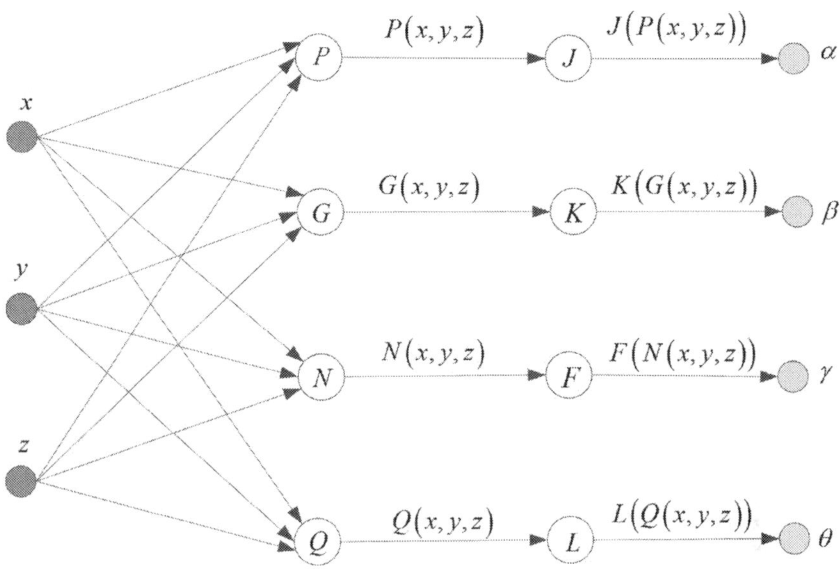

Figure 2. A basic FN topology model.

Definition 1: Assume there exists a function set F that transforms an n-dimensional input vector into an m-dimensional output vector in a complex regime $F: \mathbf{C}^n \to \mathbf{C}^m$, and

$$X \in \mathbf{C}^n, \qquad X = (x_1, x_2, \cdots, x_n), \qquad f_1 = f_1(x_1, x_2, \cdots, x_n), \qquad f_2 = f_2(x_1, x_2, \cdots, x_n), \qquad \cdots,$$

$f_m = f_m(x_1, x_2, \cdots, x_n)$, then the FN model $F = F(f_1, f_2, \cdots, f_m)$ is a basic MIMOFN model.

Definition 2: Let X be a linear combination of a column in $\mathbf{C}^n$, and $f_i = \sum_{j=1}^{n} a_{ij} x_j + c_i$, $(i = 1, 2, \cdots, m)$, $x_j \in X, j = 1, 2, ..., n$, where both a_{ij} and c_i are constant values, then $F = F(f_1, f_2, \cdots, f_m)$ is a linear MIMOFN.

Generally, FNs are driven by specific problems, that is, the initial architecture is designed based on problems in hand. Here, an MIMOFN, shown in **Figure 3**, is designed for the special issue of DSD. In this topology, $\mathbf{w}_1, \mathbf{w}_2, ..., \mathbf{w}_N$ is the input vector, and $f(.)$, $g(.)$, and $h^{-1}(.)$ denote the neuron functions of the first, second, and output layer, respectively. Re(.) and Im(.) denote the real part and imaginary part, respectively.

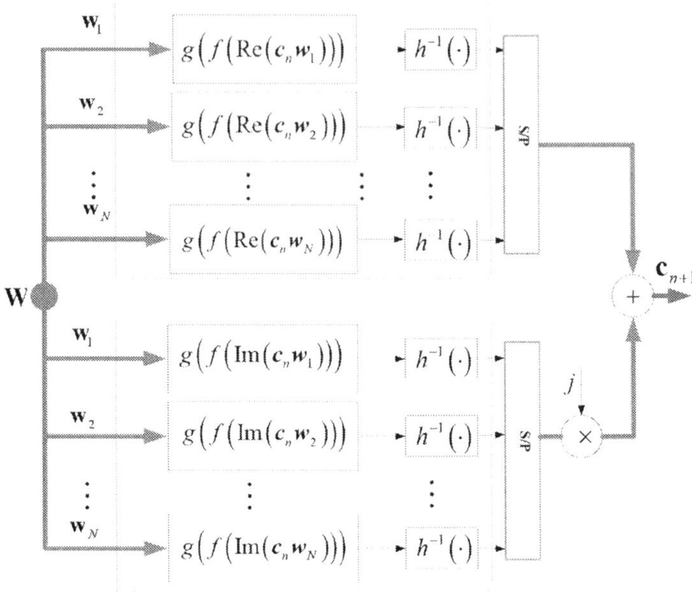

Figure 3. The MIMOFN topology for DSD.

In this case, $\mathbf{c}_{n+1}$ is the output of MIMOFN and its elements are

$$c_{n+1,1} = h^{-1}\left(g\left(f\left(\mathrm{Re}(\mathbf{c}_n\mathbf{w}_1)\right)\right)\right) + j \cdot h^{-1}\left(g\left(f\left(\mathrm{Im}(\mathbf{c}_n\mathbf{w}_1)\right)\right)\right)$$
$$c_{n+1,2} = h^{-1}\left(g\left(f\left(\mathrm{Re}(\mathbf{c}_n\mathbf{w}_2)\right)\right)\right) + j \cdot h^{-1}\left(g\left(f\left(\mathrm{Im}(\mathbf{c}_n\mathbf{w}_2)\right)\right)\right)$$
$$\dots$$
$$c_{n+1,N} = h^{-1}\left(g\left(f\left(\mathrm{Re}(\mathbf{c}_n\mathbf{w}_N)\right)\right)\right) + j \cdot h^{-1}\left(g\left(f\left(\mathrm{Im}(\mathbf{c}_n\mathbf{w}_N)\right)\right)\right)$$

(7)

where all of $f(.)$, $g(.)$, and $h^{-1}(.)$ are arbitrary continuous and strictly monotonic functions, and j is the imaginary unit.

4. DSD using MIMOFN

4.1. The input vector of MIMOFN

Our objective is to detect the source sequence directly from the observed output data by utilizing MIMOFN without training sequence and estimating the channel impulse response.

Since $\mathbf{X} \in \mathbf{C}^{N \times (L_w + 1)q}$ with $N \geq (L_w + 1)q$, QR decomposition can be applied to $\mathbf{X}$, and thus $\mathbf{X}$ can be rewritten as

$$\mathbf{X} = \overline{\mathbf{Q}}\,\overline{\mathbf{R}} \tag{8}$$

where $\overline{\mathbf{Q}} \in \mathbf{C}^{N \times (L_w + 1)q}$ is a matrix with orthonormal columns and $\overline{\mathbf{R}} \in \mathbf{C}^{(L_w + 1)q \times (L_w + 1)q}$ is an upper triangular matrix such that $\overline{\mathbf{R}}(j, j) \neq 0, j = 1, \cdots, (L_w + 1)q$ [17].

For the DSD issues, there is a well-defined gap in the singular values of $\mathbf{X}$; in other words, it exists as an index r that $\sigma(r + 1) \ll \sigma(r)$, where $\sigma(\cdot)$ denotes the singular of $\mathbf{X}$, and then the subset selection will tend to produce a subset containing the most important columns (rules) of $\mathbf{X}$.

In order to obtain the full QR factorization, we proceed with SVD and extend $\overline{\mathbf{Q}}$ to a unitary matrix $\mathbf{Q}_1$. Then, $\mathbf{X} = \mathbf{Q}_1 \mathbf{R}_1$ with unitary $\mathbf{Q}_1 \in \mathbf{C}^{N \times N}$ and upper triangular $\mathbf{R}_1 \in \mathbf{C}^{N \times (L_w + 1)q}$, with the last $N - (L_w + 1)q$ rows being zero. So we obtain

$$\mathbf{X} = \mathbf{Q}_1 \mathbf{R}_1 = [\mathbf{Q}, \mathbf{Q}_c] \cdot \begin{bmatrix} \mathbf{R} \\ \mathbf{0} \end{bmatrix} \cdot \mathbf{E} \tag{9}$$

where $\mathbf{E}$ is a permutation matrix. The $\mathbf{R}$-values are arranged in decreasing order and incline to track the singular values of $\mathbf{X}$.

Thus, the input matrix of MIMOFN W can be formulated as

$$W = \mathbf{Q}\mathbf{Q}^{H} \tag{10}$$

where superscript H denotes conjugate transpose of a matrix. Clearly, W is a non-negative definite idempotent Hermitian matrix.

Since the column vectors of W are a base set of signal space, they can be adopted to the input vector of MIMOFN and remain unchanged.

4.2. Cost function

The next issue to be considered is construction of a cost function. The cost function of MIMOFN can be formulated as

$$J(\mathbf{c}) = \frac{1}{2} E\left(\left\|\mathbf{c}_n - \mathbf{c}_{n-1}\right\|_2^2\right) = \frac{1}{2} E\left(\left\|\mathbf{c}_{n+1} - h^{-1}\left(g\left(\mathbf{Wc}_n\right)\right)\right\|_2^2\right) \tag{11}$$

where $h^{-1}(x) = x$, $E\{.\}$ is expectation operation, and $\|\cdot\|_2^2$ is two-norm. Clearly, it is true that $\mathbf{Ws}_N(t-d) = \mathbf{s}_N(t-d)$ is satisfied, here $\{s_N(t-d)\,|\,d = 0, \cdots, L_h + L\}$, the value of cost function is minimum.

4.3. Design of neural functions

Neural function $g(.)$ must be easy to compute and complement, and hence needs to satisfy the following conditions:

1. $g(.)$ should be simple, easy to calculate, continuously differentiable, and bounded.

2.   The derivative of $g(.)$ should be simple too, and it is the ordinary transformation of $g(.)$.

3.   A priori knowledge of special issue must be considered, which makes the network easy to be trained with strong generalization ability in a smaller scale.

Since both the in-phase and quadrature-part of QAM signals belong to P^N, we only consider the in-phase part of QAM signals and design the following neural function $f(.)$ as

$$g(x, N_s) = \left[2\sum_{i=1}^{N_s}\sigma_s(x + b_i)\right] - N_s \tag{12}$$

where $b_i = (N_s + 1) - 2i, i = 1, 2, \cdots, N_s$, N_s are the number of multi-levels and the unstable inflexion points of the basis function $\sigma_s(x + b_i) = \left[1 + e^{-a(x + b_i)}\right]^{-1}$, here $\sigma_s(x + b_i)$ is the arbitrary continuous and strictly monotonic function. a is the attenuation factor of the basis function. Furthermore, the derivative of $g(.)$ can be calculated by

$$g'(x, N_s) = \left\{\left[2\sum_{i=1}^{N_s}\sigma_s(x + b_i)\right] - N_s\right\}'$$
$$= 2\sum_{i=1}^{N_s}\sigma'_s(x + b_i) = 2\sum_{i=1}^{N_s}a\sigma_s^2(x + b_i)\cdot e^{-a(x+b_i)} \tag{13}$$

Figure 4 shows the curves of $g(.)$ neural function and its derivatives g'(.) for 16QAM with a in the Descartes coordinate. The value of a influences the convergence rate and performance of the algorithm significantly. A small value of a (e.g. $a = 5$) will accelerate the convergence rate of algorithm.

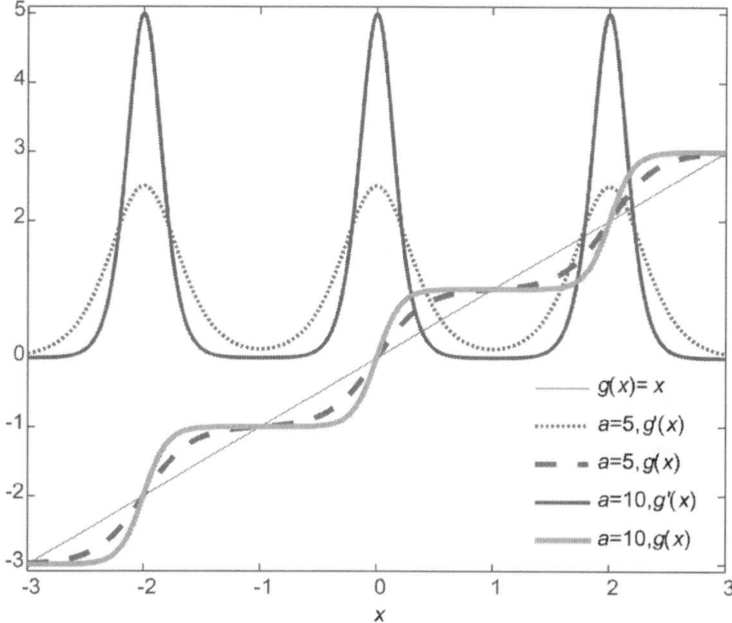

Figure 4. 16QAM, the curves of $g(.)$ neural function and its derivative $g'(.)$ with $a = 5,10$ in the x–y plane.

5. The learning rule for the parameters of neural functions

Herein, the input vector and the cost function of MIMOFN are determined, and the following mission is design of a learning strategy of the MIMOFN's neural function.

(1) The learning strategy of the parameters of $f(.)$.

A back-propagation(BP) algorithm is adopted to update the parameters of $f(.)$. Since the error function has been shown in Eq. (11), we can obtain the following equation

$$\mathbf{c}_{n+1} = \mathbf{c}_n - \mu \frac{\partial J}{\partial c_n} = \mathbf{c}_n - \mu \left(\mathbf{I} - \mathbf{W} g'\left(\mathbf{W} \mathbf{c_n} \right) \right) \tag{14}$$

where $\mu \in (0, 1]$ is the learning rate factor.

Let us look into the i-th neuron. At the first iteration, the neural functions $f(.)$ are multi-dimensional linear functions.

$$f\left(\mathrm{Re}\left(\mathbf{c}_n\mathbf{w}_N\right)\right) = \mathrm{Re}\left(c_{0,1}w_{i,1} + c_{0,2}w_{i,2} + \cdots + c_{0,N}w_{i,N}\right) \tag{15}$$

$$f\left(\mathrm{Im}\left(\mathbf{c}_n\mathbf{w}_N\right)\right) = \mathrm{Im}\left(c_{0,1}w_{i,1} + c_{0,2}w_{i,2} + \cdots + c_{0,N}w_{i,N}\right) \tag{16}$$

where $c_{0,1}, c_{0,2}, \cdots, c_{0,N}$ are the parameters of $f(.)$ and $w_{i,1}, w_{i,2}, \cdots, w_{i,N}$ denote the input variables.

At the n-th iteration, we have

$$\mathbf{c}_{n+1} = \mathbf{c}_n - \mu \frac{\partial J}{\partial c_n} = \mathbf{c}_n - \mu\left(\mathbf{I} - \mathbf{W}\mathbf{g'}\left(\mathbf{W}\mathbf{c_n}\right)\right) \tag{17}$$

and $f(.)$ become

$$f\left(\mathrm{Re}\left(\mathbf{c}_n\mathbf{w}_N\right)\right) = \mathrm{Re}\left(c_{n,1}w_{i,1} + c_{n,2}w_{i,2} + \cdots + c_{n,N}w_{i,N}\right) \tag{18}$$

$$f\left(\mathrm{Im}\left(\mathbf{c}_n\mathbf{w}_N\right)\right) = \mathrm{Im}\left(c_{0,1}w_{i,1} + c_{0,2}w_{i,2} + \cdots + c_{0,N}w_{i,N}\right) \tag{19}$$

To quicken the learning rate, an adaptive BP training algorithm with a momentum term is adopted, has shown in Eq. (20), is used

$$\mathbf{c}_{n+1} = \mathbf{c}_n - \mu\left(\mathbf{I} - \mathbf{W}\mathbf{g'}\left(\mathbf{W}\mathbf{c}_n\right)\right) + \Delta\mathbf{c}_n = \mathbf{c}_n - \mu\left(\mathbf{I} - \mathbf{W}\mathbf{g'}\left(\mathbf{W}\mathbf{c}_n\right)\right) + \left(\mathbf{c}_n - \mathbf{c}_{n-1}\right) \tag{20}$$

(2) The learning strategy of the parameters of $g(.)$.

The attenuation factor a of the $g(.)$ function is not fixed but adjusted in accordance with the value of error function. First, when the value of error function is large, a takes the small value in order to expedite the adjusting proceedings of MIMOFN output signals, in other words, to accelerate the convergence rate, making the input sequence leave the origin of coordinate quickly. As the iteration proceeds, the value of error function will become smaller and smaller, and then a large value of a should be taken to make the output sequence go to the ideal constellation points.

$$a(t) = -C \cdot \left(\frac{\sin(t-A)}{t-A} + B \right) \cdot \varepsilon(t-A) + \min\left(\frac{\sin(t-A)}{t-A} + B \right) \cdot \left(\varepsilon(t) - \varepsilon(t-A) \right) \tag{21}$$

where $\varepsilon(t)$ is the unit step function, B and C are constants, and A is the iteration times of $J(\mathbf{c}_{A+1}) < J(\mathbf{c}_A)$. The curve of $a(t)$ when $A = 10$, $B = 10$, and $C = 5$ is shown in **Figure 5**.

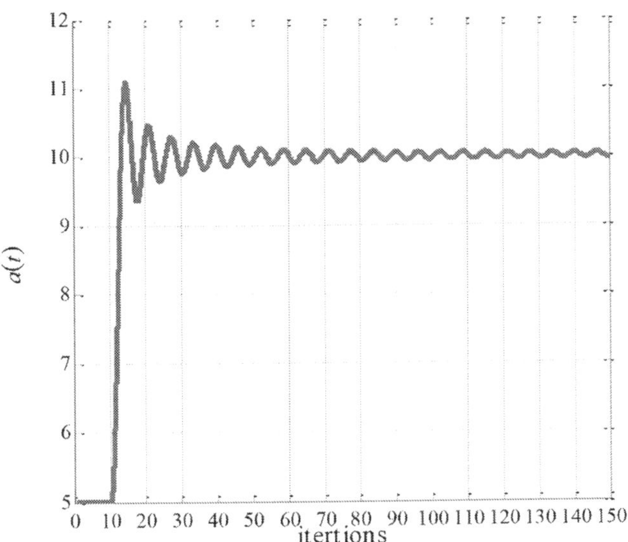

Figure 5. The curve of $a(t)$ when $A = 10, B = 10$, and $C = 5$, respectively.

6. Simulation and results

In this section, simulation results are provided to illustrate and verify the developed theory. Unless noted otherwise, these experiments are based on a multi-path channel

$$h(t) = \sum_{k=1}^{N_L} \left(\gamma_k^R \left(h^R(v, t - \tau_k^R) \right) + j \cdot \gamma_k^I \left(h^I(v, t - \tau_k^I) \right) \right),$$ with an over-sampling factor $q = 4$ and a

multi-path number $N_L = 5$. Here $h^R(v, t - \tau_k^R)$ and $h^I(v, t - \tau_k^I)$ are the raised cosine roll-off finite

impulse responses with a roll-factor $v = 0.1$, delay factors τ_k^R and τ_k^I are random constants, and

γ_k^R and $\gamma_k^I \in (0, 1]$ are random weight coefficients (see **Figure 6**). And the order L of $f(.)$ is [5,

18]. The signal modulation type is 16QAM and satisfies block-fading feature. Results are averaged over 500 Monte Carlo runs.

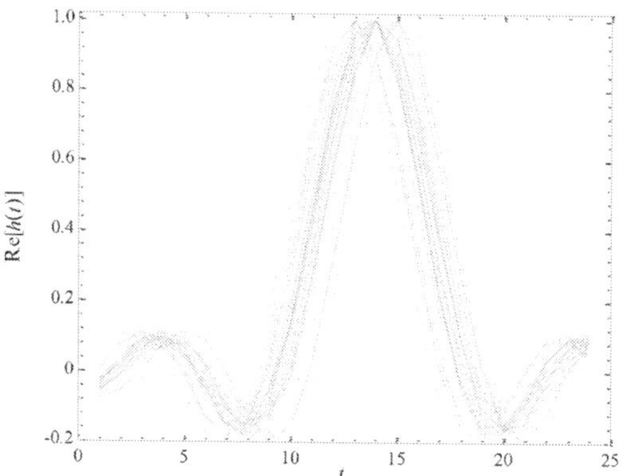

Figure 6. The sample of the real part of $h(t)$.

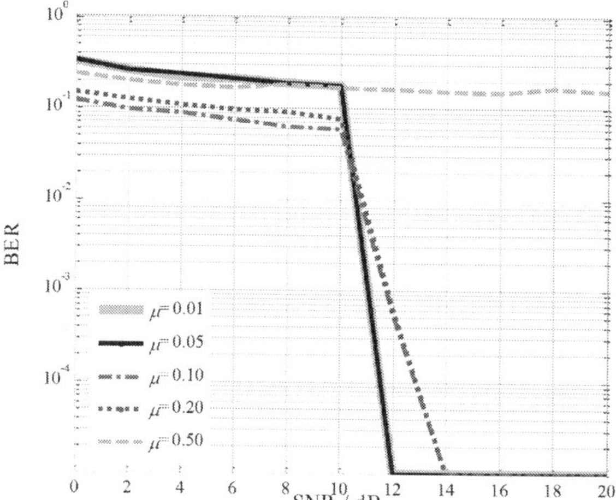

Figure 7. The average Bit Error Rate (BER) of DSD using the MIMOFN approach with the learning rate μ when data length $N = 500$.

Figure 7 shows the average BER curves of DSD using an MIMOFN approach with the learning rate μ when data length $N = 500$. This improved performance results from the decrease of μ. In the meantime, it is shown that the performance will stop improving when μ is small enough (e.g. $\mu \leq 0.05$). As we all know that increasing μ will lead to faster convergence rate of this approach, however, too large μ (e.g. $\mu = 0.5$) will make the approach fail. In the meantime, **Figure 7** also illustrates that the MIMOFN approach can work well even if the signal-to-noise ratio (SNR) = 12 dB, which is hard to reach for most existing DSD.

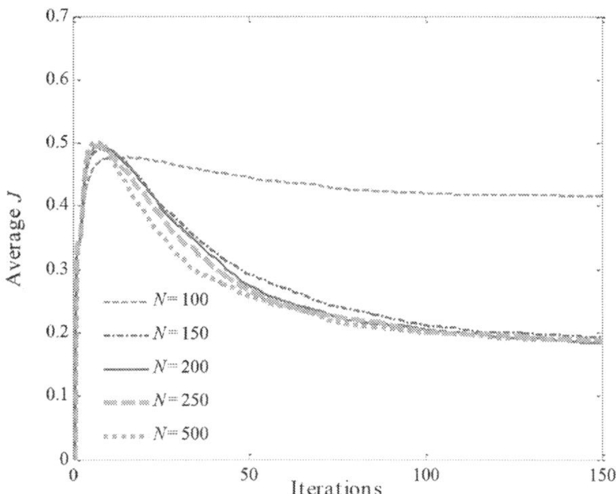

Figure 8. The curves of the average cost function J of the MIMOFN approach with several different lengths of data $N =$ (100, 150, 200, 250, 500), when $\mu = 0.05$ and SNR = 15 dB, respectively.

Figure 8 illustrates the curves of the average cost function J of the MIMOFN approach with several different lengths of data $N =$ (100, 150, 200, 250, 500), when $\mu = 0.05$ and SNR = 15 dB, respectively. In the initial iteration stage, the elements of sequence are amplified from the original point to the whole area of $[-3, 3]$. This makes the value of cost function to progressively increase. Regardless of the initial iteration stage, it is obvious that the average cost function keeps decreasing until its value is not changed, which means the algorithm is always convergent. In addition, the iteration is only about 150 times for 16QAM input case. Furthermore, it is implied that the cost function value is independent of data length.

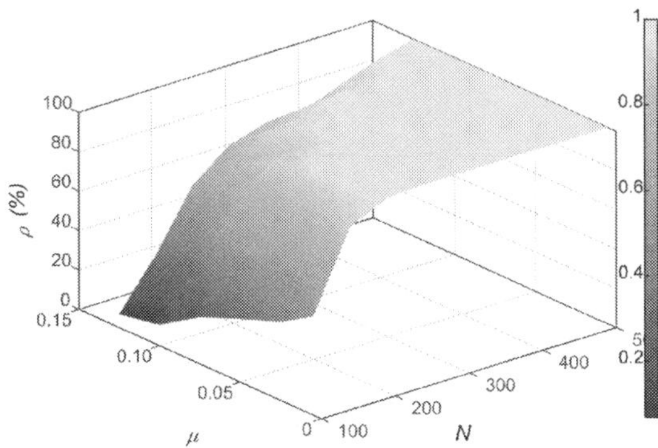

Figure 9. The 3D surface of the rate of correct recognition ρ with μ and N.

μN	N								
	100	150	200	250	300	350	400	450	500
0.01	50.4	90	98.8	100	100	100	100	100	100
0.05	40.0	84.8	97.8	100	100	100	100	100	100
0.10	32.4	80.8	96.2	100	100	100	100	100	100
0.15	24.0	73.4	90.8	93.2	100	100	100	100	100
0.20	10.8	46.0	80	91.2	93.2	100	100	100	100
0.25	6.8	30.8	60.4	75.2	80.8	80.8	88.4	95.2	100

Table 1. The relation of the rate of correct recognition ρ (%) with μ and N.

Figure 9 and **Table 1** illustrate the rate of correct recognition ρ of the MIMOFN approach with several different learning rate factors μ (= 0.01, 0.05, = 0.1, 0.15, 0.2, 0.25) and N = (100, 150 ,..., 500) for SNR = 15 dB.

$$\rho(\%) = \frac{\eta}{\xi} \times 100\% \tag{22}$$

where η, ξ are the total number of independent trials and the total number of correct recognition, respectively. The rate of correct recognition of the MIMOFN approach is inversely proportional to the values of μ and N.

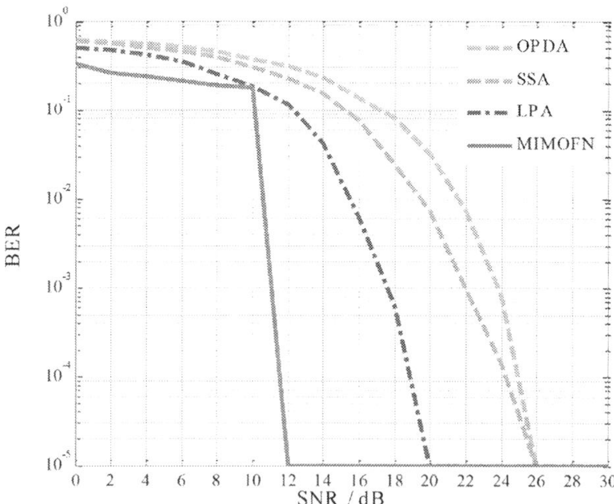

Figure 10. BER performance comparison between sequence estimation algorithms for N = 500.

We compare our method (MIMOFN) with the classical subspace algorithm (SSA), linear prediction algorithm (LPA), and outer-product decomposition algorithm (OPDA) [15], which are shown in **Figure 10**. It is found that the MIMOFN approach is superior to those of the above-mentioned DSD in performance.

The following experiments are based on 16QAM, SNR = 15 dB, N = 200, and μ = 0.05. These figures are drawn by one independent trial.

In **Figure 11**, the solid circles and hollow circles denote ideal 16QAM signal constellation points and the positions of the signal points with the iteration, respectively. **Figure 12** illustrates the phase trajectories of signal points using the MIMOFN approach. All lines denote the phase trajectories of signal points with the iteration, respectively, and the eight bold lines express the trajectories of the given different signal points, respectively. We can see that the phase trajectories are different and irregular, but all of them will reach their respective true signal points when the algorithm is convergent. In addition, the iteration is only about 150 times even for 16QAM input case.

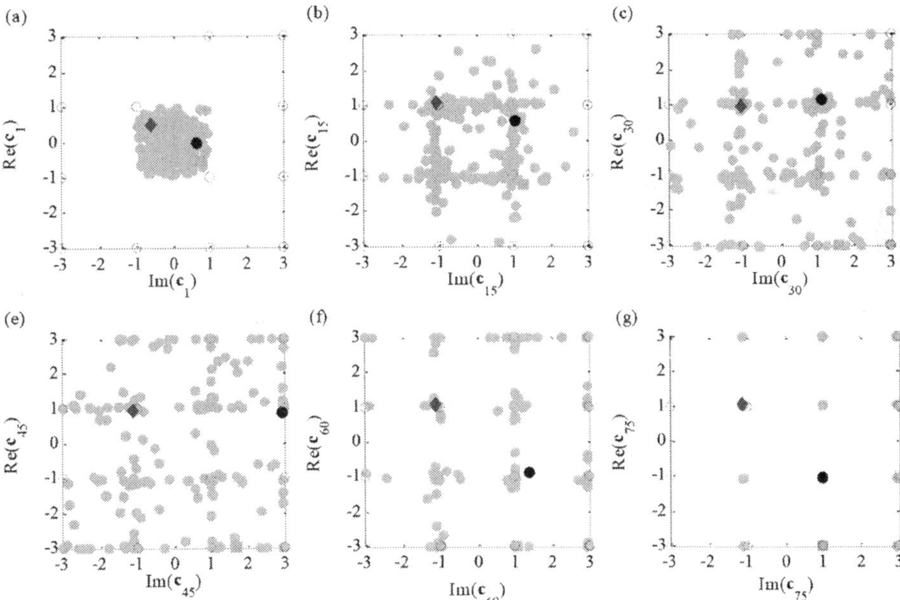

Figure 11. The constellations of input and output sequences for 16QAM signal when the MIMOFN approach is performed.

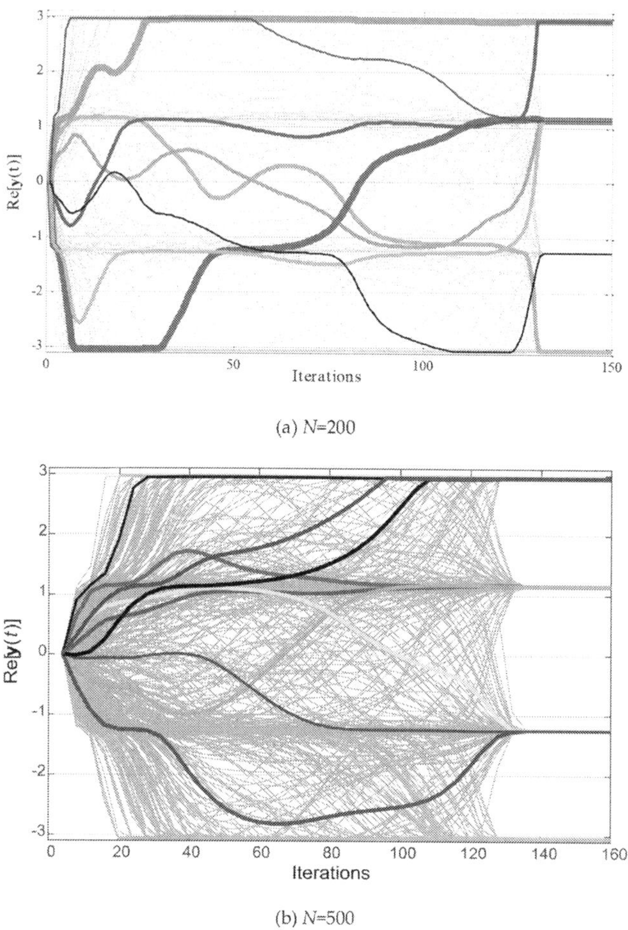

(a) N=200

(b) N=500

Figure 12. The phase trajectories of signal points using the MIMOFN approach with (a) N = 200 and (b) N=500, when μ and SNR = 15 dB, respectively.

7. Conclusions

In this chapter, a unified approach based on MIMOFN to solve DSD issues, even if the sequence is short and the training sequence is absent, is shown. The proposed method can be applied to those cases where the constellation of the source signal is dense and the data frame is short. The structure of MIMOFN not only is suitable to the DSD of square-QAM (e.g. 16QAM) issues but also can be extended to the cross-QAM (e.g. 8QAM, 32QAM) cases.

Acknowledgements

The authors would like to acknowledge the national support of this work from the National Natural Science Foundation of China (NSFC) (grant nos. 61201426, 61501331, 61303210), Zhejiang Provincial Natural Science Foundation of China (grant nos. LQ16F01001, LQ14F030007, LY16F010016), and Scientific Research Project of Education Department of Zhejiang Province of China (grant nos. Y201327231, Y201430529).

Author details

Xiukai Ruan*, Yanhua Tan, Yuxing Dai, Guihua Cui, Xiaojing Shi, Qibo Cai, Chang Li, Han Li, Yaoju Zhang and Dameng Dai

*Address all correspondence to: ruanxiukai@wzu.edu.cn

College of Physics and Electronic Information Engineering, Wenzhou University, Wenzhou, Zhejiang, China

References

[1] Robet, S., Lutz, L., & Wolfgang H.G. (2001). Noncoherent sequence estimation combined with noncoherent adaptive channel estimation. http://www.lit.lnt.de/papers/ew00cr.pdf.

[2] Pinchas, M., & Bobrovsky B.Z. (2007) A novel HOS approach for blind channel equalization. *IEEE Transactions on Wireless Communications*, 6(3): 875–886.

[3] Abra,r S., & Nandi, A.K. (2010) Blind equalization of square-QAM signal: a multimodulus approach. *IEEE Transactions on Communications*, 58(6): 1674–1685.

[4] Ruan, X. K, Jiang, X, and Li, C. (2012). A novel method of Bussgang-type blind equalization in high-order QAM systems. *Journal of Electronics and Information Technology*, 34(8): 2018–2022.

[5] Ruan, X. K, & Zhang, Y. J. (2014). Blind sequence estimation of MPSK signals using dynamically driven recurrent neural networks. *Neurocomputing*, 129: 421–427.

[6] Ruan, X. K, & Zhang, Y. J. (2012). Blind optical baseband signals detection using recurrent neural network based on continuous multi-valued neurons. *Acta Optica Sinica*, 32(11): 1106001–1106011.

[7] Ruan, X. K, and Zhang, Z. Y. (2011). Blind detection of QAM signals using continuous Hopfield-type neural network. *Journal of Electronics and Information Technology*, 33(7): 1600–1605.

[8] Castillo, E. (1998). Functional networks. *Neural Processing Letters*, 7: 151–159.

[9] Rajasekaran S.(2004). Functional networks in structural engineering. *Journal of Computing in Civil Engineering*, 18(2): 172–181.

[10] Castillo, E., Gutiérrez, J.M., Hadi, A. S., & Lacruz, B. (2001). Some applications of functional networks in statistics and engineering. *Technometrics*. 43(1): 10–24.

[11] Iglesias, A., Arcay, B., Cotos, J.M., Taboada, J.A., & Dafonte, C. (2004). A comparison between functional networks and artificial neural networks for the prediction of fishing catches. *Neural Computing and Applications*, 13: 21–31.

[12] Zhou, Y., He, D., & Nong, Z. (2007). Application of functional network to solving classification problems. *World Academy of Science, Engineering and Technology*, 12: 12–24.

[13] Emad, A.E., Asparouhov O., Abdulraheemd A.A., et al. (2012). Functional networks as a new data mining predictive paradigm to predict permeability in a carbonate reservoir. *Journal Expert Systems with Application: An International Journal*. 39(12): 10359–10375.

[14] Alonso-Betanzos, A., Castillo, E., Fontenla-Romero, O., & Sáchez-Maron˜o, N. (2004). Sheer strength prediction using dimensional analysis and functional networks. *ESANN'2004 Proceedings—European Symposium on Artificial Neural Networks Bruges (Belgium)*: 251–256.

[15] Liao, L., Khong, A. W. H.(2013). An adaptive subsystems based algorithm for channel equalization in a SIMO system. *IEEE Transactions on Circuits and Systems. Part I: Regular Papers*. 60(6): 1559–1569.

[16] Fang, J., Leyman A. R., Chew Y. H. (2006). Blind equalization of SIMO FIR channels driven by colored signals with unknown statistics. *IEEE Transactions on Signal Processing*. 54(6): 1998–2008.

[17] Franklin J. N.(2000). Matrix theory. *Dover Publications*. Chapter 4.

[18] Shen, J., Ding, Z. (2000). Direct blind MMSE channel equalization based on second-order statistics. *IEEE Transactions on Signal Processing*, 48(4): 1015–1022.

Chapter 7

From Fuzzy Expert System to Artificial Neural Network: Application to Assisted Speech Therapy

Ovidiu Schipor , Oana Geman ,

Iuliana Chiuchisan and Mihai Covasa

Additional information is available at the end of the chapter

http://dx.doi.org/10.5772/63332

Abstract

This chapter addresses the following question: What are the advantages of extending a fuzzy expert system (FES) to an artificial neural network (ANN), within a computer-based speech therapy system (CBST)? We briefly describe the key concepts underlying the principles behind the FES and ANN and their applications in assisted speech therapy. We explain the importance of an intelligent system in order to design an appropriate model for real-life situations. We present data from 1-year application of these concepts in the field of assisted speech therapy. Using an artificial intelligent system for improving speech would allow designing a training program for pronunciation, which can be individualized based on specialty needs, previous experiences, and the child's prior therapeutical progress. Neural networks add a great plus value when dealing with data that do not normally match our previous designed pattern. Using an integrated approach that combines FES and ANN allows our system to accomplish three main objectives: (1) develop a personalized therapy program; (2) gradually replace some human expert duties; (3) use "self-learning" capabilities, a component traditionally reserved for humans. The results demonstrate the viability of the hybrid approach in the context of speech therapy that can be extended when designing similar applications.

Keywords: fuzzy expert system, artificial neural network, assisted speech therapy, artificial intelligent system, hybrid expert system

1. Speech therapy: key concepts and facts

Dyslalia is a pronunciation deficiency manifested by an alteration of one or more phonemes due to several causes such as: omissions, substitutions, distortions, and permanent motor

© 2016 The Author(s). Licensee InTech. This chapter is distributed under the terms of the Creative Commons Attribution License (http://creativecommons.org/licenses/by/3.0), which permits unrestricted use, distribution, and reproduction in any medium, provided the original work is properly cited.

impairments. Dyslalia can be simple when it is related with only one sound (eventually in an attenuated form). An extension of pronunciation–articulation disorder related with more sounds and/or groups of syllables is called polymorphic dyslalia [1].

The existence of a dyslalia with defectological significance can be diagnosed after the age of four. Until that, dyslalia is called physiological and it is caused by the insufficient development of the speech-articulator apparatus and the neurological systems implicated in the speech process. This is the age that allows maximization of the therapeutic effects and offers a good prognosis for improvement/correction. The later the therapy begins, the weaker the effect [2].

There are many causes for dyslalia: the imitation of persons with deficient pronunciation, lack of speech stimulation, adults encouraging the preschool child to stabilize wrongful habits, defects in teeth implantation, different anomalies of the speech-articulator apparatus, cerebral deficiencies, hearing loss, weak development of phonetic hearing. Also, in severe dyslalias, heredity is considered an important factor in diagnosing and explaining this deficiency.

Impairment type		Number of subjects	Impairment frequency (%)	Overall impairment frequency (%)
Dyslalia		434	91.2	14.8
Dysarthria		–	–	–
Rhinolalia		7	1.5	0.2
Reading-writing difficulties		–	–	–
Rhythm and fluency difficulties		17	3.7	0.6
Language impairments	Selective mutism	4	0.8	0.1
	General development delays	8	1.6	0.3
Voice impairments		–	–	–
Language impairments in association with:	Autism	4	0.8	0.1
	Down syndrome	2	0.4	0.1
	Intellectual deficiencies	–	–	–
	Deafness	–	–	–
Total		476	100.0	16.2

Table 1. Speech and language impairments distribution (unpublished data from Suceava—Romania Regional Speech Therapy Centre).

In dyslalia, the sounds are not equally affected. Thus, the sounds most affected are the ones that appear later in the child's speech: vibrant—r (very important in Romanian language), affricates—c, g, t, hissing—s, z. In fact, the sounds mostly affected are the ones that require a greater effort to synchronize the elements of the phono-articulator apparatus (elements engaged in the emission of sounds: larynx, vocal cords, tongue, lips, teeth, and cheeks). Their pronunciation involves a certain position of all these elements and a certain intensity of the exhausted air jet [1].

Regarding the frequency of speech impediments and especially the frequency of dyslalia, the statistics from the Suceava Romanian Regional Speech Therapy Centre (**Table 1**; **Figure 1**) reveals the following aspects [2]: (i) Disorders that affect speech are more frequent that the ones affecting the language; (ii) Dyslalia is the most frequent pronunciation disorder, with sounds r and s most affected; (iii) the proportion of children with speech impediments:

- Decreases constantly until first grade;

- Suddenly decreases between first and second grade;

- Decreases slower and slower between second and fourth grade.

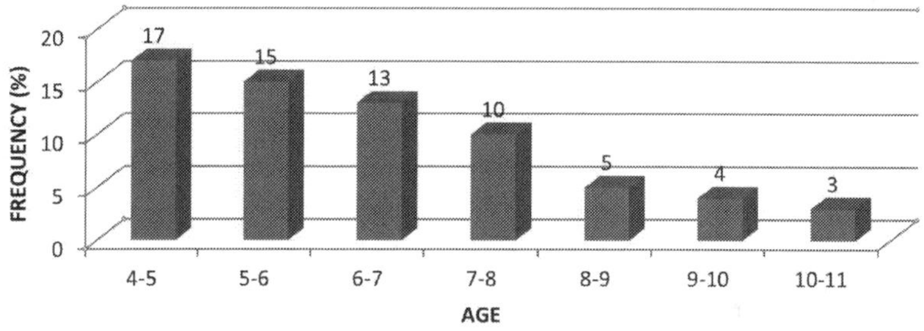

Figure 1. Evolution of speech impairments frequency across subjects' age.

The characterization of the dyslalia dynamics is of great interest also, in regard to the age of the subjects as depicted in **Figure 1**. Before age four no logopedic evaluation was conducted for children since possible speaking problems might be due to insufficient maturation of the phono-articulatory organs and of the involved cortical areas.

After this age, children with speech impairments are integrated in the speech therapy programs. The therapy determines the progressive decrease of the proportion of children with speech problems in relation to their age. At the beginning of the school, the frequency of children with speech disorders decreases suddenly, mainly because of the acquisition of writing and reading skills. Moreover, the corrective effort from the teaching community is highly emphasized. After this age, language disorders are present mainly in children with organ related disorders—structural disorders of the central or peripheral organs of speech.

The main steps of speech therapy together with the place of fuzzy expert system in therapeutic process are presented in **Figure 2**. Each therapy process contains a formative evaluation, which can be followed by the therapy within the family. After 3 months, the speech therapist can finalize the therapy or can reevaluate it [3].

The expert system incorporates information generated from social, cognitive, and affective examination, as well as from the homework reports and results' trends [4]. This allows the expert system to provide critical answers related to the length and frequency of the therapy session as well as the type of exercise to be used and its content.

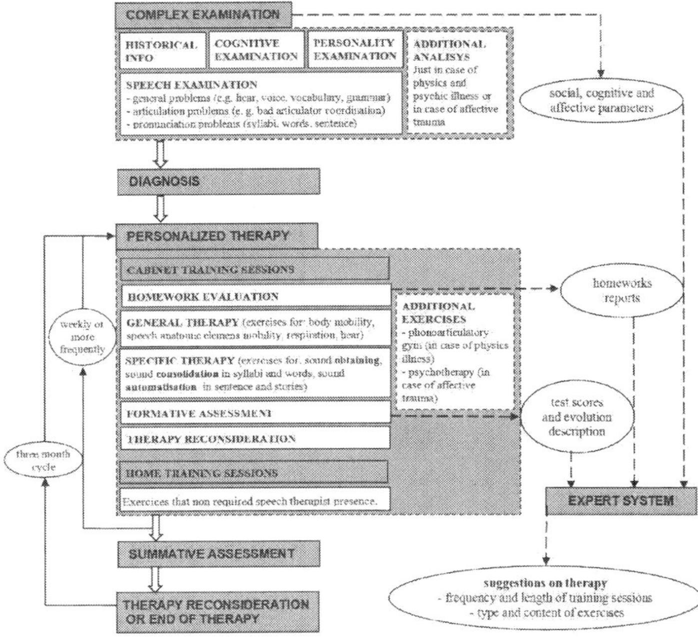

Figure 2. Speech therapy process and fuzzy expert system [3].

The therapy customization assumes a differentiated report related to the therapy stages. Thus, for each subject, there are different weights for each stage within the program structure. The therapy is generally a formative assessment because the speech therapists permanently evaluate the evolution of the patient during the exercises. The therapy is continued in familial environment during home training sessions. Thus, between the weekly sessions, family must provide the child with the adequate environment to consolidate the skills initiated at the specialty clinic.

A summative assessment is conducted every 3 months, and the child's evolution is analyzed over a longer period of time. This is the time for the reconsideration of the therapy and, eventually, for finalizing the therapeutic process.

The expert system is designed to function as a true assistant of the speech therapist. It provides suggestions based on several recordings from the integrated system. Moreover, depending on the assessments performed by the speech therapist at each session and on the homework solving, the human expert receives suggestions regarding the most appropriate exercises to recommend [5].

It is necessary for the speech therapist to have the possibility to intervene in modifying the knowledge database when the suggestion given by the expert system contradicts the speech therapist decision. The system has to self-notify the presence of a contradiction and to ask the human expert to remove the conflict. This principle is useful for the therapeutic system (in general) and for the expert system (in particular), especially in the case of the beginner speech therapist (with less practical training experience). Even if the computer decisions cannot be considered absolutely correct, they can contribute to the overall success of the therapy by raising questions which require further clarifications by consulting a human expert.

2. Expert system validation

Since 2006 we have developed Logomon, the computer-based speech therapy system (CBST) for Romanian language. The modules of the integrated system are briefly presented in **Figure 3** (modules 1,…,9). All administrative tasks are grouped in the Lab Monitor Application. The expert system takes the information it needs from the database of this module. In the first scenario, the child exercises in SLT's Lab using Lab Monitor Application.

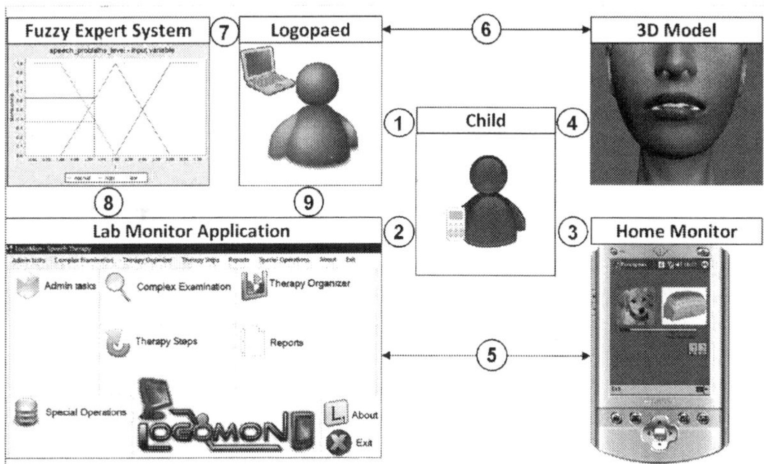

Figure 3. Architecture of Logomon CBST.

Another scenario involves the utilization of a dynamic 3D model, a module that indicates the correct positioning of elements of phono-articulator apparatus for each phoneme in Romanian language (the model can translate and rotate; the transparency of each individual elements—teeth, tongue, cheeks—can also be modified). Homework is mainly generated by the fuzzy expert system that indicates the number, the duration, and the content of home exercises. These exercises are played on a mobile device (Home Monitor), without SLT intervention [6]. The relations between input and output variables are presented in **Figure 4**.

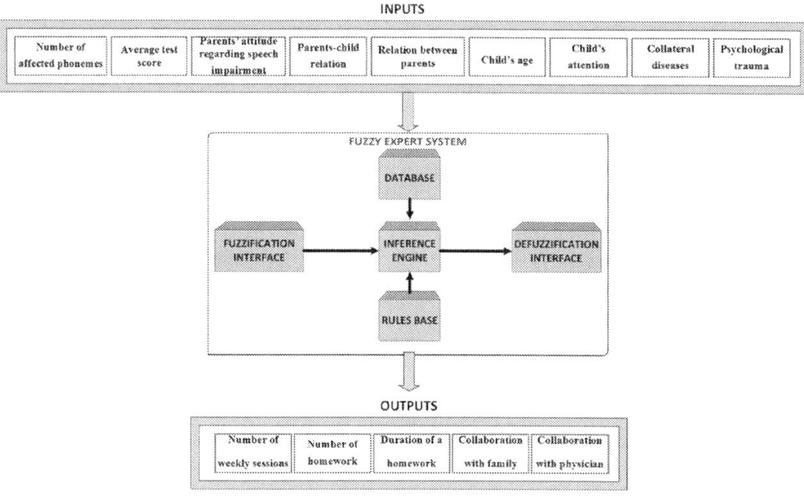

Figure 4. The relation between input and output variables.

The expert system is fed with information taken from three sources: socio-psychological parameters (Lab Monitor Application), tests scores (Lab Exercises), and homework scores (Home Monitor). These numbers are grouped in nine input variables [3].

1. number of affected phonemes (in order to differentiate between simple and polymorphic dyslalia);

2. average test score (indicates the intensity of impairment);

3. parents' attitude regarding speech impairment (the parents' attitude is a key factor in therapy prognosis);

4. parents–child relation (offer important clues regarding the importance of home training sessions);

5. relation between parents (describes the emotional quality of familial environment);

6. child's age (the therapeutical strategy largely vary with subject's age);

7. child's attention (this variable was taken into consideration due to increasing frequency of ADHD—attention deficit disorders—among the children);

8. collateral diseases (AIDS, Down syndrome, intellectual disabilities, nutrition diseases);

9. psychological trauma (shows the child's emotional health).

The expert system outputs five numbers that configure the personalized therapy:

1. number of weekly sessions (how many times in a week the child should encounter SLT?);

2. number of homeworks (how many homework sessions should be?);

3. duration of a homework (how long a homework should last?);

4. collaboration with family (should SLT rely on child's family support?);

5. collaboration with physician (does SLT have to collaborate with a physician?).

One major limitation of such a system is the inability to express and/or mimic emotions such as empathy and to recognize emotional states. To improve this, some studies used the human–computer interaction (HCI) model in which trained individuals reflecting a particular emotional state are used. In our previous work, we explored the possibility of adapting and integrating the classical techniques of emotion recognition in the assisted therapy for children with speech problems [6].

The fuzzy expert system is based on forward chaining of over 200 rules written in fuzzy control language (FCL). The expert system engine is coded in Java language and is integrated in our speech therapy platform. In order to adjust and validate the inferential process, we used our platform for more than 100 children from 2008 to 2015. The extension of our system using an artificial neural network (ANN) is demanding especially because it is relative hard for a SLT to change a fuzzy rule. Thus, in the case of a contradiction between human and artificial expert, an ANN could facilitate the re-training process [7, 8].

3. State of the art in fuzzy expert systems, artificial neural network and medical application

Because of the emergence of interdisciplinary technologies during the past few years, the interaction between doctors and engineers opened unprecedented opportunities, and the medical specialists are employing computerized technologies to assist in diagnosis of, and access to, related medical information.

3.1. Fuzzy expert systems for medical diagnosis

The rapid progress in computer technology plays a key role in the development of medical diagnostic tools that call for the need of more advanced intelligent and knowledge-based systems [9]. This is important since medical diagnosis is characterized by a high degree of uncertainty that can be improved through the application of fuzzy techniques that provide powerful decision support, expert systems knowledge, and enhanced reasoning capabilities in the decision-making process. Also, it provides a powerful framework for the combination of evidence and deduction of consequences based on knowledge stored in the knowledge base [9]. Therefore, fuzzy expert system (FES) can be used in applications for diagnosis, patient monitoring and therapy, image analysis, differential diagnosis, pattern recognition, medical data analysis [10–14].

The areas in which diversified applications are developed using fuzzy logic are fuzzy models for illness, heart and cardiovascular disease diagnosis, neurological diseases, asthma, abdominal pain, tropical diseases, medical analogy of consumption of drugs, diagnosis and treatment of diabetes, syndrome differentiation, diagnosis of lung and liver diseases, monitoring and control in intensive care units and operation rooms, diagnosis of chronic obstructive pulmonary diseases, diagnosis of cortical malformation, etc. The non-disease areas of applications are in X-ray mammography, interpretation of mammographic and ultrasound images, electrographic investigation of human body. Other areas for the applications of fuzzy logic are prediction of aneurysm, fracture healing, etc.

Recent research studies have contributed to the development of diagnostic techniques, quantification of medical expertise, knowledge technology transfer, identification of usage patterns, and applications of FES in practice by the medical practitioners [15]. According to [15], 21% of studies present the development of methodologies and models and 13% studies contributed to the development of neuro-fuzzy-based expert systems [9]. These studies contributed to the development of innovative diagnostic techniques, quantification of medical expertise, and application of fuzzy expert systems and their implementation in practice.

The rationale behind the decision-making process in medical diagnosis is a complex endeavor that involves a certain degree of uncertainty and ambiguity. The computer-assisted expert system that incorporates the fuzzy model has been used to aid the physician in this process [15]. As such, several computer-assisted applications for patient's diagnosis and treatments as well as web-based FES have been recently developed and include ways of handling vagueness

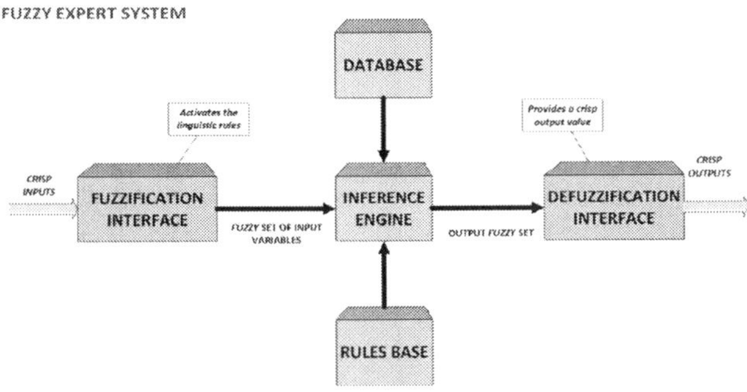

Figure 5. Fuzzy expert system architecture.

and complexity (**Figure 5**). Furthermore, disease-focused intelligent medical systems are rapidly emerging and are designed to handle more complex variables such as patient monitoring, predictive values, as well as taking into account assessment and performance parameters.

The architecture of a generic medical fuzzy expert system showing the flow of data through the system is depicted in **Figure 6** [9]. The knowledge base for developed medical FES contains both static and dynamic information. There are qualitative and quantitative variables, which are analyzed to arrive at a diagnostic conclusion. The fuzzy logic methodology involves fuzzification, inference engine, and defuzzification as the significant steps [9].

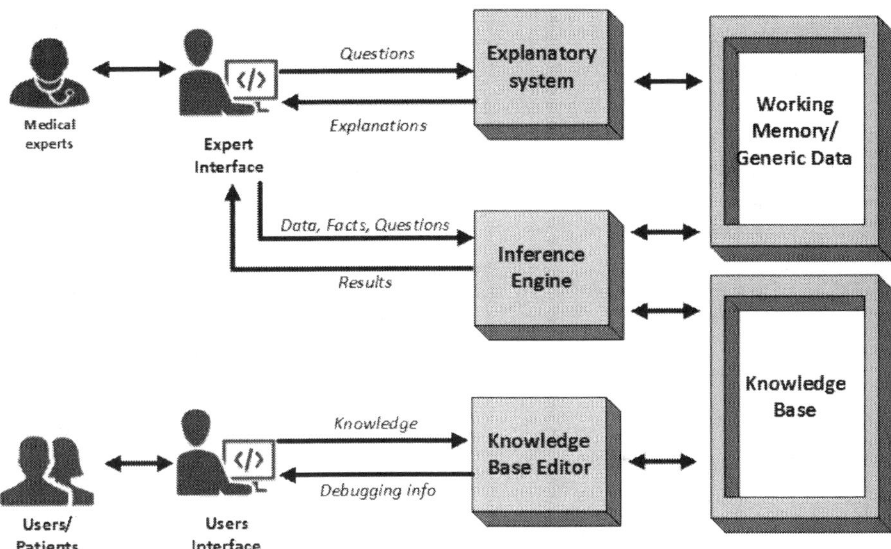

Figure 6. The architecture of a generic medical fuzzy expert system.

The FES uses both quantitative and qualitative analyses of medical data and represents a useful tool in achieving a high success rate in medical diagnosis. These computer-based diagnostic tools together with the knowledge base have proved very useful in early diagnosis of pathologies. On the other hand, the web-based applications and interfaces allow health practitioners to readily share their knowledge and know-how expertise [15].

3.2. Application of artificial neural network in medicine

An artificial neural network (ANN) is a computational model that attempts to account for the parallel nature of the human brain [16]. Analyzing approaches in different scientific procedures, the ability to learn, tolerance to data noises and capability to model incomplete data have made them unique, and once the network has been trained, new data in similar domain may be analyzed and predicted [17].

In the medical field, ANN applications that have been developed use the "classification" principle-based on which patients are assigned to a particular set of classes based on specific biological measures. For example, ANN applications have been used in the diagnosis of diabetes (using blood and urine analyses) [18, 19], tuberculosis [20, 21], leukemia [22], cardiovascular conditions [23] (such as heart murmurs [24]), liver [25], and pulmonary [26] diagnosis, as well as in urological dysfunctions [27], including expert pre-diagnosis system for automatic evaluation of possible symptoms from the uroflow results [28], and ANN applications have also been used in image analyses [29, 30] and in analysis of complicated effusion samples [31]. Finally, a neural networks-based automatic medical diagnosis system has been developed for eight different diseases [32], and in detection and diagnosis of micro-calcifications in digital format mammograms [33].

An ANN is a network of highly interconnecting processing elements (inspired by biological nervous systems—neurons) operating in parallel. The connections between elements largely determine the network function. A subgroup of processing element is a layer in the network. Each neuron in a layer is connected with each neuron in the next layer through a weighted connection [34]. The structure of a neural network is formed by layers. The first layer is the input layer, and the last layer is the output layer, and between them, there may be additional layer(s) of units (hidden layers) [16]. The number of neurons in a layer and the number of layers depend strongly on the complexity of the system studied [34]. Therefore, the optimal network architecture must be determined. The general scheme of a typical three-layered ANN architecture is illustrated in **Figure 7**.

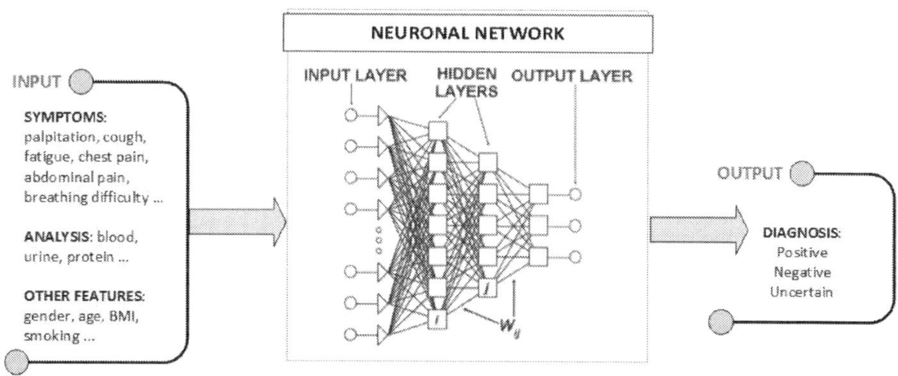

Figure 7. General structure of a neural network (modify after [34]).

Based on the way they learn, all artificial neural networks are divided into two learning categories: supervised and unsupervised. In unsupervised networks, the training procedure uses inputs only, and there are no known answers and the network must develop its own representation of the input stimuli by calculating the acceptable connection weights. On the other hand, training in the supervised learning involves both input and output patterns so that the neural weights can be changed to generate the desired output [16]. In medical applications, supervised networks may be used as alternatives to conventional response surface methodology (RSM) while the unsupervised ones can serve as alternatives to principal component analysis (PCA) in order to map multidimensional data sets onto two-dimensional spaces [17].

Models from ANNs are multifactorial models which can predict, classify, approximate function, or recognize patterns. Theoretically, ANNs are able to estimate any function and if used properly, it can be used effectively in medicine. Outputs from artificial neural networks models are generated from nonlinear combinations of input variables, and such models can be effectively employed to deal with experimental data routinely observed in medicine and to find rules governing a process from raw input data [17].

3.3. Neuro-fuzzy models

The development of intelligent systems in the health field is based on the complementarity between technologies that use the combination between fuzzy logic and neural networks models. This generated the neuro-fuzzy model that takes advantage of both the capability in modeling uncertain data by the artificial neural networks as well as of handling qualitative knowledge. The neuro-fuzzy approaches have been used in several studies to build more intelligent decision-making systems as additional supportive tools for the physicians.

For example, an application of artificial neural networks in typical disease diagnosis using a fuzzy approach was investigated in [35]. The real procedure of medical diagnosis which usually is employed by physicians was analyzed and converted to a machine implementable format. Similarly, in [16], a series of experiments were described and advantages of using a fuzzy approach were discussed.

Neuro-fuzzy (NF) computing becomes a popular framework for solving complex problems based on knowledge expressed in linguistic rules for building a FES, and on data, for learning from a simulation (training) using ANNs. For building a FES, we have to specify the fuzzy sets, fuzzy operators, and the knowledge base. For constructing an ANN for an application, the user needs to specify the architecture and the learning algorithm. Both approaches have their own drawbacks, and they should be combined when building an integrated system [36]. This way we can take advantage of the learning capabilities, which is essential for the fuzzy expert system as well as the linguistic base knowledge that constitutes part of the artificial neural networks.

Therefore, FES and ANNs have attracted the attention of many scientists, and also a huge number of successful applications of them are found in the literature, reporting problems solving in various areas of sciences, such as computing, engineering, medicine, nanotechnology, environmental science, and business.

4. Fuzzy expert system vs. neuro-fuzzy expert system

The fuzzy expert systems (FES) and artificial neuronal network (ANN) have common origin and purposes. They may carry out the logical reasoning, simulating artificial intelligence, by combining the quantitative and qualitative information and meta-knowledge. The advantages and disadvantages of these techniques are complementary. The main disadvantages of FES as regards to the acquisition of knowledge can be easily eliminated using ANN, due to its ability to learn from typical examples. On the other hand, limitations of the ANN related to the man–machine interface and capabilities to explain the reasoning leading to a certain conclusion can be theoretically compensated using the FES [10].

The FES has the following properties: (i) sequential processing; (ii) the acquisition process of knowledge takes place outside the expert system; (iii) the logic is a deducible; (iv) the knowledge is presented in the explicit form; (v) the system is based on the knowledge acquired from human experts; (vi) the rules in the chain of the rules have their origin in the logic of mathematics and fuzzy logic; and (vi) the extraction of the conclusion (implementation of the diagnosis) is done by correlating the exact amount of information and data [10].

The ANN, due to the fact that is designed according to the model of the human brain, has the ability: (i) to learn; (ii) has the advantage of a parallel processing; (iii) the acquisition of knowledge takes place inside the system; (iv) the logic is inductively; (v) the knowledge is the default and gained through examples; (vi), uses parameters and statistical methods for classification and data clustering; and (vii) the extraction of the learned conclusion is made by the approximate correlation of data.

A significant difference between the two instruments lies in the basis of reasoning. As such, the FES is based on the algorithms and deductions, while the ANN is based on the inference from simulating the learning mechanisms of specialized neurons. Based on the techniques used for processing information, the ESF uses sequential methods of processing while ANN has parallel processing, that is, each neuron performs functions in parallel with other neurons in the network.

In the case of learning processes and reasoning in the FES, learning is made outside of the system and the knowledge is obtained from outside and then coded in the knowledge base. For ANN, the knowledge accumulates in the form of weights of the connections between the nodes (neurons), the learning process being internal, permanently adjusting the knowledge deployments as new examples. The FES is based on the method of deductive reasoning, unlike the ANN, in which the methods are inductive. The algorithms of inference of the FES are based on the logic of the sequence "forward or backward" method in the knowledge base, and the ANN uses the approximate correlation of the components of the knowledge base in order to return to items previously learned. The ANN may acquire knowledge through direct learning from examples, which constitutes an advantage, on the basis of algorithms of specific learning with the possibility to learn from the incomplete or partially incorrect or contradictory input data, having the capacity to generalize. On the other hand, the FES has the advantage of a friendly user interface with the possibility of incorporating elements of heuristic reasoning.

One of the basic paradigms of artificial intelligence, with applications in the medical field, is to find a tool which will make it possible to the representation of a large number of meta-knowledge, consistent, and usable for the user. There are two approaches of a computerized system based on knowledge: the first approach is one in which the field of knowledge representation is based on the rules. This involves the necessity that human experts extract rules from its experience and express them in the form of explicit and comprehensible rules. The system has the explanatory and perfect skills and performs well with incomplete information and inaccurate (fuzzy) using the factors of trust, but the construction of such base of knowledge is a difficult task.

The second approach has a connection with the development of the theory of the neuronal networks which is automatically created by a learning algorithm from a variety of inference examples. The knowledge representation is based on the weights of the connections between the neurons. Due to the default representation of knowledge, there is no possibility to identify a problem at the level of the singular neuron. In this case, both working with incomplete information and the provision of evidence of the inference are limited.

From these considerations, combining fuzzy expert system with the neuronal networks will lay the base for the construction of a practical application for strategic decisions, (especially medical decisions), both tactical and operative, and will integrate the advantages of both types of information systems (neuro-fuzzy system expert) [10].

The main challenge in the integration of these two approaches is the creation of the knowledge base when they are only available the rules and examples of data. Additional problems may also occur when incomplete and unreliable information is encoded in neuronal networks. Therefore, it is necessary that the "learning" network is able to work with incomplete information during training in place of using of special heuristic inference.

The inputs and outputs values in a neuro-fuzzy expert system are coded using the analog statuses of neuronal values. An inference is a pair consisting of a vector of the typical inputs and the vector to the corresponding outputs obtained by the expert answers to these questions. Knowledge base of the neuro-fuzzy expert system is a multilayer neuronal network.

To solve the problems raised by the irrelevant values and unknown inputs and outputs of the expert system, the range neuron should be created. The value of the irrelevant or even unknown input and output of the expert system is coded using the full range of status of neurons.

The expert systems become effective and efficient not only to resolve problems of high complexity but also for the decision-making problems, which contain a high degree of uncertainty.

More recently, a hybrid system that includes fuzzy logic, neuronal networks, and genetic algorithms has been developed this required inclusion of additional techniques. The fundamental concept of these hybrid systems consists in complementarity and addresses the weaknesses of each other. The fuzzy expert systems are appropriate especially in the case of systems that have a mathematical model that is difficult to comprehend, for example, when the values of the inputs and of the parameters are vague, imprecise, and/or incomplete. It facilitates the decision-making process in the case of use of the estimated values for the inaccurate information (if the decision is not correct, it may be modified later when more information becomes available). Fuzzy models allow us to represent the descriptive phrases/ qualitative, which are subsequently incorporated in the symbolist instructions (fuzzy rules).

Neuro-fuzzy expert system has the following two functions: (i) the generalization of the information derived from the training data processed by the entries with fuzzy learning and incorporation of knowledge in the form of a neuronal fuzzy network; (ii) the extraction of fuzzy rules "IF THEN" using the importance of linguistic relative diversity of each sentence in a prerequisite ("IF" part), using for this purpose a trained neuro-fuzzy network. The neural network is similar to the standard multilayer network, having in addition, direct connections between the input and output nodes. Activation of nodes is muted, taking the values of +1, 0, or -1.

To work with various fuzzifications in the input and the output layers of the system, it is necessary to interpret the subjective input data. The neuronal network may include groups of fuzzy neurons and groups of non-fuzzy neurons involving shades and accurate data. The output layer will contain only fuzzy neurons.

By incorporating the factor of certainty (groups of non-fuzzy neurons) extends the traditional logic in two ways: (i) sets are labeled from the point of view of quality, and the elements in the same set are assigned different degrees of membership; (ii) any action which results from a valid premise will be executed with a weighting in order to reflect the degree of certainty.

The entrances of the system "suffer" three transformations to become exits: (i) fuzzification of the inputs which consists in the calculation of a value to represent the factor of membership in the qualitative groups; (ii) assessing the rules that consists in the elaboration of a set of rules type "IF THEN"; (iii) outputs defuzzification in order to describe the significance of vague actions through the functions of membership and to resolve the conflicts between competing actions which may trigger [10].

The factor of membership is determined by the function of membership, which is defined on the basis of intuition or experience. To implement a fuzzy system, the following data structure is required: (i) the entries in the system; (ii) the functions of the input membership; (iii) the previous values; (iv) a basis for the rules; (v) the weightings of the rules; (vi) the functions of the output membership; and (vii) exits from the system.

The use of fuzzy logic leads to finding answers and allows drawing conclusions on the basis of vague, ambiguous, and inaccurate information. Fuzzy techniques adopt reasoning similar to human, which allows a quick construction of technical, feasible, and robust systems. The application of the fuzzy methods involves less space of memory and a lot of calculation power in comparison with conventional methods. This fact leads to less expensive systems. The fuzzy expert systems should be constructed in such manner that the overall results are able to change in a way that is smooth and continuous, regardless of the type of inputs. Artificial neural networks have the advantage that it can be included in the fuzzy expert systems, becoming parts of it in the framework of a hybrid neuro-fuzzy expert system. In the majority of the medical applications, the ANN can be used for quick identification of the conditions on the base of FES rules, laying down quickly the rules that should be applied for a given set of conditions.

In conclusion, the specialized literature presents several models of integrating the FES with ANN in the hybrid systems (neuro-fuzzy expert systems), with medical applications. In the strategy of the human expert (programmer), the ANN is driven to solve a problem, and then, the responses are analyzed in order to extract a set of rules. The integrated systems jointly use the data structures and knowledge. Communication between the two components is carried out with both the symbolic and heuristic information, FES characteristics, and with their ANN structures, that is, using weighted coefficients.

5. Results and discussion

To solve issues related to classification, the objects should be grouped in clusters (in our case patients with speech disorders) based on their characteristics (feature vectors) in predefined classes. Classifiers are then built from examples of correct classification by a supervised learning process as opposed to unsupervised learning, where categories are not predefined.

For the classifier design, based on examples of classification, we grouped data into three main sets:

- Training data: data used in the training process to determine the classifier parameters (for example, in the case of the artificial neural networks, it is necessary to determine the weights of connections between neurons) (1).

- Validation data: data used to analyze the behavior during learning algorithm; the performance on the validation set during the learning process is used to decide whether or not learning should be continued (2);

- Test data: used to analyze the performance of a trained classifier (3).

ANN is composed of simple elements operating in parallel. Knowledge of ANN is stored as numerical values that are associated with connections between artificial neurons, named weights. ANN training means changing and/or adjusting the weights values. Most often, ANNs are trained so that for a given input, output returns a value as close to the desired output, a process exemplified in **Figures 8** and **9**.

For this process, a set of training data (pairs input–output) is required. To solve classification problems, we used the tools package offered by Matlab R2014, specifically the neural network Matlab package (nntool—the tool for classification).

We used a feedforward architecture characterized in [37]:

- An entry level that has as many units (attributes) as the input data;

- One or more hidden levels (the higher the number of hidden units, the greater the complexity of the model extracted from the network; however, this can be a disadvantage leading to decreased network capacity to generalization process);

- A level of output with as many units as the number of classes.

There are two main types of artificial neural networks:

- feedforward—with progressive propagation; the main characteristic of these networks is that a neuron receives signals only from neurons located in previous layer(s).

- feedback—with recurrent or regressive propagation; these networks are characterized by the fact that there is a feedback signal from the higher-order neurons, for those on lower layers or even for themselves.

We used a feedforward network for illustration (see **Figure 9**).

To design a simple Matlab neural network for classification ("Pattern Recognition"), we used *"nprtool"* tool that opens a graphical interface that allows specification of a network element characterized by the following:

- a level of hidden units (the number of hidden units can be chosen by the user);

- the logistics activation (logsig) for both hidden units and for the output [(output values ranged between (0.1)];

- the backpropagation training algorithm based on minimization method of conjugate gradient.

The artificial neural networks have the ability to learn, but the concrete way by which the process is accomplished is dictated by the algorithm used for training. A network is considered trained when application of an input vector leads to a desired output, or very close to it. Training consists of sequential application of various input vectors and adjusting the weights of the network in relation to a predetermined procedure. During this time, weights of the connections gradually converge toward certain values so that each input vector produces the desired output vector. Supervised learning involves the use of an input–output vector pair desired [37].

After input setting, the output is calculated by comparing the calculated output with the desired output, and then, the difference is used to change the weights in order to minimize the error to an acceptable level. In a backpropagation neural network, learning algorithm has two stages: the training patterns for the input layer and the updated error propagation. The ANN propagates the training pattern layer by layer, until it generates the output pattern. If this is different from the desired target pattern, it will calculate the error and will be backpropagated from the output to the input. The weights are updated simultaneously with error propagation [37].

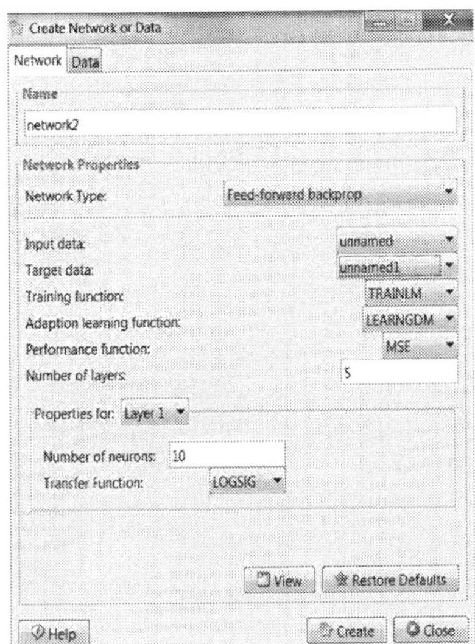

Figure 8. Create network using Matlab.

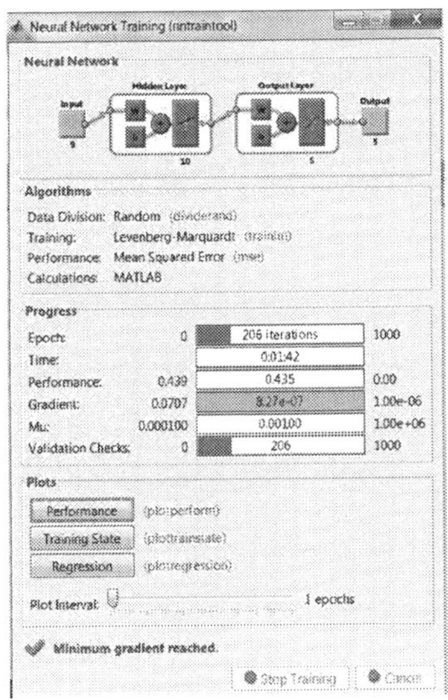

Figure 9. Neural network design and training.

The proposed artificial neural network uses supervised learning with two rules (see **Figures 10** and **11**):

1. extraction of a subset from the training dataset for testing dataset (not used during setting network parameters)

2. maintaining an acceptable level of error in the training set to avoid over learning (learning insignificant details of examples used for training).

The training process is controlled by means of a technique of cross-validation, which consists in splitting the initial random set of data in three subsets: for actual training (training); for controlling learning (validation); and for classifier's quality assurance (testing).

We used backpropagation as the correction algorithm (regressive propagation of errors) with propagation of the error signal in the opposite direction compared to how the signal travels during the working phase.

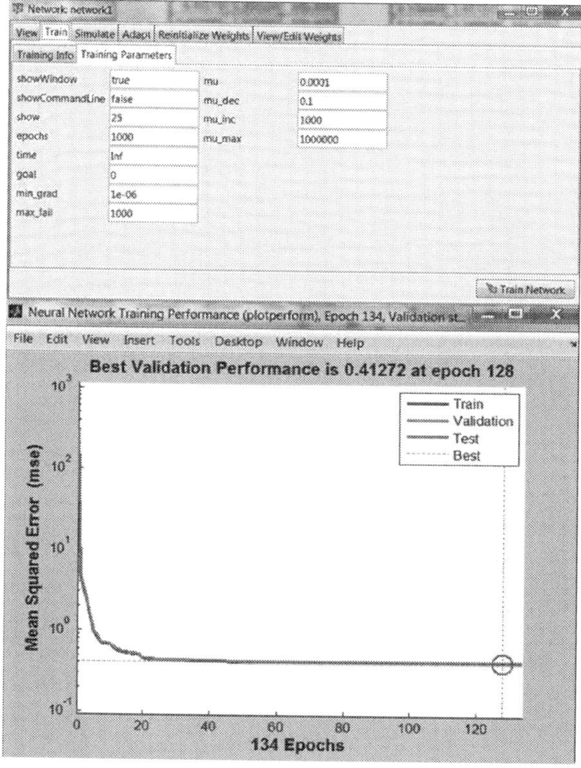

Figure 10. Network training parameters and best validation performance.

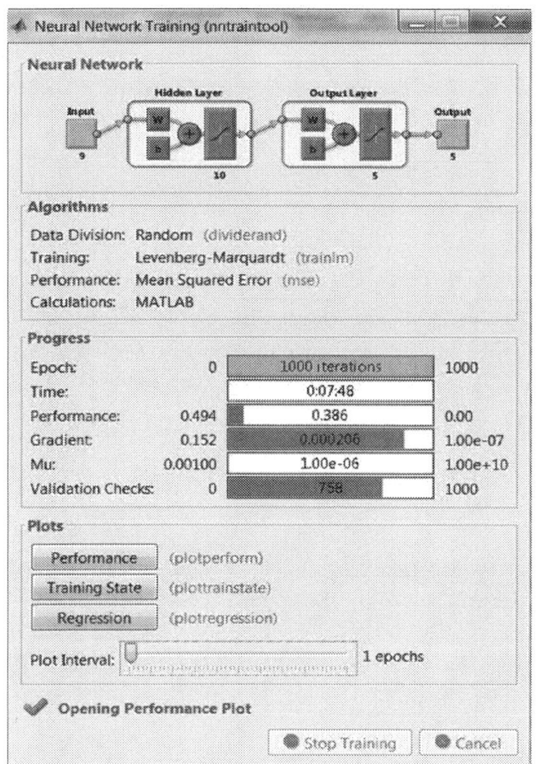

Figure 11. Neural network after 1000 iterations.

The training of the neural network lasted 1000 epochs. Matlab interface allows us to display graphs of the statistical parameters, for example, the mean square error, regression (the correlation between desired values and targets, and the values ??obtained; The R correlation close to 1 means a value very close?? to the desired one). Mean values ??for MSE and R are available after training in the main window, under Results section. Identification of classes of subjects from the dataset tested with ANN was achieved with high specificity and accuracy (see **Figures 12** and **13**).

One of the trivial artificial neural network is SOM—self-organizing map, which is mainly used for data clustering and feature mapping (see **Figures 14** and **15**).

The quality of a classifier in terms of correct identification of a class is measured using information from confusion matrix that contains the following:

- The number of data correctly classified as belonging to the class interests: true positive cases (TP);

- The number of data correctly classified as not belonging to the class of interest: true negative cases (TN);

- The number of data misclassified as belonging to the class of interest: false positive cases (FP);

- The number of data misclassified as not belonging to the class of interest: false negative cases (FN).

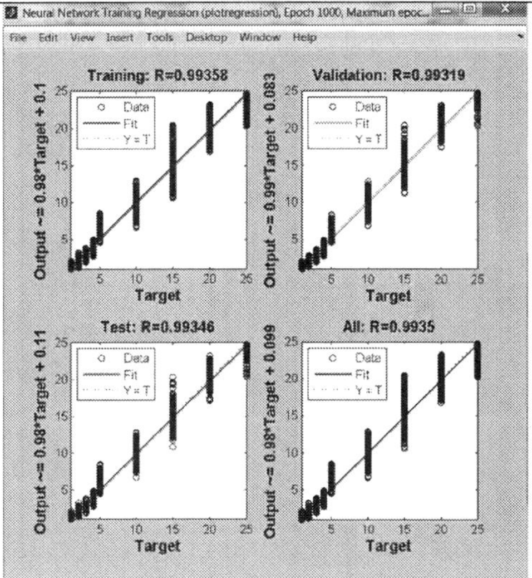

Figure 12. Neural network training regression.

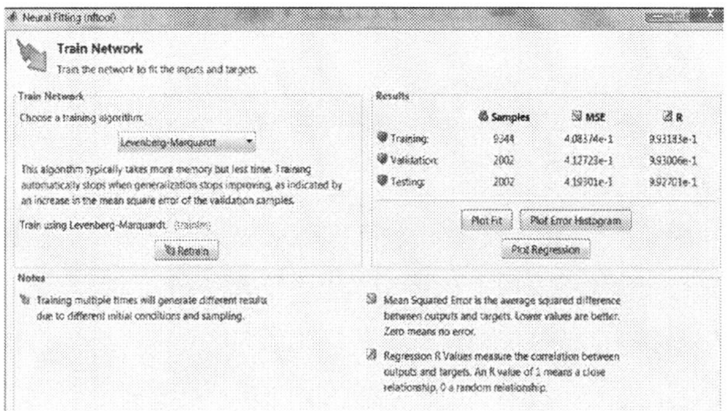

Figure 13. Train the network to fit the input and targets.

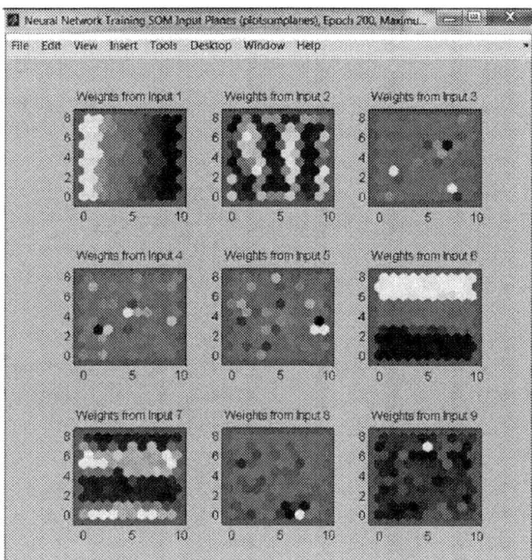

Figure 14. Neural network training self-organizing map (SOM) Input Planes, epoch 200.

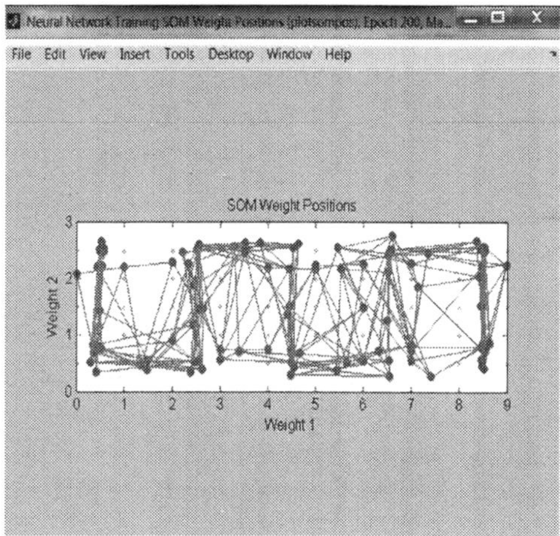

Figure 15. Neural network training Self-Organizing Map (SOM) Weight Positions, epoch 200.

Based on these values, we calculated the following measures:

Sensitivity = TP/(TP + FN)

Specificity = TN/(TN + FP)

Precision = TP/(TP + FP)

Recall = TP/(TP + FN)

F = 2 × precision × recall/(precision + recall)

Model Name	Training			Cross Validation			Testing		
	RMSE	r	MAE	RMSE	r	MAE	RMSE	r	MAE
MLPR-1-O-M (Regression MLP)	0.508933	1.402201	0.409704	0.322604	0.922972	0.255361	0.358704	0.96404	0.290742
MLPC-1-O-M (Classification MLP)	0.327037	1.220537	0.244729	0.321762	1.156201	0.219466	0.40723	1.18764	0.282503
LinR-0-B-R (Linear Regression)	0.392882	1.147459	0.321291	0.436575	1.334644	0.352292	0.55806	1.462276	0.455368
LinR-0-B-L (Linear Regression)	0.392851	1.145372	0.321291	0.436507	1.329756	0.352205	0.557872	1.453303	0.455158
LogR-0-B-R (Logistic Regression)	0.392077	1.238948	0.325784	0.428968	1.46138	0.322088	0.527981	1.59547	0.390729
LogR-0-B-L (Logistic Regression)	0.39111	1.230656	0.327396	0.423441	1.447031	0.322429	0.519991	1.579243	0.3882
MLPR-1-B-L (Regression MLP)	0.387056	1.198567	0.317948	0.421741	1.419294	0.335343	0.519126	1.529009	0.411309
MLPC-1-B-L (Classification MLP)	0.38846	1.141375	0.319109	0.394126	1.255082	0.311733	0.487495	1.489909	0.383896
PNN-0-N-N (Probabilistic Neural Network)	0.085338	0.456856	0.04353	0.271987	1.451648	0.11348	0.280823	1.952781	0.10972
RBF-1-B-L (Radial Basis Function)	0.662088	1.442092	0.534637	0.650547	1.28424	0.540903	0.616498	1.289826	0.504839
GFFR-1-B-L (Reg Gen Feedforward)	0.271436	1.084635	0.219762	0.303184	1.088514	0.240272	0.415099	1.284186	0.334125
GFFC-1-B-L (Class Gen Feedforward)	2.311805	11.90046	1.371521	4.419387	11.95021	2.995643	5.125515	13.28726	3.688224
MLPRPC-1-B-L (Reg MLP with PCA)	0.881967	2.045036	0.720389	0.813134	2.04216	0.673859	0.836139	2.042751	0.688616
MLPCPC-1-B-L (Class MLP with PCA)	0.542446	1.381137	0.477375	0.545818	1.408567	0.499732	0.593192	1.471763	0.531133
SVM-0-N-N (Classification SVM)	0.978216	3.46208	0.775134	0.57077	1.854557	0.461521	0.37726	1.215167	0.319964
TDNN-1-B-L (Time-Delay Network)	0.379655	2.001422	0.316254	0.407738	1.357801	0.318339	0.492179	1.460222	0.374016
TLRN-1-B-L (Time-Lag Recurrent Network)	0.471094	1.868466	0.393253	0.495184	1.631292	0.411436	0.547943	1.703328	0.44724
RN-1-B-L (Recurrent Network)	0.425129	1.325358	0.351005	0.398425	1.612961	0.298228	0.478658	1.58024	0.350892
MLPR-2-B-L (Regression MLP)	0.320861	1.233744	0.265915	0.331135	1.207313	0.26449	0.357926	1.260343	0.284382
MLPC-2-B-L (Classification MLP)	0.315982	1.167649	0.247558	0.357427	1.398602	0.242102	0.458333	1.542289	0.307155
MLPR-1-B-R (Regression MLP)	0.301484	1.14782	0.229342	0.33914	1.300022	0.233399	0.436376	1.420916	0.29758
MLPC-1-B-R (Classification MLP)	0.329803	1.479794	0.266462	0.33202	1.113177	0.250788	0.399761	1.220224	0.297668
MLPR-2-O-M (Regression MLP)	0.221035	1.074964	0.12011	0.113007	0.981053	0.054795	0.151261	0.932933	0.064494
MLPC-2-O-M (Classification MLP)	0.348334	1.121105	0.268159	0.318955	0.867087	0.223579	0.369996	0.924195	0.258641
MLPR-2-B-R (Regression MLP)	0.203215	0.933993	0.137048	0.231383	0.966788	0.141672	0.246501	1.069248	0.143614
MLPC-2-B-R (Classification MLP)	0.384336	1.4615	0.321085	0.432656	1.692839	0.343492	0.523127	1.739074	0.407794
MLPRPC-1-O-M (Reg MLP with PCA)	0.945582	1.954717	0.778937	0.666084	1.83967	0.536057	0.712878	1.839316	0.576275
MLPCPC-1-O-M (Class MLP with PCA)	0.545546	1.582078	0.484669	0.521149	1.344116	0.495434	0.553071	1.412793	0.514216
MLPRPC-1-B-R (Reg MLP with PCA)	0.54491	1.34828	0.467731	0.557591	1.428227	0.475297	0.613538	1.527512	0.504508
MLPCPC-1-B-R (Class MLP with PCA)	0.540359	1.434408	0.479016	0.546114	1.337124	0.501908	0.571789	1.370814	0.517757
GFFR-1-O-M (Reg Gen Feedforward)	0.454291	1.575135	0.374846	0.375064	1.214175	0.291732	0.420285	1.159984	0.329084
GFFC-1-O-M (Class Gen Feedforward)	0.324176	1.029036	0.253448	0.313517	0.903713	0.226223	0.396962	1.007077	0.281022
GFFR-1-B-R (Reg Gen Feedforward)	0.338294	1.11053	0.282375	0.39134	1.27208	0.313176	0.519232	1.459908	0.4263
GFFC-1-B-R (Class Gen Feedforward)	0.380846	1.311824	0.315869	0.418067	1.516297	0.310688	0.517929	1.633733	0.37983
RBF-1-O-M (Radial Basis Function)	0.894092	1.921294	0.741068	0.621811	1.60236	0.516025	0.665073	1.605045	0.552353
RBF-1-B-R (Radial Basis Function)	0.653407	1.435348	0.532607	0.636503	1.28697	0.533418	0.603007	1.287842	0.500127
TDNN-1-O-M (Time-Delay Network)	0.533729	1.451931	0.396164	0.340023	1.162859	0.209211	0.402151	1.168537	0.254628
TDNN-1-B-R (Time-Delay Network)	0.295563	1.069168	0.253161	0.283278	0.960019	0.233299	0.297115	0.964466	0.249916
RN-1-O-M (Recurrent Network)	0.394225	1.378934	0.319767	0.323742	1.351473	0.241807	0.385874	1.635519	0.275718
RN-1-B-R (Recurrent Network)	0.397754	1.582702	0.322333	0.428865	1.776686	0.313778	0.521978	1.855299	0.380998
TLRN-1-O-M (Time-Lag Recurrent Network)	0.294567	1.088781	0.23422	0.25323	0.93366	0.174036	0.304505	0.991213	0.210027
TLRN-1-B-R (Time-Lag Recurrent Network)	0.346775	1.28051	0.276559	0.407926	1.355195	0.291143	0.506161	1.658579	0.360642

Figure 16. A multilayer perceptron network (MLP) best performance.

The results show that the best performance was obtained using a multilayer perceptron network (MLP). MLP is a feedforward neural network comprising one or more hidden layers. Like any neural network, a network with backpropagation is characterized by the connections between neurons (forming the network architecture), activation of functions used by neurons and learning algorithm that specifies the procedure used to adjust the weights. Usually, a backpropagation neural network is a multilayer network comprising three or four layers fully connected [37].

Each neuron computes its output similar to perceptron. Then, input value is sent to the activation function. Unlike perceptron, in a backpropagation neural networks, the neurons have sigmoid-type activation functions. Derivative function is very easy to calculate and ensure the output range [0, 1]. Each layer of a MLP neural network performs a specific function. The input layer accepts input signals and computational rarely contains neurons that do not process input patterns. Output layer supports output signals (stimuli coming from the hidden layer) and lays it out on the network. Detects hidden layer neurons traits and their weight is hidden patterns of input traits. These characteristics are then used to determine the output layer to the output pattern.

The backpropagation algorithm is a supervised learning algorithm named generalized delta algorithm. This algorithm is based on minimizing the difference between the desired output and actual output by descending gradient method. The gradient tells us how the function varies in different directions. The idea of the algorithm is finding the minimum error function in relation to relative weights of connections. The error is given by the difference between the desired output and the actual output of the network. The most common error function is the mean square error (**Figures 16** and **17**).

RMSE is the mean square error and is used to characterize the scattering of the data in relation to the average. In our case, in all three stages of ANN testing, we obtained RMSE values below 0.5, with 100% identification of classes as shown in **Figure 18**.

Performance Metrics

Model Name	Training			Cross-validation			Testing		
	RMSE	r	Correct	RMSE	r	Correct	RMSE	r	Correct
MLPR-1-O-M (Regression MLP)	0.193136	0.504298	100.00%	0.40441	1.276899	100.00%	0.411551	0.828285	94.44%
MLPC-1-O-M (Classification MLP)	0.292957	0.659528	100.00%	0.423566	0.766415	100.00%	0.360862	0.77623	100.00%
LinR-0-B-R (Linear Regression)	0.334444	0.771683	100.00%	0.36981	0.774197	100.00%	0.378221	0.679267	94.44%
LinR-0-B-L (Linear Regression)	0.320609	0.723112	100.00%	0.382431	0.899123	100.00%	0.373497	0.713072	94.44%
LogR-0-B-R (Logistic Regression)	0.323498	0.802888	100.00%	0.411873	0.883485	100.00%	0.429729	0.777518	100.00%
LogR-0-B-L (Logistic Regression)	0.320243	0.756819	100.00%	0.399313	0.862804	100.00%	0.406476	0.733547	100.00%
MLPR-1-B-L (Regression MLP)	0.321919	0.701325	100.00%	0.448925	1.193378	100.00%	0.338979	0.690299	94.44%
MLPC-1-B-L (Classification MLP)	0.29544	0.929712	100.00%	0.504155	1.517705	100.00%	0.524958	1.351293	100.00%
PNN-0-N-N (Probabilistic Neural Network)	4.27E-06	2.41E-05	100.00%	0.578235	1	100.00%	0.522295	1	100.00%
RBF-1-B-L (Radial Basis Function)	0.391416	0.896709	100.00%	0.370999	0.691104	100.00%	0.468485	0.883554	100.00%
GFFR-1-B-L (Reg Gen Feedforward)	0.230875	0.608818	100.00%	0.513599	1.403539	100.00%	0.492597	1.227754	94.44%
GFFC-1-B-L (Class Gen Feedforward)	2.631665	11.12665	29.85%	2.33251	5.953767	42.11%	3.168973	10.87653	16.67%
MLPRPC-1-B-L (Reg MLP with PCA)	0.539245	1.436432	100.00%	0.505726	1.220976	100.00%	0.450536	0.946967	100.00%
MLPCPC-1-B-L (Class MLP with PCA)	0.604741	1.112989	100.00%	0.631973	1.093975	100.00%	0.440293	0.863168	100.00%
SVM-0-N-N (Classification SVM)	0.278716	0.667789	95.52%	0.324384	0.573036	94.74%	0.326518	0.558213	100.00%
TDNN-1-B-L (Time-Delay Network)	0.341169	0.862838	100.00%	0.721197	1.834166	100.00%	0.531575	0.985912	100.00%
TLRN-1-B-L (Time-Lag Recurrent Network)	1.009541	1.902801	100.00%	0.707728	1.619331	100.00%	0.906855	1.618652	100.00%
RN-1-B-L (Recurrent Network)	0.378266	0.882711	100.00%	0.465783	1.180841	100.00%	0.390453	0.773721	100.00%
MLPR-2-B-L (Regression MLP)	0.310913	0.896222	100.00%	0.476074	1.445478	100.00%	0.536759	1.04037	100.00%
MLPC-2-B-L (Classification MLP)	0.276627	0.854803	100.00%	0.497293	1.247617	100.00%	0.475513	1.028863	100.00%
MLPR-1-B-R (Regression MLP)	0.287202	0.768005	100.00%	0.406402	1.018289	100.00%	0.364087	0.870826	100.00%
MLPC-1-B-R (Classification MLP)	0.258878	0.717773	100.00%	0.414439	1.198915	100.00%	0.32167	0.687884	100.00%
MLPR-2-O-M (Regression MLP)	0.320195	0.69593	100.00%	0.445851	1.09194	100.00%	0.325504	0.728061	100.00%
MLPC-2-O-M (Classification MLP)	0.665406	1.262284	100.00%	0.586722	1.249546	100.00%	0.505312	1.243577	100.00%
MLPR-2-B-R (Regression MLP)	0.232608	0.747501	100.00%	0.410747	0.847326	100.00%	0.329586	0.68689	94.44%
MLPC-2-B-R (Classification MLP)	0.266694	0.745959	100.00%	0.344822	0.973372	100.00%	0.322039	0.714744	100.00%
MLPRPC-1-O-M (Reg MLP with PCA)	0.507237	1.213724	100.00%	0.477877	1.059424	100.00%	0.578924	1.194079	100.00%
MLPCPC-1-O-M (Class MLP with PCA)	0.57946	1.458307	100.00%	0.506006	1.161451	100.00%	0.445815	1.024323	100.00%
MLPRPC-1-B-R (Reg MLP with PCA)	0.49895	1.472947	100.00%	0.481242	0.966154	100.00%	0.355227	1.320027	100.00%
MLPCPC-1-B-R (Class MLP with PCA)	0.532171	1.479628	100.00%	0.440814	0.816954	100.00%	0.453173	0.912813	100.00%
GFFR-1-O-M (Reg Gen Feedforward)	0.270117	0.819621	98.51%	0.477297	0.929855	100.00%	0.458854	1.079618	94.44%
GFFC-1-O-M (Class Gen Feedforward)	0.3695	1.101388	100.00%	0.391554	0.822629	100.00%	0.319803	0.552367	100.00%
GFFR-1-B-R (Reg Gen Feedforward)	0.26564	0.766449	100.00%	0.486714	1.097254	100.00%	0.483942	1.302634	94.44%
GFFC-1-B-R (Class Gen Feedforward)	0.319684	0.808798	100.00%	0.37662	0.783517	100.00%	0.401291	0.794602	100.00%
RBF-1-O-M (Radial Basis Function)	0.551233	1.150324	100.00%	0.542021	0.974906	100.00%	0.393073	0.868909	100.00%
RBF-1-B-R (Radial Basis Function)	0.382085	0.841063	100.00%	0.37343	0.862982	100.00%	0.420303	0.819838	100.00%
TDNN-1-O-M (Time-Delay Network)	0.193776	0.849372	100.00%	0.541533	0.976413	100.00%	0.478353	0.881796	100.00%
TDNN-1-B-R (Time-Delay Network)	0.343289	1.009517	100.00%	0.489615	1.053666	100.00%	0.542653	0.973057	100.00%
RN-1-O-M (Recurrent Network)	0.566416	1.428649	100.00%	0.602502	1.37504	100.00%	0.653149	1.362624	100.00%
RN-1-B-R (Recurrent Network)	1.002518	2.107082	80.60%	1.266936	2.103606	73.68%	0.96296	1.911124	61.11%
TLRN-1-O-M (Time-Lag Recurrent Network)	0.403019	1.071385	100.00%	0.539168	1.007768	100.00%	0.40355	0.952376	100.00%
TLRN-1-B-R (Time-Lag Recurrent Network)	0.416302	0.921486	100.00%	0.585876	1.371814	100.00%	0.400352	0.779646	100.00%

Figure 17. Performance metrics. A multilayer perceptron network (MLP) best classification results (100% for training data vs. 100% for validation data vs. 100% for testing data).

Performance Metrics

	Training	Cross Val.	Testing
# of Rows	9344	2002	2002
RMSE	0.47151	0.281644	0.321151
Correlation (r)	1.538889	0.826787	0.84907
# Correct	9344	2002	2002
# Incorrect	0	0	0
% Correct	100.00%	100.00%	100.00%

Figure 18. Performance metrics.

In medical applications, it is required to use a neuro-fuzzy hybrid system that can be fitted with a neural network that presents many advantages such as: flexibility, speed, adaptability. The structure of a hybrid system is represented in **Figure 19**:

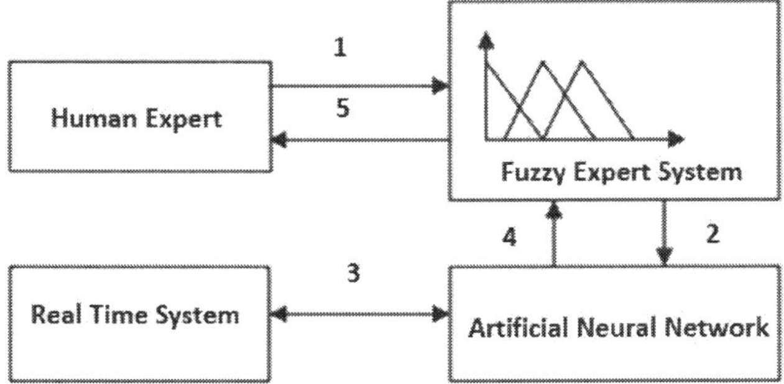

Figure 19. Hybrid neuro-fuzzy expert system [37].

The human expert knowledge is translated as symbolic (1) and is used for ANN initialization (2). The network is trained on a real inputs and outputs system (3). The knowledge obtained using ANN (4) is processed in a fuzzy manner for the determination of fuzzy rule, which are finally communicated to the human expert (5) [37]. These hybrid systems are suitable for the acquisition of knowledge and learning, and they can achieve inclusive process using weighting of the fuzzy neural network connections. Using a simple learning algorithm, such as backpropagation, neuro-fuzzy hybrid systems can identify fuzzy rules and then learn the associated functions of inferences. In summary, the hybrid system can also learn linguistic rules (fuzzy) as well as optimizing existing rules.

During generation and validation of expert system rules, we observed a positive correlation between speech disorders and eating disorders (obesity), so that a higher Body Max Index (BMI) exacerbated learning and speech difficulties in children. This is consistent with previous work demonstrating that risk of being obese in young adulthood was increased if the child had learning difficulties, scholastic proficiency below the class average, received special education, or had scholarly difficulties in childhood [38]. Therefore, our future studies will address the causal relationship between overweight, obesity, and various functions related to speech disorders and learning abilities during a longer period of time.

6. Conclusions

Each decision technique has specific advantages and drawbacks when it is used in medical field. Thus, a FES is able to make inferences with approximate data and, more importantly, it can track the decision-making process (i.e., the chain of activated rules). However, the rules must be written and, eventually, modified by human expert only. On the other hand, the artificial neural networks are the best choice when dealing with a large quantity of data and wish to obtain the related pattern but unable to provide useful information on how a specific conclusion is reached.

Due to the complementarity of expert system and artificial neural networks, several attempts to integrate these techniques have emerged. For example, combining qualitative modeling (based on fuzzy if-then rules) with quantitative modelling (used when all we have is chunks of already classified data) represents a major step forward. The hybrid neuro-fuzzy expert system is able to both learn by examples and organize knowledge and meta-knowledge in the form of fuzzy rules. For this type of system, we first fuel neural network with symbolic information and then adapt the raw model using individual examples. At the end of the process, we are able to extract symbolic information from trained neural network.

To the best of our knowledge, there are few, if any, studies based on the utilization of above-mentioned hybrid techniques in speech and language therapy of children. In this chapter, we have proposed and validated this original approach using Logomon, the first CBST for Romanian language. We have demonstrated that it is possible to use the equivalent relation between a fuzzy expert system and an artificial neural network in order to capitalize on the advantages of both techniques. The results are very encouraging and provide strong impetus to continue these studies by extending rules database and by optimizing integration between the two parts of inferential system.

Acknowledgements

These authors contributed equally to this book chapter, and the work was supported by the Romanian National Program PN-II-ID-PCE-2012–4-0608 no. 48/02.09.2013, "Analysis of novel risk factors influencing control of food intake and regulation of body weight".

Author details

Ovidiu Schipor[1], Oana Geman[2*], Iuliana Chiuchisan[3] and Mihai Covasa[2,4]

*Address all correspondence to: oana.geman@usm.ro

1 Computers Department, Integrated Center for Research, Development and Innovation in Advanced Materials Nanotechnologies, and Distributed Systems for Fabrication and Control, "Stefan cel Mare" University of Suceava, Suceava, Romania

2 Department of Health and Human Development, "Stefan cel Mare" University of Suceava, Suceava, Romania

3 Computers, Electronics and Automation Department, "Stefan cel Mare" University of Suceava, Suceava, Romania

4 Department of Basic Medical Sciences, Western University of Health Sciences, Pomona, California, USA

References

[1]   Verya E. Logopaedics Compendium. Humanitas Publisher: Bucharest, Romania; 2003.

[2]   Schipor OA, Pentiuc SG, Schipor MD. Improving computer based speech therapy using a fuzzy expert system. Computing and Informatics—Slovak Academy of Sciences. 2010; 29(2):303–318.

[3]   Schipor OA, Pentiuc SG, Schipor MD. Knowledge base of an expert system used for dyslalic children therapy. In: Proceedings of Development and Application System International Conference (DAS'08). Suceava, Romania; 2008, pp. 305–308.

[4]   Schipor MD, Pentiuc SG, Schipor OA. End-user recommendations on LOGOMON—a computer based speech therapy system for Romanian language. Advances in Electrical and Computer Engineering. 2010; 10(4):57–60.

[5]   Giza FF, Pentiuc SG, Schipor OA. Software Exercises for Children with Dyslalia. In: Proceedings of the Sixth International Scientific and Methodic Conference. Vinnytsia, Ukraine; 2008, pp. 317–326.

[6]   Schipor OA, Schipor DM, Crismariu E, Pentiuc SD. Finding key emotional states to be recognized in a computer based speech therapy system. Journal of Social and Behavioral Sciences. 2011; 30:1177–1183.

[7]   Badiru AB, Cheung JY. Fuzzy Engineering Experts Systems with Neural Network Application. John Wily & Sons: New York; 2002.

[8] Zaharia MH, Leon F. Speech therapy based on expert system. Advances in Electrical and Computer Engineering. 2009; 9(1):74–77. ISSN:1582–7445.

[9] Sikchi SS, Sikchi S, Ali MS. Design of fuzzy expert system for diagnosis of cardiac diseases. International Journal of Medical Science and Public Health. 2013; 2(1):56–61.

[10] Teodorescu HN, Zbancioc M, Voroneanu (Geman) O. Knowledge-based system applications. Performantica Publisher: Iasi; 2004, 293 p. ISBN: 973-730-014-9.

[11] Geman O. A fuzzy expert systems design for diagnosis of Parkinson's disease. In: Proceedings of the E-Health and Bioengineering Conference (EHB'11). Iasi, Romania: IEEE; 2011, pp. 122–126.

[12] Geman O. Nonlinear dynamics, artificial neural networks and neuro-fuzzy classifier for automatic assessing of tremor severity. In: Proceedings of the E-Health and Bioengineering Conference (EHB'13). Iasi, Romania: IEEE; 2013, p. 112–116.

[13] Geman O, Turcu CO, Graur A. Parkinson's disease screening tools using a fuzzy expert system. Advances in Electrical and Computer Engineering. 2013; 13(1):41–46.

[14] Geman O, Costin HN. Automatic assessing of tremor severity using nonlinear dynamics, artificial neural networks and neuro-fuzzy classifier. Advances in Electrical and Computer Engineering. 2014; 14(1):133–138.

[15] Sikchi S, Sikchi S, Ali MS. Fuzzy expert systems (FES) for medical diagnosis. International Journal of Computer Applications. 2013; 63(11):7–16. ISSN: 0975-8887.

[16] Al-Shayea QK. Artificial neural networks in medical diagnosis. IJCSI International Journal of Computer Science. 2011; 8(2):150–154. ISSN: 1694-0814.

[17] Hui C-L. Artificial Neural Networks–Application. InTech Publisher US; 2011; 586p, ISBN: 9–7895–3307–1886.

[18] Catalogna M, Cohen E, Fishman S, Halpern Z, Nevo U, Ben-Jacob E. Artificial neural networks based controller for glucose monitoring during clamp test. Plos One. 2012; 7:e44587.

[19] Fernandez de Canete J, Gonzalez-Perez S, Ramos-Diaz JC. Artificial neural networks for closed loop control of in silico and ad hoc type 1 diabetes. Computer Methods and Programs in Biomedicine. 2012; 106:55–66.

[20] Er O, Temurtas F, Tanrıkulu A. Tuberculosis disease diagnosis using artificial neural networks. Journal of Medical Systems. 2008; 34:299–302.

[21] Elveren E, Yumusak N. Tuberculosis disease diagnosis using artificial neural network trained with genetic algorithm. Journal of Medical Systems. 2011; 35:329–332.

[22] Dey P, Lamb A, Kumari S, Marwaha N. Application of an artificial neural network in the prognosis of chronic myeloid leukemia. Analytical and Quantitative Cytology and Histology. 2012; 33:335–339.

[23] Das R, Turkoglu I, Sengur A. Effective diagnosis of heart disease through neural networks ensembles. Expert Systems with Applications. 2009; 36(4):7675–7680.

[24] Higuchi K, Sato K, Makuuchi H, Furuse A, Takamoto S, Takeda H. Automated diagnosis of heart disease in patients with heart murmurs: application of a neural network technique. Journal of Medical Engineering & Technology. 2006; 30(2):61–68.

[25] Lin R. An intelligent model for liver disease diagnosis. Artificial Intelligence in Medicine. 2009; 47(1):53–62.

[26] Er O, Yumusak N, Temurtas F. Chest disease diagnosis using artificial neural networks. Expert Systems with Applications. 2010; 37(12):7648–7655.

[27] Gil D, Johnsson M, Garicia Chemizo JM, Paya AS, Fernandez DR. Application of artificial neural networks in the diagnosis of urological dysfunctions. Expert Systems with Applications. 2009; 36(3):5754–5760.

[28] Altunay S, Telatar Z, Erogul O, Aydur E. A new approach to urinary system dynamics problems: evaluation and classification of uroflowmeter signals using artificial neural networks. Expert Systems with Applications. 2009; 36(3):4891–4895.

[29] Barbosa D, Roupar D, Ramos J, Tavares A, Lima C. Automatic small bowel tumor 15 diagnosis by using multiscale wavelet based analysis in wireless capsule endoscopy 16 images. Biomed Eng Online. 2012; 17p, 11(3). doi:10.1186/1475-925X-11-3.

[30] Saghiri M, Asgar K, Boukani K, Lotfi M, Aghili H, Delvarani A, Karamifar K, Saghiri A, Mehrvarzfar P, Garcia-Godoy F. A new approach for locating the minor apical foramen using an artificial neural network. International Endodontic Journal. 2012; 45:257–265.

[31] Barwad A, Dey P, Susheilia S. Artificial neural network in diagnosis of metastatic carcinoma in effusion cytology. Cytometry Part B: Clinical Cytometry. 2012; 82:107–111.

[32] Moein S, Monadjemi SA, Moallem P. A novel fuzzy-neural based medical diagnosis system. International Journal of Biological & Medical Sciences. 2009; 4(3):146–150.

[33] Zhang G, Yan P, Zhao H, Zhang X. A computer aided diagnosis system in mammography using artificial neural networks. International Conference on BioMedical Engineering and Informatics, Sanya, China. 2008; 2:823–826. ISSN: 978–0-7695–3118–2.

[34] Amato F, Lopez A, Pena-Mendez EM, Vanhara P, Hampl A, Havel J. Artificial neural networks in medical diagnosis. Journal of Applied Biomedicine. 2013; 11:47–58.

[35] Monadjemi SA, Moallem P. Automatic diagnosis of particular diseases using a fuzzy-neural approach. International Review on Computers & Software. 2008; 3(4):406–411.

[36] Abraham A. Neuro fuzzy systems: state-of-the-art modelling techniques. In: International Work Conference on Artificial and Natural Neural Networks: Connectionist

Models of Neurons, Learning Processes and Artificial Intelligence; Granada, Spain, 2001, pp. 269–276. ISBN: 3540422358.

[37] Dosoftei C. Using computational intelligence in process management [thesis]. Romania; 2009.

[38] Lissau I, Sorensen TI. School difficulties in childhood and risk of overweight and obesity in young adulthood: a ten year prospective population study. International Journal of Obesity and Related Metabolic Disorders. 1993; 17(3):169–175.

Chapter 8

Neural Networks for Gas Turbine Diagnosis

Igor Loboda

Additional information is available at the end of the chapter

http://dx.doi.org/10.5772/63107

Abstract

The present chapter addresses the problems of gas turbine gas path diagnostics solved using artificial neural networks. As a very complex and expensive mechanical system, a gas turbine should be effectively monitored and diagnosed. Being universal and powerful approximation and classification techniques, neural networks have become widespread in gas turbine health monitoring over the past few years. Applications of such networks as a multilayer perceptron, radial basis network, probabilistic neural network, and support vector network were reported. However, there is a lack of manuals that summarize neural network applications for gas turbine diagnosis.

A monitoring system comprises many elements, and many factors influence the final diagnostic accuracy. The present chapter generalizes our investigations that are devoted to the enhancement of this system by choosing the best option for each element. In these investigations, a diagnostic process is simulated on the basis of neural networks, and we focus on reaching the highest accuracy by choosing the best network and its optimal tuning to the issue to solve. Thus, helping with enhancement of a whole monitoring system, neural networks themselves are objects of investigation and optimization. As a result of the conducted investigations, the chapter provides the recommendations on choosing and tailoring the network for a particular diagnostic task.

Keywords: gas turbines, gas path diagnosis, fault classification, pattern recognition, artificial neural networks

1. Introduction

As complex and expensive mechanical systems, gas turbine engines benefit a lot from the application of advanced diagnostic technologies, and the use of monitoring systems has

© 2016 The Author(s). Licensee InTech. This chapter is distributed under the terms of the Creative Commons Attribution License (http://creativecommons.org/licenses/by/3.0), which permits unrestricted use, distribution, and reproduction in any medium, provided the original work is properly cited.

become a standard practice. To perform effective analysis, there are different diagnostic approaches that cover all gas turbine subsystems. The diagnostic algorithms based on measured gas path variables are considered as principal and pretty complex. These variables (air and gas pressures and temperatures, rotation speeds, fuel consumption, etc.) carry valuable information about an engine's health condition and allow to detect and identify different engine abrupt faults and deterioration mechanisms (for instance, foreign object damage, fouling, erosion, tip ribs, and seal wear). Malfunctions of measurement and control systems can be diagnosed as well. Thousands of technical publications devoting to the gas path diagnosis can be found. They can be arranged according to input information and mathematical models applied.

Although advancement of instrumentation and computer science has enabled extensive field data collection, the data with gas turbine faults are still infrequent because real faults rarely appear. Some intensive and practically permanent deterioration mechanisms, for example, compressor fouling, allow their describing on the basis of real data. However, to describe the variety of all possible faults, mathematical models are widely used. These models and the diagnostic methods that use them fall into two main categories: physics-based and data-driven.

A thermodynamic engine model is a representative physics-based model. This nonlinear model is based on thermodynamic relations between gas path variables. It also employs mass, energy, and momentum conservation laws. Such a sophisticated model has been used in gas turbine diagnostics since the work of Saravanamuttoo H.I.H. (see, e.g., [1]). The model allows to simulate the gas path variables for an engine baseline (healthy engine performance) and for different faults embedded into the model through special internal coefficients called fault parameters. Applying system identification methods to the thermodynamic model, an inverse problem is solved: Unknown fault parameters are estimated using measured gas path variables. During the identification, such parameters are found that minimize the difference between the model variables and the measured ones. Besides the better model accuracy, the simplification of the diagnosing process is reached because the fault parameter estimates contain information of current engine health. The diagnostic algorithms based on the model identification constitute one of two main approaches in gas turbine diagnostics (see, for instance, [1–4]).

The second approach uses a pattern recognition theory. Since model inaccuracy and measurement errors impede a correct diagnosis, gas path fault localization can be characterized as a challenging recognition issue. Numerous applications of recognition tools in gas path diagnostics are known, for instance, genetic algorithms [5], correspondence and discrimination analysis [6], k-nearest neighbor [7], and Bayesian approach [8]. However, the most widespread techniques are artificial neural networks (ANNs). The ANNs applications are not limited by the fault recognition, they are also applied or can be applied at other diagnostic stages: feature extraction, fault detection, and fault prediction.

At the feature extraction stage, differences (a.k.a. deviations) between actual gas path measurements and an engine baseline are determined because they are by far better indicators of engine health than the measurements themselves are. To build the necessary baseline model, the multilayer perceptron (MLP), also called a back-propagation network, is usually employed [9, 10]. To filter noise, an auto-associative configuration of the perceptron is sometimes applied to the measurements [11].

At the fault localization stage, fault classes can be presented by sets of the deviations (patterns) induced by the corresponding faults. Such a pattern-based classification allows to apply the ANNs as recognition techniques, and multiple applications of the MLP (see, e.g., [4, 5]) as well as the radial basis network (RBN) [5], the probabilistic neural network (PNN) [12, 13], and support vector machines (SVM) a.k.a. Support vector network (SVN) [7, 12] were reported. In spite of many publications on gas turbine fault recognition, comparative studies, which allow to choose the best technique [4, 5, 7, 12], are still insufficient. They do not cover all of the used techniques and often provide differing recommendations.

The fault detection stage can also be presented as a pattern recognition problem with two classes to recognize: a class of healthy engines and a class of faulty engines. If the classification for the fault localization stage is available, it does not seem a challenge to use the patterns of this classification for building the fault detection classification. However, the studies applying recognition techniques, in particular the ANNs, for gas turbine fault detection are absent so far. Instead, the detection problem is solved by tolerance monitoring [14, 15].

The fault prediction stage is less investigated than the previous stages, and only few ANNs applications are known. Among them, it is worth to mention book [16] analyzing the ways to predict gas turbine faults and study [17], comparing a recurrent neural network and a nonlinear auto-regressive neural network. We can see that in total for all stages, the perceptron is by far the highest demand network. It is used for filtering the measurements, approximating the engine baseline, and recognizing the faults.

Thus, a brief observation of the neural networks applied for gas turbine diagnosis has revealed that the multiple known cases of their use need better generalization and recommendations to choose the best network. The areas of promising ANNs application were also found. In the present chapter, we generalize our investigations aimed at the optimization of a total diagnostic process through the enhancement of each of its elements. On the one hand, the neural networks help with process realization being its critical elements. On the other hand, the networks themselves are objects of analysis: For known applications, they are compared to choose the best network, and one new application is proposed. During the investigations, the rules of proper network usage have also been established.

The rest of the chapter describes these investigations and is structured as follows: description of the networks used (Section 2), network-based diagnostic approach (Section 3), diagnostic process optimization (Section 4), feature extraction stage optimization (Section 5), fault detection stage optimization (Section 6), and fault localization stage optimization (Section 7).

2. Artificial neural networks

The four networks mentioned in the introduction have been chosen for investigations: MLP, RBN, PNN, and SVN. The PNN is a realization of the Parzon Windows and has the important property of probabilistic outputs, that is, the gas turbine faults are recognized on the basis of their confidence probabilities. These probabilities are computed through numerical estimates of probability density of fault patterns. For the purpose of comparison, a similar recognition tool, the K-nearest neighbor (K-NN) method has been involved into the investigations. Foundations of the chosen techniques can be found in many books on classification theory, for example, in [18, 19, 20]. The next subsections include only a brief description of techniques required to better understand the present chapter.

2.1. Multilayer perceptron

The perceptron can solve either approximation or classification issues. The scheme shown in **Figure 1** illustrates structure and operation of the MLP [18, 19]. We can see that the perceptron presents a feed-forward neural network in which no feedback is observed, and all signals go only from the input to the output.

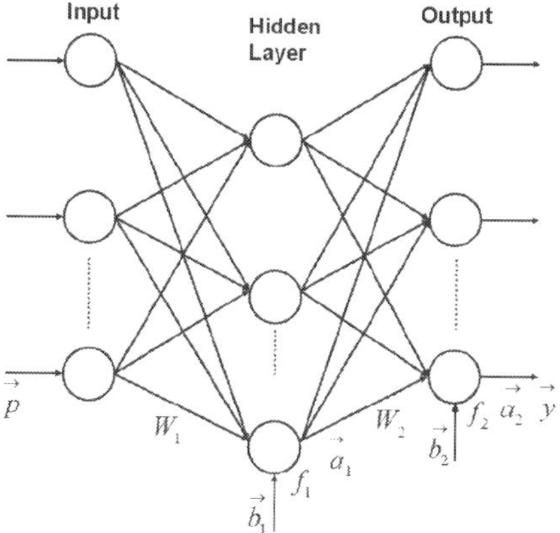

Figure 1. Multilayer perceptron.

To determine a hidden layer input vector, the product of a weight matrix W_1 and a network input vector (pattern) $\vec{p}$ is summed with a bias vector $\vec{b_1}$. A hidden layer transfer function f_1 transforms this vector in an output vector $\vec{a_1}$. A network output $\vec{a_2}$ is computed similarly considering the vector $\vec{a}_1$ as an input. In this way, perceptron operation can be expressed by $\vec{y} = \vec{a_2} = f_2\left\{W_2 f_1(W_1 \vec{p} + \vec{b_1}) + \vec{b_2}\right\}$. When we apply the MLP to classify patterns, elements of the vector $\vec{a_2}$ show how close the pattern $\vec{p}$ is to the corresponding classes. The nearest class is chosen as a class to which the pattern belongs, and such classifying can be considered as deterministic.

To find unknown matrixes W_1 and W_2 and vectors $\vec{b}_1$ and $\vec{b}_2$, a back-propagation learning algorithm distributes a network output error on these unknown quantities. In every learning iteration (epoch), they vary in the direction of error reduction. The iterations continue unless the minimum error has been reached. This algorithm requires differentiable transfer functions, and a sigmoid type is commonly used.

2.2. Radial basis network

Figure 2 illustrates operation of an RBN. It includes two layers: a hidden radial basis layer and an output linear layer. Operation of radial basis neurons is different from the perceptron neurons operation [18, 19, 20]. The neuron's input n is formed as the Euclidean norm $\|\|$ of a difference between a pattern vector $\vec{p}$ and a weight vector $\vec{w}$, multiplied by a scalar b (bias). In this way, $n = \|\vec{w} - \vec{p}\|b$. Using this input, a radial basis transfer function determines an output $a = \exp(-n^2)$. Where there is no distance between the vectors, the function has the maximum value $a=1$, and the function decreases when the distance increases. The bias b allows changing the neuron sensitivity. The output layer transforms the radial basis output $\vec{a}_1$ to a network output $\vec{a}_2$. Operation of this layer does not differ from the operation of a perceptron layer with a linear transfer function. The radial basis layer usually needs more neurons than a comparable perceptron hidden layer because the radial basis neuron covers a smaller region compared with the sigmoid neuron.

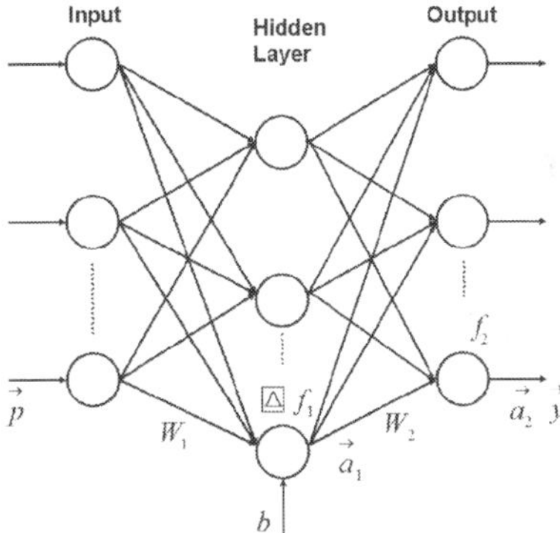

Figure 2. Radial basis network.

2.3. Probabilistic neural networks

The PNN is a specific variation of radial basis network [18]. It is used to solve classification problems. **Figure 3** presents the scheme of this network and helps to understand its operation. Like the RBN, the probabilistic neural network has two layers.

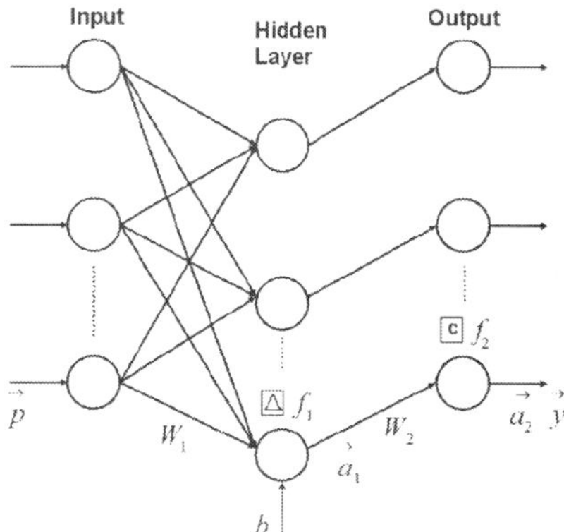

Figure 3. Probabilistic neural network.

The hidden layer is formed and operates just like the same layer of the RBN. It is built from learning patterns united in a matrix W_1. Elements of an output vector $\vec{a}_1$ indicate how close the input pattern is to the learning patterns.

The output or classification layer differs from the RBN output layer. Each class has its output neuron that sums the radial basis outputs a_j corresponding to the class patterns. To this end, a weight matrix W_2 formed by 0- and 1-elements is employed. A vector $W_2\vec{a}_1$ contains probabilities of all classes. A transfer function f_2 finally chooses the class with the largest probability. In this way, the probabilistic network classifies input patterns using a probabilistic measure that is more realistic than the perceptron classifying. The PNN is the most used realization of a Parzen Windows (PW) [18], a nonparametric method that estimates probability density in a given point (pattern) $\vec{Z}$ using the nearby learning patterns.

2.4. k-Nearest neighbors

Like the Parzen Windows (PNNs), the k-nearest neighbors is a nonparametric technique [18]. For a given class and point (pattern) $\vec{p}$, it counts the number k of class patterns in a nearby region of volume V and estimates the necessary probability density in accordance with a simple formula

$$\rho = \frac{k/n}{V} \tag{1}$$

where n stands for a total number of class patterns.

To ensure the convergence of the estimate ϱ, we need to satisfy the following requirements

$$\lim_{n\to\infty} V = 0; \lim_{n\to\infty} k = \infty; \lim_{n\to\infty} k/n = 0. \tag{2}$$

To this end, we increase n and can let V be proportional to $1/\sqrt{n}$.

In contrast to the Parzen Window method that fixes the volume V and looks for the number k, the K-nearest neighbor method specifies k and seeks for the sphere of volume V. Since the PW uses constant window size, it may not capture patterns when the actual density is low. The density estimate will be equal to zero, and the classification decision confidence will be underestimated. A solution to this problem is to use the window that depends on learning data. Using this principle, the K-NN increases a spherical window individually for each class until k patterns (nearest neighbors) fall into the window. A sphere radius will change class by class. The greater the radius is, the lower probability density estimate will be according to Eq. (1).

2.5. Support vector network

Any hyperplane can be written in the space R^P as the set of points $\vec{p}$ satisfying:

$$\vec{p}^T \vec{w} + b = 0 \tag{3}$$

where $\vec{w}$ is a vector perpendicular to the hyperplane and b is the bias. Let us present learning data of two classes as pattern vectors $\vec{p}_i \in R^P, i = 1, N$ and their corresponding labels $y_i \in (-1, 1)$, indicating the class to which the pattern $\vec{p}$ belongs.

If the learning data are linearly separable, two parallel hyperplanes without points between them can be built to divide the data. The hyperplanes can be given by $\vec{w}^T \vec{p}_i + b = 1$ and $\vec{w}^T \vec{p}_i + b = -1$. The margin is defined to be the distance between them and is equal to $2/\|\vec{w}\|$ (**Figure 4**). Intuitively, it measures how good the separation between the two classes is. The points divided in this manner satisfy the following constraint:

$$y_i(\vec{w}^T \vec{p}_i + b) \geq 1 \tag{4}$$

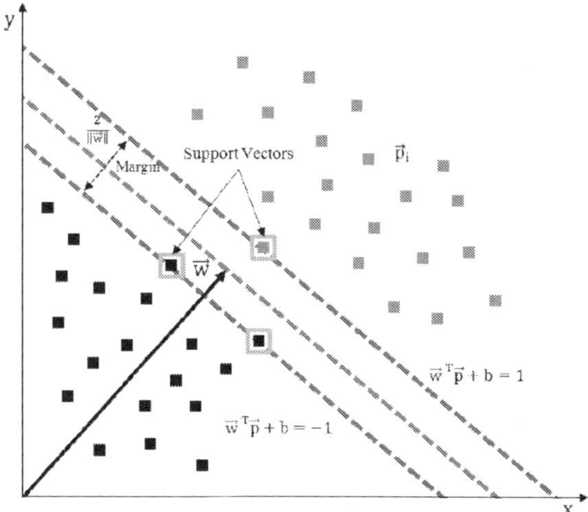

Figure 4. SVN: hyperplanes and separation margin.

The objective of the SVN is to find the hyperplanes that produce the maximal margin or minimum vector $\vec{w}$ [19, 20]. In this way, SVN needs to solve the following primal optimization problem:

$$\min \frac{1}{2}\vec{w}^T\vec{w} \tag{5}$$

subject to $y_i(\vec{w}^T\vec{p}_i + b) \geq 1$, for $i = 1, ..., N$

Introducing the Karush-Kuhn-Tucker (KKT) multipliers $\alpha_i \geq 0$, objective function (5) can be transformed to:

$$\min_{w,b} \max_{\alpha} \frac{1}{2}\vec{w}^T\vec{w} - \sum_{i-1}^{N}\alpha_i(y_i(\vec{w}^T\vec{p}_i + b) - 1) \tag{6}$$

As can be seen, expression (6) is a function of $\vec{w}$, b, and α. This function can be transformed into the dual form:

$$L = \min_{\alpha} \frac{1}{2}\sum_{i=1}^{N}\sum_{j=1}^{N}y_i y_j \alpha_i \alpha_j \vec{p}_i^T \vec{p}_j - \sum_{i=1}^{N}\alpha_i \tag{7}$$

subject to $\alpha_i \geq 0$ and $\sum_{i=1}^{N} \alpha_i y_i = 0$ for i = 1, ..., N

It can be also expressed as:

$$L = \min_{\alpha} \frac{1}{2} \vec{\alpha}^T \, Q \vec{\alpha} - 1^T \vec{\alpha} \tag{8}$$

where **Q** is the matrix of quadratic coefficients. This expression is minimized now only as a function of $\vec{\alpha}$, and the solution is found by Quadratic Programming.

In SVM classification problems, a complete separation is not always possible, and a flexible margin is suggested in reference [21] that allows misclassification errors while tries to maximize the distance between the nearest fully separable points. The other way to split not separable classes is to use nonlinear functions as proposed in reference [22]. Among them, radial basis functions are recommended [23].

SVMs were originally intended for binary models; however, they can now address multi-class problems using the One-Versus-All and One-Versus-One strategies.

A gas turbine diagnostic process using the techniques above described is simulated according to the following approach.

3. Neural networks-based diagnostic approach

The approach described corresponds to the diagnostic stages of feature extraction and fault localization and embraces the steps of fault simulation, feature extraction, fault classification formation, making a recognition decision, and recognition accuracy estimation.

3.1. Fault simulation

Within the scope of this chapter, faults of engine components (compressor, turbine, combustor, etc.) are simulated by means of a nonlinear gas turbine thermodynamic model

$$\vec{Y}(\vec{U}, \vec{\Theta}) \tag{9}$$

The model determines monitored variables $\vec{Y}$ as a function of steady-state operating conditions $\vec{U}$ and engine health parameters $\vec{\Theta} = \vec{\Theta}_0 + \Delta\vec{\Theta}$. Each component is presented in the model by its performance map. Nominal values $\vec{\Theta}_0$ correspond to a healthy engine, whereas fault parameters $\Delta\vec{\Theta}$ imitate fault influence by shifting the component maps.

3.2. Feature extraction

Although gas turbine monitored variables are affected by engine deterioration, the influence of the operating conditions is much more significant. To extract diagnostic information from raw measured data, a deviation (fault feature) is computed for each monitored variable as a difference between the actual and baseline values. With the thermodynamic model, the deviations Z_i i=1,m induced by the fault parameters are calculated for all m monitored variables according to the following expression

$$Z_i = \left(\frac{Y_i\left(\vec{U},\vec{\Theta}_0 + \Delta\vec{\Theta}\right) - Y_{0i}\left(\vec{U},\vec{\Theta}_0\right)}{Y_{0i}\left(\vec{U},\vec{\Theta}_0\right)} + \varepsilon_i \right)/a_i \tag{10}$$

A random error ε_i makes the deviation more realistic. A parameter a_i normalizes the deviation errors, resulting that they will be localized within the interval $[-1, 1]$ for all monitored variables. Such normalization simplifies fault class description.

Deviations of the monitored variables united in an (m×1) deviation vector $\vec{Z}$ (feature vector) form a diagnostic space. Every vector $\vec{Z}$ presents a point in this space and is a pattern to be recognized.

3.3. Fault classification formation

Numerous gas turbine faults are divided into a limited number q of classes $D_1, D_2, ..., D_q$. In the present chapter, each class corresponds to varying severity faults of one engine component. The class is described by component's fault parameters $\Delta\Theta_j$. Two types of fault classes are considered. The variation of one fault parameter results in a single fault class, while independent variation of two parameters of one gas turbine component allows to form a class of multiple faults.

To form one class, many patterns are computed by expression (10). The required parameters $\Delta\Theta_j$ and ε_i are randomly generated using the uniform and Gaussian distributions correspondingly. To ensure high computational precision, each class is typically composed from 1000 patterns. A learning set **Z1** uniting patterns of all classes presents a whole pattern-based fault classification. **Figure 5** illustrates such a classification by presenting four single fault classes in the diagnostic space of three deviations.

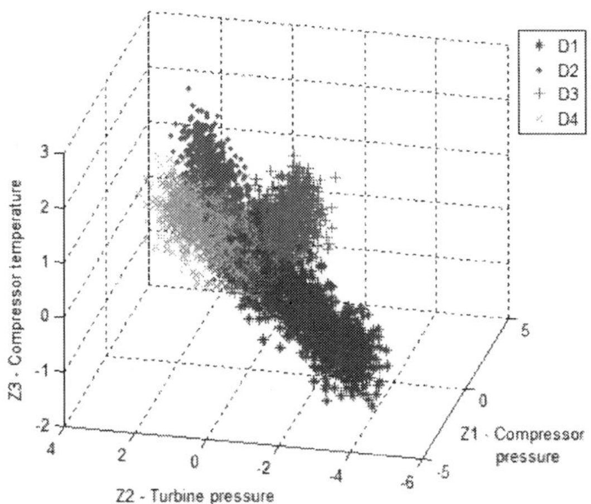

Figure 5. Pattern-based fault classification.

3.4. Making a fault recognition decision

In addition to the given (observed) pattern $\vec{Z}$ and the constructed fault classification **Z1**, a classification technique (one of the chosen networks) is an integral part of a whole diagnostic process. To apply and test the classification techniques, a validation set **Z2** is also created in the same way as set **Z1**. The difference between the sets consists in other random numbers that are generated within the same distributions.

3.5. Recognition accuracy estimation

It is of practical interest to know recognition accuracy averaged for each fault class and a whole engine. To this end, the classification technique is consequently applied to the patterns of set **Z2** producing diagnoses d_l. Since true fault classes D_j are also known, probabilities of correct diagnosis (true positive rates) $P(d_j/D_j)$ can be calculated for all classes resulting in a probability vector $\vec{P}$. A mean number $\overline{P}$ of these probabilities characterizes accuracy of engine diagnosis by the applied technique. In this chapter, the probability $\overline{P}$ is employed as a criterion to compare the techniques described in Section 2.

4. Optimization of the neural networks-based diagnostic process

The structure and efficiency of a diagnostic algorithm depend on many factors and the options that can be chosen for each factor. The classification of these factors and options is given in

Figure 6, where the factors are shown in the first line. On the basis of accumulated knowledge and experience, every research center (even a single researcher) chooses an appropriate option for each factor and develops its own diagnostic algorithm. To be optimal, this algorithm should take into account all peculiarities of a given engine, its application, and other diagnostic conditions. Thus, it is not likely that the algorithm be optimal for other engines and applications. As a result, every monitoring system needs an appropriate diagnostic algorithm.

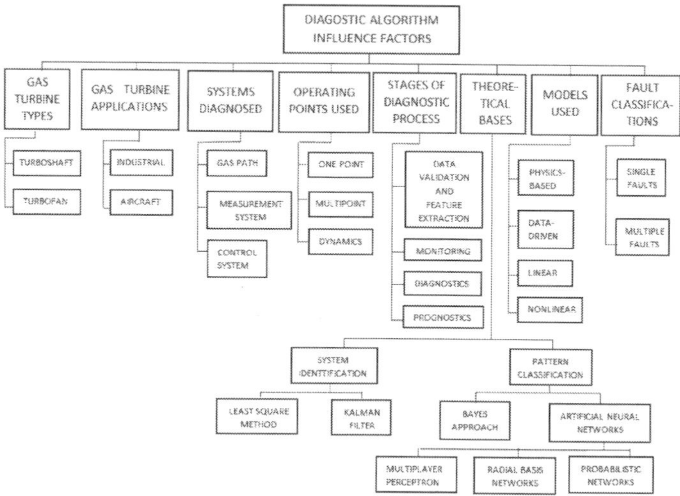

Figure 6. Factors that influence structure and efficiency of gas path diagnostic algorithms.

Thus, comparing complete diagnostic algorithms does not seem to be useful. Instead, comparing options for each above factor and choosing the best option are proposed. When options of one factor are compared, the other factors (comparison conditions) are fixed forming a comparison case. To draw sound conclusions about the best option, the comparison should be repeated for many comparison cases. To form these cases, each comparison condition varies independently according to the theory of the design of experiments. Since every new condition drastically increases the volume of comparative calculations, the most significant conditions are considered first.

To perform the comparative calculations, a test procedure based on the above-described approach has been developed in Matlab (MathWorks, Inc.). For each compared option, the procedure executes numerous cycles of gas turbine fault diagnosis by the chosen technique and finally computes a diagnosis reliability indicator, which is used as a comparison criterion.

Three gas turbine engines (Engine 1, Engine 2, and Engine 3) of different construction and application have been chosen as test cases. Engine 1 and Engine 2 are free turbine power plants. Engine 1 is a natural gas compressor driver; it is presented in the investigations by its thermodynamic model and field data recorded. Engine 2 is intended for electricity production and is given by field data. Engine 3 is a three-spool turbofan for a transport aircraft; its thermody-namic model is used. The field data called hourly snapshots present filtered and averaged steady-state values recorded every hour during about one year of operation of Engine 1 and Engine 2. Since the data include periods of compressor fouling and points of washing, they are very suitable for testing diagnostic techniques.

Using the network-based approach described in Section 3 and the information about the test case engines, many investigations have been conducted to improve the diagnostic process at the stages of feature extraction, fault detection, and fault localization. The results achieved for the feature extraction stage are described in the next section.

5. Feature extraction stage optimization

As stated in Section 3, the deviations are useful diagnostic features. Although the thermody-namic model can be used as a baseline model for computing the deviations, it is too complex for real monitoring systems and has intrinsic inaccuracy. As mentioned in the introduction, to build a simple and fast data-driven baseline model, only neural networks, in particular the MLP, are applied. On the other hand, in the previous studies we successfully used a polynomial type baseline model. It was therefore decided [24] to verify whether the application of such a powerful approximator as the MLP instead of polynomials yields higher adequacy of the baseline model and better quality of the corresponding deviations.

Given a measured value Y_i^* and data-driven baseline model $\vec{Y}_0(\vec{U})$, the deviation is written as

$$\delta Y_i^* = \frac{Y_i^* - Y_{0i}(\vec{U})}{Y_{0i}(\vec{U})} \tag{11}$$

For one monitored variable, a complete second-order polynomial function of four arguments (operating conditions) is written as

$$Y_0(\vec{U}) = a_0 + a_1 u_1 + a_2 u_2 + a_3 u_3 + a_4 u_4 + a_5 u_1 u_2 + a_6 u_1 u_3 + a_7 u_1 u_4 + $$
$$a_8 u_2 u_3 + a_9 u_2 u_4 + a_{10} u_3 u_4 + a_{11} u_1^2 + a_{12} u_2^2 + a_{13} u_3^2 + a_{14} u_4^2 \tag{12}$$

For all m monitored variables and measurements at n operating points, equation (12) is transformed to a linear system $\mathbf{Y}=\mathbf{VA}$ with matrixes $\mathbf{Y}$ ($n \times m$) and $\mathbf{V}$ ($n \times k$) formed from these data, where $k=15$ is number of coefficients. To enhance coefficient estimates (matrix $\mathbf{A}$), great volume of input data ($n \gg k$) is involved and the least-squares method is applied.

As to the perceptron, its typical input is formed by four operating conditions, and the output consists of seven monitored variables. Hidden layer size determines a network's capability to approximate complex functions and varies in calculations. As a result of MLP tuning, we chose 12 nodes at this layer. Thus, the perceptron structure is written as 4×12×7. Since the MLP has tan-sigmoid transfer functions, and the output varies within the interval (−1, 1), all monitored quantities are normalized.

Many cases of comparison on the simulated and real data of Engines 1 and 2 were analyzed. The MLP was sometimes more accurate at the learning step. At the validation step, the deviations computed with the MLP had a little worse accuracy for Engine 1. For Engine 2, the best MLP validation results are illustrated in **Figure 7** . As can be seen here, both polynomial deviations dTtp and network deviations dTtn reflect the fouling and washing effects equally well. However, in many other cases the polynomials outperformed. Why does the network approximate well a learning set and frequently fail on a validation set? The answer seems to be evident because of an overlearning (overfitting) effect. Due to a greater flexibility, the network begins to follow data peculiarities induced by measurement errors in the learning set and describes worse a gas turbine baseline performance for the validation set.

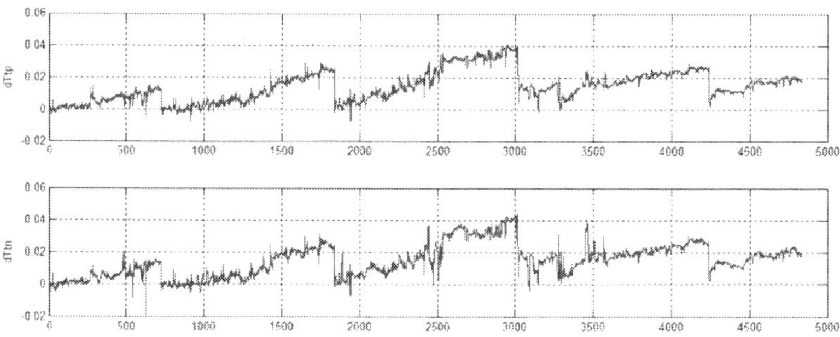

Figure 7. EGT deviations computed on the Engine 2 real data validation set (dTtn—network-based deviation; dTtp—polynomial-based deviation).

Although the MLP as a powerful approximation technique promised better gas turbine performance description, the results of the comparison have been somewhat surprising. No manifestations of network superiority were detected. When comparing these techniques, it is also necessary to take into consideration that an MLP learning procedure is more complex because it is numerical in contrast to an analytical solution for polynomials. Thus, a polynomial baseline model can be successfully used in real monitoring systems along with neural networks. At least, it seems to be true for simple cycle gas turbines with gradually changed performance, like the turbines considered in this chapter.

6. Fault detection stage optimization

As mentioned in the Introduction, the fault detection is actually based on tolerances (thresholds). However, it seems reasonable to present it as a pattern recognition problem like we do at the fault recognition stage. Classification $D_1, D_2, ..., D_q$ created for the purpose of fault localization and presented in **Figure 5** corresponds to a hypothetical fleet of engines with different faults of variable severity. To form the classification for fault detection, we can reasonably accept that the engine fleet and the distributions of faults are the same. Paper [25] explains how to use patterns of the existing classification $D_1, D_2, ..., D_q$ for two new classes of healthy and faulty engines. The boundary between these classes corresponds to maximal error of the normalized deviations and is determined as a sphere of radius $R = 1$. The patterns, for which a vector of true deviations (without errors) is situated inside the sphere, form the healthy engine class; the others create the faulty engine class. It is clear that the patterns (deviation vectors with noise) of these two classes are partly intersected, resulting in α- and β-errors during the detection. **Figure 8** illustrates the new classification; the intersection is clearly seen. Two variations of the new classification based on single and multiple original classes have been prepared.

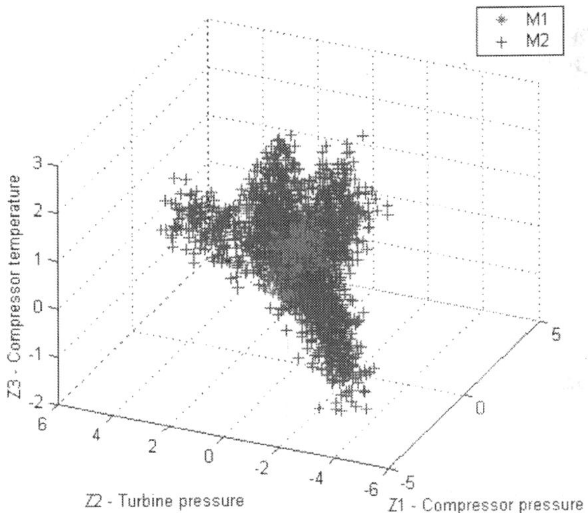

Figure 8. Patterns-based classification for monitoring.

Since new patterns-based classification (learning and testing sets) is ready, we can use any recognition technique to perform fault detection, and the MLP has been selected once more. It conserved sigmoid transfer functions and the hidden layer size of 12. Given that a threshold-based approach, which classifies pattern vectors according to their length, is traditionally used in fault detection, the algorithm with a distance measure (r-criterion) was also developed and compared with the MLP. Since the consequences of α- and β-errors are quite different (α-error is always considered as more dangerous), reduced losses $\bar{c} = P_\beta + \dfrac{c_\alpha}{c_\beta} P_\alpha$ were introduced to quantify monitoring effectiveness, where P_α and P_β are probabilities of α- and β-errors, c_α and c_β denote the corresponding losses, and $\dfrac{c_\alpha}{c_\beta}$ are equal to 10.

Figure 9 shows the plots of the reduced losses versus the radius r. For the MLP the change of r was simulated by the corresponding change of the boundary radius R during pattern separation in the learning set. It can be seen that the introduction of an additional threshold r, which is different from the boundary, reduces monitoring errors for both techniques. The best results correspond to the minimums of the curves. By comparing them, we can conclude that the network (MLP) provides better results for single classes, and the techniques are equal for multiple classes. In general for all comparison cases, the MLP slightly outperforms the r-criterion-based technique. Thus, the perceptron can be successfully applied for real gas turbine fault detection.

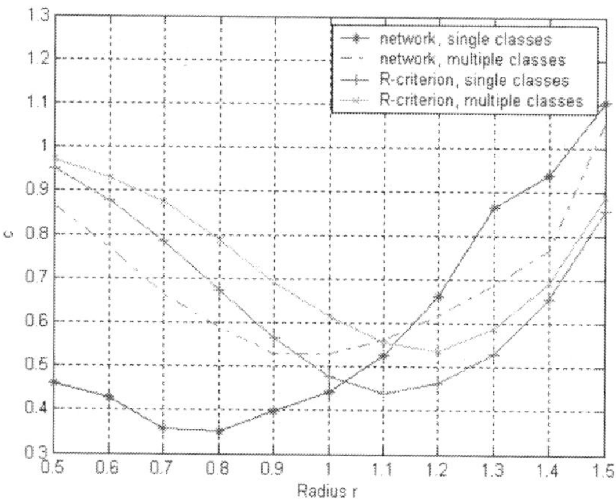

Figure 9. Reduced losses due to monitoring errors versus the threshold radius r.

7. Fault localization stage optimization

To draw sound conclusions about the ANN applicability for gas turbine fault localization, the comparison of the chosen networks was repeated for many comparison cases formed by independent variation of the main influencing factors: engines, operating modes, simulated or real information, and class types. In this way not only the best network is chosen but also the influence of these factors on diagnosis results is determined helping with the optimization of a total diagnostic process. For the purpose of correct comparison, the networks were tailored to a concrete task to solve.

7.1. Neural network tuning

We started to use ANNs applications and their tuning with the MLP [26]. The numbers of monitored variables and fault classes unambiguously determine the size of input and output layers of this network. As to the hidden layer, the number of 12 nodes was estimated as optimal using the probability $\overline{P}$ as a criterion. To choose a proper back-propagation algorithm, 12 variations were compared by accuracy and execution time. The resilient back-propagation ("rp"-algorithm) provided the best results and has been chosen. It was also found that 200 batch mode training epochs are sufficient for good learning; however, a learning stop by an Early Stopping Option may be useful as well.

Figure 10 illustrates other example of the tuning. Averaged probabilities computed for the PNN are plotted here against spread b, unique PNN tuning parameter. To determine this probability that has high precision of about ±0.001, calculations of $\overline{P}$ were repeated 100 times for each spread value, each time with a different seed (quantity that determines a consequence of random numbers), and an average value was computed. Such computations to find the best value b were repeated for two operating modes of Engine 1 and for two fault class types. It can be seen in the figure that the highest values of probability $\overline{P}_{av}$ does not depend on operating mode. These values are $b=0.35$ for the single fault type and $b=0.40$ for the multiple one.

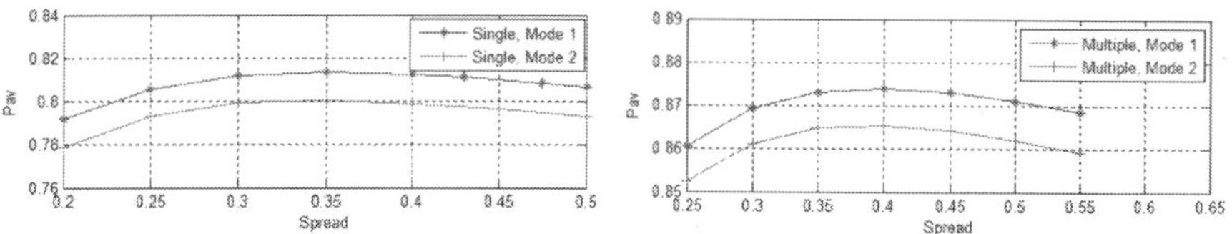

Figure 10. Probabilities versus spread parameter.

For all networks, the value 1000 simulated patterns per fault class has been selected as tradeoff between the required computer resources and the accuracy of the probabilities $\overline{P}$ and $\overline{P}_{av}$.

It is worth mentioning that the networks tuning is very time consuming. A tuning time can occupy up to 80% of a total investigation time, leaving 20% for the calculations related to final learning and validation of the networks.

7.2. Neural network comparison

The comparison of three tuned networks: MLP, RBN, and PNN, was firstly performed in reference [27], then the SVN was also evaluated. The variations of comparison conditions embraced independent changes of two engines, two operating modes, and two classification variations. The resulting probabilities $\overline{P}_{av}$ are given in **Table 1**. We can see that all networks are practically equal in accuracy for all comparison cases.

Paper [28] provides some additional results extending the comparison on the K-NN technique. The data given in **Table 2** confirm the conclusion about equal performances, now for five different techniques.

Class type	ANN	Engine 1		Engine 3	
		Mode 1	Mode 2	Mode 1	Mode 2
Single	MLP	0.8184	0.8059	0.7338	0.7470
	RBN	0.8186	0.8058	0.7349	0.7485
	PNN	0.8134	0.8004	0.7287	0.7456
	SVN	0.8190	0.8064	-	-
Multiple	MLP	0.8765	0.8686	0.7749	0.7596
	RBN	0.8783	0.8701	0.7787	0.7643
	PNN	0.8739	0.8653	0.7730	0.7617
	SVN	0.8770	0.8698	-	-

Table 1. Results of the network comparison (probabilities computed for Engine 1 and Engine 3).

Technique	Class type	
	Single	Multiple
PNN	0.8134	0.8739
K-NN	0.8154	0.8735
MLP	0.8193	0.8765

Table 2. Additional results of the technique comparison (probabilities for Engine 1).

The PNN and K-NN have probabilistic output, and every pattern recognition decision is accompanied with a confidence probability. This is an important advantage for gas turbine diagnosticians and maintenance staff. It can be taken into account for choosing the best technique when mean diagnosis reliability $\bar{P}$ is equal for all techniques considered. The PNN and K-NN are nonparametric techniques that estimate a probability density for each fault class by counting the patterns that fall into a given volume (window). To accurately estimate the probability density in a multidimensional diagnostic space, the number 1000 of available patterns can be insufficient. To assess possible imprecision of the density and confidence probability estimation by the PNN and K-NN techniques, a more precise analytical density estimation (ADE) technique has been proposed and developed [28]. It analytically determines the density and is employed as a reference to assess imprecision of the PNN and K-NN. To verify the newly developed technique, it was firstly compared with the others by the criterion $\bar{P}_{av}$. The results were reasonably good: the performances of all the techniques remained very close, but the ADE had the highest probability with the increment of 0.366–0.771 relatively the others.

The results of comparison by the estimated confidence probability are illustrated in **Figure 11** , when the PNN, K-NN, and MLP errors are plotted for 100 patterns. One can see that the bias and scatter for the K-NN estimates are by far greater. As to the MLP outputs, these non-probabilistic quantities look by far more precise than the K-NN probability estimates and seem to have the same precision level as the PW-PNN estimates.

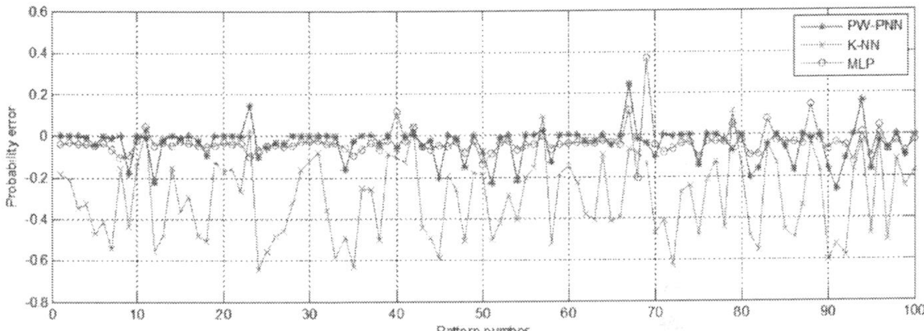

Figure 11. Errors of probability estimation by PW-PNN, K-NN, and MPL techniques (Engine 1, first 100 patterns of the first single fault class).

Table 3 presents the mean estimations errors for the case of the single fault classification. The table data confirm the above conclusion on the compared techniques: The bias and standard deviation of the K-NN errors are by far greater. The table also shows that on average the MLP outputs are even more exact than the PNN probabilities. It is one more argument to apply the perceptron in real gas turbine monitoring systems.

Bias			σ		
PNN	K-NN	MLP	PW-PNN	K-NN	MLP
-0.0444	-0.3293	-0.0419	0.0845	0.2020	0.0791

Table 3. Mean errors of confidence probability estimation (Engine 1, single fault classification).

7.3. Fault classification extension

In the investigations previously described, only two rigid classifications were maintained: one formed by single fault classes and the other constituted from multiple fault classes created by two fault parameters. However, the classification can vary a lot in practice even for the same engine, and it is difficult to predict what classification variation will be finally used in a real monitoring system. To verify and additionally compare the networks for different classification variations, the test procedure was modified for easily creating any new fault classification, more complex and more realistic than the classifications previously analyzed.

Twelve classification variations have been prepared and three networks: MLP, RBN, and PNN, were examined in reference [29]. These classifications have from 4 to 18 gas path and sensor fault classes, 1 to 4 fault parameters to form each class, positive and negative fault parameter changes. All the networks operated successfully for all fault classifications. **Table 4** shows the resulting averaged probabilities of correct diagnosis. Analyzing them, one can state that the differences between the networks within the same classification remain not great (except variation 6), about 0.015 (1.5%), while the difference between the variations can reach the value 0.10. Thus, these results reaffirm once more the conclusion drawn before that many recognition techniques may yield the same gas turbine diagnosis accuracy.

Variation	MLP	RBN	PNN
1	0.8172	0.8169	0.8099
2	0.8732	0.8759	0.8720
3	0.8091	0.8072	0.8037
4	0.8490	0.8524	0.8474
5	0.8033	0.8080	0.8036
6	0.6805	0.7319	0.7316
7	0.7362	0.7616	0.7567
8	0.7828	0.7965	0.7910
9	0.9279	0.9280	0.9260
10	0.7909	0.8017	0.7930
11	0.8075	0.7867	0.7775
12	0.8209	0.8184	0.8076

Table 4. Technique comparison for new classification variations (probabilities $\bar{P}_{av}$ for Engine 1).

7.4. Real data-based classification

Gas path mathematical models are widely used in building fault classification required for diagnostics because faults rarely occur during field operation. In that case, model errors are transmitted to the model-based classification. Paper [30] looks at the possibility of creating a mixed fault classification that incorporates both model-based and data-driven fault classes. Such a classification will combine a profound common diagnosis with a higher diagnostic accuracy for the data-driven classes. Engine 1 has been chosen as a test case. Its real data with two periods of compressor fouling were used to form a data-driven class of the fouling. **Figure 12** illustrates simulated (without errors) and real data.

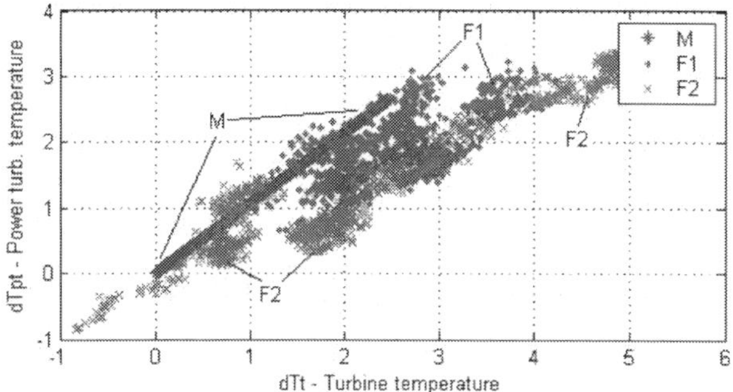

Figure 12. Simulated and real compressor fouling deviations (Engine 1: M—simulated deviations, F1 and F2—real deviations for the first and second fouling periods).

Different variations of the classification were considered and compared using the MLP. In spite of irregular distribution of real patterns, the MLP normally operated at the learning and validation steps. We also found that the perceptron trained on simulated data has 30% recognition errors when applied to real compressor fouling data. However, the use of mixed learning data allows to reduce these errors up to 3%. It was shown as well how to form a representative real fault class, which ensures minimal recognition errors.

Paper [31] presents another way to enhance gas turbine fault classification using real information. Diagnostic algorithms widely use theoretical random number distributions to simulate measurement errors. Such simulation differs from real diagnosis because the diagnostic algorithms work with the deviations, which have other error components that differ from simulated errors by amplitude and distribution. As a result, simulation-based investigations might result in too optimistic conclusions on gas turbine diagnosis reliability. To make error presentation more realistic, it was proposed in reference [31] to extract an error component from real deviations and to integrate it in fault description.

Using simulated and real data of Engine 1, six alternative variations of deviation error were integrated in the fault classification. Diagnosis was performed by the MLP, and the diagnosis reliability was estimated for each variation. Despite irregular real error distribution, the MLP successfully operated for all the variations. Experiments with error representation variations have shown what can happen when the classification formed with accurate simulated deviations is applied to classify less accurate real deviations. In that case, the diagnosis accuracy can fall from $\bar{P} \approx 92\%$ to $\bar{P} \approx 54\%$, but this low diagnostic accuracy can be considerably elevated by including real errors into the description of fault classes.

The fault classifications with integrated real errors were used in reference [32] to compare three networks: MLP, RBN, and PNN, one more time. All networks operated well and they differed in accuracy indicators $\bar{P}_{av}$ by less than 1%, thus confirming again the conclusion about equality of recognition techniques.

7.5. Different operating conditions

Many known studies show that grouping the data collected at different engine operating modes for making a single diagnosis (multipoint diagnosis) yields higher diagnostic accuracy than the accuracy provided by traditional one-point methods. But it is of a practical interest to know how significant the accuracy increment is and how it can be explained. The diagnosis of engines at dynamic modes poses the similar questions. To make one diagnosis, this technique combines data from successive measurement sections of a transient operation mode and in this regard looks like multipoint diagnosis.

Paper [33] analyzes the influence of the operating conditions on the diagnostic accuracy by comparing the one-point, multipoint, and transient options. The MLP is used as a pattern recognition technique. In spite of significant increase of the input dimensionality, the perceptron operated well for all options.

The calculations have revealed that the process of network training has peculiarities for multipoint diagnosis. They are illustrated in **Figure 13**, which shows the plots of the perceptron error versus training epochs for the cases of one-point and multipoint diagnosis. As can be seen, the curves of the error function for the training and validation processes almost coincide for the one-point option, they slow down along with training epochs, and a total epoch number 300 is relatively large. These are indications of no over-training effect. The behavior of the perceptron applied for the multipoint diagnosis is quite different. We can see that the validation curve falls behind the training curve after the 30th epoch, this gap rapidly increases, and the training process stops earlier (108 epochs) because of the over-training phenomenon. We can conclude that the Early Stopping Option is more required here. The differences indicated above can be explained by the ratio of input data volume to the unknown perceptron parameter number. For both cases, the volume of the training set is equal to 7000 patterns, but the numbers of unknown quantities significantly differ: 144 for the first case and 1540 for the second. Consequently, in the case of multipoint diagnosis, the trained network is much more flexible and the over-training becomes possible. An increase of the reference set volume can improve the training process; however, this increase is presently limited by the computation time.

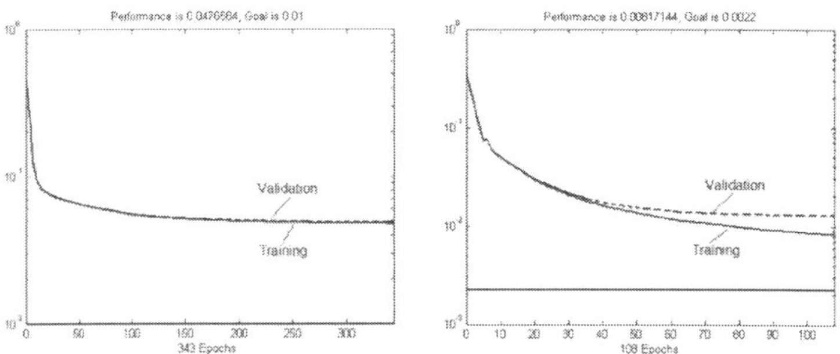

Figure 13. Training process (Engine 1, left plot—one-point diagnosis, right plot—multipoint diagnosis).

The results of the option comparison (probabilities $\bar{P}$) are grouped in **Table 5**. One can see that a total growth of diagnosis accuracy due to switching to the multipoint diagnosis and data joining from different steady states is significant: The diagnosis errors decrease by two to five times. The diagnosis at transients causes further accuracy growth, but it is not great. It has been found that this positive effect of the data joining is mainly explained by averaging the input data and smoothing the random measurement errors.

Option	Single fault classification	Multiple fault classification
One-point	0.7316	0.7351
Multipoint	0.8915	0.9444
Transient	0.9032	0.9561

Table 5. Comparison of the one-point, multipoint, and transient options (Engine 1).

8. Conclusions

A monitoring system comprises many elements, and many factors influence the final diagnostic accuracy. The present chapter has generalized our investigations aimed to enhance this system by choosing the best option for each element. In every investigation, a diagnostic process was simulated mainly on the basis of neural networks, and we focused on reaching the highest accuracy by choosing the best network and its optimal tuning to the issue to solve. As can be seen, all the examined techniques (MLP, RBN, PNN, SVN, and K-NN) use a pattern-based classification. Such a classification can be formed from complex classes in which faults are simulated by the nonlinear thermodynamic model. Moreover, this classification allows its description by real fault displays that completely exclude a negative effect of model inaccuracy. Thus, being objects of investigation and optimization, neural networks help with enhancement of a whole monitoring system. As a result of the conducted investigations, some methods to elevate diagnostic accuracy were proposed and proven. The chapter also provides the recommendations on choosing and tailoring the networks for different diagnostic tasks. For solving many tasks, the utility of the multilayer perceptron has been proven on simulated and real data.

Acknowledgements

The work has been carried out with the support of the National Polytechnic Institute of Mexico (research project 20150961).

Author details

Igor Loboda

Address all correspondence to: igloboda@gmail.com

National Polytechnic Institute, Mexico

References

[1] Saravanamuttoo, H.I.H., MacIsaac, B.D., 1983, Thermodynamic models for pipeline gas turbine diagnostics, *ASME Journal of Engineering for Power*, Vol. 105, pp. 875–884.

[2] Doel, D.L., 2003, Interpretation of weighted-least-squares gas path analysis results, *Journal of Engineering for Gas Turbines and Power*, Vol. 125, Issue 3, pp. 624–633.

[3] Aretakis, N., Mathioudakis, K., Stamatis, A., 2003, Nonlinear engine component fault diagnosis from a limited number of measurements using a combinatorial approach, *Journal of Engineering for Gas Turbines and Power*, Vol. 125, Issue 3, pp. 642–650.

[4] Volponi, A.J., DePold, H., Ganguli, R., 2003, The use of Kalman filter and neural network methodologies in gas turbine performance diagnostics: a comparative study, *Journal of Engineering for Gas Turbines and Power*, Vol. 125, Issue 4, pp. 917–924.

[5] Sampath, S., Singh, R., 2006, An integrated fault diagnostics model using genetic algorithm and neural networks, *ASME Journal of Engineering for Gas Turbines and Power*, Vol. 128, Issue 1, pp. 49–56.

[6] Pipe K., 1987, Application of advanced pattern recognition techniques in machinery failure prognosis for turbomachinery, *Condition Monitoring 1987 International Conference*, British Hydraulic Research Association, UK, pp. 73–89.

[7] Lokesh Kumar S., et al., 2007, Comparison of a few fault diagnosis methods on sparse variable length time series sequences, *IGTI/ASME Turbo Expo 2007*, Montreal, Canada, 8 p., ASME Paper GT2007-27843.

[8] Romessis, C., Mathioudakis, K., 2006, Bayesian network approach for gas path fault diagnosis, *ASME Journal of Engineering for Gas Turbines and Power*, Vol. 128, Issue 1, pp. 64–72.

[9] Fast, M., Assadi, M., De, S., 2008, Condition based maintenance of gas turbines using simulation data and artificial neural network: a demonstration of feasibility, *IGTI/ASME Turbo Expo 2008*, Berlin, Germany, 9 p., ASME Paper GT2008-50768.

[10] Palme, T., Fast, M., Assadi, M., Pike, A., Breuhaus, P., 2009, Different condition monitoring models for gas turbines by means of artificial neural networks, *IGTI/ASME Turbo
Expo 2009*, Orlando, Florida, USA, 11 p., ASME Paper GT2009-59364.

[11] Palme, T., Breuhaus, P., Assadi, M., Klein, A., Kim, M., 2011, Early warning of gas
turbine failure by nonlinear feature extraction using an auto-associative neural network
approach, *IGTI/ASME Turbo Expo 2011*, Vancouver, British Columbia, Canada, 12 p.,
ASME Paper GT2011-45991.

[12] Butler, S.W., Pattipati, K.R., Volponi, A., et al., 2006, An assessment methodology for
data-driven and model based techniques for engine health monitoring, ASME Paper
No. GT2006-91096.

[13] Romessis, C., Mathioudakis, K., 2003, Setting up of a probabilistic neural network for
sensor fault detection including operation with component fault, *Journal of Engineering
for Gas Turbines and Power*, Vol. 125, pp. 634–641.

[14] Jaw, L. C., Wang, W., 2006, Mathematical formulation of model-based methods for
diagnostics and prognostics, *IGTI/ASME Turbo Expo 2006*, Barcelona, Spain, 7 p., ASME
Paper GT2006-90655.

[15] Borguet, S., Leonard, O., Dewallet, P., 2015, Regression-based modelling of a fleet of
gas turbine engines for performance trading, *IGTI/ASME Turbo Expo 2015*, Montreal,
Canada, 12 p., ASME Paper GT2015-42330.

[16] Vachtsevanos, G., Lewis, F.L., Roemer, M., Hess, A., Wu, B., 2006, *Intelligent Fault
Diagnosis and Prognosis for Engineering Systems*, John Wiley & Sons, Inc., New Jersey,
434 p.

[17] Vatani, A., Korasani, K., Meskin, N., 2015, Degradation prognostics in gas turbine
engines using neural networks, *IGTI/ASME Turbo Expo 2015*, Montreal, Canada, 13 p.,
ASME Paper GT2015-44101.

[18] Duda, R.O., 2001, *Pattern Classification*, Wiley-Interscience, New York, 654 p.

[19] Haykin, S., 1994, *Neural Networks*, Macmillan College Publishing Company, New York.

[20] Bishop, C.M., 2006, *Pattern Recognition and Machine Learning*, Springer Science, New
York.

[21] Cortes, C., Vapnik, V., 1995, Support-vector networks, *Machine Learning*, Vol. 20, pp.
273–297.

[22] Boser, B.E., Guyon, I.M., Vapnik, V.N., 1992, A training algorithm for optimal margin
classifiers, Fifth Annual Workshop on Computational Learning Theory—COLT '92,
ACM Press, New York, USA, pp. 144–152.

[23] Hsu, C.W., Chang, C.C., Lin, C.J., 2010, A practical guide to support vector classification,
National   Taiwan   University.   http://www.csie.ntu.edu.tw/~cjlin/papers/guide/
guide.pdf

[24] Loboda, I., Feldshteyn, Y., 2011, Polynomials and neural networks for gas turbine monitoring: a comparative study, *International Journal of Turbo & Jet Engines*, Vol. 28, Issue 3, pp. 227–236 (also see ASME paper GT2010-23749).

[25] Loboda, I., Yepifanov, S., Feldshteyn, Y., 2009, An integrated approach to gas turbine monitoring and diagnostics, *International Journal of Turbo & Jet Engines*, Vol. 26, Issue 2, pp. 111–126 (also see ASME paper GT2008-51449).

[26] Loboda, I., Yepifanov, S., Feldshteyn, Y., 2007, A generalized fault classification for gas turbine diagnostics on steady states and transients, *Journal of Engineering for Gas Turbines and Power*, Vol. 129, Issue 4, pp. 977–985.

[27] Loboda, I., Yepifanov, S., 2013, On the selection of an optimal pattern recognition technique for gas turbine diagnosis, *IGTI/ASME Turbo Expo 2013*, San Antonio, Texas, USA, 11 p., ASME Paper GT2013-95198.

[28] Loboda, I., 2014, Gas turbine fault recognition using probability density estimation, *ASME Turbo Expo 2014*, Dusseldorf, Germany, 13 p., ASME Paper GT2014-27265.

[29] Perez Ruiz, J.L., Loboda, I., 2014, A flexible fault classification for gas turbine diagnosis, *Aerospace Techniques and Technology*, Vol. 113, Issue 6, pp. 94–102.

[30] Loboda, I., Yepifanov, S., 2010, A mixed data-driven and model based fault classification for gas turbine diagnosis, *International Journal of Turbo & Jet Engines*, Vol. 27, Issue 3–4, pp. 251–264 (also see ASME Paper GT2010-23075).

[31] Loboda, I., Yepifanov, S., Feldshteyn, Y., 2013, A more realistic scheme of deviation error representation for gas turbine diagnostics, *International Journal of Turbo & Jet Engines*, Vol. 30, Issue 2, pp. 179–189 (also see ASME Paper GT2012-69368).

[32] Loboda, I., Olivares Robles, M.A., 2015, Gas turbine fault diagnosis using probabilistic neural networks, *International Journal of Turbo & Jet Engines*, Vol. 32, Issue 2, pp.175–192.

[33] Loboda, I., Feldshteyn, Y., Yepifanov, S., 2007, Gas turbine diagnostics under variable operating conditions, *International Journal of Turbo & Jet Engines*, Vol. 24, Issues 3–4, pp. 231–244 (also see ASME Paper GT2007-28085).

Statistical property	Formula
Sum average	$$f_6 = \sum i = 22Nip_{x+y}(i)$$
Sum variance	$$f_7 = \sum_{i=2}^{2N} (i - f_6)^2 p_{x+y}(i)$$
Sum entropy	$$f_8 = -\sum_{i=2}^{2N} p_{x+y}(i)\log(p_{x+y}(i))$$
Entropy	$$f_9 = -\sum_i \sum_j p(i,j)\log(p(i,j))$$
Difference variance	$$f_{10} = -\sum_{i=0}^{N-1} \left(i - \mu_{x-y}\right)^2 p_{x-y}(i)$$
Difference entropy	$$f_{11} = -\sum_{i=0}^{N-1} p_{x-y}(i)\log(p_{x-y}(i))$$
Information measure of correlation 1	$$f_{12} = \frac{f_9 - HXY1}{\max\{HX,HY\}}$$
Information measure of correlation 2	$$f_{13} = (1 - \exp[-2.0(HXY2 - f_9)])^{\frac{1}{2}}$$

Table 2. Second-order statistics [14].

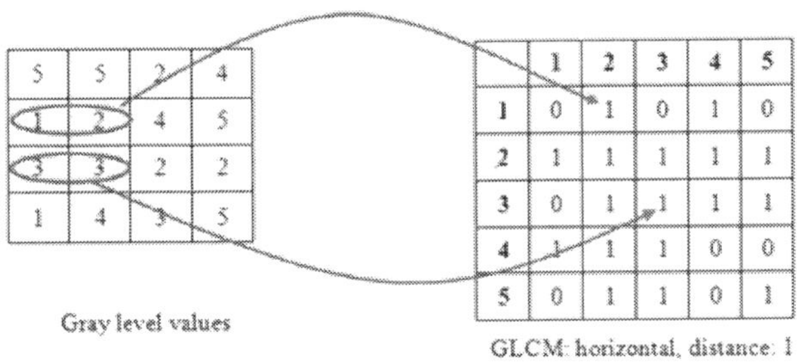

Figure 3. GLCM calculation.

The second-order statistics are derived from GLCM of images by using the methodology proposed by Haralick [26]. GLCM is the statistical method of examining texture that considers the spatial relationship of pixels [29]. GLCM measures how often a pixel p_1 occurs in specific spatial relationship to a pixel p_2 as shown in **Figure 3**. GLCM is a square matrix of size $N \times N$ where N is the number of gray level. Generally, the statistical measures are made from this matrix. When a single GLCM is not enough to describe the textural features of the input image, an additional parameter "*offset*" could be specified to allow detection of patterns in different direction [29]. The offsets define pixel relationships of varying direction and distance given in **Figure 4**. An offset array is defined to create a different GLCM for multiple directions.

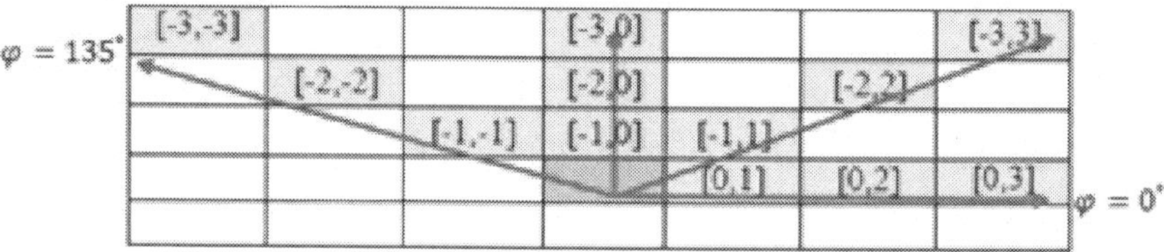

Figure 4. Offset directions.

The notations given in the following (Eqs. (3)–(6)) are used in the formulas for the second-order statistics of the image texture [26–28],

$p(i, j)$: (i,j)-th entry in a GLCM, and called as "*probability density*" with N being the number of gray levels.

$$p_x(i) = \sum_{j=1}^{N} p(i, j) \tag{3}$$

$$p_y(j) = \sum_{j=1}^{N} p(i, j) \tag{4}$$

$$p_{x+y}(k) = \sum i, j : i + j = k^{p(i,j)} \quad \text{for } k = 2,3,4\ldots\ldots\ldots 2N \tag{5}$$

$$p_{x-y}(k) = \sum i, j : |i - j| = k^{p(i,j)} \quad \text{for } k = 0,1,2\ldots\ldots\ldots N - 1 \tag{6}$$

where μ is the mean of $p(i, j)$, μ_x, μ_y are the means of p_x and p_y, respectively, and

$$\mu_{x-y} = \sum_{i=0}^{N-1} ip_{x-y} \cdot \sigma_x \quad \text{and} \quad \sigma_y$$ are the standard deviations, and HX and HY are the

entropies of p_x and p_y, respectively. They are calculated as follows:

$$HXY1 = -\sum_{i=1}^{N}\sum_{j=1}^{N} p(i, j) \log(p_x(i) p_y(j)) \tag{7}$$

$$HXY2 = -\sum_{i=1}^{N}\sum_{j=1}^{N} p_x(i) p_y(j) \log(p_x(i) p_y(j)) \tag{8}$$

4.3. Description of texture feature extraction method

The algorithm consisting of Discrete Wavelet Transform (DWT), Soft Wavelet Thresholding (SWT) and GLCM methods is formed to extract the required texture features of the defective fabric images. The procedure of the algorithm includes seven steps as follows:

i.   The image noises are removed by means of Wiener filter to get a smoother image.

ii.   The image is then decomposed into sub-images by applying DWT at level 2 with "*db3*" wavelet base. The approximation image is then applied to SWT (Eq. (9)) [30]:

$$Y = \begin{cases} sgn(X)(|X| - T_0), & |X| \geq T_0 \\ 0, & |X| < T_0 \end{cases} \tag{9}$$

where Y is the *wavelet coefficient* and T_0 is the threshold level. The *threshold value* "T_0" is determined according to Eq. (10):

$$T_{1,2} = mean[a(i, j)] \pm w * mean[std(a(i, j))] \tag{10}$$

T_1 is the upper limit, T_2 is the lower limit of the double thresholding processes, and "w" is the weighting factor which is determined experimentally between 2 and 4. The upper and lower thresholding limits are determined by using a defect-free fabric image as a template.

iii.   The regular texture patterns should be made smoother and the defective regions should be accentuated in order to distinguish the defect boundaries. The image frame applied to soft thresholding is convolved with *"Laplacian"* operator.

iv.   The first-order statistics (**Table 1**) are then extracted from the convolved image.

v.   The woven fabric pattern is produced by interlacing the warp and weft yarns with a perpendicular angle. They are arranged to the horizontal (weft yarns) and vertical (warp yarns) directions in the fabric. The co-occurrence matrices with offset [0, 1] are formed for horizontal and vertical detail coefficients of the defective fabric. Basically, they represent the latitude and the longitude properties of the fabric.

vi.   The second-order statistics are extracted from the co-occurrence matrices by using Haralick method.

vii.   The feature column vector having 32 elements is then formed by using the first- and second-order statistics.

The procedure given above is repeated for each defective fabric image.

5. Preparation of defect database

The material selected for defect classification is *"undyed denim fabric."* Denim is a strong and heavy warp-faced cotton cloth. The classical denim is made from 100% cotton and woven from coarse indigo dyed warp and gray undyed weft yarn. Weft yarn passes under two or more warp yarns and three and one twill construction is obtained. Generally, brown- or blue-colored yarns are used in warp and bleached yarns are used in weft [31, 32]. The name of denim comes from a strong fabric called serge, originally made in Nimes, France, which is then shortened to denim [31, 32]. Denim fabric is first produced as *"working cloths."* Since the denim fabric is strong and durable, it was used as a working cloth in the 18th century and as a mineworker cloth in the 19th century. The mass production of the denim fabrics was begun in 1853 by Levi Strauss. Overtime, the denim fabric was used in the production of different cloth types such as short, shirt, skirt, jacket, and different products such as hat and bag. It is being estimated that 85% of the produced denim fabric is used in the production of trousers.

The sample fabric used in this study has got the specifications given in **Table 3**. The material is supplied by Prestij Weaving Company in Gaziantep/Turkey, as an undyed denim fabric. It is woven on Picanol Gammax rapier weaving machines with a production speed of 450 rpm and a production efficiency of 85%. The fabric has got a size of 2000 cm length and 43 cm width. The fabric sample has four types of defects: warp lacking, weft lacking, hole, and soiled yarn (**Figure 5**). Since the required number of defect cannot be encountered on a fabric with such a length, some of the defects are made randomly with different widths and lengths on the sample [14].

Pattern	3/1 (s) twill
Warp yarn number	Ne 16/1 Open end
Weft yarn number	Ne 10/1 Open end
Warp sett	45 ends/cm
Weft sett	20 picks/cm
Warp crimp (%)	12
Weft crimp (%)	1.5
Weight per square meter (with sizing)	323 g/m^2
Cover factor	33.8
Reed number	110 dents/10cm

Table 3. Fabric sample specifications [14].

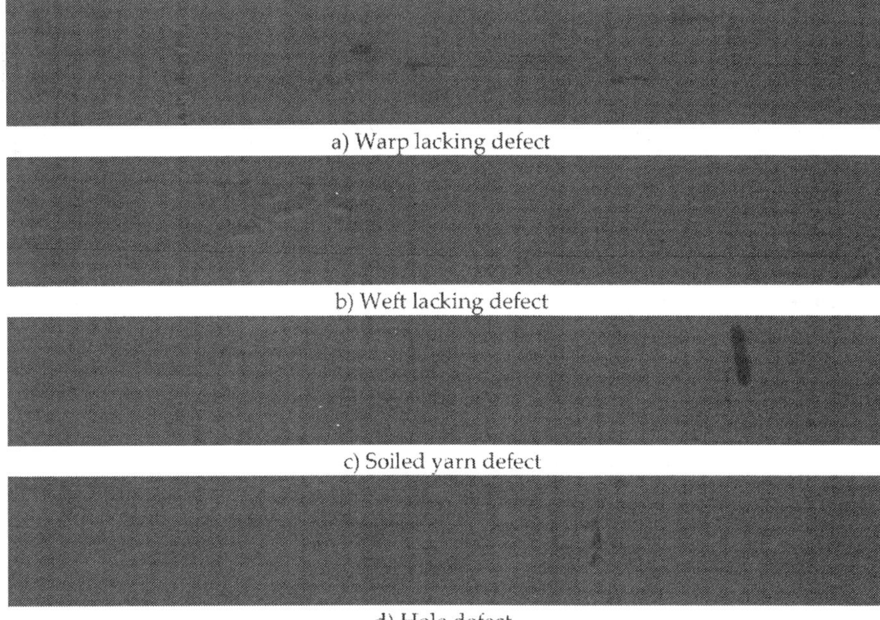

a) Warp lacking defect

b) Weft lacking defect

c) Soiled yarn defect

d) Hole defect

Figure 5. Fabric defect samples.

The image frames of the defective fabrics that will be used for network training and testing are acquired by using a prototype machine vision system [14] (**Figure 6**). The system consists of

an industrial fabric inspection machine, a camera system, camera attachment equipment, an additional lightening unit, a rotary encoder, and host computer. The camera system includes charge-coupled device (CCD) line-scan camera, frame grabber card, lens, and camera link cable. The fabric sample was placed on a fabric inspection machine. As the fabric was wound, the image frames were captured and then memorized on the computer. The fabric motion and the camera exposure are synchronized with a rotary encoder via a frame grabber card.

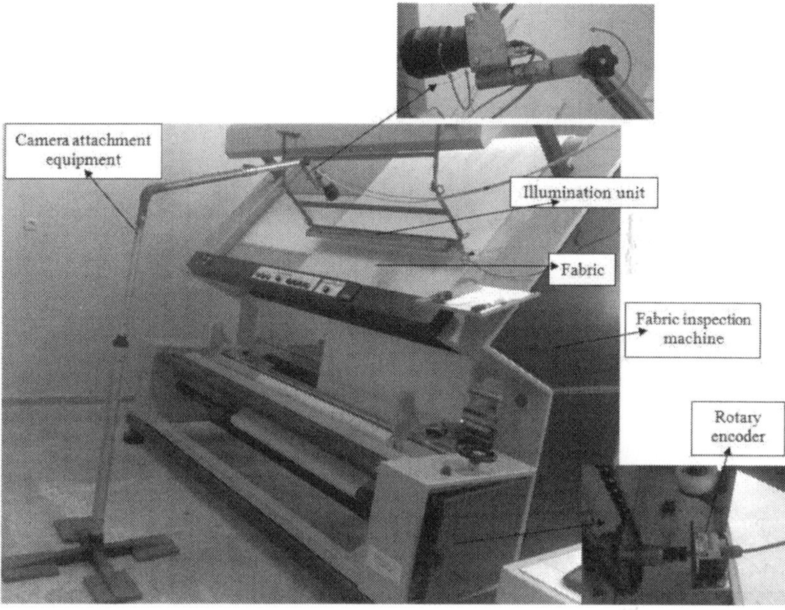

Figure 6. Machine vision system for fabric inspection.

6. Case study: neural network architecture for fabric defect classification

The most commonly preferred method in AI among the studies on fabric defect classification problem [9–13] is Artificial Neural Network. In this study, four defect types, hole, warp lacking, weft lacking, and soiled yarn are classified by using MATLAB® Neural Network Toolbox. The toolbox consists of some tools such as neural fitting, neural clustering, pattern recognition, and neural network. The pattern recognition tool is used to classify inputs into a set of target categories for the fabric defect classification problem. The pattern recognition tool consists of a two-layer feed-forward network (**Figure7**). The network is trained with scaled conjugate gradient back propagation. Tan-sigmoid transfer function is used in both the hidden and the output layers [21].

The input and target matrices are formed for each defect type. Twenty-five defective fabric images for each defect type are taken to be used for the feature extraction. This results in an input matrix with 32 × 100 size. Each feature vector of the input matrix is assigned to the target vector, which has a size of 4 × 1 (binary vector). It is defined in **Table 4**.

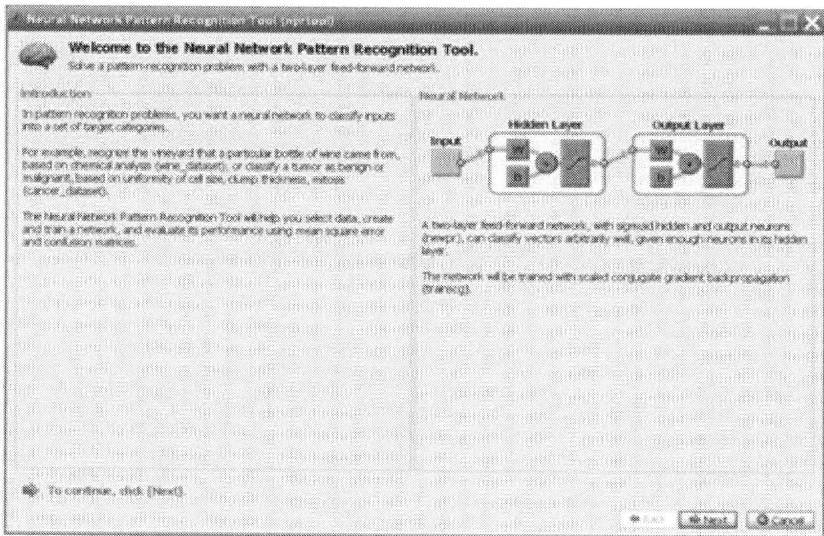

Figure 7. Pattern Recognition Tool GUI of MATLAB® NN toolbox.

Defect type	Column vector
Hole	[1; 0; 0; 0]
Warp lacking	[0; 1; 0; 0]
Weft lacking	[0; 0; 1; 0]
Soiled yarn	[0; 0; 0; 1]

Table 4. Defect type and corresponding vector definition.

Target vector is formed for each defective fabric image and the target matrix's size is 4 × 100. The input and target matrices are introduced into Neural Network Pattern Recognition Tool (nprtool) (**Figure 8**). The input data set is randomly divided as 80, 10, and 10% for training, validation, and testing samples, respectively (**Figure 9**). The number of neurons is then determined for the hidden layer of the network (**Figure 10**). The number of neurons in the output layer is determined automatically according to the number of elements in the target vector, and it is taken as four in this study. Since four defect types are to be classified having

performed many trials, the best results are obtained for 37 neurons in the hidden layer after many trials. The network is finally trained using the scaled conjugate gradient back propagation (**Figure 11**). The Mean-Square-Error (MSE) algorithm adjusts the biases and weights so as to minimize the mean square error. MSE of training, testing, and validation operations is calculated by using Eq. (11). They are determined as 0.0021, 0.00014, and 0.00027, respectively (**Figure 12**):

$$E = \sum_j (t_i - o_i)^2 \tag{11}$$

where t_i is the desired output and o_i is the actual output of neuron "i" in the output layer [10].

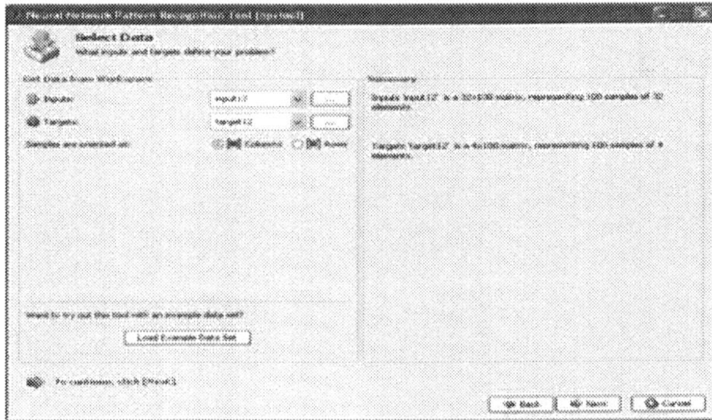

Figure 8. Input and target matrix introduction.

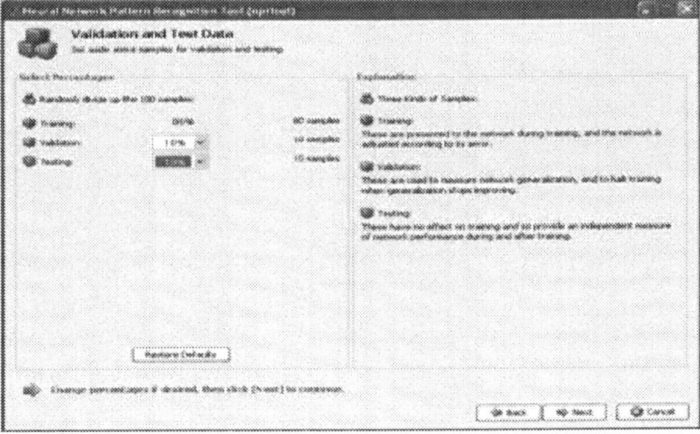

Figure 9. Random division of data set.

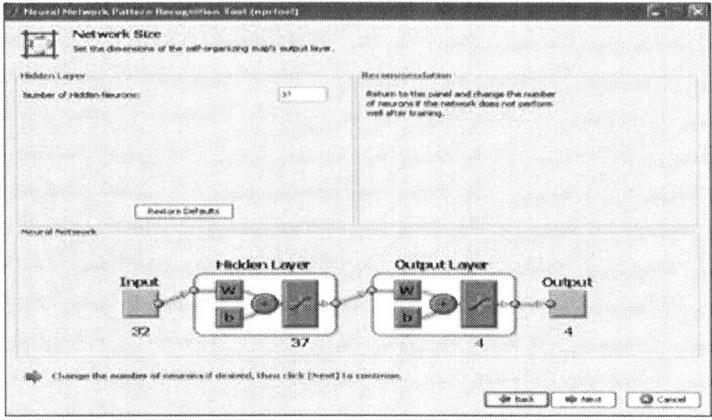

Figure 10. Number of neurons in the hidden layer.

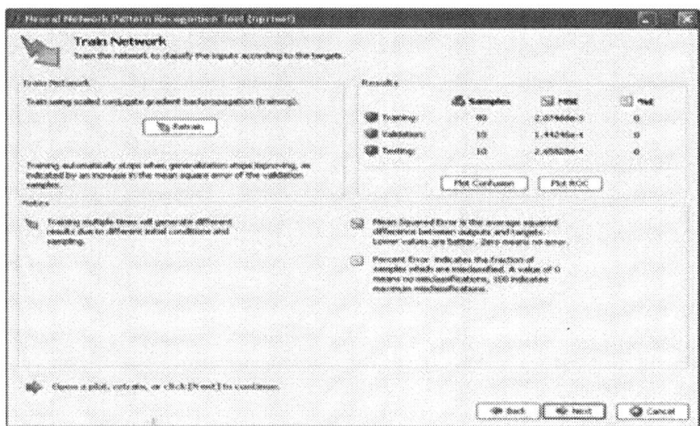

Figure 11. Network training.

6.1. Classification accuracy of the network

The classification accuracy of the network is specified by confusion matrices (**Figure 12**), and Receiver Operating Characteristic (ROC) curves (**Figure 13**) for training, testing, validation, and overall (three kinds of data combined). In the confusion matrices, the green squares indicate the correct response and the red squares indicate the incorrect responses. The lower-right blue squares illustrate the overall accuracies. As the number of green squares gets higher, the classification accuracy of the network increases. As in **Figure 12**, 100% correct responses are obtained for all confusion matrices with this network.

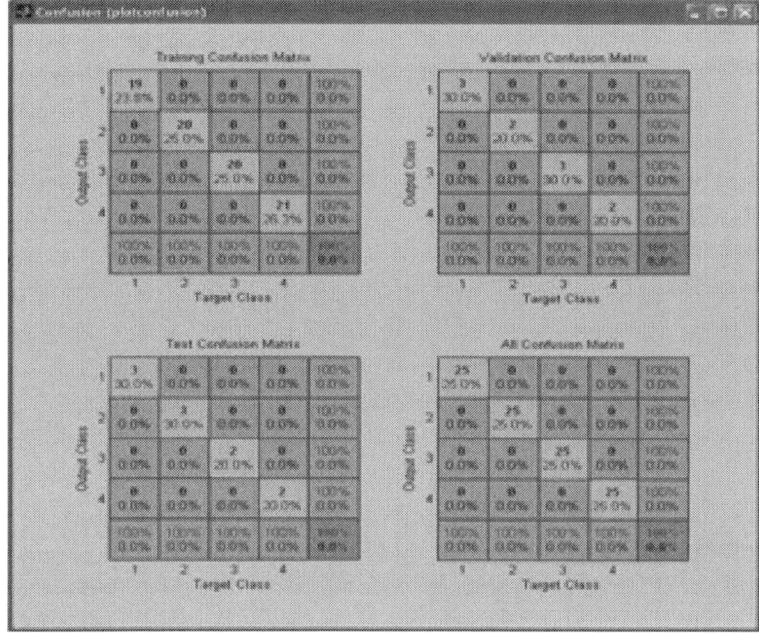

Figure 12. Confusion matrices [14].

Receiver Operating Characteristic curve is useful for recognizing the accuracy of predictions [33]. ROC curve illustrates the classification performance of a binary system as its distinguishing threshold level is varied. It is plotted as *True-Positive Rate* (TPR) versus *False-Positive Rate* (FPR). TPR is also known as sensitivity, and FPR is one minus the specificity. Four possible outcomes are seen as follows:

i.   If the sample is positive and it is classified as positive, it is counted as a *true positive* (TP).

ii.   If the sample value is positive and it is discriminated as negative, it is counted as a false negative (FN).

iii.   If the sample is negative and it is detected as negative, it is counted as a true negative (TN).

iv.   If the sample has a negative value and it is detected as positive, it is counted as a false positive (FP).

As the curve gets closer to the left upper corner, it means that the higher classification accuracy is obtained. A perfect test shows points in the upper-left corner, with 100% sensitivity and 100% specificity. When the true-positive rate of ROC value is 1, it means the true positives are perfectly separated from the false positives. For this classification problem, ROC value 1 is

obtained for training, testing, validation, and overall (**Figure 13**). The network performs almost perfectly [34].

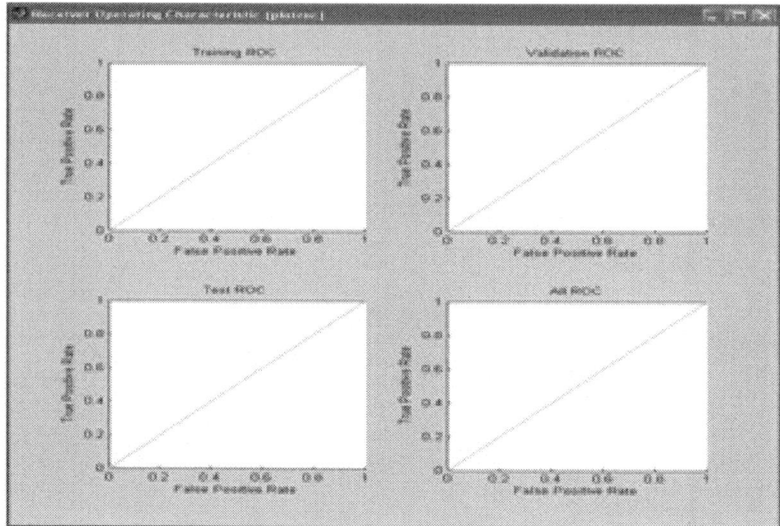

Figure 13. Receiver Operating Characteristic (ROC) curves.

6.2. Defect classification software

Finally, a user interface is prepared for the classification of the defective fabric images. It is automatically used to determine the defect type of a selected defective image. The user interface consists of three buttons as *"Exit," "Reset Data,"* and *"Load-Defective Image"* as shown in **Figure 14**.

The exit button is used to exit the window. After the required image samples are classified, the counters of the defect classes can be made zero by using *"reset data"* button (**Figure 15**). The counts of the defect classes come to the initial zero number. The classification operation can be continued with a different defective image folder. The image to be classified is selected from the directory by using the *"load-defective image"* button. The folder browser window is opened and the required fabric image is selected when this button is activated (**Figure 16**). The selected image is applied to the feature extraction algorithm. The statistical texture features of the image are then extracted. The feature column vector is formed and it is simulated with the network previously built above. The selected image is displayed on the screen. The detect type is then titled for the image. The related defect-type counter is increased by one. These steps are shown in **Figures 17–20** [14].

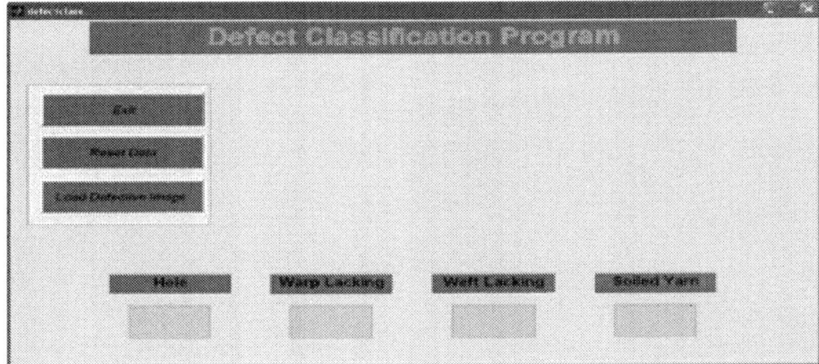

Figure 14. Defect classification program user interface.

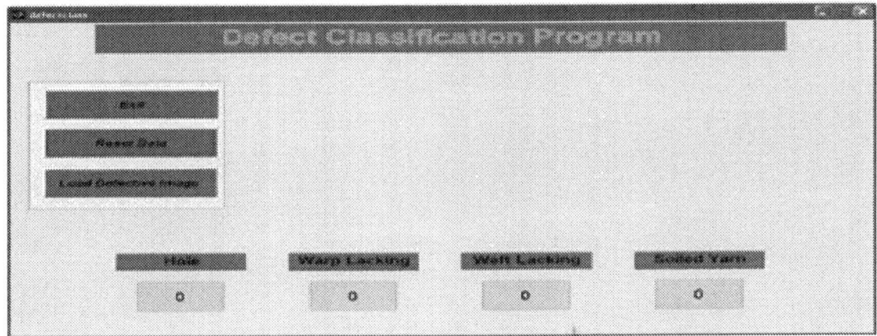

Figure 15. Reset the counters.

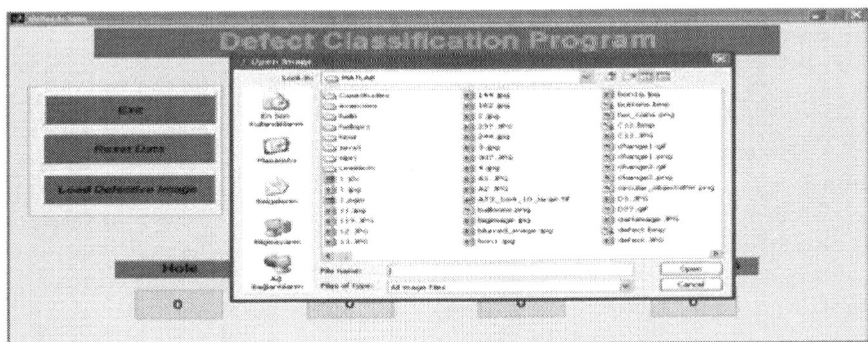

Figure 16. Selection of the defective image.

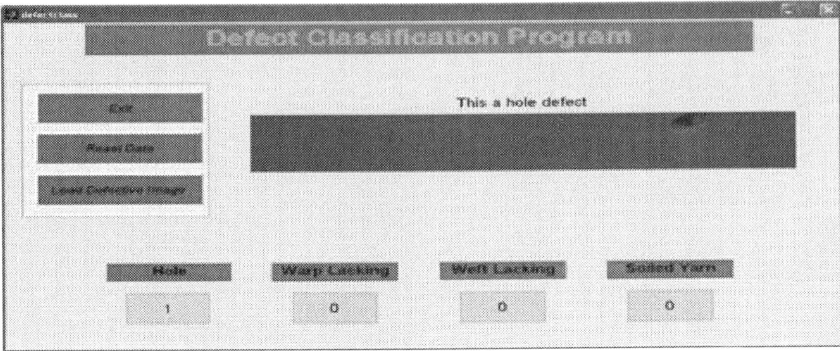

Figure 17. Classification of hole defect.

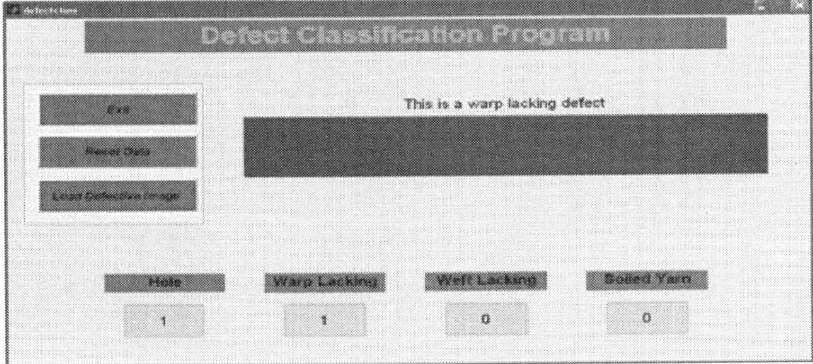

Figure 18. Classification of warp-lacking defect.

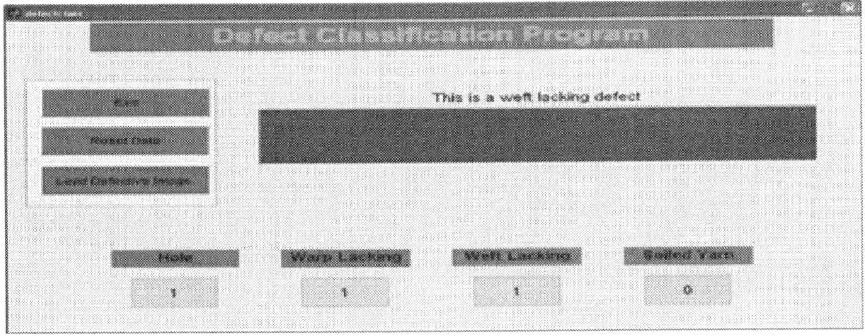

Figure 19. Classification of weft-lacking defect.

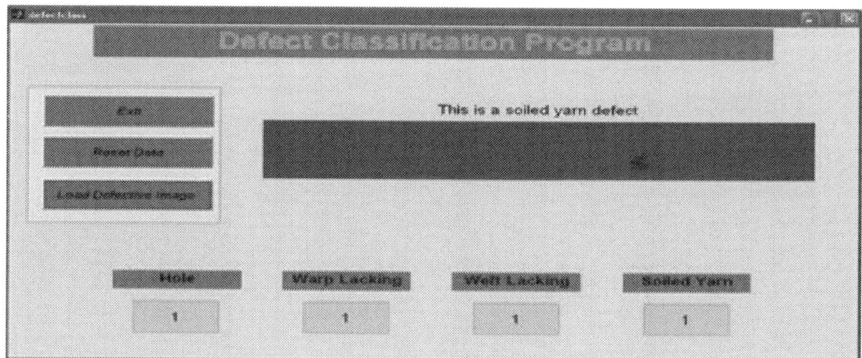

Figure 20. Classification of soiled yarn defect.

7. Statistical evaluation of network testing results

The defective fabric images are stored. They are then used for network training and testing. The features of the 25 defective fabric images are extracted for each defect type and the input matrix of the network is formed. After the neural network is trained successfully, 20 samples of each type of defects are used to test the network classification accuracy.

The neural network simulation results of hole, warp-lacking, weft-lacking, and soiled yarn defects are given in **Tables 5–8**, respectively. The overall accuracy rate of each type of defect is then presented in **Table 9** and **Figure 21** [14].

The defective images are classified with an average accuracy rate of 96.3%. As the hole defect is recognized with 100% accuracy rate, the others are recognized with a rate of 95%. Since many weft yarns are removed and the large spaces occur between the yarns, one of the weft-lacking images is recognized as the hole. One of the soiled yarn images is recognized as warp lacking because of having large vertical soil. Since only a small part of the fabric image is different from the regular pattern, it is more difficult to classify them than the classification of completely different textures.

1	1.0000	0.0090	0.0000	0.0000
2	1.0000	0.0004	0.0000	0.0000
3	1.0000	0.0000	0.0000	0.0000
4	1.0000	0.0000	0.0000	0.0000
5	0.9999	0.0001	0.0000	0.0000
6	1.0000	0.0000	0.0000	0.0000

1	1.0000	0.0090	0.0000	0.0000
7	0.9750	0.0000	0.0000	0.0495
8	0.9995	0.0000	0.0000	0.0009
9	0.9995	0.0000	0.0000	0.0005
10	0.9997	0.0000	0.0000	0.0022
11	0.6396	0.0033	0.0000	0.0036
12	0.8833	0.0003	0.0000	0.0311
13	1.0000	0.0009	0.0000	0.0000
14	0.9997	0.1108	0.0000	0.0000
15	0.8559	0.0087	0.0001	0.0000
16	0.9993	0.0004	0.0000	0.0000
17	1.0000	0.0001	0.0001	0.0000
18	0.9992	0.0025	0.0001	0.0000
19	0.8551	0.0020	0.3635	0.0000
20	1.0000	0.0000	0.0000	0.0001

Table 5. Classification results of *"hole"* defect.

1	0.0084	0.9601	0.0002	0.0000
2	0.0024	0.7283	0.0012	0.0000
3	0.0000	0.8354	0.1381	0.0000
4	0.0000	0.9938	0.0033	0.0000
5	0.0000	0.9997	0.0000	0.0001
6	0.0030	0.1955	0.0035	0.0001
7	0.0369	0.9362	0.0000	0.0000
8	0.0000	0.9824	0.0005	0.0024
9	0.0000	0.8589	0.5104	0.0000
10	0.0000	0.9983	0.0000	0.0003
11	0.0000	0.7221	0.0000	0.5606
12	0.0000	0.9999	0.0000	0.0000
13	0.0000	0.8850	0.0225	0.0000
14	0.0285	0.9988	0.0000	0.0000
15	0.0013	0.9998	0.0000	0.0000
16	0.0000	0.9910	0.0098	0.0000
17	0.0010	0.0099	0.0367	0.0042

1	0.0084	0.9601	0.0002	0.0000
18	0.0013	0.9238	0.0000	0.0001
19	0.0000	0.9993	0.0011	0.0000
20	0.0000	0.8986	0.1990	0.0000

Table 6. Classification results of *"warp-lacking"* defect.

1	0.0001	0.0015	0.9996	0.0000
2	0.0001	0.0017	0.9999	0.0000
3	0.9989	0.0003	0.0265	0.0000
4	0.0037	0.0127	0.9974	0.0000
5	0.0249	0.0467	0.9831	0.0000
6	0.0000	0.0014	1.0000	0.0000
7	0.0020	0.0094	0.2899	0.0000
8	0.0000	0.5929	0.8806	0.0000
9	0.0000	0.0001	1.0000	0.0000
10	0.0122	0.0476	0.8142	0.0000
11	0.0145	0.0004	0.9565	0.0000
12	0.0000	0.0000	1.0000	0.0000
13	0.0000	0.0001	1.0000	0.0000
14	0.0003	0.0010	1.0000	0.0000
15	0.0241	0.0846	0.5240	0.0000
16	0.0000	0.0001	1.0000	0.0000
17	0.0000	0.0036	1.0000	0.0000
18	0.0011	0.0007	0.9999	0.0000
19	0.0005	0.0006	0.9999	0.0000
20	0.0001	0.0007	0.9997	0.0000

Table 7. Classification results of *"weft–lacking"* defect.

1	0.0000	0.0000	0.0000	1.0000
2	0.0001	0.0024	0.0000	0.9991
3	0.0000	0.0003	0.0000	1.0000
4	0.0000	0.0002	0.0000	1.0000
5	0.0000	0.0233	0.0000	0.9897

1	0.0000	0.0000	0.0000	1.0000
6	0.0033	0.0916	0.0000	0.4757
7	0.0000	0.0010	0.0000	0.9999
8	0.0000	0.1733	0.0000	0.7789
9	0.0000	0.0392	0.0000	0.8368
10	0.0000	0.0008	0.0000	0.9995
11	0.0000	0.0000	0.0000	1.0000
12	0.0000	0.0000	0.0000	1.0000
13	0.0000	0.1266	0.0000	0.8657
14	0.0064	0.0073	0.0000	0.9998
15	0.0002	0.7885	0.0000	0.1102
16	0.0009	0.0000	0.0000	1.0000
17	0.0000	0.0075	0.0000	0.9987
18	0.0004	0.0000	0.0000	1.0000
19	0.0005	0.0149	0.0000	0.9924
20	0.0000	0.0001	0.0000	1.0000

Table 8. Classification results of *"soiled yarn"* defect.

Defect type	Hole	Warp lacking	Weft lacking	Soiled yarn	Number of sample	Classification accuracy (%)
Hole	20	0	0	0	20	100
Warp lacking	0	19	1	0	20	95
Weft lacking	1	0	19	0	20	95
Soiled yarn	0	1	0	19	20	95

Table 9. Defect classification accuracy rates.

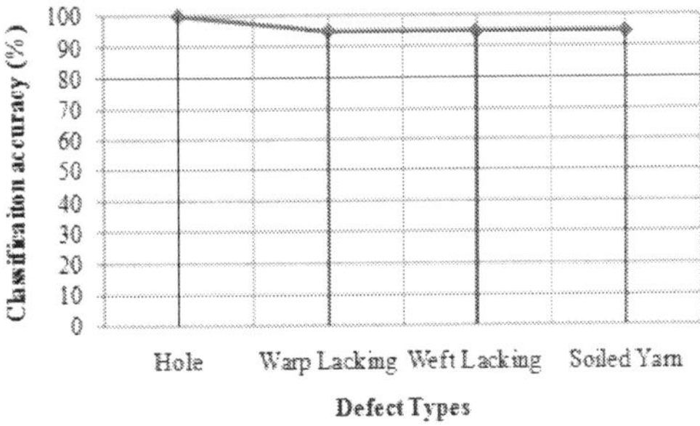

Figure 21. Classification accuracy rates of defects [14].

8. Conclusion

The experimental setup developed in this study has an operation speed of 7.5 m/min and it can detect the defects as small as 0.5 mm. This system was designed for the inspection of denim fabrics. The defective fabric images acquired via the developed machine vision system were classified by using ANN method. The classification was achieved according to their texture properties like a pattern recognition problem. The texture features of each defective image were extracted by using an algorithm based on DWT, SWT, and GLCM methods. Four defect types, hole, warp lacking, weft lacking, and soiled yarn, were classified. The first- and second-order statistical properties were extracted and the feature vector was formed for each defective fabric image. The feature extraction algorithm is applied for 25 images of each defect type. The input matrix with the size of 32 × 100 is obtained. The target vector indicated to which the input vector was assigned. It was made of a binary vector T (size = 4 × 1). The network was built by using MATLAB® Neural Network Toolbox and Pattern Recognition Tool.

Two layers were included in the network. The best results were obtained for 37 neurons in the hidden layer after many trials. The number of neurons in the output layer was determined automatically according to the number of elements in the target vector; it was taken as four in this study. The network was finally trained by using the scaled conjugate gradient BP method. Having trained the neural network successfully, 20 samples of each type of defects were used to test the network classification accuracy. The defective images were then classified with an average accuracy rate of 96.3%. As the hole defect was recognized with 100% accuracy rate, the others were recognized with a rate of 95%.

Acknowledgements

This study is a project supported by the Gaziantep University Scientific Research Projects Management Unit. The name of the project is "Development an Intelligent System for Fabric Defect Detection" and the project number is MF.10.12. The authors also thank Prestij Weaving Company in Gaziantep/Turkey for providing samples during tests.

Author details

H. İbrahim Çelik[1]*, L. Canan Dülger[2] and Mehmet Topalbekiroğlu[1]

*Address all correspondence to: hcelik@gantep.edu.tr

1 Gaziantep University, Department of Textile Engineering, Gaziantep, Turkey

2 Gaziantep University, Department of Mechanical Engineering, Gaziantep, Turkey

References

[1] Stojanovic, R., Mitropulos, P., Koulamas, C., Karayiannis, Y., Koubias, S., and Papadopoulos, G. (2001). Real-time vision-based system for textile fabric inspection. Real-Time Imaging. 7, 507–518.

[2] Guruprasad, R. and Behera, B. K. (2010). Soft computing in textiles. Indian Journal of Fibre and Textile Research. 35, 75–84.

[3] Chattopadhyay, R. and Guha, A. (2004). Artificial neural networks: applications to textiles. Textile Progress. 35, 1, 1–42.

[4] Huang, C. C. and Chen, C. I. (2001). Neural-fuzzy classification for fabric defects. Textile Research Journal. 71(3), 220–224.

[5] Tilocca, A., Borzone, P., Carosio, S., and Durante, A. (2002). Detecting fabric defects with a neural network using two kinds of optical patterns. Textile Research Journal. 72(6), 745–750.

[6] Kumar, A. (2003). Neural network based detection of local textile defects. Pattern Recognition. 36, 1645–1659.

[7] Islam, A., Akhter, S., and Mursalin, T. E. (2006). Automated textile defect recognition system using computer vision and artificial neural networks. World Academy of Science, Engineering and Technology. 13, 1–6.

[8] Liu, S. Y., Zhang, L. D., Wang, Q., and Liu, J. J. (2008). BP neural network in classification of fabric defect based on particle swarm optimization. In: Proceedings of the 2008 International Conference on Wavelet Analysis and Pattern Recognition, Hong Kong. 216–220.

[9] Suyi, L., Liu Jingjing, L., and Leduo, Z. (2008). Classification of fabric defect based on PSO-BP neural network. In: Proceedings of the 2008 Second International Conference on Genetic and Evolutionary Computing. Hubei, China. 137–140.

[10] Suyi, L., Qian, W., and Heng, Z. (2009). Edge detection of fabric defect based on fuzzy cellular automata. In: Intelligent Systems and Applications. Wuhan, China. 1–3.

[11] Jianli, L. and Baoqi, Z. (2007). Identification of fabric defects based on discrete wavelet transform and back-propagation neural network. Journal of the Textile Institute. 98(4), 355–362.

[12] Kuo, C. J. and Su, T. (2003). Gray relational analysis for recognizing fabric defects. Textile Research Journal. 73(5), 461–465.

[13] Kuo, C. J. and Lee, C. J. (2003). A back-propagation neural network for recognizing fabric defects. Textile Research Journal. 73(2), 147–151.

[14] Çelik, H. I. Development of an intelligent fabric defect inspection system. Ph.D Thesis, Mechanical Engineering, University of Gaziantep Graduate School of Natural & Applied Sciences. 2013.

[15] Çelik, H. İ., Topalbekiroğlu, M., and ve Dülger, L. C. (2015). Real-time denim fabric inspection using image analysis. Fibers and Textiles in Eastern Europe. 3(111), 85–90.

[16] Çelik, H. İ., Dülger, L. C., and Topalbekiroğlu, M. (2014). Fabric defect detection by using linear filtering and morphological operations. Indian Journal of Fibre & Textile Research. 39, 254–259.

[17] Çelik, H. I., Dülger, L. C., and Topalbekiroğlu, M. (2013). Developing an algorithm for defect detection of denim fabric: Gabor filter method. Tekstil ve Konfeksiyon. 23(3), 255–260.

[18] Çelik, H. İ., Dülger, L. C., and Topalbekiroğlu, M. (2013). Development of a machine vision system: real-time fabric defect detection and classification with neural networks. The Journal of the Textile Institute. 105(6), 575–585.

[19] Graupe, D. (2007). Principles of artificial neural networks. 2nd edition. Advanced Series on Circuits and Systems. Vol. 6. Singapore: World Scientific Publishing Co. Pte. Ltd.

[20] Munakata, T. (2008). Fundamentals of the new artificial intelligence; neural, evolutionary, fuzzy and more. 2nd edition. London: Springer-Verlag London Limited.

[21] Beale, M. H. and Hagan, M. T. (2012). Neural network toolbox™ user's guide. Natick, MA: The MathWorks, Inc.

[22] Jain, A. K., Mao, J., and Mohiuddin, K. M. (1996). Artificial neural networks: a tutorial. Computer. 29(3), 31–44.

[23] Sonka, M., Hlavac, V., and Boyle, R. (2008). Image processing, analysis and machine vision. International student edition. Toronto, Ontario, USA: Thomson Corporation.

[24] Heijden, F. V., Duin, R. P. W., Ridder, D., and Tax, D.M.J. 2004. Classification, parameter estimation and state estimation an engineering approach using MATLAB. West Sussex, UK: John Wiley & Sons, Ltd.

[25] Gonzalez, R. C., Woods, R. E., and Eddins, S. L. (2004). Digital image processing using Matlab. Upper Saddle River, NJ: Prentice-Hall Inc.

[26] Haralick, R. M. (1979). Statistical and structural approaches to texture. Proceedings of the IEEE. 67(5), 786–804.

[27] Alam, F. I. and Uddin Faruqui, R. U. (2011). Optimized calculations of haralick texture features. European Journal of Scientific Research. 50(4), 543–553.

[28] Haralick, R. M., Shanmugam, K., and Dinstein, I. (1973). Textural features for image classification. IEEE Transactions on Systems, Man and Cybernetics, SMC 3(6), 610–621.

[29] The MathWorks. (2009). Image processing toolbox™ 6 user's guide. Natick, MA: The MathWorks, Inc.

[30] Misiti, M., Misiti, Y., Oppenheim, G., and Poggi, J. M. (1997). Wavelet toolbox for use with Matlab. Natick, MA: The MathWorks, Inc.

[31] Wikipedia the free encyclopedia. Available at: https://en.wikipedia.org/wiki/Denim. Accessed 17.02.2016.

[32] Gokarneshan, N. (2004). Fabric structure and design. New Delhi: New Age International (P) Ltd.

[33] Wikipedia. Available at: http://en.wikipedia.org/wiki/Receiver_operating_characteristic. Accessed 15.02.2016.

[34] Fawcett, T. (2006). An introduction to ROC analysis. Pattern Recognition Letters. 27, 861–874.

Chapter 10

Thunderstorm Predictions Using Artificial Neural Networks

Waylon G. Collins and Philippe Tissot

Additional information is available at the end of the chapter

http://dx.doi.org/10.5772/63542

Abstract

Artificial neural network (ANN) model classifiers were developed to generate ≤ 15 h predictions of thunderstorms within three 400-km² domains. The feed-forward, multi-layer perceptron and single hidden layer network topology, scaled conjugate gradient learning algorithm, and the sigmoid (linear) transfer function in the hidden (output) layer were used. The optimal number of neurons in the hidden layer was determined iteratively based on training set performance. Three sets of nine ANN models were developed: two sets based on predictors chosen from feature selection (FS) techniques and one set with all 36 predictors. The predictors were based on output from a numerical weather prediction (NWP) model. This study amends an earlier study and involves the increase in available training data by two orders of magnitude. ANN model perform-ance was compared to corresponding performances of operational forecasters and multi-linear regression (MLR) models. Results revealed improvement relative to ANN models from the previous study. Comparative results between the three sets of classifiers, NDFD, and MLR models for this study were mixed—the best performers were a function of prediction hour, domain, and FS technique. Boosting the fraction of total positive target data (lightning strikes) in the training set did not improve generalization.

Keywords: thunderstorm prediction, artificial neural networks, correlation-based fea-ture selection, minimum redundancy maximum relevance, multi-linear regression

1. Introduction

A *thunderstorm or convective storm* is a cumulonimbus cloud that produces the electric discharge known as lightning (which produces thunder) and typically generates heavy rainfall, gusty

---

© 2016 The Author(s). Licensee InTech. This chapter is distributed under the terms of the Creative Commons Attribution License (http://creativecommons.org/licenses/by/3.0), which permits unrestricted use, distribution, and reproduction in any medium, provided the original work is properly cited.

surface wind, and possibly hail [1]. Meteorologists use the term convection/convective to refer to the vertical component of convective heat transfer owing to buoyancy [2–4]. The term *deep moist convection* (DMC), which refers to the overturning of approximately the entire troposphere due to convective motions and involving condensation of water vapor associated with rising parcels [5], is part of the literature and includes both thunderstorms and moist convection not involving thunder [4]. The terms *thunderstorm, convective storm*, and *convection* are used interchangeably in this chapter to refer to thunderstorms. Thunderstorms adversely affect humans and infrastructure. An estimated 24,000 deaths and 240,000 injuries worldwide are attributable to lightning [6, 7]. In the USA, lightning is the third leading cause of storm-related deaths based on averages during the period 1985–2014 [8]. Additional hazards that can occur include large hail, flash flooding associated with heavy rainfall, and damage from wind from tornadoes and/or non-rotational (straight-line) wind. During the period 1980–2014, 70 severe thunderstorm events each totaling ≥ 1 billion US dollar damage occurred in the USA, which totaled to 156.3 billion US dollars (adjusted for inflation to 2014 dollars) [9]. Further, convection exacts an economic cost on aviation in terms of delays [10]. Given the adverse socioeconomic impact associated with thunderstorms, there is motivation to predict thunderstorm occurrence and location to inform the public with sufficient lead time.

However, the complexity of thunderstorm generation (hereafter *convective initiation*, or CI), given the myriad of processes (operating on different scales) that influence the vertical thermodynamic structure of the atmosphere (that directly influences the thunderstorm development) and the CI itself [11], the characteristic Eulerian (with respect to a fixed point at the surface) time and linear space scales of individual thunderstorms [12], and the inherent predictability limitations of atmospheric phenomena on the scale of individual thunderstorms [13, 14], renders the skillful prediction of thunderstorm occurrence, timing, and location very difficult. This chapter begins by explaining the thunderstorm development process in order to help the reader understand the predictor variables used in the artificial neural network (ANN) models. Next, the variety of methods used to predict thunderstorms are presented in order to acquaint the reader with the relative utility of the ANN model option. The main section starts with an account of the previous methods developed by the authors and presents a new approach to the development of ANN models to predict thunderstorms with high temporal and spatial resolution. Finally, concluding remarks, including a discussion of future research.

2. Thunderstorm development

To properly understand the process of thunderstorm development, it is essential to define the terms *parcel* and *environment*. The environment refers to the ambient atmospheric conditions. In general, a parcel is an imaginary volume of air that can be assigned various properties [1]. A parcel in this discussion is infinitesimal in dimension and is assumed to be thermally insulated from the surrounding environment which allows for adiabatic temperature changes owing to vertical displacement, and it has a pressure that immediately adjusts to the environmental pressure [15]. One method used by meteorologists to assess the potential for the development of thunderstorms is the *parcel method* [3]. This method is used to assess atmospheric stability and involves the finite vertical displacement of a parcel from hydrostatic equilibrium (balance between vertical pressure force and gravity) while the environment remains unchanged. After the displacement, the temperature contrast between the parcel and the environment at the same level results in buoyancy forces that determine stability.

Consider an environment of depth H with a temperature lapse rate (decrease in temperature with height) Γ satisfying the condition $\Gamma_m < \Gamma < \Gamma_d$, where $\Gamma_d = 9.8°\text{Ckm}^{-1}$ and $\Gamma_m = 6.5°\text{Ckm}^{-1}$ are the dry and moist adiabatic/pseudoadiabatic lapse rates, respectively. Now consider a *surface-based parcel*, defined as a parcel originating in the convective *planetary boundary layer* (PBL) (also called *mixing layer*) that eventually contribute to the primary thunderstorm updraft if thunderstorms develop [16]. The convective PBL refers to the bottom layer of the atmosphere in contact with the earth surface with a diurnal depth varying between tens of meters (near sunrise) to 1–4 km (near sunset) [1]. Let us begin with an unsaturated parcel located at a particular position $(x, y, z = h)$ within the PBL and at the same temperature, density, and pressure as the environment (hydrostatic equilibrium.) Consider an upward vertical displacement of this parcel and apply the parcel method. Since the parcel is unsaturated, it will initially cool at the dry adiabatic lapse rate. Since $\Gamma < \Gamma_d$, the parcel will become cooler than its surrounding environment. Applying the ideal gas law and the assumption that the parcel's pressure instantly adjusts to the environmental pressure, the parcel's density becomes greater than environmental air density. Thus, the parcel is negatively buoyant, a condition known as *positive static stability* [15]. If this parcel is released, it will return to its original height h with negative buoyancy acting as the restoring force. However, let us assume that the parcel overcomes this negative buoyancy via certain upward-directed external force. The parcel eventually reaches the *lifted condensation level* (LCL), whereby the parcel becomes saturated followed by condensation. (The condensation of parcels is manifested by the development of cumulus clouds.) Due to the associated latent heat release, the parcel cools at the pseudoadiabatic rate during subsequent lift. Since $\Gamma_m < \Gamma$, the parcel now cools at a lesser rate than the environmental rate and (with the help of the external force) will eventually reach the environmental temperature at the level referred to as the *level of free convection*. Afterward, the parcel becomes warmer than the environment and thus positively buoyant. If the parcel is released, it will continue to rise without the aid of an external force, a condition known as *static instability*. Thus, a parcel with sufficient vertical displacement within an environment with lapse rates following the $\Gamma_m < \Gamma < \Gamma_d$ constraint may become positively buoyant. This condition is known as *conditional instability*.

The parcel will remain positively buoyant until it reaches the *equilibrium level* (EL). The magnitude of the energy available to a given parcel for convection is the *convective available potential energy* (CAPE) [3] which is the integrated effect of the parcel's positive buoyancy between its original height h and the EL:

$$CAPE_h = \int_{p_{EL}}^{p_h} R_d\left(T_{vp} - T_{ve}\right) d\ln p \tag{1}$$

The variables T_{vp}, T_{ve}, R_d, and p refer to the virtual temperatures of the parcel and environment, specific gas constant for dry air, and air pressure, respectively. Recall that before the surface-based parcel reached the LFC, an external force was needed. The amount of energy required of the external force to lift the parcel to its LFC is known as *convective inhibition* (CIN) [1], represented as follows:

$$CIN_h = - \int_{p_h}^{p_{LFC}} R_d \left(T_{vp} - T_{ve} \right) d\ln p \tag{2}$$

Now, consider a separate case whereby the environment is *absolutely stable* with respect to a surface-based parcel ($\Gamma_m > \Gamma$). This condition is characterized by negative buoyancy during the parcel's entire vertical path of depth H within the troposphere. Hence, the parcel method would suggest that convection is not possible. However, consider a layer of depth $l \le H$ within this environment where water vapor content decreases rapidly with height. Owing to this moisture profile, if the entire layer l is lifted, parcels at the bottom of the layer will reach their LCL before parcels at the top of the layer. The differential lapse rates within this layer resulting from continued lifting will transform the layer from absolutely stable to conditionally unstable. This condition is known as *convectively (or potential) instability* [3, 15]. A convectively unstable layer is identified as one that satisfies:

$$\frac{\partial \theta_e}{\partial z} < 0 \tag{3}$$

The symbols θ_e and z refer to *equivalent potential temperature* and geometric height, respectively. It must be emphasized that CAPE is necessary for the potential for convection [3]. Recall that a convectively unstable layer is not necessarily unstable. In this example, the environment is absolutely unstable, devoid of positive buoyancy, and thus CAPE = 0. A mechanism is required to lift the convectively unstable layer to one characterized by conditional instability.

Air parcels extending above the LFC accelerate upward owing to positive buoyancy and draw energy for acceleration from CAPE. The relationship between maximum updraft velocity (w_{max}) and CAPE (parcel theory) is as follows:

$$w_{max} = \left(2CAPE \right)^{1/2} \tag{4}$$

The moist updraft is integral to the development of a supersaturated condition that results in excess water vapor that (with the aid of hygroscopic aerosols that serve as cloud condensation nuclei or CNN) condenses to form water in liquid and solid form (condensate) manifested as the development of a *cumulus cloud,* followed by the transition to *cumulus congestus,* then ultimately to *cumulonimbus.* With respect to the production of rain during convection, the stochastic *collision-coalescence* mechanism is likely the predominant process that transforms cloud droplets (with broad drop-size distribution) to liquid hydrometeors large enough (diameter 500 μm) to combine with gravity and fall as rain on convective time scales [17].

As saturated parcels rise to the region with environmental temperatures colder than −4°C, the likelihood that ice crystals will develop within the cloud increases. Further, a fraction of water remains in liquid form (supercooled water) until around −35°C [15]. Thus, a region character‐ ized by water in all three phases (vapor, liquid, and solid) develops. The development of the solid hydrometeors known as *ice crystals* and *graupel* within this mixed phase region contribute to the development of lightning. In particular, ice-graupel collisions contribute to the transfer of negative (positive) charge to the larger graupel (smaller ice crystal) particles with charge separation caused by gravity, resulting in a large-scale positive dipole within the cumulonim‐ bus [18]. A smaller positively charged region exists near the cloud base. *Intracloud* (IC) lightning occurs in response to the foregoing dipole, *cloud-to-ground* (CTG) lightning involves a transfer of negative charge from the dipole to the earth surface, and the less common *cloud-to-air* (CTA) lightning variety links the large-scale negative charge with the smaller positive charge near cloud base [18]. The temperatures in the air channel through which lightning occurs exceed the surface of the sun and result in a shockwave followed by a series of sound waves recognized as thunder that is heard generally 25 km away from the lightning occurrence [1, 15].

Straight-line thunderstorm surface winds develop as negative buoyancy (owing to cooling associated with evaporation of water/melting of ice), condensate loading (weight of precipi‐ tation dragging air initially downward before negative buoyancy effects commence), and/or downward-directed pressure gradient force (associated with convection developing within strong environmental vertical wind shear) contribute to the generation of the *convective downdrafts* which are manifested as *gust fronts* (also called *outflow boundaries*) after contact with the earth surface [19]. Hail associated with a thunderstorm involves a complex process whereby graupel and frozen raindrops serve as pre-existing hail embryos and transition to hailstones by traveling along optimal trajectories favorable for rapid growth within the region of the cumulonimbus composed of supercooled water [20].

Given the foregoing thunderstorm development process, the simultaneous occurrence of three conditions are necessary for CI: sufficient atmospheric moisture, CAPE, and a lifting/triggering mechanism. Moisture is necessary for the development of the cumulonimbus cloud condensate which serves as a source material for the development of hydrometeors rain, ice crystals, graupel, and hail. The environmental moisture profile contributes to the development conditional and convective instability. CAPE provides the energy for updraft to heights necessary for the development of the cumulonimbus cloud and the associated mixed phase region that contributes to lightning via charge separation. A mechanism is necessary to lift surface-based parcels through the energy barrier to their LFC, and to lift convectively unstable layers necessary for the development of conditional instability. A myriad of phenomena can provide lift, including fronts, dry lines, sea breezes, gravity waves, PBL horizontal convective rolls, orography, and circulations associated with local soil moisture/vegetation gradients [11, 21].

A myriad of synoptic scale [12] patterns/processes can alter the thermodynamic structure of the environment at a particular location to one favorable for the development of CAPE or convective instability [22]. One scenario in the USA involves the advection of lower-level moist air toward the north across the Southern Plains from the Gulf of Mexico in advance of an upper-level disturbance approaching from the west and advecting midtropospheric dry air originating from the desserts of northern Mexico. The thermodynamic profile over a location influenced by those air masses (e.g., Oklahoma City, Oklahoma) would become one characterized by both conditional and convective instabilities owing to the dry air mass moving over the moist air mass [3].

The foregoing discussion is not exhaustive with respect to thunderstorms. The transition to *severe* convective storms (defined as thunderstorms which generate large hail, damaging straight-line wind, and/or tornadoes), flash flooding, and convective storm mode (squall lines, single cells, multi-cells, supercells, etc.) are not relevant to the development of *non-severe* (also called *ordinary*) thunderstorms in general and are not discussed. Further, *slantwise convection* owing to *conditional symmetric instability* due to the combination of gravitational and centrifugal forces [1] is not considered.

3. Thunderstorm prediction methods

We classify thunderstorm prediction based on the following methods: (1) numerical weather prediction (NWP) models, (2) post-processing of NWP model ensemble output, (3) the post-processing of single deterministic NWP model output via statistical and artificial intelligence (AI)/machine learning (ML), and (4) classical statistical, AI/ML techniques.

3.1. Secondary output variables/parameters from Numerical Weather Prediction (NWP) models

NWP models are based on the concept of determinism which posits that future states of a system evolve from earlier states in accordance with physical laws [23]. Meteorologists describe atmospheric motion by a set of nonlinear partial differential conservation equations —derived from Newton's second law of motion for a fluid, the continuity equation, the equation of state, and the thermodynamic energy equation—that describe atmospheric heat, momentum, water, and mass referred to as *primitive equations, Euler equations,* or *equations of motion* [24–26]. These equations cannot be solved analytically and are thus solved numerically. Further, the earth's atmosphere is a continuous fluid with 10^{44} molecules (Appendix A) which the state-of-the-art NWP models cannot resolve. Thus, NWP model developers undertake the process known as *discretization,* which involves the representation of the atmosphere as a three-dimensional (3D) spatial grid (which divides the atmosphere into volumes or grid cells), the representation of time as finite increments, and the substitution of the primitive equations with corresponding numerical approximations known as *finite difference equations* solved at the grid points [26]. Atmospheric processes resolved by the NWP equations are termed *model dynamics* while unresolved processes are *parameterized* via a series of equations collectively known as *model physics* [25]. Parameterization involves using a set of equations on the resolved scale to implicitly represent the unresolved process. These unresolved (sub-grid-scale) processes include solar/infrared radiation and microphysics (which occur on the molecular scale), cumulus convection, earth surface/atmosphere interactions, and planetary boundary layer/ turbulence [27]. If these primary unresolved processes are not taken into account, the quality of NWP output would deteriorate in less than 1 h when simulating the atmosphere at horizontal grid scales of 1–10 km [25]. The NWP model prediction process is an *initial value problem*. A process known as *data assimilation* is used to provide the requisite initial values. A predominate data assimilation technique involves the use of balanced (theoretical and observed winds in phase) short-term output from an earlier NWP model run to serve as a first guess, followed by the incorporation of meteorological observations to create a balanced *analysis* which serve as the initial condition for the NWP model [26]. Next, the finite difference equations are solved forward in time. The primary output variables include temperature, wind, pressure/height, mixing ratio, and precipitation. At the completion of the NWP model run, *post-processing* is performed which includes the calculation of secondary variables/parameters (CAPE, relative humidity, etc.) and the development of techniques to remove model biases [25, 26, 28].

The state-of-the-art high-resolution NWP models have the ability to explicitly predict/simulate individual thunderstorm cells rather than parameterize the effects of sub-grid-scale convection [29]. NWP output identified as thunderstorm activity involves assessment of NWP output parameter/secondary variable known as *radar reflectivity* defined as the efficiency of a radar target to intercept and return of energy from radio waves [1]. Operational meteorologists in the NWS use radar technology to diagnose/analyze thunderstorms. With respect to hydrometeor targets (rain, snow, sleet, hail, graupel, etc.), radar reflectivity is a function of hydrometeor size, number per volume, phase, shape, and is proportional to six times the effective diameter of the hydrometeor [1]. Radar reflectivity magnitudes ≥ 35dB at the −10°C level are generally regarded as a proxy for CI and for the initial CG lightning flash [30, 31]. Further, the increase in the reflectivity within the mixed-phase region of cumulonimbus clouds correlates strongly with lightning rate [32]. An example of a high-resolution (≤4-km) NWP model that can simulate/predict *radar reflectivity* is version 1.0.4 of the 3-km High-Resolution Rapid Refresh (HRRR) Model, developed by National Oceanic and Atmospheric Administration (NOAA)/ Oceanic and Atmospheric Research (OAR)/Earth Systems Research Laboratory implemented by the National Weather Service (NWS) National Centers for Environmental Prediction (NCEP) Environmental Modeling Center (EMC) on 30 September 2014 to support NWS operations [33]. The specific model dynamical core, physics, and other components are detailed in Appendix B. Yet, we emphasize here that the HRRR does not incorporate cumulus/ convective parameterization (CP), thus allowing for the explicit prediction of thunderstorm activity. One of the output parameters relevant to thunderstorm prediction is *simulated radar reflectivity 1-km (dBZ)*, which is an estimate of the *radar reflectivity* at the constant 1-km level.

Despite the utility of NWP models, there exist fundamental limitations. In particular, the atmosphere is chaotic—a property of the class of deterministic systems characterized by sensitive dependence on the system's initial condition [13, 14, 23]. Thus, minor errors between the initial atmospheric state and the NWP model representation of the initial state can result in a future NWP solution divergent from the future true atmospheric state. Unfortunately, a true, exact, and complete representation of the initial state of the atmosphere using the state-of-the-art NWP models is not possible. Even if the NWP model could perfectly represent the initial atmospheric state, errors associated with imperfections inherent in model formulation and time integration would grow. Model discretization and physics parameterizations introduce errors. Further, the gradient terms in the finite difference equations are approximated using a Taylor series expansion of only a few orders [26, 34], thus introducing *truncation* error. Errors associated with the initial condition, discretization, truncation, and parameterization limits predictability; an intrinsic finite range of predictability exists that is positively correlated to spatial scale [14]. A high-resolution NWP simulation of a tornadic thunderstorm can result in inherent predictability with lead times as short as 3–6 h [35].

Accurately predicting the exact *time* and *location* of individual convective storms is extremely difficult [36]. High-resolution (≤4-km) NWP models can accurately simulate/predict the *occurrence* and *mode* of convection (e.g., whether a less common left-moving and devastating *supercell thunderstorm* will develop), yet have difficulty with regard to the *time* and *location* (exactly when and where will the *supercell* occur) [37, 38]. Even very high-resolution (≤1-km) NWP models that can resolve and predict individual convective cells [29] will not necessarily provide greater accuracy and skill relative to coarser resolution NWP models [39].

3.2. Post processing of NWP model ensembles

Methods exist to generate more optimal or skillful thunderstorm predictions/forecasts when using NWP models. One such method is known as ensemble forecasting [40], which is essentially a Monte Carlo approximation to *stochastic dynamical forecasting* [28, 41]. Stochastic dynamical forecasting is an attempt to account for the uncertainty regarding the true initial atmospheric state. The idea is to run an NWP model on a probability distribution (PD) that describes initial atmospheric state uncertainty. Due to the impracticability of this technique, a technique was proposed whereby the modeler chooses a small random sample of the PD describing initial state uncertainty [41]; the members are collectively referred to as ensemble of initial conditions. The modeler then conducts an NWP model run on each member of the ensemble, hence the term ensemble forecasting [28]. In practice, each member of the ensemble represents a unique combination of model initial condition, dynamics, and/or physics [27, 42]. An advantage of ensemble forecasting over prediction with single deterministic NWP output is the ability to assess the level of forecast uncertainty. One method to assess this uncertainty is to assume a positive correlation between uncertainty and the divergence/spread in the ensemble members [28]. Prediction probabilities can be generated by post-processing the ensemble. Applying ensembles to thunderstorm forecasting, the NWS Environmental Modeling Center developed the *short-range ensemble forecast (SREF)*, a collection of selected output from an ensemble of 21 mesoscale (16-km) NWP model runs. The NWS Storm Prediction Center (SPC) post-processes SREF output to create a quasi-real-time suite of products that includes the *calibrated probabilistic prediction of thunderstorms* [42]. There exist utility in the use of ensembles in thunderstorm forecasting. According to [16], the timing of CI within selected mesoscale regions can be predicted accurately using an ensemble-based approach.

One limitation of NWP ensembles to support operational forecasters is the tremendous computational cost necessary to run since each ensemble member is a separate NWP model run. Another limitation is the realization that the true PD of the initial condition uncertainty is unknown and changes daily [28].

3.3. Post-processing of single deterministic NWP model output using other statistical and artificial intelligence/machine learning techniques

Statistical methods can be utilized to post-process NWP output to correct for certain systematic NWP model biases and to quantify the level of uncertainty in single NWP deterministic output [28, 43]. Statistical post-processing methods include *model output statistics* (MOS) [44] and *logistic regression* [28].

MOS involves the development of data-driven models to predict the future state of a target based on a data set of past NWP output (features/predictors) and the corresponding target/ predictand. Following [28], a regression function f_{MOS} is developed to fit target Y at future time t to a set of predictors/features (from NWP output known at $t = 0$) represented by vector x. The development and implementation is as follows:

$$Y_t = f_{MOS}\left(x_t\right) \tag{5}$$

One limitation of the MOS technique involves NWP model changes made by the developers. If NWP model adjustments alter *systematic errors*, new MOS equations should be formulated [28]. Model changes can occur somewhat frequently. Consider the North American Mesoscale (NAM), which is the placeholder for the official NWS operational mesoscale NWP model for the North American domain. On 20 June 2006, the NAM representative model switched from the *hydrostatic Eta* to the *Weather Research and Forecasting (WRF)-Non-hydrostatic Mesoscale Model (NMM)*, a change in both the model dynamical formulation and modeling framework. Then, on 1 October 2011, the NAM representative model switched to *NOAA Environmental Modeling System Non-hydrostatic Multiscale Model on the B-grid (NEMS-NMMB)* resulting in changes to the model framework (WRF to NEMS) and model discretization (change from Arakawa E to B grid) (Appendix C).

The NWS uses multiple linear regression (MLR) (with forward selection) applied to operational NWP model predictors and corresponding weather observations (target) to derive MOS equations to support forecast operations [43]. The NWS provides high-resolution gridded MOS products which include a 3-h probability of thunderstorms [45] and thunderstorm probability forecasts as part of the NWS *Localized Aviation Model Output Statistics Program* (LAMP) [46].

Logistic regression is a method to relate the predicted probability p_j of one member of a binary target to the jth set of n predictors/features $\left(x_1, x_2, ..., x_n\right)$ to the following nonlinear equation:

$$p_j = \frac{1}{1 + exp\left(-b_0 - b_1 x_1 - b_2 x_2 - \dots - b_n x_n\right)} \tag{6}$$

The regression parameters are determined via the method of *maximum likelihood* [28].

Logistic regression models were used by [47] to develop MOS equations to generate probability of thunderstorms and the conditional probability of severe thunderstorms in twelve 7200 km^2 regions at 6-h projections out to 48-h in the Netherlands. The NWP output was provided by both the High-Resolution Limited-Area Model (HIRLAM) and the European Centre for Medium-Range Weather Forecasts (ECMWF) NWP model. The Surveillance et d'Alerte Foudre par Interférométrie Radioélectrique (SAFIR) lightning network provided the target data. Verification results suggest that the prediction system possessed good skills.

Artificial intelligence (AI) involves the use of computer software to reproduce human cognitive processes such as learning and decision making [1, 48]. More recently, the term *machine learning* (ML) is used to describe the development of computer systems that improve with experience [1, 49]. Specific AI/ML techniques involving the post-processing of NWP output include *expert systems* [50], *adaptive boosting* [51], *artificial neural networks* [52, 53], and *random forests* [31].

A random forest [54] is a classifier resulting from an ensemble/forest of tree-structured classifiers, whereby each tree is developed from independent random subsamples of the data set (including a random selection of features from which the optimum individual tree predictors are selected) drawn from the original training set. The generalization error (which depends on individual tree strength and tree-tree correlations) convergences to a minimum as the number of trees becomes large, yet overfitting does not occur owing to the law of large numbers. After training, the classifier prediction is the result of a synthesis of the votes of each tree.

In one study, selected thermodynamic and kinematic output from an Australian NWP model served as input for an expert system using the decision tree method to assess the likelihood of thunderstorms and severe thunderstorms [50]. Further, an artificial neural network model to predict significant thunderstorms that require the issuance of the Convective SIGMET product (called WST), issued by the National Weather Service's Aviation Weather Center, for the 3–7 h period after 1800 UTC; the model demonstrated skill, including the ability to narrow the WST outlook region while still capturing the subsequent WST issuance region [52]. Logistic regression and random forests were used to develop models to predict convective initiation (CI) ≤1 h in advance. The features/predictors included NWP output and selected Geostationary Operational Environmental Satellite (GOES)-R data. The performance of these models was an improvement of an earlier model developed based on GOES-R data alone [31].

3.4. Classical statistical and artificial intelligence/machine learning techniques

Statistical methods not involving the use of NWP model output (classical statistical) that have been used to predict thunderstorm occurrence include *multiple discriminate analysis (MDA)*, *scatter diagrams*, and *multiple regression*. Corresponding AI/ML techniques include *expert systems, artificial neural networks*, and *logistic regression*.

MDA is essentially a form of multiple linear regression used to predict an event. In particular, a discriminant function relates a nonnumerical predictand to a set of predictors; the value of the function that distinguishes between event groups [1, 55]. An MDA was used to obtain 12 h prediction functions to distinguish between the following two or three member groups within selected domains in portions of the Central and Eastern USA: thunderstorm/no-thunderstorm, thunderstorm/severe thunderstorm, and thunderstorm/severe thunderstorm/no-thunderstorm. The verification domains were within 1° latitude radius relative to the position of the data source that provided the predictor variables. The MDA prediction system provided skill in the 0-12 h period [55].

In one study, the utility of both a graphical method and multiple regression was tested to predict thunderstorms [56]. The graphical method involved scatter diagrams that were used to analyze multiple pairs of atmospheric stability index parameters in order to discover any diagram(s) whereby the majority of thunderstorm occurrence cases were clustered within a zone while the majority of the non-thunderstorm occurrence cases were outside of the zone. Two such diagrams were found—scatter diagrams of Showalter index versus Total Totals index, and Jefferson's modified index versus the George index. The multiple regression technique involved the stepwise screening of 274 potential predictors to 9 remaining. Both prediction models provided thunderstorm predictions in probabilistic terms. Objective techniques were used to convert probabilistic predictions to binary predictions for the purpose of verification. Results indicate that the multiple regression model performed better.

An expert system is a form of artificial intelligence that attempts to mimic the performance of a human expert when making decisions. The expert system includes a knowledge base and an inference engine. The knowledge base contains the combination of human knowledge and experience. Once the system is developed, questions are given to the system and the inference engine uses the knowledge base and renders a decision [57]. An expert system was developed using the decision tree method to forecast the development of thunderstorms and severe thunderstorms [58]; the tree was based on physical reasoning using the observation of meteorological parameters considered essential for convective development. An expert system named *Thunderstorm Intelligence Prediction System (TIPS)* was developed to predict thunderstorm occurrence [59]. Selected thermodynamic sounding data from 1200 UTC and forecaster assessment of likely convective triggering mechanisms were used to forecast thunderstorm occurrence for the subsequent 1500–0300 UTC period. Critical values of five (5) separate atmospheric stability parameters for thunderstorm occurrence and corresponding consensus rules served as the knowledge base. The forecaster answer regarding trigger mechanism and the values of the stability parameters served as input to the inference engine, which interrogated the knowledge base and provided an answer regarding future thunder-storm occurrence. Verification of TIPS revealed utility.

The artificial neural network (ANN) has been used to predict thunderstorms. Thermodynamic data from Udine Italy rawinsondes, surface observations, and lightning data were used to train/optimize an ANN model to predict thunderstorms 6 h in advance over a 5000-km^2 domain in the Friuli Venezia Giulia region [60]. An ANN model was developed (also using thermo-dynamic data) to predict severe thunderstorms over Kolkata India during the pre-monsoon season (April–May) [61].

Logistic regression was used to develop a binary classifier to predict thunderstorms 6–12 h in advance within a 6825-km^2 region in Spain. A total of 15 predictors (combination of stability indices and other parameters) were chosen to adequately describe the pre-convective environment. The classifier generated satisfactory results on the novel data set [62].

A limitation of classical statistics to weather prediction is that utility is bimodal in time; confined to very short time periods (less than a few hours) or long time periods (10 days) [28]. The utility of AI/ML techniques without NWP may not be as restrictive. Convective storm prediction accuracies associated with expert systems may be similar to that of NWP models [36].

4. The utility of post-processing NWP model output with artificial neural networks to predict thunderstorm occurrence, timing, and location

The rapid drop in prediction/forecast accuracy per unit time for classical statistical techniques renders it less than optimal for thunderstorm predictions over time scales greater than nowcasting (≤ 3 h).

Predicting thunderstorms with the use of deterministic NWP models allows for the prediction of atmospheric variables/parameters in the ambient environment that directly influence thunderstorm development. As discussed previously, limitations of NWP models include predictability limitations owing to a chaotic atmosphere and inherent model error growth [13, 14, 23]. NWP model ensembles attempt to account for the uncertainty in the NWP model's initial condition which contributes to predictability limitations in NWP models [40]. The post-processing of NWP model ensembles can generate useful probabilistic thunderstorm output [42]. However, there is a much greater computational cost to generate an ensemble of deterministic runs relative to a single run. The post-processing of output from a single deterministic NWP model can improve skill by minimizing certain systematic model biases, yet predictability limitations associated with single deterministic NWP model output remain.

The authors explored the use of the artificial neural network (ANN) to post-process output from a single deterministic NWP model in an effort to improve thunderstorm predictive skill, based on an adjustment to the author's previous research [53]. As mentioned earlier, this approach involves a much lower computational cost relative to model ensembles. In particular, the single NWP model used in the development of the thunderstorm ANN (TANN) models discussed in this chapter is the 12-km NAM (North American Mesoscale), which refers to either the Eta, NEMS-NMMB, or WRF-NMM model (only one model used at a time; see Appendix C). The model integration cost to run the 21-member SREF ensemble would be of the order of 20 times the cost required to run the 12-km NAM (Israel Jirak 2016, personal communication.)

Given that ANN was developed to capture the parallel distributed processing thought to occur in the human brain and has tremendous pattern recognition capabilities [63–65], we posit that the ANN will learn the limitations/errors associated with a single NWP deterministic model solution to generate skillful forecasts, notwithstanding NWP predictability limitations. Thus, AI/ML rather than NWP model ensembles would be utilized to deal with atmospheric chaos. The remainder of this chapter focuses on the development of ANN models to predict thunderstorms (TANN) that are part of the ongoing research.

5. Artificial neural network models to predict thunderstorms within three South Texas 400-km^2 domains based solely on a data set within the same domain of each

In an earlier study [53], a thunderstorm ANN (TANN) was developed to predict thunderstorm occurrence in three separate 400-km^2 square (box) domains in South Texas (USA), 9, 12, and 15 h (+/–2 h) in advance, by post-processing 12-km NWP model output from a single deterministic NWP model (Appendix C) and 4-km sub-grid-scale output from soil moisture magnitude and heterogeneity estimates. A framework was established to predict thunderstorms in 286 box domains (**Figure 1**), yet predictions were only performed for three. The three box regions were strategically located to access model performance within the *Western Gulf Coastal Plain* region (boxes 103 and 238), the more arid *Southern Texas Plains* region (box 73), and within the region with the greatest amount of positive target data/thunderstorm occurrences based on CTG lightning density (box 238.) A skillful model was envisioned based on the combination of the deterministic future state of ambient meteorological variables/parameters related to thunderstorm development and sub-grid-scale data related to CI. TANN models were trained with the foregoing NWP model output and sub-grid data as predictors and corresponding CTG lightning data as the target. Each TANN model was trained using the feed-forward multi-layer perceptron topology with one hidden layer, the log-sigmoid and linear transfer functions in the hidden and output layers, respectively, and the scaled conjugate gradient (SCG) learning algorithm. The SCG algorithm makes implicit use of the second-order terms of the Hessian, searches the weight space/error surface in conjugate directions, avoids problems associated with line searches, and converges more efficiently than gradient descent [66]. The nomenclature X-Y-Z was used to describe the topology, where X, Y, and Z are the number of neurons in the input, hidden, and output layers, respectively. The data set consisted of a training/validation set (2004–2006; 2009–2012) and a testing set (2007–2008) for final performance and comparison with human forecasters and MLR. For each TANN model variant, the number of neurons in the hidden layer was determined iteratively For Y hidden layers, where $Y = \{1 - 10, 12, 15, 17, 20, 25, 30, 35, 40, 45, 50, 60, 70, 80, 90, 100\}$, the TANN model was trained 50 times. After each training, receiver operating characteristic (ROC) curves were generated to determine the optimal threshold, defined as the case where the Peirce Skill Score (PSS) was greatest [67]. The trained ANN with optimal threshold was then used to make predictions on the testing set (2007–2008); the corresponding performance results were calculated. The mean PSS of the 50 results from both the training and testing sets, for each Y, was archived. The chosen Y corresponded to the least number of hidden layer neurons with a PSS standard error which overlaps the standard error associated with the maximum PSS. Once Y is chosen, the performance results of the TANN are simply the mean of the 50 runs previously archived that corresponds to the chosen Y.

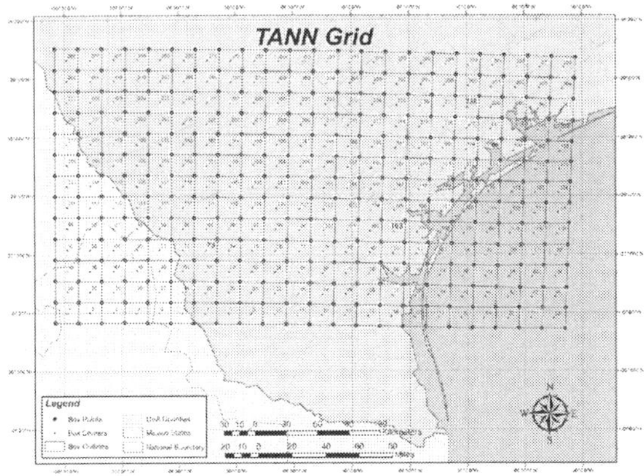

Figure 1. TANN and TANN2 grid domain. This grid is represented as 286 20 km× 20 km regions (boxes). The label inside each box is the identification number (ID). The boxes with ID values in larger font (73, 103, and 238) are the subject of this study. Image from Collins and Tissot [53].

Eighteen (18) TANN classifiers were developed with half based on a reduced set of predictors/features due to feature selection (FS) and the other half using the full set of 43 potential predictors. FS involves a determination of the subset of potential predictors that describes much of the variability of the target/predictand. This is very important for very large dimensional models which may suffer from the *curse of dimensionality*, which posits that the amount of data needed to develop a skillful data-driven model increases exponentially as model dimension increases linearly [68]. When the features in the subset generated by the FS method are used to train an ANN model, it is important that such features are both relevant and non-redundant. Irrelevant features can adversely affect ANN model learning by introducing noise, and redundant features can result in reduced ANN model predictive skill by increasing the likelihood of convergence on local minima on the error surface during training [69]. The FS technique used was *correlation-based feature selection* (CFS) [70–72]. CFS is a filtering-based FS technique, meaning that statistical associations between the features and the target are assessed outside of the model. Specifically, CFS uses an information theory-based heuristic known as *symmetric uncertainty* to assess feature-target and feature-feature correlations to assess relevance and redundancy, respectively. The search strategy is the *Best First search* with a stopping criterion of five consecutive non-improving feature subsets.

The optimized TANN binary classifiers were evaluated on a novel data set (2007–2008), and performance was compared to MLR-based binary classifiers, and to operational forecasts from the NWS (National Digital Forecast Database, NDFD, Appendix D).

The MLR models were developed via stepwise forward linear regression (SFLR). For each MLR model, the SFLR process began with an empty set of features (constant value $y = \beta_0$. At each subsequent forward step, a predictor is added (from the list of 36 predictors in **Tables 2** and **3**, less the predictors already chosen) based on the change in the value of the Akaike information criterion (AIC) [73], while also considering removal of previously selected predictors based on the same criterion. The optimal MLR model chosen has the smallest AIC which is essentially a trade-off between model size and accuracy based on the training data. The MATLAB® function *stepwiselm* was used to perform SFLR to determine the regression equation coefficients. The resultant MLR models in this study are of the form:

$$y_i = \beta_0 + \sum_{j=1}^{k} \beta_j x_{ij} + \varepsilon_i \tag{7}$$

where y_i is the ith predictand response, β_j is the jth regression coefficient, β_0 is a constant, x_{ij} is the ith observation for the jth predictor, for $j = 1, \ldots, k$. Finally, ε_i represents error. Each MLR model was transformed into a binary classifier using the same method used in ANN classifier development, except that each MLR model was calibrated on the entire training sample to determine the coefficients, unlike ANN calibration which involved the splitting of the training sample into training and validation data sets. (However, one could argue that the ANN is also using the entire training sample as the validation set is inherently necessary to properly calibrate a model.)

The results were mixed—the TANN, MLR, and human forecasters performed better than the other two depending on the domain, prediction hour, and performance metric used. Results revealed the utility of an automated TANN model to support forecast operations with the limitation that a larger number of individual ANNs must be calibrated in order to generate operational predictions over a large area. Further, the utility of sub-grid-scale soil moisture data appeared limited given the fact that only 1/9 of the TANN models with reduced features retained any of the sub-grid parameters as a feature. The NWP model convective precipitation (CP) feature was retained in all the nine feature selection TANN models, suggesting that CP adequately accounted for the initiation of sub-grid-scale convection. This result is consistent with another study [47] which found that model CP was the most relevant predictor of thunderstorm activity.

6. Artificial neural network models to predict thunderstorms within three South Texas 400-km² domains based on data set from two-hundred and eighty-six 400-km² domains

With respect to TANN skill, the endeavor to predict thunderstorms in a small domain relative to domains used in other studies restricted the amount of CG lightning cases. A large number of thunderstorm cases would be beneficial to the model calibration and verification process; the amount of target data in [53] may have been insufficient to train this data-driven model with sufficient skill owing to the curse of dimensionality [67]. Further, the method of training/optimizing TANN models for each 400-km² domain limits operational applicability since it would require the development of literally thousands of TANN models at a country scale. In order to retain thunderstorm predictions in 400-km² domains while increasing predictive skill, a new approach was developed (TANN2), whereby for each prediction hour (9, 12, 15), a single TANN model is trained over all two-hundred and eighty six 400-km² continuous domains. This approach dramatically increased the amount of positive target data (thunderstorm cases) and total cases/instances. **Table 1** depicts the quantity of data utilized in this project. The total number of cases over the study period was 1,148,576 with 939,510 cases used for model calibration and 209,066 cases contained in the 2007–2008 testing set.

Prediction hour	Total instances (training sample)	Positive target data	Percent positive target
9	663,519	22,139	3.3
12	646,073	16,904	2.6
15	659,801	12,682	1.9

Table 1. Quantity of data available to train TANN2 models.

Relative to the previous study [53], only the NWP model and Julian date predictor variables (features) were retained (resulting in 36 potential features used in this study; see **Tables 2** and **3**.) Given that in [53], only one sub-grid parameter was chosen for only 1/9 of the box/prediction hour combinations, and that the model including this sub-grid-scale parameter did not result in classifier performance improvement, the utility of the sub-grid-scale data appeared very limited. As mentioned in [53], the NWP model CP parameter was a ubiquitous output of the FS technique and thus considered a skillful predictor of convection. Physically, it was surmised that CP adequately accounted for the effects of sub-grid-scale convection. The use of FS was retained in order to eliminate irrelevant and redundant features to improve model skill and to reduce model size. The reduction in model size/dimension (owing to FS) and the increase in both the training data set and the amount of target CG lightning cases are expected to result in a more accurate/skillful model when considering the curse of dimensionality.

Abbreviation	Description (Units)	Justification as thunderstorm predictor
PWAT	Total precipitable water (mm)	Atmospheric moisture proxy
MR_{850}	Mixing ratio at 850 hPa (g kg^{-1})	Lower level moisture necessary for convective cell to reach horizontal scale ≥4 km in order to overcome dissipative effects [84]
RH_{850}	Relative humidity at 850 hPa (%)	When combined with CAPE, predictor of subsequent thunderstorm location independent of synoptic pattern [85]
CAPE	Surface-based convective available potential energy (J kg^{-1})	Instability proxy; the quantity $(2CAPE)^{0.5}$ is the theoretical limit of thunderstorm updraft velocity [11]

Abbreviation	Description (Units)	Justification as thunderstorm predictor
CIN	Convective inhibition (J kg^{-1})	Surface-based convective updraft magnitude must exceed $(CIN)^{0.5}$ for parcels to reach level of free convection [11]
LI	Lifted index (K)	Atmospheric instability proxy; utility in thunderstorm prediction [86]
U_{LEVEL}, V_{LEVEL}	U,V wind components at surface, 850 hPa (LEVEL = surface, 850 hPa) (ms^{-1})	Strong wind can modulate or preclude surface heterogeneity induced mesoscale circulations [87, 88]
VV_{LEVEL}	Vertical velocity at 925, 700, and 500 hPa (LEVEL = 925, 700, 500 hPa) (Pa s^{-1})	Account for mesoscale and synoptic scale thunderstorm triggering mechanisms (sea breezes, fronts, upper level disturbances) that are resolved by the NAM
DROPOFF$_{PROXY}$	Potential temperature dropoff proxy (K)	Atmospheric instability proxy; highly sensitive to CI [89]
LCL	Lifted condensation level (m)	Proxy for cloud base height; positive correlation between cloud base height and CAPE to convective updraft conversion efficiency [90]
T_LCL	Temperature at the LCL (K)	T_LCL $\geq$ −10°C essential for presence of supercooled water in convective cloud essential for lightning via graupel-ice crystal collision mechanism [91]
CP	Convective precipitation (kg m^{-2})	By-product of the *Betts-Miller-Janjic* convective parameterization scheme [92] when triggered; proxy for when the NAM anticipates existence of sub-grid-scale convection
VSHEARS8	Vertical wind shear: 10 m to 800 hPa layer (×10^{-3} s^{-1})	The combination of horizontal vorticity (associated with ambient 0–2 km vertical shear), and density current (e.g., gust front) generated horizontal vorticity (associated with 0–2 km vertical shear of opposite sign than that of ambient shear can trigger new convection [93]
VSHEAR86	Vertical wind shear: 800–600 hPa layer (×10^{-3} s^{-1})	Convective updraft must exceed vertical shear immediately above the boundary layer for successful thunderstorm development [58, 89]

Table 2. Description of NAM predictor variables/parameters used in TANN and TANN2 (from [53]).

Abbreviation	Description (units)	Justification as thunderstorm predictor
U_{LEVEL}, V_{LEVEL}	U,V wind at the surface, 900, 800, 700, 600, 500 hPa levels (LEVEL= surface, 900, 800, 700, 600, 500) (ms^{-1})	Thermodynamic profile modification owing to veering of wind (warming) or backing of wind (cooling); backing (veering) of wind in the lowest 300 hPa can suppress (enhance) convective development [94]
HI$_{LOW}$	Humidity index (°C)	Both a constraint on afternoon convection and an atmospheric control on the interaction between soil

Abbreviation	Description (units)	Justification as thunderstorm predictor
		moisture and convection [94]
CTP Proxy	Proxy for convective triggering potential (dimensionless)	Both a constraint on afternoon convection and an atmospheric control on the interaction between soil moisture and convection [95]
VSHEARS7	Vertical wind shear: surface to 700 hPa layer ($\times 10^{-3}$ s^{-1})	Strong vertical shear in the lowest 300 hPa can suppress convective development [94]
VSHEAR75	Vertical wind shear: 700 to 500 hPa layer ($\times 10^{-3}$ s^{-1})	Convective updraft must exceed vertical shear immediately above the boundary layer for successful thunderstorm development [58, 89]

Table 3. Description of NAM initialization variables/parameters used in TANN and TANN2 (from [53]).

With respect to model training, validating, optimizing, and testing, the same strategy was utilized as in [53], with two differences. First, when determining the optimal number of hidden layer neurons, the range of neurons was extended to $Y = \{1–10, 12, 15, 17, 20, 25, 30, 35, 40, 45, 50, 60, 70, 80, 90, 100, 125, 150, 200\}$. Second, before each split of the training sample into training and validation components, a training set of the same size of the total training data available was drawn randomly from the training set with replacement. This technique allows for an exploration of training data set variability.

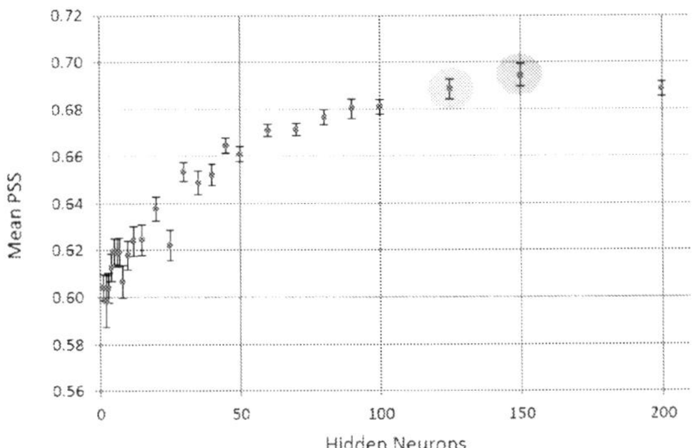

Figure 2. Determination of the optimal number of hidden layer neurons (Y) for the 12 h TANN2 36-Y-1 model (all 36 potential predictors used). Each point and corresponding error bar represents the mean Peirce Skill Score (PSS) and standard error resulting from 50 iterations with results computed based on the training portions of the training sample including the generation of ROC curves based on the same data; the selected thresholds/models correspond to the maximum PSS along the respective ROC curve. The number of hidden layer neurons chosen is the least number of hidden layer neurons with a PSS standard error which overlaps the standard error corresponding to the maximum PSS. Thus, in this example, 150 hidden layer neurons corresponds to the maximum mean PSS = 0.694 ± 0.005 (within the red circle.) The performance of the TANN2 model with 125 hidden neurons, PSS = 0.689 ± 0.005, overlapped with the 150 hidden neuron confidence interval and hence was selected as the optimum number of hidden neurons, thus TANN 36-125-1.

Figure 2 depicts an example of how the optimal Y is chosen. The light red highlight identifies the number of hidden neurons leading to the largest mean PSS while the green highlight indicates the number of hidden neurons selected as the two cases standard errors overlap. **Table 4** depicts the optimal topologies for the TANN2 X-Y-1 and 36-Y-1 models.

With respect to FS, an exhaustive search involving the 36 potential features, although ideal, would have been computationally unrealistic. The FS methods used for this work were filter based, information theoretic, and designed to choose feature subsets relevant to the corresponding target while non-redundant to each feature in the subset. The methods used were multi-variate in the sense that feature-feature relationships were also considered, rather than the univariate strategy of assessing only feature-target relationships sequentially. The methods used are CFS (described earlier) and *minimum Redundancy Maximum Relevance* (mRMR) [74]. The *mRMR classic* function from the **mRMRe** package as part of the **R** programming language [75] was used to calculate mRMR. The following is an explanation of the mRMR technique in the context of mRMR classic as described in [76]: Consider $r(x, y)$ the correlation coefficient between features x and y. The mRMR technique uses the information-theoretic parameter known as *mutual information* (MI), defined as

$$1 - r\left(x,y\right)^2 \ MI\left(x,y\right) = \frac{-1}{2} ln \tag{8}$$

Let t be the target/predictand and $X = \left\{x_1, ..., x_n\right\}$ represent the set of n features. We desire to rank X such that we maximize relevance (maximize MI with t) and minimize redundancy (minimize mean MI with all previously selected features.) First, we selected x_i, the feature with the greatest MI with t:

$$x_i = arg \ \max_{x_i \in X} MI\left(x_i,t\right) \tag{9}$$

Thus, we initialize the set of selected features S with x_i. For each subsequent step j, features are added to S by choosing the feature with the greatest relevance with t and lowest redundancy with previously selected features to maximize score Q:

$$Q_j = MI\left(x_j,t\right) - \frac{1}{|S|} \sum_{x_k \in S} MI\left(x_j,x_k\right) \tag{10}$$

The mRMR classic function requires the user to select the size of S, which we chose to equal the maximum number of features. We then choose the subset by choosing only those features corresponding to $Q_j > 0$.

Table 4 depicts the reduced set of features chosen via CFS and mRMR. **Table 5** summarizes the resulting TANN2 topologies.

Prediction hour	CFS	mRMR
9 h	PWAT, CP	$U_{800}(0)$, HI_{LOW}, CP, VV_{925}, VV_{500} RH_{850}, CIN, LCL, T_LCL, CAPE, VSHEAR86, $V_{600}(0)$, PWAT, CTP_PROXY, VSHEAR75(0)
12 h	CP	CP, VV_{500}, VV_{925}, PWAT, RH_{850}, CTP_PROXY, CAPE, VSHEAR86, HI_{LOW}, $DROPOFF_{PROXY}$, $U_{800}(0)$, VV_{700}
15 h	CP	CP, LI, CAPE, VV_{925}, PWAT, RH_{850}, CTP_PROXY, VV_{700} $V_{500}(0)$, $U_{SFC}(0)$, VV_{500}, HI_{LOW}

Table 4. Variables/parameters chosen by the CFS and mRMR feature selection techniques; variables followed by zero depict NAM initialization variables.

Prediction hour	Optimal 36-Y-1 topology	Optimal X-Y-1 topology (CFS)	Optimal X-Y-1 topology (mRMR)
9	36-150-1	2-60-1	15-100-1
12	36-125-1	1-1-1	12-90-1
15	36-70-1	1-1-1	12-90-1

Table 5. Optimal TANN2 topologies based on iterative method to determine the optimal number of hidden layer neurons.

Forecast	Observed		
	Yes	No	Total
Yes	a *(hit)*	b *(false alarm)*	$a + b$
No	c *(miss)*	d *(correct rejection)*	$c + d$
Total	$a + c$	$b + d$	$a + b + c + d = n$

Table 6. Contingency Matrix from which scalar performance metrics (**Table 7**) were derived (from [53]).

Performance metric (value range)	Symbol	Equation
Probability of detection [0,1]	POD	$a/(a + c)$
False alarm rate [0,1]	F	$b/(b + d)$
False alarm ratio [0,1]	FAR	$b/(a + b)$
Critical success index [0,1]	CSI	$a/(a + b + c)$
Peirce skill score [−1,1]	PSS	$(ad - bc)/(b + d)(a + c)$
Heidke skill score [−1,1]	HSS	$2(ad - bc)/[(a + c)(c + d) + (a + b)(b + d)]$
Yule's Q (odds ratio skill score) [−1,1]	ORSS	$(ad - bc)/(ad + bc)$
Clayton skill score [−1,1]	CSS	$(ad - bc)/(a + b)(c + d)$
Gilbert skill score [−1/3,1]	GSS	$\left(a - a_r\right)/\left(a + b + c - a_r\right);\ a_r = (a + b)(a + c)/n$

Table 7. Relevant scalar performance metrics for binary classifiers used to evaluate TANN2 and MLR Models and NDFD (from [53]).

Tables 6 and **7** depict the contingency matrix and the corresponding performance metrics for binary classifiers used in this study.

Tables 8–11 depict the performance results of the TANN2 models, trained over all 286 boxes, and applied to boxes 73, 103, 238, and 1–286 (all boxes.) For each skill-based performance metric (PSS, CSI, HSS, ORSS, CSS, GSS), the *Wilcoxon Sign Rank* Test was used to determine whether TANN2 median performance (based on the 50 runs on the 2007–2008 testing set corresponding to the optimal number of hidden neurons) was statistically significantly different (5% level) than the corresponding MLR model and human forecaster performances. The relevant human forecasters were operational forecasters from the National Weather Service (NWS) (Appendix D). A summary of the results follow.

There is a significant improvement in the value of selected performance metrics for TANN2 over TANN in absolute terms. For example, with respect to the TANN models developed without FS, the PSS metric for the TANN2 models increased over the corresponding TANN models, by approximately 10–70%, 55–74%, and 10–120%, respectively, for boxes 238, 103, and 73.

When comparing TANN2 model performance relative to the operational forecasters (NDFD), and defining superior performance as statistically significant superior performance with respect to at least one skill-based performance metric (PSS, CSI, HSS, ORSS, CSS, and GSS), the results are as follows: For *box 238*, at least one of the TANN2 model performances exceeded that of the forecasters (NDFD), for all three prediction hours; all three TANN2 models (TANN 36-150-1, TANN 2-60-1 CFS, and TANN 15-100-1 mRMR) performed superior to NDFD for prediction hour 9, both TANN 36-150-1 and TANN 2-60-1 CFS performed better for prediction hour 12, and only TANN 2-6-1 CFS performed better for prediction hour 15. With respect to *box 103*, results were mixed. None of the TANN2 models performance was superior to NDFD for prediction hour 9, the TANN 36-125-1 and TANN 12-90-1 mRMR performed better for prediction hour 12, and only the TANN 1-1-1 CFS performed superior to the forecasters for prediction hour 15. Results were again mixed with regard to *box 73*. TANN 36-150-1 and TANN 15-100-1 mRMR performed superior to NDFD for prediction hour 9, none of the TANN2 models performed better than NDFD for prediction hour 12, and only TANN 36-70-1 performed superior to NDFD for prediction hour 15.

Conducting the same analysis with respect to TANN2 model compared to MLR, namely assessing statistically significant superior performance with respect to at least one skill-based performance metric, the results are as follows: For *box 238*, all three TANN2 models performed better than MLR at 9 h, none of the TANN2 models performed better at 12 h, and only the TANN 1-1-1 CFS model performed superior to MLR at 15 h. Regarding *box 103*, the TANN 36-125-1 and TANN 15-100-1 mRMR performed better than MLR for both 9 h and 12 h, while TANN 36-70-1 and TANN 1-1-1 CFS performed better than MLR for 15 h. For *box 73*, only TANN 36-150-1 performs better than MLR at 9 h, only TANN 1-1-1 CFS performs better at both 12 h and 15 h.

	POD	FAR	F	PSS	CSI	HSS	ORSS	CSS	GSS
9 h Model predictions									
TANN 36-150-1	0.94	0.80	0.30	0.63	0.20	0.24	0.94	0.19	0.13
TANN 2-60-1 CFS	0.98	0.81	0.33	0.65	0.19	0.22	0.98	0.19	0.13
TANN 15-100-1 mRMR	0.91	0.80	0.30	0.63	0.20	0.23	0.93	0.19	0.13
MLR	0.96	0.80	0.32	0.64	0.19	0.23	0.96	0.19	0.13
9 h Operational public forecasts									
NDFD	0.94	0.81	0.35	0.59	0.19	0.21	0.93	0.18	0.12
12 h Model predictions									
TANN 36-125-1	0.81	0.93	0.28	0.53	0.07	0.09	0.83	0.06	0.04
TANN 1-1-1 CFS	0.56	0.93	0.20	0.36	0.06	0.08	0.67	0.05	0.04
TANN 12-90-1 mRMR	0.75	0.94	0.32	0.42	0.05	0.06	0.71	0.05	0.03
MLR	0.88	0.93	0.30	0.57	0.07	0.09	0.88	0.07	0.05
12 h Operational public forecasts									
NDFD	0.67	0.92	0.28	0.39	0.07	0.08	0.67	0.06	0.04
15 h Model predictions									
TANN 36-70-1	0.64	0.95	0.23	0.41	0.05	0.06	0.71	0.04	0.03
TANN 1-1-1 CFS	0.45	0.91	0.08	0.37	0.08	0.13	0.81	0.08	0.07
TANN 12-90-1 mRMR	0.64	0.96	0.28	0.36	0.04	0.04	0.63	0.03	0.02
MLR	0.73	0.95	0.27	0.46	0.05	0.06	0.76	0.04	0.03
15 h Operational public forecasts									
NDFD	0.92	0.92	0.23	0.69	0.08	0.11	0.95	0.07	0.06

Values corresponding to each TANN X-Y-Z model represent the median of 50 separate trial runs of the model. Yellow (blue) denotes TANN X-Y-Z median values of skill-based metrics (PSS, CSI, HSS, ORSS, CSS, and GSS only) NOT statistically significantly different (based on the Wilcoxon Sign Rank Tests, 2 sided, 1 sample, 5% significant level) from the NDFD (MLR) values.

Table 8. Performance results of TANN X-Y-Z models for box 238 for the 2007–2008 independent data set and corresponding comparisons to the WFO CRP forecasters (NDFD), multi-linear regression (MLR) models.

	POD	FAR	F	PSS	CSI	HSS	ORSS	CSS	GSS
9 h Model predictions									
TANN 36-150-1	0.93	0.87	0.31	0.62	0.13	0.15	0.93	0.12	0.08
TANN 2-60-1 CFS	0.90	0.88	0.33	0.57	0.12	0.14	0.89	0.11	0.07
TANN 15-100-1 mRMR	0.87	0.87	0.29	0.56	0.13	0.15	0.87	0.12	0.08
MLR	0.97	0.88	0.36	0.61	0.12	0.14	0.96	0.12	0.08
9 h Operational public forecasts									
NDFD	1.00	0.85	0.31	0.69	0.15	0.19	1.00	0.15	0.10

	POD	FAR	F	PSS	CSI	HSS	ORSS	CSS	GSS
12 h Model predictions									
TANN 36-125-1	0.80	0.95	0.23	0.58	0.05	0.07	0.87	0.05	0.04
TANN 1-1-1 CFS	0.50	0.96	0.18	0.32	0.04	0.05	0.64	0.03	0.03
TANN 12-90-1 mRMR	0.90	0.95	0.27	0.63	0.05	0.07	0.92	0.05	0.04
MLR	0.80	0.95	0.25	0.55	0.05	0.06	0.85	0.05	0.03
12 h Operational public forecasts									
NDFD	0.80	0.94	0.24	0.56	0.06	0.08	0.86	0.06	0.04
15 h Model predictions									
TANN 36-70-1	0.83	0.96	0.21	0.62	0.04	0.05	0.90	0.03	0.03
TANN 1-1-1 CFS	0.50	0.92	0.06	0.44	0.07	0.12	0.89	0.07	0.06
TANN 12-90-1 mRMR	0.83	0.97	0.29	0.55	0.03	0.04	0.86	0.03	0.02
MLR	0.83	0.97	0.24	0.60	0.03	0.05	0.88	0.03	0.02
15 h Operational public forecasts									
NDFD	1.00	0.97	0.19	0.81	0.04	0.07	1.00	0.04	0.04

Values corresponding to each TANN X–Y–Z model represent the median of 50 separate trial runs of the model. Yellow (blue) denote TANN X–Y–Z median values of skill-based metrics (PSS, CSI, HSS, ORSS, CSS, and GSS only) NOT statistically significantly different (based on the Wilcoxon Sign Rank Tests, 2 sided, 1 sample, 5% significant level) from the corresponding NDFD (MLR).

Table 9. Performance results of TANN X-Y-Z models for box 103 for the 2007–2008 independent data set and corresponding comparisons to the WFO CRP forecasters (NDFD), multi-linear regression (MLR) models.

	POD	FAR	F	PSS	CSI	HSS	ORSS	CSS	GSS
9 h Model predictions									
TANN 36-150-1	0.94	0.81	0.22	0.71	0.19	0.25	0.96	0.19	0.14
TANN 2-60-1 CFS	0.94	0.85	0.30	0.64	0.14	0.18	0.95	0.14	0.10
TANN 15-100-1 mRMR	0.97	0.83	0.26	0.70	0.17	0.22	0.98	0.17	0.12
MLR	0.97	0.82	0.25	0.72	0.18	0.23	0.98	0.17	0.13
9 h Operational public forecasts									
NDFD	0.91	0.83	0.26	0.65	0.16	0.21	0.93	0.16	0.12
12 h Model predictions									
TANN 36-125-1	0.86	0.90	0.29	0.57	0.10	0.12	0.88	0.09	0.07
TANN 1-1-1 CFS	0.77	0.88	0.21	0.56	0.11	0.15	0.85	0.11	0.08
TANN 12-90-1 mRMR	0.91	0.91	0.35	0.56	0.08	0.10	0.90	0.08	0.05
MLR				0.68	0.10	0.13	1.00	0.10	0.07

	POD	FAR	F	PSS	CSI	HSS	ORSS	CSS	GSS
12 h Operational public forecasts									
NDFD	0.91	0.86	0.23	0.68	0.14	0.19	0.94	0.14	0.11
15 h Model predictions									
TANN 36-70-1	0.92	0.93	0.25	0.68	0.07	0.10	0.95	0.07	0.05
TANN 1-1-1 CFS	0.33	0.96	0.15	0.18	0.04	0.04	0.47	0.03	0.02
TANN 12-90-1 mRMR	0.83	0.96	0.34	0.47	0.04	0.05	0.79	0.04	0.02
MLR	0.92	0.94	0.30	0.62	0.06	0.07	0.93	0.05	0.04
15 h Operational public forecasts									
NDFD	0.85	0.93	0.24	0.61	0.07	0.10	0.89	0.07	0.05

Values corresponding to each TANN X-Y-Z model represent the median of 50 separate trial runs of the model. Yellow (blue) denote TANN X-Y-Z median values of skill-based metrics (PSS, CSI, HSS, ORSS, CSS, and GSS only) NOT statistically significantly different (based on the Wilcoxon Sign Rank Tests, 2 sided, 1 sample, 5% significant level) from the corresponding NDFD (MLR) value.

Table 10. Performance results of TANN X–Y–Z models for box 73 for the 2007–2008 independent data set and corresponding comparisons to the WFO CRP forecasters (NDFD), multi-linear regression (MLR) models.

	POD	FAR	F	PSS	CSI	HSS	ORSS	CSS	GSS
9 h Model predictions									
TANN 36-150-1	0.92	0.86	0.24	0.68	0.14	0.18	0.95	0.13	0.10
TANN 2-60-1 CFS	0.93	0.89	0.31	0.62	0.11	0.14	0.93	0.11	0.07
TANN 15-100-1 mRMR	0.93	0.87	0.27	0.66	0.13	0.17	0.94	0.12	0.09
MLR	0.92	0.87	0.27	0.65	0.13	0.16	0.94	0.12	0.09
12 h Model predictions									
TANN 36-125-1	0.85	0.93	0.26	0.59	0.07	0.10	0.89	0.07	0.05
TANN 1-1-1 CFS	0.68	0.92	0.19	0.49	0.07	0.10	0.80	0.07	0.05
TANN 12-90-1 mRMR	0.88	0.94	0.31	0.58	0.06	0.08	0.89	0.06	0.04
MLR	0.88	0.93	0.27	0.61	0.07	0.09	0.90	0.07	0.05
15 h Model predictions									
TANN 36-70-1	0.83	0.94	0.24	0.59	0.06	0.08	0.88	0.06	0.04
TANN 1-1-1 CFS	0.53	0.92	0.11	0.42	0.08	0.11	0.80	0.07	0.06
TANN 12-90-1 mRMR	0.81	0.95	0.30	0.51	0.05	0.06	0.82	0.04	0.03
MLR	0.88	0.95	0.28	0.59	0.05	0.07	0.89	0.05	0.04

Table 11. Performance results of TANN X–Y–Z models for all 286 boxes for the 2007–2008 independent data set and corresponding comparisons to the NWS forecasters (NDFD), multi-linear regression (MLR) models.

	9-h Prediction	*12-h Prediction*	*15-h Prediction*
ORSS			
Box 73		NDFD	TANN 36-70-1
Box 103	NDFD		NDFD
Box 238	TANN 2-60-1	TANN 36-125-1	NDFD
PSS			
Box 73	TANN 36-150-1	NDFD	TANN 36-70-1
Box 103	NDFD		NDFD
Box 238	TANN 2-60-1	TANN 36-125-1	NDFD
HSS			
Box 73	36-150-1	NDFD	NDFD
Box 103	NDFD	NDFD	TANN 1-1-1
Box 238			TANN 1-1-1

Gray boxes indicate that a single performer did not distinguish itself.

Table 12. Best performers (based on the equitable ORSS, PSS, and HSS performance metrics) between the TANN2 models and NWS forecasters (NDFD) using the combination of Wilcoxon Sign Rank Tests (2 sided, 1 sample, 5% significant level) to compare each TANN model to NDFD, and the Nemenyi post-hoc analyses of pairwise combination of TANN2 models (5% significance level).

An alternative analysis was performed to determine the single best-performing classifiers for each box and prediction hour based only on performance metrics PSS, HSS, and ORSS. HSS and PSS are truly equitable and ORSS is asymptotically equitable (approaches equitability as size of the data set approaches infinity) and truly equitable for the condition $\frac{(a+c)}{n} = 0.5$ (see contingency matrix.) [77]. Equitability includes the desirable condition whereby the perform-ance metric is zero for random or constant forecasts. For each of the three performance metrics and for each box and prediction hour combination, comparisons were made between the TANN2 models and NDFD. Such a comparison was performed separately between the TANN2 models and MLR. The best performers were determined in the following manner: First, the output from the *Wilcoxon sign rank test* was used to determine statistically significant differ-ences between the TANN2 models and NDFD or MLR (**Tables 8–10**). Next, the *Friedman rank sum test* was used to determine whether significant differences existed only between the three TANN2 models. If differences existed, the *Nemenyi post-hoc test* [78] was performed to deter-mine statistical significance between pairwise combinations of TANN2 models. The best performer was based on a synthesis of the Wilcoxon and Friedman/Nemenyi results (see Appendix E). The Friedman and Nemenyi post-hoc tests were performed using the *fried-man.test* and *posthoc.friedman.nemenyi.test* functions from the Pairwise Multiple Comparison of Mean Rank (*PMCMR*) package in the **R** programming language [74]. Results are depicted in **Tables 12** and **13**. The results are mixed. With respect to comparisons between the TANN2 models and NDFD, the best performer is a function of the performance metric, box number, and prediction hour. The same is true for the TANN2 model-MLR comparisons. However, it is noteworthy to mention that none of the TANN2 models based on the mRMR FS method were determined to be the single best performer for 15 h (**Tables 12** and **13**).

	9-h Prediction	12-h Prediction	15-h Prediction
ORSS			
Box 73	MLR	MLR	TANN 36-70-1
Box 103	MLR		
Box 238	TANN 2-60-1	MLR	TANN 1-1-1
PSS			
Box 73		MLR	TANN 36-70-1
Box 103			
Box 238	TANN 2-60-1	MLR	MLR
HSS			
Box 73	TANN 36-150-1	TAN 1-1-1	TAN 36-70-1
Box 103			TANN 1-1-1
Box 238			TANN 1-1-1

Gray boxes indicate that a single performer did not distinguish itself.

Table 13. Best performers (based on the equitable ORSS, PSS, and HSS performance metrics) between the TANN2 models and MLR using the combination of Wilcoxon Sign Rank Tests (2 sided, 1 sample, 5% significant level) to compare each TANN model to MLR, and the Nemenyi post-hoc analyses of pairwise combination of TANN2 models (5% significance level).

The increase in data as compared to the previous study [53] likely contributed to performance enhancements. **Figure 3** depicts the change in performance of the 36-Y-1 12 h model as a function of training data used. Note that performance improvement was positively correlated with the quantity of training data. This adds credence to the argument that the amount of data in [53] may have been insufficient. Further, note that for ≤1% of available data (~6000 instances), performance decreased after the number of neurons in the hidden layer (Y) exceeded 100, possibly due to the curse of dimensionality. **Figure 4** depicts the relationship between an overfitting metric, defined as $\left(AUC_{val} - AUC_{train}\right)/AUC_{train}$, and the number of hidden layer neurons. Note that overfitting generally increases with the number of hidden layer neurons when the training set is reduced to ≤ 10 of the total available training data, and particularly apparent when only 1 of available, or about 6000 cases. In [53], only a few thousand cases were available. This partially explains why the original TANN models are relatively smaller ($Y \leq 35$) than the TANN2 models. The ability to obtain similar performance while training on a smaller portion of the data set would have allowed substantial gains in computational efficiency. ANNs were trained using MATLAB® R2015b on several multi-core personal computers (PCs) and on a computer cluster with compute nodes with two Xeon E5 with 10 core processors each and

256 gigabytes (GB) of memory. For the full data set (**Table 1**), training times varied from less than 1 h to more than two days per batch of 50 ANNs when increasing the number of hidden layer neurons from 1 to 200. When reducing the size of the training set to 1%, training times decreased to less than 3 min for each Y case (not shown.) evaluated. Reducing the size of the training set to 10% of the full set decreased training times by about one order of magnitude for each Y case.

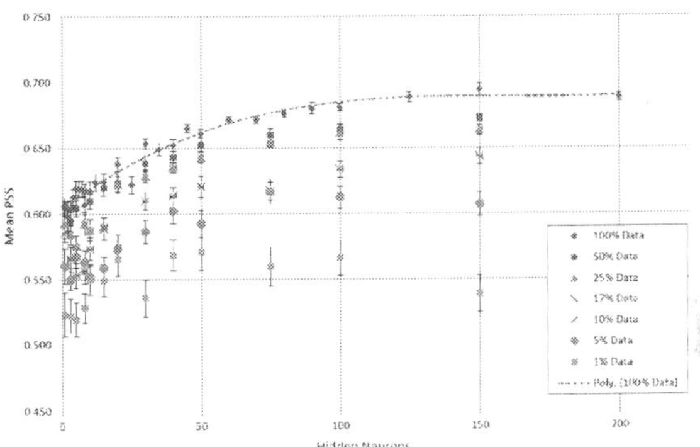

Figure 3. 12 h 36-Y-1 TANN performance versus hidden layer neuron quantity (Y) as a function of the percentage of total training data available.

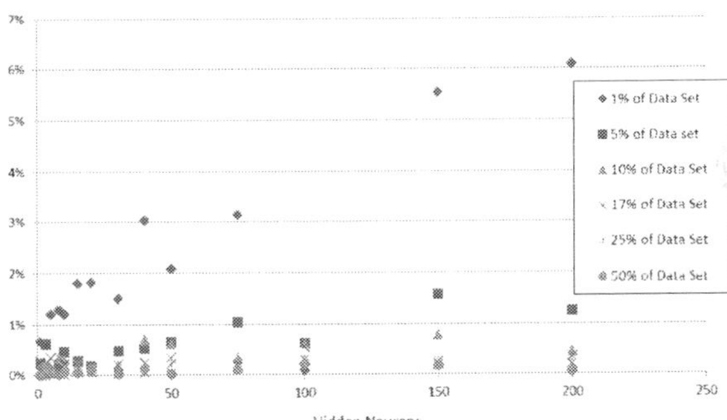

Figure 4. 12 h 36-Y-1 TANN overfitting index versus hidden layer neuron quantity (see text).

With regard to data set size and composition, it was hypothesized that performance gains may be obtained when artificially increasing the proportion of positive targets (CTG lightning strikes) in the training set. All possible inputs were included and the total number of training cases was maintained constant with positive and negative cases randomly selected (with replacement) to create target vectors with 5, 10, 25, and 50% of CTG lightning strikes. Substantial increases in performance were obtained for the training sets for all prediction lead times; **Figure 5** depicts the 12 h prediction example. Maximum PSS increased progressively while increasing proportion of lightning strikes in the data set. However, as the percent of positive targets was raised, the performance over the 2007–2008 independent testing decreased. Efforts are continuing to further modify the training of the TANN to improve performance.

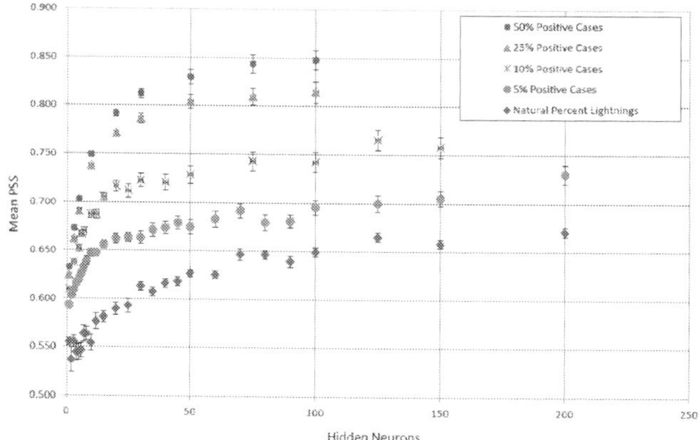

Figure 5. 12 h 36-Y-1 TANN performance versus hidden neuron quantity (*Y*) as a function of the proportion of positive target (CG lightning) data in the training set.

7. Conclusion

We presented here the results of an ANN approach to the post processing of single deterministic NWP model output for the prediction of thunderstorms at high spatial resolution, 9, 12, and 15 h in advance (TANN2.) ANNs were selected to take advantage of a large data set of over 1 million cases with multiple predictors and attempt to capture the complex relationships between the predictors and the generation of thunderstorms. This study represents an adjustment to a previous ANN model framework, resulting in the generation of a significantly larger data set. The larger data set allowed for more complex ANN models (by increasing the number of neurons in the hidden layer). Three groups of TANN2 model variants were generated based on two filtering-based feature selection methods (designed to retain only relevant and non-redundant features) and one group based on models calibrated with all predictors.

The skills of these TANN2 models within each of the three 400-km² boxes were substantially improved over previous work with the improvements attributed to the increase of the size of the data set. TANN2 model performance was compared to that of NWS operational forecasters and to MLR models. Results regarding the best-performing classifiers per prediction hour and box were mixed. Several attempts were made to further improve model performance or decrease training time. Training the models using a small fraction of the data set reduced model calibration time yet resulted in lower performance skill. Altering the target by artificially boosting the proportion of positive outcomes (lightning strikes) resulted in substantial performance improvements over the training sets but did not lead to substantial improvements of performance on the independent 2007–2008 cases.

Given that the atmosphere is chaotic, or deterministic with highly sensitive dependence on the initial condition, one future research plan includes the prediction of thunderstorms by the post-processing of single deterministic NWP model output using ANN models that account for chaotic systems [79]. Such a strategy would be an alternative to the state of the art practice of using NWP model ensembles to account for the sensitive dependence on the initial condition. In addition, another plan involves the development of ensemble ANN models [80]. Specifically, an optimal TANN prediction can be developed by integrating output from 50 unique TANN models.

Appendix A

The total mean mass of the atmosphere: 5.1480×10^{21}g [81]

Total mol of dry air: $5.1480 \times 10^{21}\text{g} \times \dfrac{1}{28.97\text{gmol}^{-1}} = 1.777 \times 10^{20}\text{mol}$

Total molecules of dry air: $1.777 \times 10^{20}\text{mol} \times 6.02214 \times 10^{23}\text{mol}^{-1} = 1.0701 \times 10^{44}\text{molecules}$

(Mass of dry air: 28.97gmol^{-1}; Avogadro's number: $6.02214 \times 10^{23}\text{mol}^{-1}$)

Appendix B

Version 1.04 of the HRRR uses the Advanced Research WRF (ARW) dynamic core within the WRF modeling framework (version 3.4.1 WRF-ARW). The HRRR uses GSI 3D-VAR data assimilation. With respect to parameterizations, the RRTM longwave radiation, Goddard shortwave radiation, Thompson microphysics (version 3.4.1), no cumulus/convective parameterization, MYNN planetary boundary layer, and the rapid update cycle (RUC) land surface model [33].

Appendix C

At any given time, only one NWP model was utilized in the TANN. Yet, three different modeling systems were used, each during a unique time period—the hydrostatic Eta model [82] (1 March 2004 to 19 June 2006), the Weather Research and Forecasting Non-hydrostatic

Mesoscale Model (WRF-NMM) [83] (20 June 2006 to 30 September 2011), and the NOAA Environmental Modeling System Non-hydrostatic Multiscale Model (NEMS-NMMB) (October 2011 to December 2013.)

Appendix D

NWS operational forecasts were obtained from the NWS *National Digital Forecast Database* [96] (NDFD) [96], a database of archived NWS forecasts; the forecasts are written to a 5-km coterminous USA (CONUS) grid (or to 16 pre-defined grid sub-sectors) and provided to the general public in Gridded Binary Version 2 (GRIB2) format [97]. The forecasts for most of the 286 boxes (**Figure 1**) originated from the NWS Weather Forecast Office (WFO) in Corpus Christi, Texas (CRP) in the USA.

Appendix E

The following are three examples to explain how the "best performers" where determined in **Tables 12** and **13**.

Example 1: Table 12 (Determining the best performers between the three TANN model variants and NDFD) Box 238 Prediction Hour 9 ORSS: Step 1: Based on the Wilcoxon Sign Rank Test, the performer with the largest ORSS value was TANN 2-60-1, and that value (0.98) was statistically significantly larger than the corresponding NDFD value (0.93) (**Table 8**). Step 2: Based on the Nemenyi post-hoc analysis of the pairwise combination of the three TANN model variants, the TANN 2-60-1 ORSS value was statistically significantly different than the corresponding ORSS values from the TANN 36-150-1 and TANN 15-100-1 models. *Thus, the best performer is TANN 2-60-1.*

Example 2: Table 12 (Determining the best performers between the three TANN model variants and NDFD) Box 103 Prediction Hour 12 PSS: Step 1: Based on the Wilcoxon Sign Rank test, the performer with the largest PSS value was TANN 12-90-1, and that value (0.63) was statistically significantly larger than the corresponding NDFD value (0.56) (**Table 9**). Step 2: Based on the Nemenyi post-hoc analysis of the pairwise combination of the three TANN model variants, there was no statistically significant difference between the PSS values for TANN 12-90-1 (0.63) and TANN 36-125-1 (0.58). *Thus, there is no single best performer.*

Example 3: Table 13 (Determining the best performers between the three TANN model variants and MLR) Box 73 Prediction Hour 12 PSS: Step 1: Based on the Wilcoxon Sign Rank Test, the performer with the largest PSS value was MLR, and that value (0.68) was statistically significantly greater than the corresponding PSS values from each of the three TANN variants (**Table 10**.) *Thus, the best performer is MLR. No additional steps are required.*

Author details

Waylon G. Collins[1*] and Philippe Tissot[2]

*Address all correspondence to: Waylon.Collins@noaa.gov

1 National Weather Service, Weather Forecast Office Corpus Christi, TX, USA

2 Texas A&M University—Corpus Christi, Conrad Blucher Institute, Corpus Christi, TX, USA

References

[1] Glickman TS. Glossary of Meteorology. 2nd ed. Boston: American Meteorological Society; 2011. 1132 p.

[2] Byers HR. General Meteorology, 3rd ed. New York: McGraw Hill Book Company; 1959. 540 p.

[3] Emanuel KA. Atmospheric Convection. New York: Oxford University Press; 1994. 580 p.

[4] Doswell CA, editor. Severe Convective Storms (Meteorological Monographs, Volume 28, Number 50). Boston: American Meteorological Society; 2001. 561 p.

[5] Groenemeijer, P. Sounding-derived parameters associated with severe convective storms in the Netherlands [thesis]. Utrecht: Utrecht University; 2005.

[6] Holle RL. Annual rates of lightning fatalities by country. In: 20th International Lightning Detection Conference; 21–23 April 2008; Tucson.

[7] Holle RL, Lopez RE. A comparison of current lightning death rates in the U.S. with other locations and times. In: International Conference on Lightning and Static Electricity; 2003; Blackpool. p. 103–134.

[8] NWS. Natural Hazards Statistics National Weather Service Office of Climate, Water, and Weather Services [Internet]. 2015. Available from: http://www.nws.noaa.gov/om/hazstats.shtml [Accessed 2015-10-26].

[9] NOAA. Billion-Dollar Weather and Climate Disasters: Summary Stats, National Oceanic and Atmospheric Administration (NOAA) National Centers for Environmental Information [Internet]. 2016. Available from: https://www.ncdc.noaa.gov/billions/summary-stats [Accessed 2016-01-28].

[10] Wolfson MM, Clark DA. Advanced Aviation Weather Forecasts. Lincoln Lab. J. 2006; 16: 31–58.

[11] Trier SB. Convective storms – Convective Initiation. In: Holton Jr, editor. Encyclopedia of Atmospheric Sciences. New York: Oxford University Press; 2003. p. 560–570.

[12] Orlanski I. A Rational Subdivision of Scales for Atmospheric Processes. Bull. Am. Meteorol. Soc. 1975; 56: 527–530.

[13] Lorenz EN. Deterministic nonperiodic flow. J. Atmos. Sci. 1963; 20: 130–141.

[14] Lorenz EN. The predictability of a flow which possesses many scales of motion. Tellus. 1969; 3: 1–19.

[15] Wallace JM, Hobbs PV. Atmospheric Science: An Introductory Survey. New York: Academic Press; 1977. 466 p.

[16] Kain JS, Coniglio MC, Correia J, Clark AJ, Marsh PT, Ziegler CL, Lakshmanan V, Miller SD, Dembek SR, Weiss SJ, Kong F, Xue M, Sobash RA, Dean AR, Jirak IL, CJ Melick. A feasibility study for probabilistic convection initiation forecasts based on explicit numerical guidance. Bull. Amer. Meteor. Soc. 2013; 94: 1213–1225.

[17] Lamb D. Rain Production in Convective Storms. In: Doswell CA, editor. Severe Convective Storms. Boston: American Meteorological Society; 2001. p. 299–321.

[18] Williams ER. The Electrification of Severe Storms. In: Doswell CA, editor. Severe Convective Storms. Boston: American Meteorological Society; 2001. p. 527–561.

[19] Wakimoto RM. Convectively Driven High Wind Events. In: Doswell CA, editor. Severe Convective Storms. Boston: American Meteorological Society; 2001. p. 255–298.

[20] Knight CA, Knight NC. Hailstorms. In: Doswell CA, editor. Severe Convective Storms. Boston: American Meteorological Society; 2001. p. 223–254.

[21] Taylor CM, Gounou A, Guichard F, Harris PP, Ellis RJ, Couvreux F. Frequency of Sahelian storm initiation enhanced over mesoscale soil-moisture patterns. Nat. Geosci. 2011; 4: 430–433.

[22] Doswell CA, Bosart LF. 2001. Extratropical synoptic-scale processes and severe convection. In: Doswell CA, editor. Severe Convective Storms. Boston: American Meteorological Society; 2001. p. 27–70.

[23] Lorenz, EN. The Essence of Chaos. Seattle: University of Washington Press; 1993. 227 p.

[24] Bjerknes V. Das Problem der Wettervorhersage, betrachtet vom Stanpunkt der Mechanik und der Physik. Meteor. Zeits. 1904; 21: 1–7.

[25] Kalnay E. Atmospheric Modeling, Data Assimilation and Predictability. Cambridge: Cambridge University Press; 2003.

[26] Stull R. Meteorology for Scientists and Engineers. 3rd ed. Pacific Grove: Brooks Cole; 2015.

[27] Stensrud DJ. Parameterization Schemes, Keys to Understanding Numerical Weather Prediction Models. New York: Cambridge University Press; 2007. 459 p.

[28] Wilks DS. Statistical Methods in the Atmospheric Sciences. 2nd ed. Oxford: Elsevier; 2006.

[29] Bryan GH, Wyngaard JC, Fritsch JM. Resolution Requirements for the Simulation of Deep Moist Convection. Mon. Wea. Rev. 2003; 131: 2394–2416.

[30] Hodanish S, Holle RL, Lindsey DT. A Small Updraft Producing a Fatal Lightning Flash. Wea. Forecasting. 2004; 19: 627–632.

[31] Mecikalski JR., Williams JK, Jewett CP, Ahijevych D, LeRoy A, Walker JR. Probabilistic 0–1-h convective initiation nowcasts that combine geostationary satellite observations and numerical weather prediction model data. J. Appl. Meteor. Climatol. 2015; 54: 1039–1059.

[32] Pessi AT, Businger S. Relationships among lightning, precipitation, and hydrometeor characteristic over the North Pacific Ocean. J. Appl. Meteorol. Climatol. 2009; 48: 833–848.

[33] Earth System Research Laboratory. The High-Resolution Rapid Refresh [Internet]. 2016. Available from: http://rapidrefresh.noaa.gov/hrrr [Accessed: 2016-01-14]

[34] Pielke RA. Mesoscale Meteorological Modeling. International Geophysics Series. San Diego: Academic Press; 2002. 676 p.

[35] Zhang Y, Zhang R, Stensrud DJ, Zhiyong M. Intrinsic Predictability of the 20 May 2013 Tornadic Thunderstorm Event in Oklahoma at Storm Scales. Mon. Wea. Rev. 2016; 144: 1273–1298

[36] Wilson JW, Crook NA, Mueller CK, Sun J, Dixon M. Nowcasting Thunderstorms: A Status Report. Bull. Am. Meteorol. Soc. 1998; 79: 2079–2099.

[37] Fowle MA, Roebber PJ. Short-range (0–48 h) Numerical predictions of convective occurrence, model and location. Wea. Forecasting. 2003; 18: 782–794.

[38] Weisman ML, Davis C, Wang W, Manning KW, Klemp JB. Experiences with 0-36-h explicit convective forecasts with the WRF-ARW model. Wea. Forecasting. 2008; 23: 407–437.

[39] Elmore KL, Stensrud DJ, Crawford KC. Explicit cloud-scale models for operational forecasts: a note of caution. Wea. Forecasting. 2002; 17: 873–884.

[40] Leith C.E. Theoretical skill of Monte Carlo forecasts. Mon. Wea. Rev. 1974; 102: 409–418.

[41] Epstein ES. Stochastic dynamic prediction. Tellus. 1969; 21: 739–759.

[42] Storm Prediction Center. Short Range Ensemble Forecast (SREF) Products [Internet]. 2015. Available from: URL http://www.spc.noaa.gov/exper/sref [Accessed: 2015-10-23].

[43] Meteorological Development Laboratory. Model Output Statistics (MOS) [Internet.]. 2016. Available from http://www.weather.gov/mdl/mos_home [Accessed: 2016-03-01].

[44] Glahn HR, Lowry DA. The use of model output statistics (MOS) in objective weather forecasting. J. Appl. Meteorol. 1972; 11: 1203–1211.

[45] Glahn B, Gilbert K, Cosgrove R, Ruth DP, Sheets K. The gridding of MOS. Wea. Forecast. 2009; 24: 520–529.

[46] Ghirardelli JE, Glahn B. The Meteorological Development Laboratory's aviation weather prediction system. Wea. Forecast. 2010; 25: 1027–1051.

[47] Schmeits MJ, Kok KJ, Vogelezang DHP. Probabilistic forecasting of (severe) thunderstorms in the Netherlands using model output statistics. Wea. Forecast. 2005; 20: 134–148.

[48] Costello RB. Random House Webster's College Dictionary. New York: Random House; 1992.

[49] Mitchell, T. The discipline of machine learning. Carnegie Mellon University Technical Report, CMU-ML-06-108, 2006.

[50] Mills GA, Colquhoun JR. Objective prediction of severe thunderstorm environments: preliminary results linking a decision tree with an operational regional NWP model. Wea. Forecast. 1998; 13: 1078–1092.

[51] Perler D, Marchand O. A study in weather model output postprocessing: using the boosting method for thunderstorm detection. Wea. Forecast. 2009; 24: 211–222.

[52] McCann DW. A neural network short-term forecast of significant thunderstorms. Wea. Forecast. 1992; 7: 525–534.

[53] Collins W, Tissot P. An artificial neural network model to predict thunderstorms within 400km^2 South Texas domains Meteorol. Appl. 2015; 22: 650–665.

[54] Breiman L. Random forests. Machine Learn. 2001; 45: 5–32.

[55] McNulty RP. A statistical approach to short-term thunderstorm outlooks. J. Appl. Meteorol. 1981; 20: 765–771.

[56] Ravi N. Forecasting of thunderstorms in the pre-monsoon season at Delhi. Meteorol. Appl. 1999; 6: 29–38.

[57] de Silva CW. Intelligent Machines: Myths and Realities. Boca Raton: CRC Press LLC; 2000.

[58] Colquhoun JR. A decision true method of forecasting thunderstorms serve a thunderstorms and tornados. Wea. Forecast. 1987; 2: 337–345.

[59] Lee RR, Passner JE. The development and verification of TIPS: an expert system to forecast thunderstorm occurrence. Wea. Forecast. 1993; 8: 271–280.

[60] Manzato A. The use of sounding-derived indices for a neural network short-term thunderstorm forecast. Wea. Forecast. 2005; 20: 896–917.

[61] Chaudhuri S. Convective energies in forecasting severe thunderstorms with one hidden layer neural net and variable learning rate back propagation algorithm. Asia Pac. J. Atmos. Sci. 2010; 46: 173–183.

[62] Sanchez JL, Ortega EG, Marcos JL. Construction and assessment of a logistic regression model applied to short-term forecasting of thunderstorms in Leon (Spain). Atmos. Res. 2001; 56: 57–71.

[63] Rumelhart DE, McClelland JL. Parallel Distributed Processing: Explorations in the Microstructure of Cognition: Foundations. Vol 1. Cambridge: MIT Press; 1986.

[64] Haykin S. Neural Networks, A Comprehensive Foundation. 2nd ed. New Jersey: Prentice Hall; 1999.

[65] Bishop CM. Neural Networks for Pattern Recognition. New York: Oxford University Press; 2005.

[66] Moller M. A scaled conjugate gradient algorithm for fast supervised learning. Neural Netw. 1993; 6: 525–533.

[67] Manzato A. A note on the maximum peirce skill score. Wea. Forecast. 2007; 22: 1148–1154.

[68] Bellman R. Adaptive Control Processes: A Guided Tour. Princeton: Princeton University Press; 1961.

[69] May R., Dandy G, Maier H. Review of input variable selection methods for artificial neural networks. In: Suzuki K, editor. Artificial Neural Networks- Methodological Advances and Biomedical Applications. Rijeka: InTech Europe; 2011. P. 19–44.

[70] Hall MA. Correlation-based feature selection for machine learning [thesis]. Hamilton: University of Waikato; 1999.

[71] Hall MA, Smith LA. Feature selection for machine learning: comparing a correlation-based filter approach to the wrapper. In: Proceedings of the Twelfth International Florida Artificial Intelligence Research Society Conference; 1–5 May 1999; Orlando.

[72] Arizona State University. Feature Selection at Arizona State University [Internet]. 2016. Available from: http://featureselection.asu.edu/index.php# [Accessed: 2016-02-16].

[73] Akaike H. Information theory and an extension of the maximum likelihood principle. In: 2nd International Symposium on Information Theory; 1973; Budapest: Akademiai Kiado. p. 267–281.

[74] Ding C, Peng H. Minimum redundancy feature selection from microarray gene expression data. J. Bioinform. Comput. Biol. 2005; 3: 185–205.

[75] A Language and Environment for Statistical Computing. R Foundation for Statistical Computing [Internet]. Available from: https://www.r-project.org [Accessed: 2005-12-14].

[76] De Jay N, Papillon-Cavanagh S, Olsen C, El-Hachem N, Bontempi G, Haibe-Kains. mRMRe: An R package for parallelized mrmr ensemble feature selection. Bioinformatics. 2013; 29: 2365–2368.

[77] Hogan RJ, Ferro CAT, Jolliffe IT, Stephenson DB. Equitability revisited: why the "equitable threat score" is not equitable. Wea. Forecast. 2010; 25: 710–726.

[78] Nemenyi P. Distribution-free multiple comparisons [thesis]. Princeton: Princeton University; 1963.

[79] Pan S-T, Lai C-C. Identification of chaotic systems by neural network with hybrid learning algorithm. Chaos Soliton Fract. 2008; 37: 233–244.

[80] Maqsood I, Khan MR, Abraham A. An ensemble of neural networks for weather forecasting. Neural Comput. Appl. 2004; 13: 112–122.

[81] Trenberth KE, Smith L. The Mass of the Atmosphere: A Constraint on Global Analyses. J. Climate. 2005; 18: 864–875.

[82] Rogers E, Black TL, Deaven DG, DiMego GJ. Changes to the operational "early" eta analysis/forecast system at the National Centers for Environmental Prediction. Wea. Forecast. 1996; 11: 391–413.

[83] Janjic ZI, Gerrity JP, Nickovic S. An alternative approach to nonhydrostatic modeling. Mon. Wea. Rev. 2001; 129: 1164–1178.

[84] Khairoutdinov M, Randall D. High-resolution simulation of shallow-to-deep convection transition over land. J. Atmos. Sci. 2006; 63: 3421–3436.

[85] Ducrocq V, Tzanos D, Sénési S. Diagnostic tools using a mesoscale NWP model for the early warning of convection. Meteorol. Appl. 1998; 5: 329–349.

[86] Haklander AJ, Van Delden A. Thunderstorm predictors and their forecast skill for the Netherlands. Atmos. Res. 2003; 67–68: 273–299.

[87] Dalu GA, Pielke RA, Baldi M, Zeng X. Heat and momentum fluxes induced by thermal inhomogeneities with and without large-scale flow. J. Atmos. Sci. 1996; 53: 3286–3302.

[88] Wang JR, Bras L, Eltahir EAB. A stochastic linear theory of mesoscale circulation induced by thermal heterogeneity of the land surface. J. Atmos. Sci. 1996; 53: 3349–3366.

[89] Crook NA. Sensitivity of moist convection forced by boundary layer processes to low-level thermodynamic fields. Mon. Wea. Rev. 1996; 124: 1767–1785.

[90] Williams ER, Mushtak V, Rosenfeld D, Goodman S, Boccippio D. Thermodynamic conditions favorable to superlative thunderstorm updraft, mixed phase microphysics and lightning flash rate. Atmos. Res. 2005; 76: 288–306.

[91] Saunders CPR. A review of thunderstorm electrification processes. J. Appl. Meteorol. 1993; 32: 642–655.

[92] Janji'c ZI. The step-mountain eta coordinate model: further developments of the convection, viscous sublayer, and turbulence closure schemes. Mon. Weather Rev. 1994; 122: 927–945.

[93] Rotunno RJ, Klemp B, Weisman ML. A theory for strong, long-lived squall lines. J. Atmos. Sci. 1998; 45: 464–485.

[94] Findell KL, Eltahir EAB. Atmospheric controls on soil moisture-boundary layer interactions: three-dimensional wind effects. J. Geophys. Res. 2003b; 108 (D8), 8385.

[95] Findell KL, Eltahir EAB. Atmospheric controls on soil moisture-boundary layer interactions: Part I: Framework development. J. Hydrometeorol. 2003a; 4: 552–569.

[96] National Weather Service National Digital Forecast Database [Internet]. 2016. Available from: http://www.nws.noaa.gov/ndfd/ [Accessed: 2016-03-23]

[97] World Meteorological Organization. WMO Manual on Codes, WMO Publication No. 306, Vol. 1, Part B. Geneva: WMO; 2001.

Chapter 11

Analyzing the Impact of Airborne Particulate Matter on Urban Contamination with the Help of Hybrid Neural Networks

Daniel Dunea and Stefania Iordache

Additional information is available at the end of the chapter

http://dx.doi.org/10.5772/63109

Abstract

In this study, particulate matter (PM), total suspended particulate (TSP), PM_{10}, and $PM_{2.5}$ fractions) concentrations were recorded in various cities from south of Romania to build the corresponding time series for various intervals. First, the time series of each pollutant were used as inputs in various configurations of feed-forward neural networks (FANN) to find the most suitable network architecture to the PM specificity. The outputs were evaluated using mean absolute error (MAE), mean absolute percentage error (MAPE), root mean square error (RMSE), and Pearson correlation coefficient (r) between observed series and output series. Second, each time series was decomposed using Daubechies wavelets of third order into its corresponding components. Each decomposed component of a PM time series was used as input in the optimal feed-forward neural networks (FANN) architecture established in the first step. The output of each component was re-included to form the modeled series of the original pollutant time series.

The final step was the comparison of FANN outputs with wavelet-FANN results to retrieve the wavelet utilization outcomes. The last section of the study describes the ROkidAIR cyberinfrastructure that integrates a decision support system (DSS). The DSS system uses artificial intelligence techniques and hybrid algorithms for assessing children's exposure to the pollution with particulate matter, in order to elaborate PM forecasted values and early warnings.

Keywords: air pollution, wavelet transformation, batch-learning algorithm, respiratory health, cyberinfrastructure

© 2016 The Author(s). Licensee InTech. This chapter is distributed under the terms of the Creative Commons Attribution License (http://creativecommons.org/licenses/by/3.0), which permits unrestricted use, distribution, and reproduction in any medium, provided the original work is properly cited.

1. Air pollution with particulate matter in urban areas

Quantifying the human exposure to air pollutants is a challenging task because air pollution is characterized by high spatial and temporal variability. The atmospheric physicochemical parameters of interest from the point of view of air pollution in urban areas are carbon monoxide (CO), sulfur dioxide (SO_2), nitric oxide (NO), nitrogen dioxide (NO_2), various fractions of particulate matter (PM_{10}, $PM_{2.5}$, PM_1, and UFPs or ultrafine particles), ozone (O_3), volatile organic compounds (VOCs), and polycyclic aromatic hydrocarbons (PAHs). The levels of these parameters are significantly influenced by meteorological factors (such as speed and direction of wind, precipitations, temperature, relative humidity, and solar radiation), seasonal and diurnal fluctuations, geographical factors (e.g., local topography, buildings), emission sources i.e., industrial activities and traffic in the area, as well as the air mass trajectories (e.g., long-range transport of pollutants).

Class	Description	Size (in diameter)
TSP	Airborne particles or aerosols that constantly enter the atmosphere from many sources having below 100 μm are collectively referred to as total suspended particles (TSP). TSP is assessed with high-volume samplers.	Below 100 microns (<100 μm)
Large particulates	Particles are retained by the nasopharynx area.	Over 10 microns (>10 μm)
PM_{10}	Particulates that can be inhaled below the nasopharynx area (nose and mouth) and are thus called inhalable particulates (coarse fraction).	Below 10 microns (0–10 μm)
$PM_{2.5}$	Fine particulates travel down below the tracheobronchial region, that is, into the lungs (fine fraction).	below 2.5 microns (0–2.5 μm)
UFP	Ultrafine particulates can penetrate into the deepest parts of lungs and can be dissolved into blood (ultrafine fraction).	below 0.1 microns (0–0.1 μm)

The most hazardous size classes to humans are $PM_{2.5}$ and UFP as they penetrate into the lungs and can even be dissolved into the blood.

Table 1. Airborne particulate matter classification depending on particle size [8].

In many urban agglomerations around Europe, the concentrations of airborne particles, NO_x, and O_3 exceed at least occasionally the limit or target values. Therefore, air pollution control focuses mostly on the surveillance of the above-mentioned pollutants [1]. Urban agglomerations are areas of increased emissions of anthropogenic pollutants into the atmosphere having adverse health effects on population.

Consequently, a major issue of environmental policy at regional level is the reduction of their concentrations in the ambient air [2].

Particle sizes range from a few nanometers up to more than 100 μm, and depending on particle size, there are several classes of particles (**Table 1**). However, epidemiological studies have shown that the most hazardous size classes to human health are $PM_{2.5}$ and UFP, as they penetrate into the lungs and can even enter into the blood following the gas exchange. Diseases caused by UFP exposure primarily relates to lung cancer and heart disorders. Since the measurement of UFP is a difficult task requiring sophisticated equipment, one can monitor the submicrometric fraction that includes UFP using a reliable optical system, for example, Dusttrak DRX 8533 [3].

In the recent years, the most common size fraction that is usually monitored in the national air quality infrastructures at large scales in urban areas is $PM_{2.5}$. Recent long-term studies show the associations between PM and mortality at levels significantly below the current annual WHO air quality guideline level for $PM_{2.5}$, that is, 10 $\mu g/m^3$ (WHO, 2013).

The issue of studying the fine particulate matter is very complex and has many unknown variables mainly due to the multitude of sources from which it directly originate, as well as due to the physicochemical transformations that occur in the atmosphere, resulting in the formation of secondary $PM_{2.5}$ particulates [4–6]. Other major setbacks are the difficulties of compliance assessment and the setup of measurement methods equivalence. Furthermore, the methods of $PM_{2.5}$ measurement are still in the development period and the reference method was recently revised in EN 12341: 2014 standard [7].

2. Forecasting of particulate matter using neural networks

The analysis of environmental processes involves highly complex phenomena, random variations of parameters, and difficulty to perform accurate measurements in certain situations. In these conditions, the available data are incomplete, imprecise, and current applied models require further improvements.

Measuring and forecasting of atmospheric conditions is important for understanding the processes of formation, transformation, dispersion, transport, and removal of the pollutants. Reliable overall estimates regarding the identification of sources, effects on mixing, transformation, and transportation support the control of air quality and the implementation of preventive actions to reduce the anthropogenic emissions [8].

The performance of environmental management can be improved using forecasting tools of the potential pollution episodes that can affect the population from inner and surrounding areas where the episode might occur. Prediction of the evolution of an atmospheric parameter can be done for short term (1 h, 1 day, 1 month) or long term (1 or more years).

The interest in improving the forecasting performances of time series algorithms and models in air pollution studies has considerably grown. The applied methods may vary from statistical methods, artificial intelligence (AI) techniques, and probabilistic approaches to hybrid algorithms and complex models. The final purpose is to supplement monitored data and/or to complete the missing values in the time series of air pollutants.

The field of statistics, which deals with the analysis of time dependent data, is called time series analysis (TSA). One of the most widespread types of processing is the *time series forecasting*.

Many of these techniques are used in practice. We can mention, for example, random walks, moving averages, trend models, seasonal exponential smoothing, autoregressive integrated moving average (ARIMA) parametric models, Boltzmann composite lattice, etc.

Some of the traditional statistical models such as the moving average, exponential smoothing, and ARIMA model are linear techniques, which have been in the past the main research and application tools in air pollution research. Predictions of future values are constrained to be linear functions of past observations, under the assumption that the data series is stationary [9]. The general model ARIMA introduced by Box and Jenkins [10] involves the autoregressive and moving averages parameters, and explicitly includes differentiations in the formulation of the model. Three types of parameters are required in the model as follows: autoregressive parameter; differentiation passes, and moving averages parameters [10]. The ARIMA model assumes that a parametric model relating the most recent data value to previous data values and previous noise gives the best forecast for future data. However, one weakness of the ARIMA model resides in the assumption that the examined time series is stationary and linear, and therefore has no structural changes [9].

Air pollutants have a random evolution, which requires non-deterministic approaches. Advantages of neural computing techniques over conventional statistical approaches rely on faster computation, learning ability, and noise rejection [11]. Artificial neural networks (ANN), for example, succeeded to give good results for time series processing when the data present noise and nonlinear components. Their capacity of learning and generalization recommend them as valuable tools in a wide area of applications. The most popular architecture used in practice is the multilayer feed-forward neural network. Their processing units (neurons) are organized in layers and there exist only forward connections (i.e., their orientation is from the input layer toward the output). This type of networks started to be extensively used in the late 1980s when the standard back-propagation algorithm was introduced. Since that time, the multilayer feed-forward ANNs had a large applicability in various domains, that is, financial, health, meteorology, environmental protection, etc.

The research has been oriented to find faster algorithms for training the network and to provide algorithms to automate the design of an optimal network topology for a specific problem. We can mention the standard back-propagation with momentum or with variable learning rate, the adaptive Rprop, or algorithms based on the standard numerical optimization techniques (Fletcher-Powel, conjugate gradient, quasi-Newton algorithm, Levenberg-Marquardt, etc.).

Rprop algorithm introduced by Riedmiller and Braun [12] is a supervised batch learning which accelerates the training process in the flat regions of the error function and when the iterations get nearby a local minimum. This algorithm allows different learning rates for each weight. These rates are changed adaptively with the change of sign in the corresponding partial derivative of the error function. They change progressively but without getting out of an initially prescribed interval. The algorithm is described by four parameters denoted by η^+, η^-, Δ_{max} and Δ_{min}. The first two parameters give the increasing and decreasing factor for adjusting the update size and they are chosen such that $0 < \eta^- < \eta^+ < 1$. The size step of the update is bounded by Δ_{min} and Δ_{max} . The following values of the parameters were used in our tests: $\eta^+ = 1.25, \eta^- = 0.5, \Delta_{max} = 50, \Delta_{min} = 0$ [13].

Quickprop is a batch training algorithm introduced by Fahlman [14], which takes in consideration the information about the second-order derivative of the performance error function. Literature showed that Quickprop is a particular case of the multivariate generalization of the secant method for nonlinear equation [15]. The local minimum of the batch error function reached a critical point that is a zero of the gradient [13]. In practice, Newton's iteration is replaced by a quasi-Newton iteration, which uses an approximate of the Jacobian and saves the involved amount of computation. The approximation of the Jacobian by a diagonal matrix with its entries computed with finite difference formulas proves that Quickprop belongs to this category of quasi-Newton iterations. Its convergence is not anymore quadratic, but it remains linear in the vicinity of the solution. We have used the same value (equal to 1.75) for the maximum growth factor denoted by μ in [14], in all our tests with Quickprop algorithm.

3. Experimental setup

We used the resources of an AI forecasting system called RNA-AER [13] for the domain of air pollution forecasts in urban regions. RNA-AER stands for the Romanian abbreviation of ANN for air pollution. This is a part of a complex system for $PM_{2.5}$ forecasting based on various techniques of artificial intelligence (multi-agents, knowledge base system, ANNs, and neuro-fuzzy) and that is designed to analyze the pollution level of air within ROkidAIR system (http://www.rokidair.ro/en) [16]. A feed-forward neural network with a single hidden layer was used to perform the tests presented in this work (**Figure 1**).

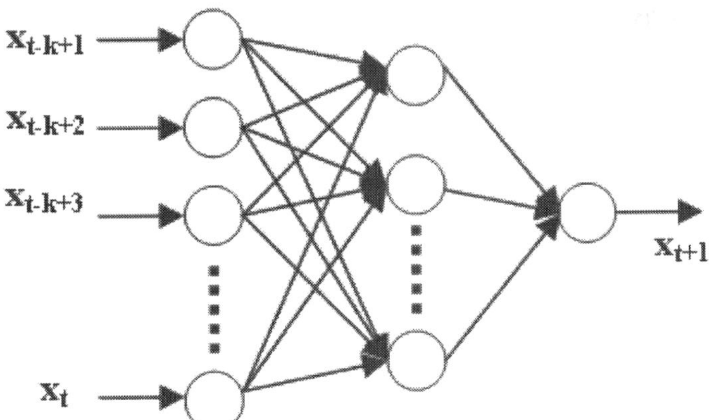

Figure 1. Example of feed-forward artificial neural network with one hidden layer.

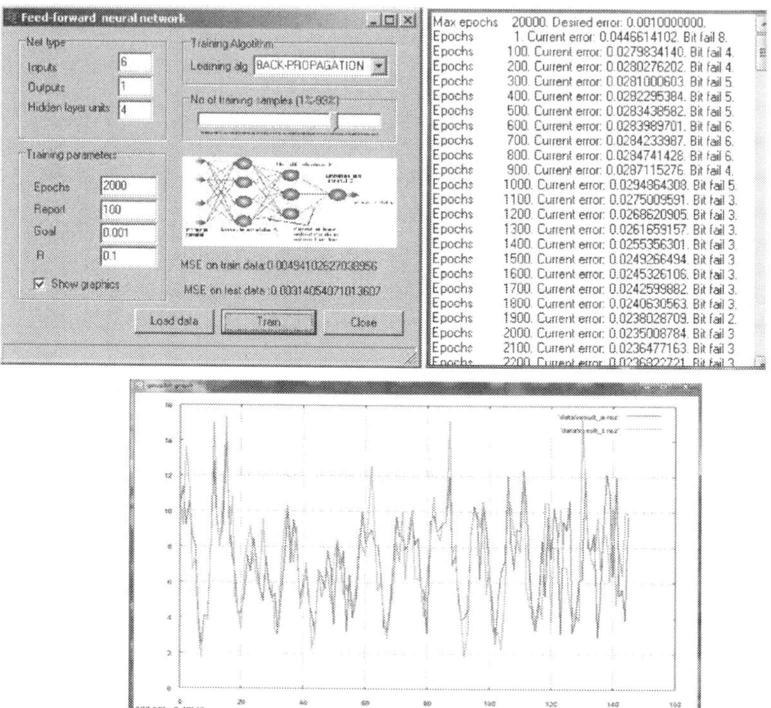

Figure 2. Front panel of the RNA-AER software with the feed-forward ANN configuration settings, error analysis, and observed and simulated time series.

The activation function used for the hidden and output layers was the symmetric sigmoid function (*tanh*). Since this function transforms the real axis into the range of (-1,1), the data were normalized before their use and transformed back in their real values after simulation.

In the training stage, we used various learning algorithms, but the most satisfactory results were obtained with Rprop and Quickprop. The application offers a friendly user interface from which one may choose various parameters that describe the network and the training algorithm. The program takes the raw data from one column text file and applies the necessary transformations in the preprocessing stage. After training, the application tests the network on the validation set of samples and shows the error. Then, the user is able to see the graphics for the evolution of the error in the training process and the observed and forecasted data (**Figure 2**). Best results were obtained with 4 or 6 units in the input layer, 6 neurons in the hidden layer and 1 output neuron. The output represents the one value ahead forecasted data. The network training comprised four learning algorithms. The first two were given by the batch and incremental implementations of the standard back-propagation learning [17]. These standard algorithms were tested with different values of the learning rate and momentum.

The other two algorithms were the resilient back-propagation Rprop and Quickprop. In this study, we present only the Rprop and Quickprop algorithms, which provided better results.

3.1. Steps for the development of a feed-forward neuronal model (FANN)

The use of raw data may rarely give satisfactory outputs. In this case, the training of the ANN will catch only general properties of the data series without being able to identify characteristics that are more refined. Therefore, a preprocessing step is often required in which the initial data are transformed such that the new data series eliminates some redundant characteristics from the analysis (e.g., interpolation, smoothing, wavelet decomposition, etc.).

The resulted series is then used to extract the required samples for training the network. Since our goal was to obtain one value ahead forecasting, each sample had the form $\left(x_{t-k+1}, x_{t-k+2}, ..., x_t, x_{t+1} \right)$, and the whole set of samples was obtained by moving window technique. Here, x_{t+1} represents the forecasting data while the other numbers are the corresponding inputs. Three-fourth of this set was used for training, while the rest was used in the validation process.

Inputs: particulate matter measurements of various PM fractions made in a certain default time window; outputs: one-step-ahead forecast of the PM pollutant.

Step 1. *Data preprocessing.* This stage involves the data processing, elimination of incomplete records, data interpolation to complete the missing values in the time series, data normalization validated by experts, and their redirection so that the database is compatible with the software used for forecasting.

Step 2. *Establishing the method of avoiding the overtraining of the ANN.* A common method is to divide the database into three sets of data: one for training (e.g., 75%), one for validation (e.g., 15%) and another one for testing (e.g., 15%). In some cases, the proportions that include the data in one of the datasets differ slightly around the value of 70–80% for the training set, 18–28% for the validation, and about 2% for the testing set. Alternatively, the cross-validation with 10 sets—9 sets used for training and the 10th for validation might be considered. This process is repeated until each of the 10 sets is used for validation.

Step 3. *Setting the ANN architecture.* This involves the establishing of the number of nodes in the input layer (optimal window time for the next value forecast of the pollutant), the number of nodes in the hidden layer, activation functions, etc.

Step 4. *Adjustment of training parameters.* The optimal number of epochs for network training, the learning rate, and momentum parameter are established experimentally, avoiding the overtraining of the network or an undertrained situation.

Step 5. *Network training* taking into account the parameters established in step 4 and step 5.

Step 6. *Validation of the resulted network architecture.*

Step 7. *Testing of the ANN.*

Step 8. *Analysis of the ANN performances*. At this stage, statistical parameters can be used such as the correlation coefficient between variables, mean absolute error (MAE), root mean square error (RMSE), the training error (MSE), and mean absolute percentage error (MAPE). The values of these parameters can be compared with the conventional limits established in the literature and those obtained with other models developed for forecasting the amount of particulate matter fractions.

The following tests present how different parameters, which describe the neural network model, affect the accuracy of the forecasted data. The topology of the neural network is denoted as $n_1-n_2-n_3$, where n_1 is the number of nodes in the input layer, n_2 is the number of nodes in the hidden layer, and n_3 is the number of nodes in the output layer. Since the training is sensitive to the initial values of the weights, 10 tests for each algorithm were performed and the mean of the resulted values was considered for all tables provided.

4. Results and discussion

4.1. Analysis of total suspended particulates time series

In the first test, we present the monthly average concentrations values of total suspended particulate (TSP) recorded between 1995 and 2006 in Targoviste, Romania. During that period, TSP often exceeded the limit value (75 $\mu g/m^3$) and the city was considered as a PM risk area at national level due to emissions from metallurgical industries. Later on, Romanian technical norms replaced the earlier TSP air quality standard with a PM_{10} standard.

We compared various (p, d, q) setups of ARIMA model [10] to identify the statistical model with the smallest magnitude of the errors during the estimation period. ARIMA (4,0,3) presented the smallest MAE and MAPE. A significant relationship ($p < 0.001$) with a correlation coefficient of 0.8 was noticed between the ARIMA (4,0,3) forecasted variables and observed data [9].

The tests performed with the feed-forward neural network using the TSP observed series provided good forecasting results with the Quickprop (4,6,1) algorithm. The correlation coefficient of ANN Quickprop (4,6,1) indicated a strong relationship between the forecasted variables and observed data (**Table 2**).

Indicator	ARIMA statistical model (4,0,3)	ANN model (4,6,1)	ANN model (4,6,1)	ANN model (6,6,1)
		Quickprop	Incremental	Rprop
r	0.801	0.946	0.779	0.652

Table 2. Correlation coefficients of forecasted/observed series of the ARIMA model and ANN algorithms using the time series of total suspended particulates (TSP) concentrations in Targoviste city.

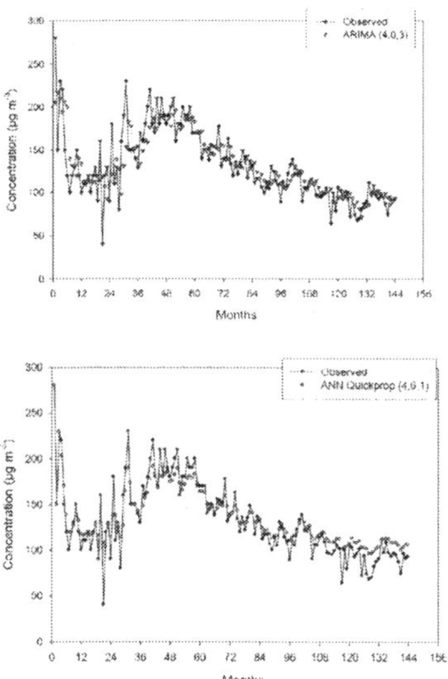

Figure 3. Comparison of monthly averages of total suspended particulates observations vs. the ARIMA (4,0,3) and Quickprop (4,6,1) simulations in Targoviste city (1995–2006) [9].

The ANN Quickprop (4,6,1) model presented a higher correlation coefficient ($r = 0.94$) than ARIMA (4,0,3) model. The neural network prediction algorithm provided a better fit to the TSP measured time series (**Figure 3**). Consequently, we observed that the use of a proper configuration of ANN could provide better results for TSP prediction than linear statistical models [9].

4.2. Analysis of PM_{10} time series

In the next test, we used daily time series of PM_{10} recorded by an optical analyzer in Targoviste city. We present a case with a time series of 101 values to test the influence of a short time series on the efficiency of the training.

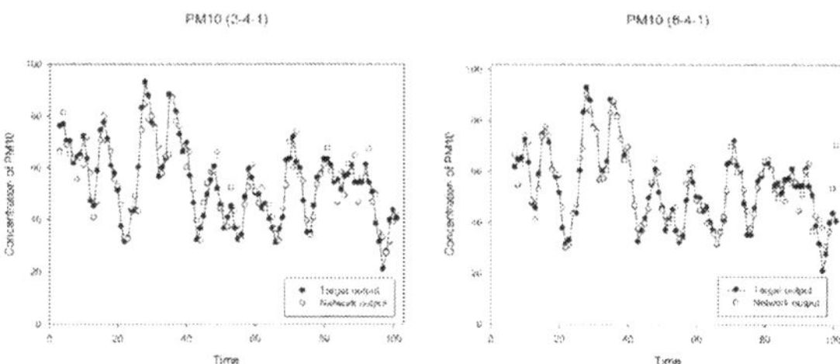

Figure 4. Observed and forecasted concentrations of PM_{10} (2-4-1) and PM_{10} (6-4-1) ANN configurations [13].

ANN	Rprop		Quickprop	
Network configuration	MSE	MSE	MSE	MSE
	Training data	Validation data	Training data	Validation data
2-4-1	0.00993	0.01095	0.01153	0.00866
4-4-1	0.00498	0.01659	0.00957	0.00950
6-4-1	0.00412	0.02069	0.00881	0.00949
8-4-1	0.00314	0.02285	0.00738	0.01368

Table 3. Dependence of training and validation errors with various topologies of feed-forward artificial neural network using short PM_{10} time series.

Figure 4 presents the graphics for the utilization of 2 and 6 neurons in the input layer.

We observed that the number of network inputs has a major influence over the forecasting performances. **Table 3** shows how the training error depends on the number of network inputs. For each case, we used the same number of values, that is, 80. Increasing the number of network inputs results in the decrease in the number of testing samples. Yet, the table shows an increase in the MSE of the validation data. This suggests that increasing the number of input neurons will improve the capability of the network to have a better response for the data close to ones used in the training process. On the other hand, the network loses its generalization abilities.

Table 4 shows how the network training and testing depend on the number of training samples. The selected network topology was 2-4-1.

The error of training data decreases with the increase in the number of samples, while the error of validation data increases for both tested algorithms.

ANN	Rprop		Quickprop	
No of training samples	MSE	MSE	MSE	MSE
	Training data	Validation data	Training data	Validation data
70	0.01060	0.00968	0.01242	0.00748
80	0.00991	0.01093	0.01151	0.00864
90	0.00962	0.01306	0.01075	0.01270

Table 4. Dependence of training and validation errors with the number of samples used in training a feed-forward artificial neural network (2-4-1).

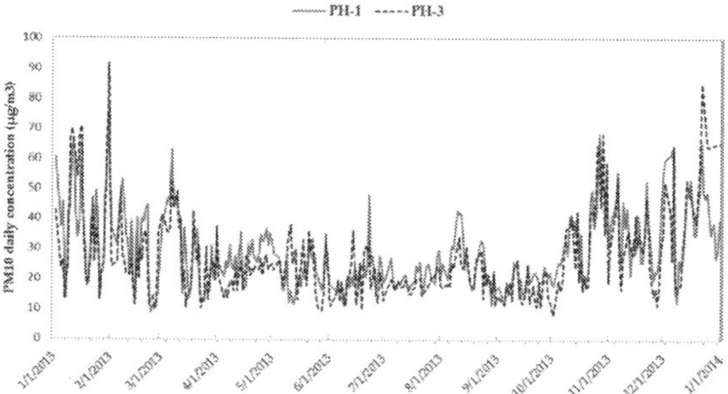

Figure 5. Plots of observed PM_{10} time series with daily averages from two automated stations i.e. PH-1 and PH-3 located in Ploieşti city in 2013.

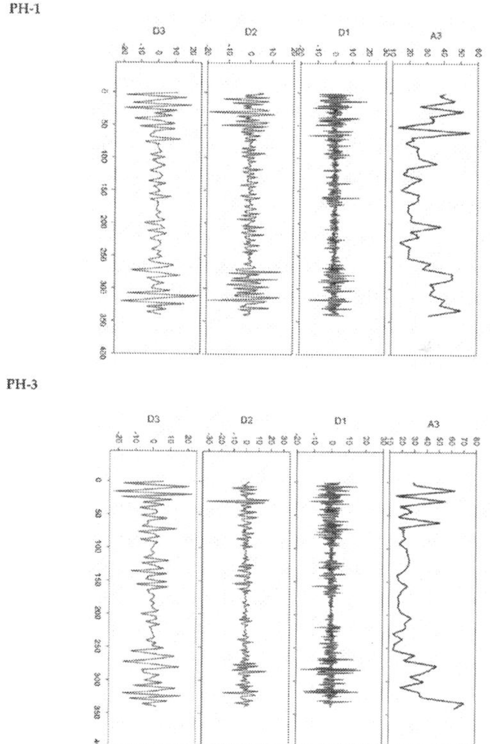

Figure 6. Decompositions of PM_{10} time series recorded at PH-1 and PH-3 automated stations in four components i.e. A3, D1, D2, and D3 using Daubechies wavelets of third order.

4.3. Analysis of PM_{10} time series

In this test, the daily averaged PM_{10} time series recorded at two automated stations located in Ploieşti city in 2013, that is, PH-1 and PH-3 were analyzed using the method of wavelet processing described in [11]. Data gaps (missing values 4 at PH-1 and 15 at PH-3) were interpolated based on existing measured values (**Figure 5**). Each air pollutant series ($n = 365$ values) was decomposed using the MATLAB Wavelet Toolbox in four components, that is, A3, D1, D2, and D3 using Daubechies wavelets of third order (**Figure 6**).

Automated station for monitoring air quality	PH-1 (F)	PH-1 (WF)	PH-3 (F)	PH-3 (WF)
Training data MSE	0.0098	A3: 0.00099	0.0067	A3: 0.00096
		D1: 0.00355		D1: 0.00289
		D2: 0.00099		D2: 0.00104
		D3: 0.00099		D3: 0.00099
Validation data MSE	0.0312	A3: 0.00053	0.0498	A3: 0.00263
		D1: 0.00677		D1: 0.01225
		D2: 0.00335		D2: 0.00238
		D3: 0.00274		D3: 0.00214
RMSE	7.7	3.4	9.9	4.4
MAE	5.5	2.5	6.8	3.2
Pearson coefficient (r)	0.78	0.96	0.75	0.95
Forecasted value ($\mu g\ m^{-3}$)	33.2	36.7	56.8	61.5
Observed value ($\mu g\ m^{-3}$)	39.9		65.6	
Studentized residuals >3.0	6	4	10	5

Table 5. Averages of 10 validation tests resulted from the Rprop (6-4-1) application to PM_{10} time series recorded in Ploiesti vs. Daubechies db3 wavelet—Rprop (6-4-1) results after recomposing the series; F—Rprop FANN, WF—Daubechies db3 wavelet—Rprop FANN.

The components resulted from decomposition of time series (A3, D1, D2, and D3) was used as input in an optimal FANN architecture established prior to this analysis, that is, Rprop (6-4-1). The simulated FANN output of each component was recomposed to form the modeled series of the original pollutant time series and the network performance was analyzed using MSE, MAE, RMSE, and r. The comparison of outputs when FANN is solely used with wavelet-FANN results allowed the evaluation of wavelet contribution to the improvement of forecasting abilities [11].

The application of Daubechies db3 wavelet as a decomposing preprocessor of daily averages time series has significantly improved the out-of-sample forecasted values (**Table 5**). The results showed that the exclusive use of Rprop (6-4-1) configuration was less fitted to the observed data at both stations. Wavelet preprocessing followed by the individual training of resulted components has substantially increased the r coefficient from 0.7 to 0.9 and decreased the error indicators for both time series as compared to the exclusive use of FANN. Furthermore, the forecasted values were closer to the corresponding real observations.

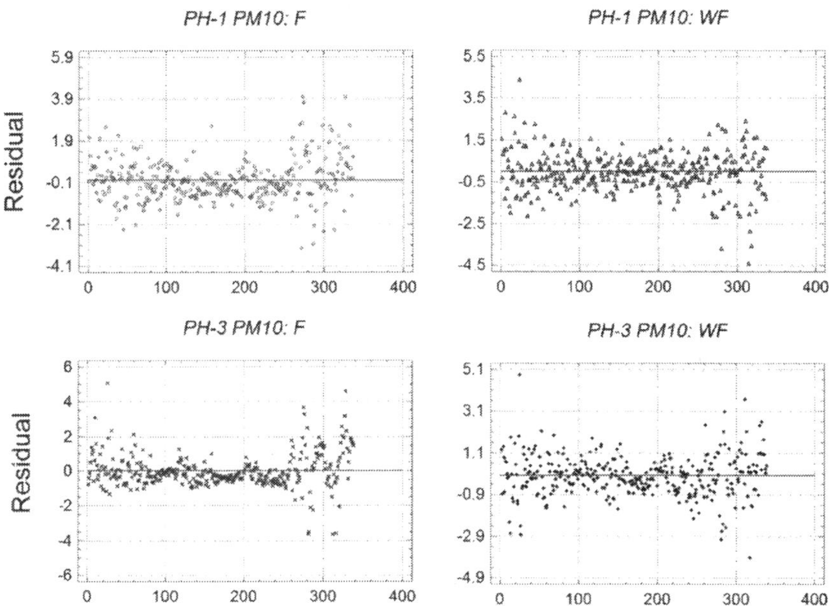

Figure 7. Plots of residuals resulted after correlating the daily averages of PM_{10} (μg m^{-3}) and Rprop FANN (6-4-1) modeled data, and Daubechies db3 wavelet—Rprop WFANN (6-4-1) data, respectively, recorded at two automated monitoring stations in Ploiesti.

A reduction of Studentized residuals number greater than 3.0 was observed using the wavelet processing of data from both stations compared to FANN (**Figure 7**), that is, from 6 Studentized residuals to 4 (PH-1), and from 10 to 5 (PH-3).

These aspects suggested that wavelet integration in processing of daily averages of PM_{10} series provided significant improvements of the forecasting ability recommending the use of the hybrid model. Compared to these results, the application of the hybrid model to hourly recorded PM_{10} time series at other Romanian stations showed also the improvements of correlation coefficient. However, the wavelet processing increased errors and provided more potential outliers [11]. Wavelet integration did not provide computational benefits taking into account the increase in time required for data processing. On the other hand, application of Rprop FANN to hourly recorded PM_{10} produced overfitting. For improved results when neural network is solely used, overfitting is required to be adjusted by using additional techniques, for example, early stopping [18], dropout [19], etc.

We observed in our study that wavelet integration diminished the overfitting tendencies.

4.4. Analysis of $PM_{2.5}$ time series

The section presents the results of Daubechies db3 wavelet—Rprop neural network (6-4-1) modeling using $PM_{2.5}$ time series of 24-h daily averaged concentrations recorded in Râmnicu Vâlcea city, south-west of Romania at VL-1 monitoring station. We selected this station for tests because VL-1 station was one of the two stations that recorded a substantial exceeding of the annual limit value (25 $\mu g/m^3$) at national level in 2012. The maximum value reached 149.13 $\mu g/m^3$ and the annual geometric mean was 23.8 $\mu g/m^3$.

Automated monitoring station in Ramnicu Valcea city (VL-1)	2012 (F)	2012 (WF)
RMSE	6.3	26.1
MAE	3.8	16.3
MAPE	31.6	50.4
Pearson coefficient (r)	0.86	0.93
Studentized residuals > 3.0	7	7

Table 6. Averages of 10 validation tests resulted from the Rprop (6-4-1) application to $PM_{2.5}$ time series recorded at VL-1 station vs. Daubechies db3 wavelet—Rprop (6-4-1) results after recomposing the series; F—Rprop FANN, WF—Daubechies db3 wavelet—Rprop FANN.

A significant increasing of the r coefficients was observed after the application of wavelet preprocessing. RMSE, MAE, and MAPE showed higher values compared to the exclusive use of Rprop configuration (**Table 6**). Both models overestimated the forecasted values in the last quarter of time series. However, the fluctuations observed in the original time series were simulated better by using Daubechies wavelets [11].

These results suggest that other models or algorithms with noise-filtering/smoothing proper-ties may be applied in various stages of the simulation in conjunction with the Daubechies db3 wavelet—Rprop FANN utilization. The expected outcome would be a superior refining of the initial $PM_{2.5}$ forecasted values [11].

5. A cyberinfrastructure for the protection of children's respiratory health by integrating hybrid neural networks for PM forecasting—ROkidAIR

ROkidAIR cyberinfrastructure is currently developed in a European Economic Area (eea-grants.org) research project to facilitate the protection of children's respiratory health in two Romanian cities, that is, Targoviste and Ploiesti.

Recent developments in the management of urban atmospheric environment demonstrated the imperative need to ensure quick, efficient, and easy-to-understand information regarding the status of air quality. The negative impact of air pollution on human health requires improvements of contemporary systems for air quality management to reduce the human exposure to various pollutants. Providing full and comprehensive information concerning the air quality is regarded as a mandatory service for citizens in the current air quality management systems. The authorities should establish an appropriate framework, especially in urban areas, where adverse health effects caused by poor air quality are more pronounced, to ensure the integration of relevant data regarding the maintaining of air quality at required standards. The systems for air quality management need to be adapted to decision makers' requirements (in order to reduce the ambient air quality issues through adequate policies) and citizens (for early warning and for providing useful recommendations). Aiming to reduce their exposure, citizens should receive adequate information on the spatiotemporal variation of air quality or the forecasts on short, medium, and long term. To achieve this goal, it is necessary to collect, integrate, and analyze data from multiple sources. Air quality forecast is one of the essential elements of modern air quality management in urban areas. However, the efficiency of the used forecasting methods is limited by the complex relationships between air quality, mete-orological parameters, and specific characteristics of each study area. In addition, an important issue that needs to be considered in choosing the forecasting method is the variation of the input data quality. The methods to be used should be less sensitive to this factor [20]. Infor-mation related to air quality in urban areas is obtained by using specific methods and tools for processing the time series recorded by the monitoring stations. Mathematical methods and tools can provide air quality forecasting, so that decision makers can act with preventive measures that would "mitigate" or change the results of a foreseen critical pollution episode. There is an increasing demand regarding the development of cyber-platforms that may facilitate the air quality management providing real health benefits to the end user (e.g., ROkidAIR, *http://www.rokidair.ro*).

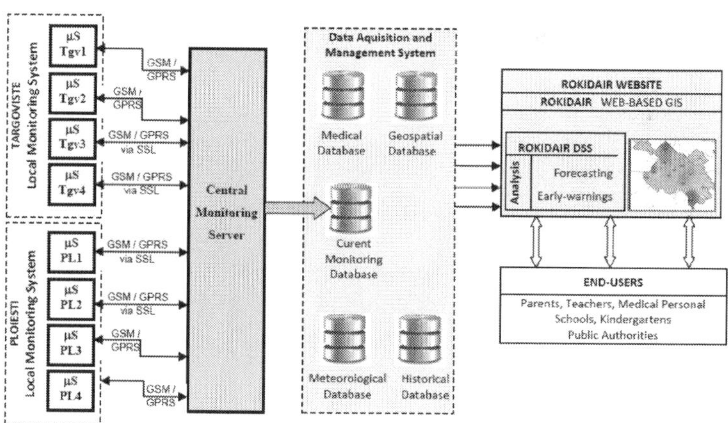

Figure 8. The architecture of the ROkidAIR system.

The main goal of the ROkidAIR project is to develop and deploy a monitoring network system and an adjacent early warning structure that provide synthesized data concerning the $PM_{2.5}$

levels obtained from simplified but reliable monitoring micro-stations and AI forecasting algorithms developed within the project . The architecture of the ROkidAIR system is presented in **Figure 8**. The ROkidAIR cyberinfrastructure is a pilot system, which is focused on fine particulate matter effects on children's health in two towns of Romania, that is, Targoviste and Ploiesti. It provides early warnings concerning the PM levels, tailored to the end-user requirements via several communication channels [3]. Collected time series obtained from the self-developed monitoring network system, based on PM micro-stations, are preprocessed and adapted to feed the forecasting module based on AI algorithms. All data are presented in a dedicated geo-portal adapted to be used by smartphones and other portable equipment. The main stream of information is transmitted both to the responsible authorities and to the sensitive persons, who are registered in the system. The expert advises and recommendations are transmitted via e-mails and SMSs to the registered users providing support for children's health management under the impact of air quality stressors and pressures. Early warnings are developed in cooperation with pediatric specialists, which synthesize the most relevant information concerning the protection of children's health against air pollution threats. The early warning data packages are also transmitted to the authorities (e.g., local EPAs—Environmental Protection Agencies and DPH—Public Health Protection Directions) for informational purposes. The monitoring network comprises eight PM micro-stations (four in each city), which are developed during the implementation of ROkidAIR project. These micro-stations provide continuous PM monitoring data that are processed to be used as inputs in forecasting algorithms based on AI. The raw data obtained from the eight micro-stations are also used in other modules of the cyber-platform: the ROkidAIR web-based geographic information systems (GIS) geoportal, and the decision support system (DSS) including the early warning module. The DSS system uses artificial intelligence techniques (ANNs and predictive data mining) and hybrid algorithms and models (Neuro-fuzzy ANFIS, and wavelet neural network, WNN) for assessing children's exposure to the pollution with particulate matter, in order to elaborate forecasted values and early warnings [16].

In ROkidAIR AI model, forecasting knowledge is extracted by using ANFIS (generating the fuzzy rules set), and other methods (e.g., a combination between some machine learning techniques) on the specific datasets (continuous monitoring data, historical data, meteorological data, and medical data). All the extracted forecasting rules and knowledge are included in a forecasting knowledge base that provide expert knowledge (heuristics) for a faster and optimal air pollution forecasting in a critical polluted area [21].

6. Conclusions

The contribution of artificial intelligence to the air quality monitoring systems under development relates to evolutionary computing, which provides stochastic search facilities that can efficiently assess complex spaces described by mathematical, statistical, neural network, or fuzzy inference models applied to assess the population exposure to air pollution in urban environments. Machine-learning techniques are currently contributing to the *online* air quality monitoring and forecasting. Statistical and neural modeling techniques can also provide approximations to supplement results from computationally expensive analytic methods.

Significant results for PM data forecasting were obtained with Rprop ($PM_{10}10$ and $PM_{2.5}$), and Quickprop (TSP) algorithms. The exclusive use of the ANN algorithms showed difficulties in predicting pollutant peaks and limitations due to limited continuous observations and large local-scale variations of concentrations. WNNs is an alternative to overcome these drawbacks related to time series predictions by integrating a proper wavelet in the hidden nodes of WNNs or as a preprocessing step. The results of numerical tests provided that the application of wavelet transformation is a significant factor for improving the accuracy of forecasting. Further investigations are required using hourly, daily, and monthly air-quality data from other locations and regional level, by assessing and verifying the reliability, relevance, and adequacy of ANN data forecasting. An important step for reliable air quality forecasting is the optimal selection of ANN learning algorithm. The automation of this component is required to optimize the informational fluxes and to facilitate the decision-making process.

Acknowledgements

This study received funding from the European Economic Area Financial Mechanism 2009–2014 under the project ROkidAIR *Towards a better protection of children against air pollution threats in the urban areas of Romania* contract no. 20SEE/30.06.2014

Author details

Daniel Dunea* and Stefania Iordache

*Address all correspondence to: dan.dunea@valahia.ro

Valahia University of Târgoviste, Aleea Sinaia, Târgoviste, Romania

References

[1] Ianache C., Dumitru D., Predescu L., Predescu M. (2015), Relationship between airborne particulate matter and weather conditions during cold months, In Proceedings of 15th International Multidisciplinary Scientific Geoconference SGEM 2015, June 18–24, 2015, Albena, Bulgaria, 1017–1024, DOI: 10.5593/SGEM2015/B41/S19.131

[2] Langner M., Draheim T., Endlicher W. (2011), Particulate matter in the urban atmosphere: concentration, distribution, reduction—results of studies in the Berlin metro-

politan area, In W. Endlicher et al. (eds.), Perspectives in Urban Ecology, Berlin, Heidelberg, Springer-Verlag, 15–41. DOI: 10.1007/978-3-642-17731-6_2

[3] Iordache St., Dunea D., Lungu E., Predescu L., Dumitru D., Ianache C., Ianache R. (2015), A cyberinfrastructure for air quality monitoring and early warnings to protect children with respiratory disorders, In Proceedings of the 20th International Conference on Control Systems and Computer Science (CSCS20-2015), Bucharest, 789–796.

[4] Dunea D., Iordache St., Alexandrescu D.C., Dincă N. (2014), Screening the weekdays/weekend patterns of air pollutant concentrations recorded in southeastern Romania, Environmental Engineering and Management Journal, 14(12), 3105–3115.

[5] WHO (2014), World Health Organization, Ambient (outdoor) air quality and health—Fact sheet N°313, Updated March 2014, http://www.who.int/mediacentre/factsheets/fs313/en, Accessed 10 February 2016.

[6] AQEG (2012), Fine Particulate Matter (PM2.5) in the United Kingdom, Defra, London.

[7] Dunea D., Iordache St. (2015), Time series analysis of air pollutants recorded from Romanian EMEP stations at mountain sites, Environmental Engineering and Management Journal, 14(11), 2725–2735.

[8] Vaisala (2016), Weather monitoring and urban air quality, Application note, http://www.vaisala.com/Vaisala%20Documents/Application%20notes/Urban%20air%20application%20note%20B210959EN-A.pdf, Accessed 10 February 2016.

[9] Dunea D., Oprea M., Lungu E. (2008), Comparing statistical and neural network approaches for urban air pollution time series analysis. In L. Bruzzone (ed.), Proceedings of the 27th IASTED International Conference on Modelling, Identification and Control, Acta Press, Innsbruck, Austria, February 11–13, 93–98.

[10] Box G.E.P., Jenkins G.M. (1970), Time Series Analysis: Forecasting and Control, Holden-Day, San Francisco, CA.

[11] Dunea D., Pohoață A., Iordache St. (2015), Using wavelet—feed forward neural networks to improve air pollution forecasting in urban environments, Environmental Monitoring and Assessment, 187, 477, 1–6.

[12] Riedmiller M., Braun H. (1993), A direct adaptive method for faster backpropagation learning: The RPROP algorithm, In H. Ruspini (ed.), Proceedings of the IEEE International Conference on Neural Networks, San Francisco, 586–591.

[13] Lungu E., Oprea M., Dunea D. (2008), An application of artificial neural networks in environmental pollution forecasting, In Proceedings of the 26th IASTED International Conference on Artificial Intelligence and Applications, Acta Press, Innsbruck, Austria, February 11–13, 187–193.

[14] Fahlman S.E. (1988), Faster learning variations on back-propagation: an empirical study, In D.S. Touretzky, G.E. Hinton, and T.J. Sejnowski (eds.), Proceedings of the 1988 Connectionist Models Summer School, Morgan Kaufmann, San Mateo, CA, 38–51.

[15] Vrahatis M.N., Magoulas G.D., Plagianakos V.P. (1999), Convergence analysis of the Quickprop method, In Proceedings of the International Joint Conference on Neural Networks (IJCNN'99), Washington DC, 848, Session: 5.3.

[16] Oprea M., Ianache C., Mihalache S., Dragomir E., Dunea D., Iordache Şt., Savu T. (2015), On the development of an intelligent system for particulate matter air pollution monitoring, analysis and forecasting in urban regions, In 19th International Conference on System Theory, Control and Computing (ICSTCC), 711–716.

[17] Oprea M. (2005), A case study of knowledge modelling in an air pollution control decision support system, AiCommunications, 18(4), 293–303.

[18] Guo X. (2010), Learning gradients via an early stopping gradient descent method, Journal of Approximation Theory, 162(11), 1919–1944.

[19] Srivastava N., Geoffrey H., Krizhevsky A., Sutskever I., Salakhutdinov R. (2014), Dropout: a simple way to prevent neural networks from overfitting, Journal of Machine Learning Research, 15, 1929–1958.

[20] Zhang Y., Bocquet M., Mallet V., Seigneur C., Baklanov A. (2012), Real-time air quality forecasting, part I: history, techniques, and current status, Atmospheric Environment, 60, 632–655.

[21] Mihalache S.F., Popescu M., Oprea M. (2015), Particulate matter prediction using ANFIS modelling techniques, In 19th International Conference on System Theory, Control and Computing (ICSTCC), 895–900.

Chapter 12

Neural Networks Applications for the Remote Sensing of Hydrological Parameters

Emanuele Santi

Additional information is available at the end of the chapter

http://dx.doi.org/10.5772/63165

Abstract

The main artificial neural networks (ANN)-based retrieval algorithms developed at the Institute of Applied Physics (IFAC) are reviewed here. These algorithms aim at retrieving the main hydrological parameters, namely the soil moisture content (SMC), the plant water content (PWC) of agricultural vegetation, the woody volume of forests (WV) and the snow depth (SD) or snow water equivalent (SWE), from data collected by active (SAR/scatterometers) and passive (radiometers) microwave sensors operating from space. Taking advantage of the fast computation, ANN are able to generate output maps of the target parameter at both local and global scales, with a resolution varying from hundreds of meters to tens of kilometres, depending on the considered sensor. A peculiar strategy adopted for the training, which has been obtained by combining satellite measurements with data simulated by electromagnetic models (based on the radiative transfer theory, RTT), made these algorithms robust and site independent. The obtained results demonstrated that ANN are a powerful tool for estimating the hydrological parameters at different spatial scales, provided that they have been trained with consistent datasets, made up by both experimental and theoretical data.

Keywords: microwave satellite sensors, soil moisture content, vegetation water content, snow water equivalent, woody volume

1. Introduction

Nowadays, global phenomena such as climate warning, stratospheric ozone depletion and troposphere pollution are threatening the long-term habitability of the planet. The Earth is a complex evolving system where regional as well as global processes at all spatial and temporal scales are strongly interrelated. These include surface exchanges of water, energy, carbon and

© 2016 The Author(s). Licensee InTech. This chapter is distributed under the terms of the Creative Commons Attribution License (http://creativecommons.org/licenses/by/3.0), which permits unrestricted use, distribution, and reproduction in any medium, provided the original work is properly cited.

other bio-geological processes, and exchange between land surface atmosphere, ocean and ground water. The human activity further complicated all these processes, because it transforms continuously the land surface to meet human needs associated with basic food production, population expansion and economic development.

Consequently, an ever-increasing interest in meteorological events and climate changes has led to a greater focus on the study of hydrological processes and their dynamics. The hydrological cycle involves the circulation of water from ocean to water vapour through the evaporation processes, the transformation of water vapour into precipitation and its return to the cycle through infiltration and evapotranspiration again. However, considering the spatial and temporal coverage needed to have reliable estimates, direct measurements of all the parameters involved in the hydrological cycle are difficult and extremely expensive. This led to an increasing interest for the observation from space, since it can meet the temporal and spatial requirements for an operational monitoring of the parameters related to the hydrological cycle. Earlier initiatives, such as the launch of a number of satellites having on-board sensors dedicated to the Earth's parameters observation, have already developed long-term applications and provided fundamental contributions in understanding global and regional ocean processes and enhancing land surface studies.

Among the instruments operating from space for the Earth surface observation, the sensors operating in the microwave portion of the electromagnetic (e.m.) spectrum have a great potential because these frequencies are capable of estimating some parameters of atmosphere, vegetation and soil that cannot be observed in the visible/near-infrared and thermal wavelength. Moreover, the scattering and emission at microwaves are related directly to the water content of the observed target. Microwave sensors, which can be classified in active (real aperture radar—RAR, and synthetic aperture radar—SAR), and passive (radiometers) are therefore particularly suitable for monitoring the key parameters of the hydrological cycle. In particular, these sensor represent a powerful tool for monitoring the soil water content or soil moisture content (SMC), the vegetation biomass, expressed as plant water content (PWC) for agricultural crops and woody volume (WV) for forests, and the snow depth (SD) or its water equivalent (SWE).

SMC is one of the driving factors in the hydrological cycle, being able to influence the runoff, the evapotranspiration, the surface heat fluxes and the biogeochemical cycles. The knowledge of SMC and its dynamics is mandatory in a wide range of activities concerning the forecasting of weather and climate, the prevention of natural disasters such as floods and landslides, the management of water resources and agriculture-related activities and many others. A huge amount of experimental and theoretical studies on the SMC retrieval from microwave acquisitions was therefore carried out since the late 1970s. The dielectric constant of soil (DC) at microwave frequencies is strongly dependent on the water content of the observed soil. At L-band, for example, the large variation in real part of the dielectric constant from dry to saturated soil results in a change of about 10 dB in radar backscatter and of 100 K in the radiometric brightness temperature. An important component required in the soil moisture inverse problem is the knowledge of the relationship between the soil dielectric constant to its moisture content: widely adopted empirical models for assessing such relationship are given in [1, 2].

Snow is another driving factor of the hydrological cycle, since it is able to influence the Earth's climate and its response to global changes. Snow is the main component of the cryosphere, and its accumulation and extension are related to the global climate variations. The monitoring of the snow parameters, and in particular SD and SWE, is essential for the forecasting of snow–water runoffs (flash floods) and for the management of the water resources. Currently, satellite microwave radiometers are employed for generating low-resolution SD or SWE products at global scale, while the operational mapping of snow at high resolution mainly rely with optical sensors, being the microwave application still at the research stage for this application. In both cases, the currently available snow products are based on the single sensors, and thus, the temporal and spatial coverage is given by the sensor characteristics, which may not fulfil the requirements for the operational use of remote sensing data in monitoring and management of snow.

Vegetation cover on the Earth's surface is an important variable in the study of global changes, since vegetation biomass is the most influential input for carbon cycle models. The frequent and timely monitoring of vegetation parameters (such as vegetation biomass and leaf area index) is therefore of vital importance to the study of climate changes and global warming.

The retrieval of the aforementioned parameters from active and/or passive microwave measurements is nonetheless not trivial, due to the nonlinearity of the relationships between radar and radiometric acquisitions and target parameters. Moreover, in general, more than one combination of surface parameters (SMC, surface roughness—HSTD, PWC and so on) give the same electromagnetic response. Thus, in order to minimize the uncertainties and enhance the retrieval accuracy from remote sensing data, statistical approaches based on the Bayes theorem and learning machines are widely adopted for implementing the retrieval algorithms [3–5].

In this framework, the artificial neural networks (ANN) represent an interesting tool for implementing accurate and flexible retrieval algorithms, which are able to operate with radar and radiometric satellite measurements and to easily combine information coming from different sources. ANN can be considered a statistical minimum variance approach for addressing the retrieval problem, and, if properly trained, they are able to reproduce any kind of input-output relationships [6, 7].

During the training, sets of input data and corresponding target outputs are provided sequentially to the ANN, which iteratively adjusts the interconnecting weights of each neuron, in order to minimize the difference between actual outputs and corresponding targets, basing on the selected learning algorithm.

Many examples of ANN application to inverse problems in the remote-sensing field can be found in literature, in particular concerning the retrieval of soil moisture at local scale from SAR [8–10] or radiometric [11] observations. The comparison of retrieval algorithms carried out in [9] demonstrated that ANN, with respect to other widely adopted statistical approaches based on Bayes theorem and Nelder–Mead minimization [12], offer the best compromise between retrieval accuracy and computational cost. Other comparison between ANN, Bayesian, SVM and other retrieval approaches can be found in [13–15]. All these works demonstrated that the ANN are able to provide accuracy results in line with (or better than) the other methods, with the advantages of a fast computation, that is mandatory for the online processing of high-resolution images, and the possibility of updating the training if new data are available. The cited publications refer to the retrieval of soil moisture; however, these considerations remain valid for the retrieval of the other parameters investigated here.

Basing the training on data simulated by forward electromagnetic models, namely models that are able to simulate the microwave signal emitted or scattered by the target surface, the ANN can be regarded as a method for estimating the hydrological parameters from satellite microwave acquisitions through the inversion of the given model. Following this approach, the ANN act for inverting the forward model, similarly to other physically based algorithms, but without the approximations needed for an analytical inversion. Moreover, the additional inclusion of experimental data in the training set allows retaining the advantages of the experimental-driven approaches in adapting the algorithm to the particular features of a given test site [16].

The main advantages of this technique consist of the possibility of quick updating the training with new datasets, thus adapting the algorithm to work on a given test area, but without losing the accuracy on a larger scale. Moreover, the method has the capability of easily merging data coming from different sources for improving the retrieval accuracy. The poor robustness to outliers represents instead the main disadvantage of ANN: outliers are input data out of the range of the training set. In such case indeed, the ANN may return large errors or fail completely the retrieval, requiring therefore a 'robust' training, which has to be representative of a variety of surface conditions as wide as possible.

Besides the other considerations, it should be remarked that the strategy adopted for setting up and training the ANN is fundamental for obtaining a valid retrieval algorithm. An inappropriate training can turn indeed the ANN from a powerful retrieval instrument into an inadequate approach to the given problem. Some examples can be found in literature, in which the training set is insufficient for defining all the interconnection weights of the complex architecture proposed, or in which the architecture definition and the related overfitting and underfitting have not been properly addressed. Another fundamental consideration is that ANN are able to represent any kind of input–output relationships, and therefore, a deep knowledge of the physic of the problem is mandatory for avoiding the risk of relating input and output quantities that are instead completely uncorrelated, thus generating relationships that have no physical basis.

In this work, a review of the main ANN-based algorithms developed at IFAC for estimating the soil moisture (SMC, in m^3/m^3), the water content of agricultural vegetation (PWC, in kg/m^2), the forest woody volume (WV, in t/ha) and the snow depth/water equivalent (SD, in cm, and SWE, in mm) is presented. These algorithms take advantage of an innovative training strategy, which is based on the combination of satellite measurements with data simulated by electromagnetic models, based on the radiative transfer theory (RTT).

2. Implementing and training the Artificial Neural Networks

The ANN considered in this work are feed-forward multilayer perceptron (MLP), having two or three hidden layers of nine to twelve neurons each between the input and the output. The training was based on the back-propagation learning rule, which is an iterative gradient-descent algorithm able to adjust the connection weights of each neuron, in order to minimize the mean square error between the outputs generated by the ANN at every iteration and the corresponding target values.

It should be noted that the gradient-descent method sometimes suffers from slow convergence, due to the presence of one or more local minima, which may also affect the final result of the training. This problem can be solved by repeating the training several times, with a resetting of the initial conditions and a verification that each training process led to the same convergence results in terms of R and RMSE, by increasing it until negligible improvements were obtained.

2.1. Defining architecture

In order to define the optimal ANN architecture in terms of number of neurons and hidden layers, the most suitable strategy is to start with a simple ANN architecture, generally with one hidden layer of few neurons. These ANN are trained by means of a subset of the available data, tested on the rest of the dataset, and the training and testing errors are compared. The ANN configuration is then increased by adding neurons and hidden layers; training and testing are repeated and errors compared again, until a further increase of the ANN architecture is found to have a negligible decrease of the training error and an increase in the test error. This procedure allows defining the minimal ANN architecture capable of providing an adequate fit of the training data, preventing overfitting or underfitting problems. NNs, like other flexible nonlinear estimation methods, can be affected indeed by either underfitting or overfitting. ANN configurations not sufficiently complex for the given problem can fail to reproduce complicated data set, leading to underfitting. ANN configurations too complex may fit also the noise, leading to overfitting. Overfitting is especially dangerous because it can easily lead to predictions that are far beyond the range of the training data. In other words, the ANN are able to reproduce the training set with high accuracy but fails the test and validation phases.

2.2. Selecting the transfer function

Another key issue for defining the ANN best architecture is in the selection of the most appropriate transfer function: in general, linear transfer functions give less accurate results in training and testing; however, they are less prone to overfitting and are more robust to outliers, that is input data out the range of the input parameters included in the training set. Logistic Sigmoid (logsig) and Hyperbolic Tangent Sigmoid (tansig) transfer functions are instead characterized by higher accuracies in the training and test; however, they may lead to large errors when the trained ANN are applied to new datasets. Logsig generates outputs between 0 and 1 as the neuron's net input goes from negative to positive infinity and describes the nonlinearity, g(a), as $1/(1 + e^{-a})$. Alternatively, multilayer networks can use the tansig function, $\tanh(a) = (e^a - e^{-a})/(e^a + e^{-a})$.

2.3. Generating the training set

Nevertheless, besides these problems, the main constraint for obtaining good accuracies with the ANN approach consists of the statistical significance of the training set, which shall be representative of a variety of surface conditions as wide as possible, in order to make the algorithm able to address all the situations that can be encountered on a global scale. The datasets derived from experimental activities are in general site dependent and cannot be representative of the large variation of the surface features that can be observed on a larger scale. Therefore, a training set only based on experimental data is not sufficient for training the ANN for global monitoring applications.

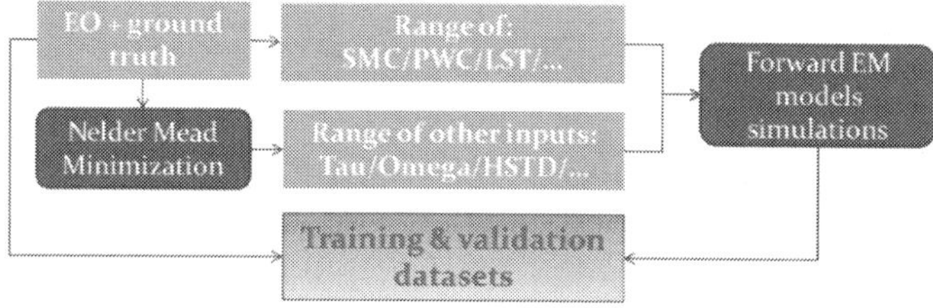

Figure 1. Strategy adopted for defining the raining and validation datasets, starting from the experimental data and using the forwards e.m. models (after [16]).

By combining the experimental in situ measurements with simulated data obtained from the e.m. models, it is possible to fill in the gaps of the experimental datasets and to better characterize the microwave signal dependence on the target parameter for a variety of surface conditions as wide as possible. The consistency between experimental data and model simulations can be obtained by deriving the range of model input parameters from the available measurements. After defining the minimum and maximum of each parameter required by the model, namely SMC, PWC, soil moisture, surface roughness (HSTD) and surface temperature (LST), the input vectors are generated by using a pseudorandom function, rescaled in order to cover the range of each parameter. Thousands of inputs vectors for running the model simulations can be generated by iterating this procedure, thus obtaining datasets of surface parameters and corresponding simulated microwave data for training and testing the ANN. The flowchart of **Figure 1** represents the main steps for generating the training from the experimental data. The same procedure allows generating the independent dataset for validating the ANN after training. In general, the available data are divided in two subsets with a random sampling; the first subset is divided again in 60–20–20% for training, test and validation phases, respectively, and the second subset is reserved for an independent test of the algorithm. The random sampling of the dataset is reiterated 5–6 times, and the training is repeated each time, in order to avoid any dependence of the obtained results on the sampling process.

This strategy has been successfully adopted for implementing and training the ANN-based algorithms that are presented in the following sections.

3. HydroAlgo ANN algorithm for AMSR-E and AMSR2

The 'HydroAlgo' algorithm [11] applies the ANN for estimating simultaneously SMC, PWC and SD from the acquisitions of the low-resolution spaceborne radiometers, like the Advanced Microwave Scanning Radiometer for the Earth observing system (AMSR-E) [17], which is no more operating, and its successor, AMSR2 [18]. We refer to [11] for a detailed algorithm description. The main characteristic of the algorithm is the exclusive use of AMSR-E/2 data, taking advantage of the multifrequency acquisitions of these sensors. It includes a disaggregation procedure, based on the smoothing filter-based intensity modulation (SFIM) technique [19], which is able to enhance the spatial resolution of the output SMC product up to the nominal sampling of AMSR-E/2 ($\sim 10 \times 10$ km^2). The algorithm flowchart is represented in **Figure 2**: it should be noted that the algorithm applies the already trained ANN to the input data, without repeating the training for each new set of satellite acquisitions. The trained ANN are generated once, saved and recalled for processing the available data. In particular, specific ANN have been trained for each given output product, basing on training sets composed by a combination of experimental data and simulations from e.m. models, obtained following the scheme of Section 2.

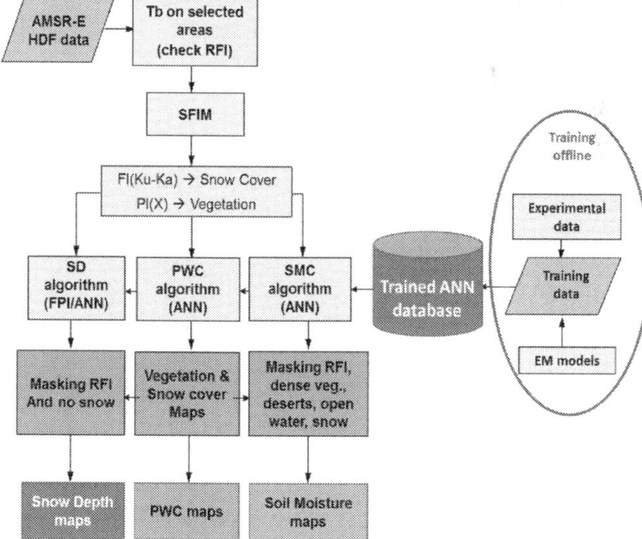

Figure 2. HydroAlgo flowchart.

3.1. SMC processor

The SMC processor was developed and tested using a set of several thousand of data, which was obtained by combining the experimental data collected in Mongolia and Australia with 10,000 values of Tb simulated by the 'tau-omega' model [20]. The experimental dataset was provided by JAXA, within the framework of the JAXA ADEOS-II/AMSR-E and GCOM/AMSR2 research programs.

The core of the algorithm is composed by two feed-forward multilayer perceptron (MLP) ANN, trained independently for the ascending and descending orbits, and using the back-propagation learning rule. Inputs of the algorithm are the brightness temperature at C-band in V-polarization, the polarization indices (PI) at 10.65 and 18.7 GHz (X- and Ku-bands), defined as $PI = 2 \times (TbV - TbH)/(TbV + TbH)$, and the brightness temperature at Ka-band (36.5 GHz) in V-polarization. C-band, that is the lowest AMSR-E frequency, was chosen for its sensitivity to the SMC, which is slightly influenced by sparse vegetation. The polarization indices at X- and Ku-bands are considered for compensating the effect of vegetation on soil emission [21], and for flagging out the densely vegetated targets, where SMC cannot be retrieved. The brightness temperature at Ka-band, V-polarization, was assumed as a proxy of the surface physical temperature, to account for the effect of diurnal and seasonal variations of the surface temperature on microwave brightness [22].

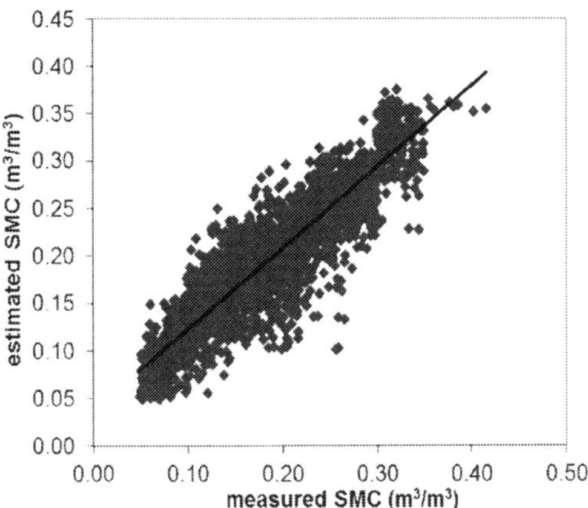

Figure 3. HydroAlgo SMC product validation (after [11]).

The SMC product validation on the Australian and Mongolian data, which were not used for the training, resulted in a determination coefficient $R^2 = 0.8$ (ANN output vs estimated SMC), root-mean-square error RMSE = 0.03 m³/m³, and BIAS = 0.02 m³/m³ (**Figure 3**).

The peculiar characteristics of ANN allowed adapting this algorithm for working on given test areas with a specific updating of the training process, which is devoted to maximize the performances of the algorithm on the area, losing something of the algorithm capabilities for the global retrieval. Following this approach, it was possible to obtain the algorithm for the SMC retrieval in central Italy, which was presented in [23]. In that work, HydroAlgo-derived SMC has been compared with simulated SMC data obtained from the application of a well-established soil water balance model (SWBM) [24] in central Italy (Umbria region), with the aim of exploiting the potential of AMSR-E/2 for SMC monitoring on a regional scale and in heterogeneous environments too. For this application, the 10% of about 450,000 AMSR-E acquisitions collected over the test area and corresponding SMC values simulated by SWBM, obtained with a random sampling, were added to the training set of the original HydroAlgo implementation. The algorithm trained with this updated dataset was validated on the remaining 90% of the available data, allowing an appreciable improvement of the accuracy with respect to the original implementation. In detail, this 'supervised' approach allowed obtaining an overall increase of the average R from 0.71 to 0.84 and a corresponding decrease of RMSE from 0.058 to 0.052 m^3/m^3, with respect to the original implementation of HydroAlgo applied to the same dataset.

3.2. PWC processor

The PWC processor was based on the well-demonstrated sensitivity of the polarization difference, expressed as the polarization index, at various AMSR-E frequencies to PWC. Past research has shown that the microwave polarization index (PI), defined as the difference of the first two Stokes parameters (H- and V-polarization) divided by their sum, especially at X- and Ku-bands, is directly related to τ and therefore to the seasonal changes in PWC and LAI.

It is generally known indeed that microwave emission, expressed as brightness temperature (Tb), depends on canopy growth but also on plant geometry and structure. Therefore, Tb temporal trends vary according to the vegetation type in terms of scatterer dimensions and observation frequency. Tb tends to increase as the biomass of plants characterized by small leaves and thin stems increases, whereas it has an opposite behaviour for crops characterized by large leaves and thick stalks. On the other hand, the PI at the same frequency usually decreases as the biomass of different vegetation types increases, resulting rather independent on crop type [25, 26].

This allowed using PI at higher frequencies with the twofold purpose of compensating the vegetation effect on soil emission at lower frequencies and of estimating directly the PWC.

The capabilities of ANN in merging different inputs into a single retrieval algorithm allowed making synergistic use of PI at C-, X- and Ku-bands from the AMSR-E acquisitions. In order to implement, train and validate the algorithm, we identified a suitable test area in a wide portion of Africa (0–20°N/16°–17°E), which extended from the Sahara desert to Equatorial forest, and therefore included a wide range of vegetation types, biomass amount and land-scapes. The area was also chosen for the presence of large and homogeneous regions, which allowed mitigating the effects related to the coarse resolution of AMSR-E. Several AMSR-E swaths on the area have been collected and resampled on a fixed grid, in order to be repre-sentative of the entire seasonal cycle of vegetation. This process resulted in a dataset of about 10,000 radiometric acquisitions at the considered frequencies, from C- to Ka-bands. Consid-ering the difficulties in obtaining 'ground truth' data of PWC for validating the algorithm on large or global scale, the validation was carried out referring to PWC values derived from NDVI thanks to the relationship established by [22]. Although this relationship was initially developed for corn and soybean crops, it can be considered valid for other types of vegetation too.

In detail, the 'reference' PWC was derived from NDVI data obtained from http://free.vgt.vito.be/home.php, resulting from 10 days of SPOT4 acquisitions on the African continent. These data were resampled on the fixed grid and compared with the corresponding satellite acquisitions, in both ascending and descending orbits. Two different ANN have been defined and trained independently, in order to better account for the large differences between Tb data collected in ascending and descending orbits.

A subset of 15% of the data available was considered for generating the datasets for training, testing and validating each ANN (60–20–20%, randomly sampled), and the remaining 85% of data (about 8500 samples) was considered for the independent validation of the algorithm, to which the result presented in **Figure 4** is referred.

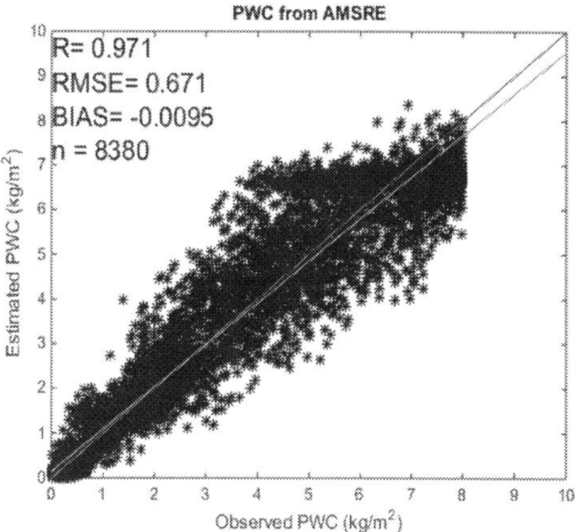

Figure 4. Validation results: PWC estimated by the algorithm as a function of the PWC derived from NDVI and considered as ground truth.

The ANN optimization process resulted in an architecture with two hidden layers of $11 + 11$ neurons, with a transfer function of type 'tansig'. The validation returned encouraging results, with a RMSE error on the PWC retrieval <1 kg/m², and a correlation coefficient $R = 0.97$.

3.3. SD processor

As per the SMC processor, the implementation of the SD processor was based on a dataset provided by JAXA and composed of AMSR-E acquisitions and direct SD and air temperature measurements collected in the eastern part of Siberia. The measurements covered a flat area of about 20′ in latitude, 45′ in longitude, at an average altitude of 300 m asl, covered by low vegetation. In this region, snow was generally present from the beginning of October to the end of May, with a depth that did not exceed 50 cm. The ground measurements were covering seven winter seasons, from October 2002 to May 2009. By combining the AMSR-E acquisitions and the related direct measurements of SD and air temperature, it was possible to obtain a dataset of 17,000 values for training and testing the ANN. As for the previously described processors, two ANN have been developed and trained separately for the ascending and descending orbits.

The validation was carried out on a different area of about 200 × 200 km located between Finland and Norway, obtaining the following statistics: R = 0.88, RMSE = 9.13 cm and BIAS = -0.95 cm.

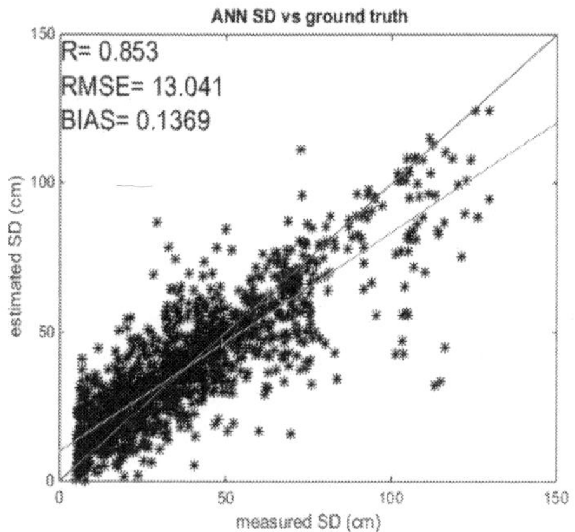

Figure 5. Validation results: SD estimated by the ANN algorithm as a function of the SD derived from ground measurements (after [26]).

The algorithm was then adapted for working on alpine areas, in which snow properties suffer dramatic spatial variations that cannot be easily reproduced by spaceborne microwave radiometers, due to their coarse spatial resolution. This limitation was overcome by setting up a method for evaluating and correcting the effects of the complex orography, of the different footprint in the different AMSR-E channels, and of the forest coverage. The detailed description of this method can be found in [27]. The test and validation were carried out on a test area of about 100 × 100 km^2 located in the eastern Italian Alps, using AMSR-E data collected during the winters between 2002 and 2011. The obtained results were encouraging: the correlation between SD estimated by the algorithm and the corresponding ground truth resulted in R = 0.85 and RMSE = 13 cm considering the descending orbits, while the retrieval accuracy worsened when considering the ascending ones (**Figure 5**).

In this case, the training of the ANN was updated by adding to the original training set a subset of the data collected on the area and the validation was carried out on the remaining part of the dataset, for a total of more than 1400 daily AMSR-E acquisitions and corresponding ground truth.

4. The SAR ANN algorithm for SMC, PWC and SWE

Similarly to HydroAlgo, a further ANN-based algorithm has been implemented for working with SAR data at C- and X-bands, aiming at generating SMC maps of bare or slightly vegetated soils, PWC maps of agricultural vegetation and SWE maps of snow covered surfaces. The algorithm takes advantage of the high resolution of the considered sensors, which can, however, provide data at local or regional scale, since SAR images cover usually areas not larger than 100×100 km^2. The other main difference in respect to HydroAlgo is that the existing SAR systems work at a single frequency and the obtainable product depends on the frequency, polarizations and ancillary information available. For instance, C-band cannot retrieve SD and it is more suitable for monitoring SMC, being less affected to the vegetation effects which drive instead the scattering mechanism at X-band. Depending on the input SAR data, the output resolution ranges between 10×10 and 100×100 m^2. **Figure 6** represents the algorithm flowchart: after a common pre-processing, the algorithm splits in three different branches, one for each output product. Details on the implementation of each processor can be found in [28, 29] for SMC processor [30], for PWC processor and [30] for SWE processor.

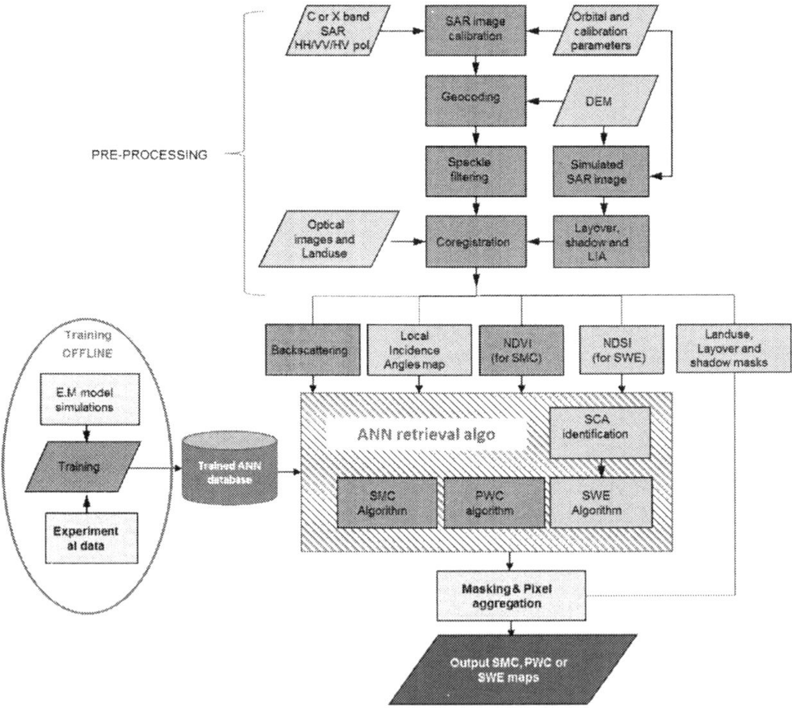

Figure 6. Flow chart of the SAR algorithm.

4.1. SMC processor

The recent generation of SAR sensors can operate in several acquisition modes and provide images at different polarizations and acquisition geometries. For enhance the retrieval accuracy, the algorithm has been implemented with a dedicated ANN for each configuration of inputs, namely the backscattering coefficients ($\sigma°$) in VV- or HH-polarization with and without the ancillary information on vegetation, represented by co-located NDVI from optical sensor, and VV + VH or HH + HV combinations. Consequently, the algorithm was composed by 6 + 6 ANN trained independently for C- and X-band, respectively. Following the strategy presented in Section 2, the dataset implemented for the ANN training was obtained by combining the available SAR images, the corresponding direct measurements of the surface parameters, and a large set of data simulated using e.m. forwards models.

Simulated backscattering values at all polarizations were obtained by coupling OH [31] and vegetation water cloud [33] models. This quite simple but widely validated combination offers several advantages with respect to more sophisticated formulations, namely the reduced set of input parameters needed for simulating the backscatter, the fast computation and the reliable accuracy. In detail, the OH model simulates the surface scattering from bare rough surfaces: with respect to IEM/AIEM, it is able to simulate both co- and cross-polarizations, accounting for the soil surface roughness by only using the height standard deviation (HSTD, in cm) parameter. The VWC model is a simplified implementation of RTT. It accounts for volume scattering of vegetation over the soil, for the attenuation effect on the soil scattering (simulated by OH model) and for the soil—vegetation interaction, requiring as inputs PWC and observation angle only. Inputs of the 'coupled' model are SMC, HSTD, PWC and the observation angle theta.

Minimum and maximum values of the soil parameters measured during the experimental campaigns (SMC, HSTD and PWC) were considered in order to define the range of variability of each soil parameter. Using a pseudorandom function drawn from the standard uniform distribution on the open interval (0, 1), rescaled in order to cover the range of each soil parameter, we generated input vectors for the e.m. model, in order to simulate the backscattering at VV, HH and HV/VH-polarizations.

This procedure was then iterated 10,000 times, thus obtaining a set of backscattering coefficients for each input vector of the soil parameters. The consistency between the experimental data and the model simulations was verified before proceeding to the training phase. The ANN training was carried out by considering the simulated $\sigma°$ at the various polarizations and the incidence angle as input of the ANN, and the soil parameters, in particular the SMC, as outputs. It should be remarked that the soil surface roughness parameter HSTD was added to the ANN outputs in order to enhance the training performances. However, an operational retrieval of surface roughness is not in the scopes of this algorithm and the roughness parameters are then disregarded in the algorithm. After training, the ANN were tested on a different dataset that was obtained by re-iterating the model simulations as described above. The use of a pseudorandom function prevented a correlation between these two datasets: this fact was particularly important in order to evaluate the capabilities of ANN to generalize the training phase and to prevent the overfitting problem. Incorrect sizing of the ANN or inadequate training could cause the overfitting: the ANN return outputs outside the training range (outliers) when tested with input data that are not included in the training set.

The algorithm was validated using a set of experimental data collected on several test areas, mainly agricultural fields and grasslands, located worldwide. The total dataset was composed by about 700 field-averaged values of σ° at C-band from Envisat/ASAR and about 600 at X-band from Cosmo-SkyMed (CSK), collected at various polarizations.

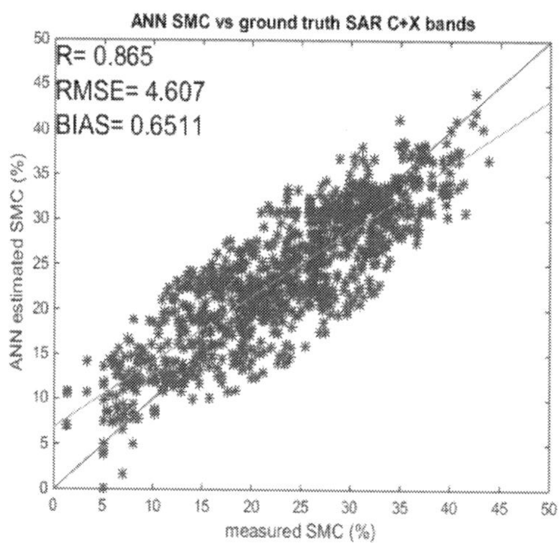

Figure 7. Validation of the SAR SMC algorithm.

Figure 7 shows the overall validation obtained by comparing the SMC values retrieved by the algorithm with the corresponding ground truth, and it corresponds to R = 0.86, RMSE = 4.6 and BIAS = 0.65. Analysing separately the two frequencies, the best results were achieved at C-band, which is more sensitive to SMC and less influenced by the vegetation than X-band. At the latter frequency, instead, the vegetation effect is dominant, although some sensitivity to SMC is detectable at least for bare and scarcely vegetated surfaces.

4.2. PWC processor

The algorithm for PWC estimate was very similar to the one for estimating SMC, and it is based on a feed-forward multilayer perceptron (MLP) ANN, trained by using the back-propagation (BP) learning rule and a RTT discrete element model, more sophisticated than the WCM [29].

The model was first validated with the experimental data collected in the 'Sesto' agricultural area located in central Italy, close to the city of Florence, mainly covered by wheat crops, and then used for generating the training set of ANN in combination with experimental data. Model simulations were iterated 10,000 times by randomly varying each input parameter in the range derived from experimental data, thus obtaining a training set able to complete the training phase and fully define all the neurons and weights of the ANN. The dataset was split randomly in two parts, the first part for training and the second one for testing the ANN. A configuration with two hidden layers of ten perceptrons each was finally chosen as the optimal one. The validation results gave R = 0.97 and RMSE = 0.345 kg/m^2 (**Figure 8**).

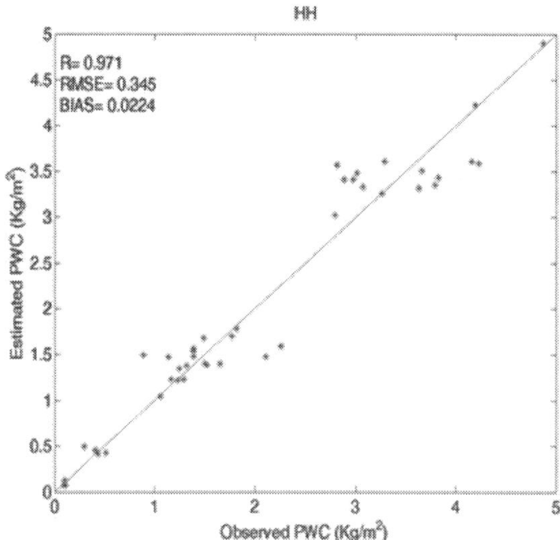

Figure 8. PWC algorithm validation: PWC estimated vs. PWC observed.

4.3. SWE processor

In the last years, the remote-sensing community has shown a growing interest in the new generation X-band SAR satellites, such as CSK and Terra-SARX (TSX), with the aim of better understanding if at this frequency, the information on snow parameters can be retrieved and under which conditions. Although X-band is not the most suitable frequency for the retrieval of SD or SWE, since the dry snow is almost transparent at this frequency, the freezing of dedicated missions such as the ESA cold regions hydrology high-resolution observatory (CoReH$_2$O), put more interest in evaluating the potential of such a frequency for snow parameter retrieval. Basing on encouraging experimental results pointing out the relationship between $\sigma°$ and SD for several winter seasons in the Italian Alps [30, 34], we have implemented an ANN-based retrieval algorithm able to estimate the SWE/SD of snow-covered surfaces from X-band SAR data.

This algorithm, which has been preliminary described in [30], is composed of two steps: first, the dry snow is identified and separated from the wet snow and from the snow-free surfaces using a well-known threshold criterion [35]. Then, the SWE retrieval by means of the ANN algorithm is attempted on the areas of the image identified as dry snow.

Inputs to the ANN are the X-band $\sigma°$ measured in the available polarizations, the corresponding reference value measured in snow-free conditions, and the local incidence angle information. SWE is the ANN output.

The main problem we had to face in developing this algorithm was related to the lack of extensive sets of measurements of snow parameters, which posed some constraints in defining the training set. The available measurements are indeed sparse, and, besides being site dependent, are numerically inadequate for training the ANN and define all its neurons and weights. The training of the ANN was therefore performed by using data simulated by the dense medium radiative transfer model implementation [36, 37]. As for the other algorithms, the training set was generated by running the model simulation for the input values of snow parameters in a range derived from the direct measurements, obtaining output backscattering coefficients at the given polarizations for each input vector of snow parameters. In order to match all the acquisition modes of CSK, several ANN have been set up and trained separately, according to the combination of polarizations available from the dataset.

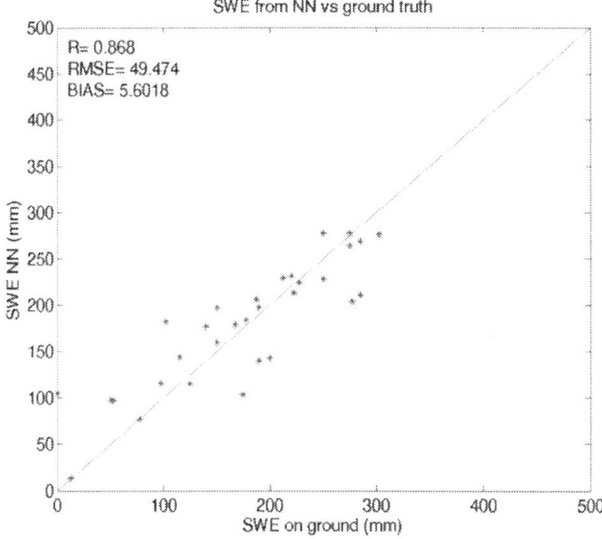

Figure 9. Validation of the SAR SWE algorithm.

Although the algorithm is not able to consider some model parameters, such the average crystal dimension, which are unavailable from in situ measurements, the training process converged successfully. In particular, for a configuration with 2 hidden layers of 13 neurons each and an activating function of 'tansig' type, assuming the availability of CSK data in two polarizations (co- and cross-polar), the validation resulted in $R > 0.9$, with an associated probability value (P-value) of 95% and RMSE = 50 mm of equivalent water [30]. After the test on simulated data, the algorithm was validated considering CSK images and corresponding ground truth available on the Cordevole and Bardonecchia test areas, located in the eastern and western part of Italian Alps, respectively. The direct comparison with ground truth data resulted in an R > 0.85, RMSE = 50 mm and Bias = 5.6 mm (**Figure 9**).

5. The P + L-band SAR ANN algorithm for WV

A final example of the ANN capabilities in adapting to the retrieval of hydrological parameters from microwave remote-sensing acquisitions is represented by this ANN application to the forest WV retrieval. The algorithm takes advantage of the well-known sensitivity of low microwave frequencies such as L- and P-bands to forest biomass. However, L- and P-band SAR data available from satellite and corresponding in situ measurements were not sufficient for implementing and validating such algorithm. Therefore, we selected a dataset of airborne SAR measurements derived from the ESA project BioSAR 2010, which has been obtained through the ESA eopi portal: https://earth.esa.int/web/guest/pi-community. The dataset was composed of airborne SAR fully polarimetric images at P- and L-bands acquired in fall 2010 in Sweden by the airborne system ONERA SETHI and corresponding LiDAR measurements of forest height, which were considered as target values for training and testing the algorithm.

The WV ANN algorithm considers as inputs the co- and cross-polarized backscattering at both P- and L-bands, along with the corresponding incidence angles, without any ancillary information from other sensors. The training set was implemented by considering as ground truth the WV estimated by LiDAR. In this case, the model simulations considered for increasing the training set were based on an implementation of the water cloud model with gaps, which was initially proposed in [38, 39] and it was based on the original VWC by [32]. The model has been modified by adding a term able to account for the backscattering dependence on the observation angle. The independent validation of this algorithm was carried out on some plots for which conventional measurements of WV were available. Although the validation set was limited, the results were encouraging, with R = 0.98, RMSE = 22 t/ha and Bias = 11 t/ha.

6. Generation of maps of the target parameter at regional and global scale

The fast computation is another important advantage of the ANN-based algorithms with respect to other statistical methods. The training represents indeed the only time-consuming process; however, it is only once carried out at the beginning and it deals with the algorithm implementation, not with its application. A trained ANN are indeed able to process the input satellite data in real or near-real time. This characteristic allows an operational application of the ANN for generating maps of the target parameter at high resolution and large or global coverage. In [27], the ANN retrieval algorithm was demonstrated to be able to process 200,000 pixels/s, which correspond to about 80 s for generating a SMC map at 25×25 m^2 resolution from an input SAR image of 100×100 km^2. Besides these considerations, the output maps represent also an effective tool for verifying qualitatively the validity of the training process, although these maps cannot be considered a real validation of the retrieval algorithms, since adequate ground truth for comparing extensively the algorithm outputs at large and global scale is barely available.

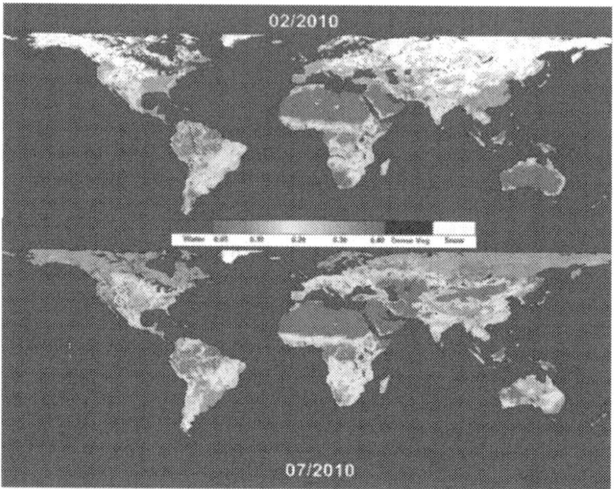

Figure 10. Global SMC and snow extent maps obtained as weekly average of AMSR-E acquisitions collected in February and June 2010 (after [11]).

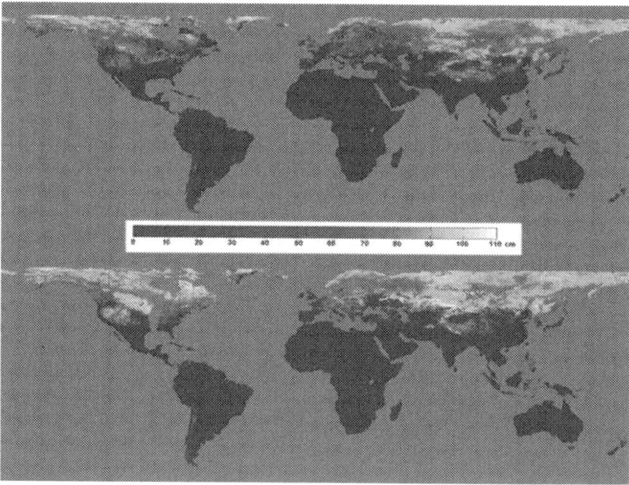

Figure 11. SD maps obtained as weekly average of AMSR-E acquisitions collected in different seasons between December 2009 and February 2010 (after [11]).

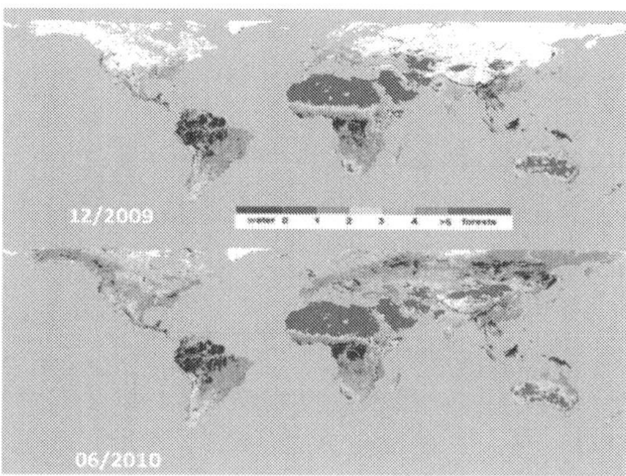

Figure 12. Global PWC maps (kg/m²) of agricultural and herbaceous vegetation from a weekly average of AMSRE ascending and descending orbits in February (top) and June (bottom) 2010.

Extreme variations of the target parameter between adjacent pixels, the presence of large percentages of outliers, and the absence of clearly detectable patterns indicate indeed that the training was not achieved successfully, although the validation in the control points resulted satisfactory. In these cases, the ANN should be retrained, by verifying that the training set is representative of the entire range of the input microwave data and output parameters considered for the specific application.

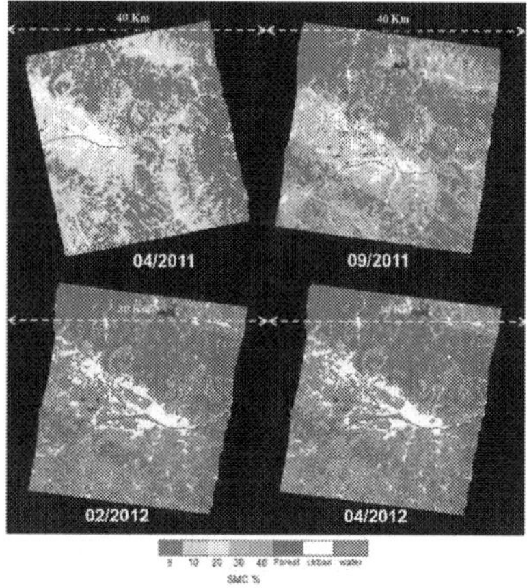

Figure 13. SMC maps from CSK images (© ASI)" for four different dates between 2011 and 2012 in the 'Sesto' test area.

As an example of the operational capabilities of the algorithms proposed here, **Figures 10** and **11** represent some examples of SMC and SD maps generated by using microwave radiometric data through HydroAlgo and reprojected on a fixed grid spaced $0.1° × 0.1°$, while examples of outputs generated by the PWC processor are represented in **Figure 12**.

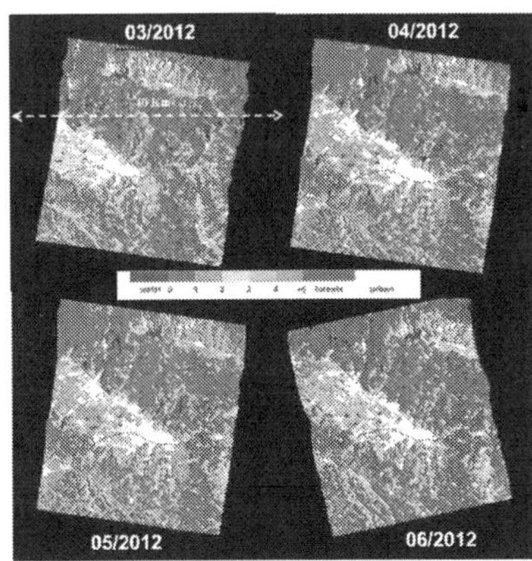

Figure 14. PWC maps from CSK images (© ASI) covering the entire seasonal cycle of wheat from march to June 2012 in the 'Sesto' test area.

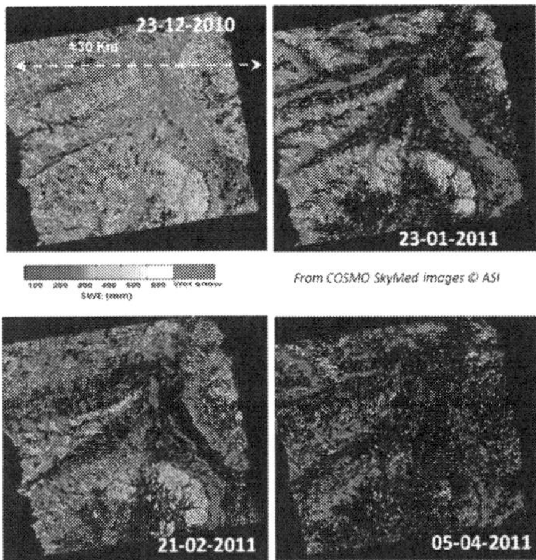

Figure 15. Maps of SWE derived from the proposed algorithm for a test area in the Italian Alps.

Maps have been obtained as weekly average of the AMSR-E acquisitions in both ascending and descending orbits for different seasons: winter and summer for SMC and PWC and two different winter periods for SD, in order to point out the sensitivity to the global spatial and temporal variations of the investigated parameter.

Examples of outputs maps generated by the SAR SMC and PWC algorithm from CSK images are represented in **Figures 13** and **14**, while maps of SWE derived from the proposed algorithm for a test area in the Italian Alps are shown in **Figure 15**. Map dimensions range between 30 × 30 and 40 × 40 km², depending on the input images. White and blue colours represent masking for urban areas and water bodies respectively.

Finally, a WV map (t/ha) has been produced for the area where SAR data at P-and L-bands have been acquired (**Figure 16**). Different colours represent different levels of forest biomass in accordance with the ground truth data collected simultaneously to the BioSAR acquisitions.

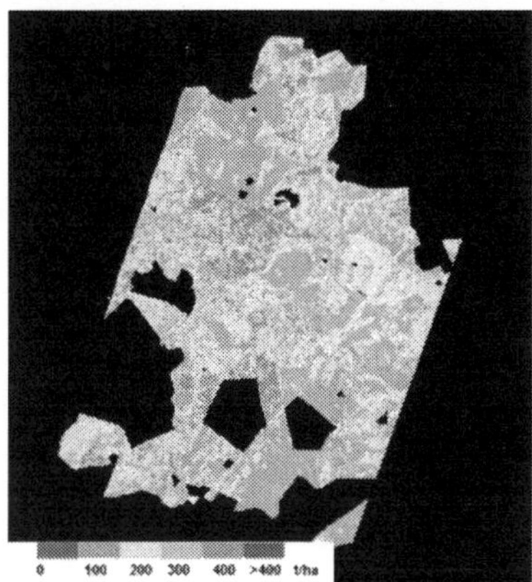

Figure 16. Forest biomass map (WV, in t/ha) from BioSAR data on the Sweden test site.

7. Conclusions

The overview of the retrieval algorithms presented here demonstrated that ANN are a powerful tool for implementing inversion algorithm, which are able to estimate the hydrological parameters from microwave satellite acquisitions, provided ANN have been trained with consistent datasets made up by both experimental and theoretical data. The flexibility of this method and the possibility of using it for both active and passive sensors with high accuracy and computational speed were confirmed. Moreover, the possibility of repeating the training with new datasets easily enables the improvement of the retrieval accuracy, making this technique flexible and adaptable to new datasets and sensors.

A further advantage of these algorithms is in their capability of merging data coming from different sources, as other sensors or ancillary information, into a unique retrieval approach. It was the case of the algorithm implemented for C- and X-band SAR, which takes advantage of the NDVI information from optical sensors (Landsat/Modis), when available, for improving the SMC retrieval accuracy.

The main constraint for accurate retrievals is due to the training process: the retrieval error may be large if the ANN are tested with data not correctly represented in the training. Large datasets are therefore needed for properly training the ANN, in order to cover the whole range of the microwave data and corresponding surface parameters. It should be noted that there is not a unique way for defining the training set. Some a priori knowledge and the support of model simulations help in setting the range of each surface parameter, in order to make the training set as representative as possible of the observed surface. Testing and validation on independent datasets (i.e. not related to the data considered for training) may indicate if the training has been achieved properly. In particular, the use of electromagnetic models for generating large training dataset is one of the best methods for avoiding the danger of 'black box' algorithms and to make sure that the results are based on physical assumptions. Since the training is performed off-line, before starting the data processing, the computational speed of ANN is not hampered by this procedure.

Acknowledgements

This research work was partially supported by the JAXA ADEOS-II/AMSR-E and GCOM/AMSR2 research programs, by the ESA/ESTEC Contract No. 4000103855/11/NL/MP/fk on GMES Sentinel-1 Soil Moisture algorithm development, by the EUMETSAT Contract No. EUM/C0/14/4600001368/JF on the use of SCA cross-pol for the Soil Moisture retrieval and by the ASI Hydrocosmo Proposal No. 1720 on the retrieval and monitoring of Land Hydrological parameters for Risk and Water Resources Management.

Author details

Emanuele Santi

Address all correspondence to: e.santi@ifac.cnr.it

Institute of Applied Physics, National Research Council (IFAC-CNR), Florence, Italy

References

[1] Dobson C., Ulaby F., Hallikainen M., El-Rayes M. 1985. Microwave dielectric behaviour of wet soil — Part II: Four component dielectric mixing models. IEEE Transactions on Geoscience and Remote Sensing. 23(4):35–46.

[2] Mironov V. L., Kosolapova L. G., Fomin S. V. 2009. Physically and mineralogically based spectroscopic dielectric model for moist soils. IEEE Transactions on Geoscience and Remote Sensing. 47(7):2059–2070.

[3]   Notarnicola C. 2014. A Bayesian change detection approach for retrieval of soil moisture variations under different roughness conditions. IEEE Geoscience and Remote Sensing Letters. 11(2):414–418.

[4]   Pasolli L., Notarnicola C., Bruzzone L., Bertoldi G., Della Chiesa S., Hell V., Niedrist G., Tappeiner U., Zebisch M., Del Frate F., Vaglio Laurin G. 2011. Estimation of soil moisture in an alpine catchment with RADARSAT2 images. Applied and Environmental Soil Science. Article ID 175473:12. doi:10.1155/2011/175473

[5]   Pierdicca N., Pulvirenti L., Pace G. 2014. A prototype software package to retrieve soil moisture from Sentinel-1 data by using a Bayesian multitemporal algorithm. IEEE Journal of Selected Topics in Applied Earth Observations and Remote Sensing. 7(1): 153–163.

[6]   Hornik K. 1989. Multilayer feed forward network are universal approximators. Neural Networks. 2(5):359–366.

[7]   Linden A., Kinderman J. 1989. Inversion of multi-layer nets. Proceedings of the International Joint Conference on Neural Networks. 2:425–443.

[8]   Del Frate F., Ferrazzoli P., Schiavon G. 2003. Retrieving soil moisture and agricultural variables by microwave radiometry using neural networks. Remote Sensing of Environment. 84(2):174–183. doi:10.1016/S0034-4257(02)00105-0

[9]   Elshorbagy A., Parasuraman K. 2008. On the relevance of using artificial neural networks for estimating soil moisture content. Journal of Hydrology. 362:1–18. Available at: http://www.sciencedirect.com/science/article/pii/S0022169408004204

[10]   Paloscia S., Pampaloni P., Pettinato S., Santi E. 2008. A comparison of algorithms for retrieving soil moisture from ENVISAT/ASAR images. IEEE Transactions on Geoscience and Remote Sensing. 46(10):3274–3284.

[11]   Santi E., Pettinato S., Paloscia S., Pampaloni P., Macelloni G., Brogioni M. 2012. An algorithm for generating soil moisture and snow depth maps from microwave spaceborne radiometers: HydroAlgo. Hydrology and Earth System Sciences. 16:3659–3676. doi:10.5194/hess-16-3659-2012

[12]   Nelder J. A., Mead R. 1965. A simplex method for function minimization. Computer Journal. 7:308–313.

[13]   Gruber A., Paloscia S., Santi E., Notarnicola C., Pasolli L., Smolander T., Pulliainen J., Mittelbach H., Dorigo W., Wagner W. 2014. Performance inter-comparison of soil moisture retrieval models for the MetOp-A ASCAT instrument. Proceedings of the 2014 IEEE International Geoscience and Remote Sensing Symposium (IGARSS), pp. 2455–2458. doi:10.1109/IGARSS.2014.6946969

[14]   Mladenova I. E., Jackson T. J., Njoku E., Bindlish R., Chan S., Cosh M. H., Holmes T. R. H., de Jeu R. A. M., Jones L., Kimball J., Paloscia S., Santi E. 2014. Remote monitoring of soil moisture using passive microwave based techniques—theoretical basis and

overview of selected algorithms for AMSR-E. Remote Sensing of Environment. 144:197–213. doi:10.1016/j.rse.2014.01.013

[15] Paloscia S., Santi E., Pettinato S., Mladenova I. E., Jackson T. J., Bindlish R., Cosh M. H. 2015. A comparison between two algorithms for the retrieval of soil moisture using AMSR-E data. Frontiers in Earth Sciences. 3(16):1–10. doi:10.3389/feart.2015.00016

[16] Santi E., Paloscia S., Pettinato S., Fontanelli G. 2015. Application of artificial neural networks for the soil moisture retrieval from active and passive microwave spaceborne sensors. International Journal of Applied Earth Observations and Geoinformation. doi: 10.1016/j.jag.2015.08.002

[17] Lobl E. 2001. Joint advanced microwave scanning radiometer (AMSR) science team meeting. Earth Observer. 13(3):3–9.

[18] Imaoka K., Takashi M., Misako K., Marehito K., Norimasa I., Keizo N. 2012. Status of AMSR2 instrument on GCOM-W1, earth observing missions and sensors: development, implementation, and characterization II. Proceedings of SPIE 2012, 852815. doi: 10.1117/12.977774

[19] Santi E. 2010. An application of SFIM technique to enhance the spatial resolution of microwave radiometers. International Journal of Remote Sensing. 31(9–10):2419–2428.

[20] Mo, T., Choudhury, B. J., Schmugge, T. J.,Wang, J. R., and Jackson, T. J. A model for microwave emission from vegetation covered fields. J. Geophys. Res., 87, 11229–11237, 1982

[21] Paloscia S., Pampaloni P. 1988. Microwave polarization index for monitoring vegetation growth. IEEE Transactions on Geoscience and Remote Sensing. 26(5):617–621.

[22] Jackson T. J., Cosh M. H., Bindlish R., Starks P. J., Bosch D. D., Seyfried M. S., Goodrich D. C., Moran M. S. 2010. Validation of advanced microwave scanning radiometer soil moisture products. IEEE Transactions on Geoscience and Remote Sensing. 48(12):4256–4272.

[23] Santi E., Paloscia S., Pettinato S., Brocca L., Ciabatta L. 2015. Robust assessment of an operational algorithm for the retrieval of soil moisture from AMSR-E data in central Italy. Proceedings of IEEE International Geoscience and Remote Sensing Symposium (IGARSS). pp. 1288–1291. doi:10.1109/IGARSS.2015.7326010

[24] Brocca L., Camici S., Melone F., Moramarco T., Martinez-Fernandez J., Didon-Lescot J.-F., Morbidelli R. 2014. Improving the representation of soil moisture by using a semi-analytical infiltration model. Hydrological Processes. 28(4):2103–2115. doi:10.1002/hyp.9766

[25] Choudhury B. J., Tucker C. J. 1987. Monitoring global vegetation using Nimbus-7 37 GHz Data Some empirical relations. International Journal of Remote Sensing. 8:1085–1090.

[26] Paloscia S., Pampaloni P. 1992. Microwave vegetation indexes for detecting biomass and water conditions of agricultural crops. Remote Sensing of Environment. 40:15–26.

[27] Santi E., Pettinato S., Paloscia S., Pampaloni P., Fontanelli G., Crepaz A., Valt M. 2014. Monitoring of Alpine snow using satellite radiometers and artificial neural networks. Remote Sensing of Environment. 144:179–186. doi:10.1016/j.rse.2014.01.012

[28] Paloscia S., Pettinato S., Santi E., Notarnicola C., Pasolli L., Reppucci A. 2013. Soil moisture mapping using Sentinel-1 images: Algorithm and preliminary validation. Remote Sensing of Environment. 134:234–248. doi:10.1016/j.rse.2013.02.02721

[29] Santi E., Paloscia S., Pettinato S., Notarnicola C., Pasolli L., Pistocchi A. 2013. Comparison between SAR soil moisture estimates and hydrological model simulations over the Scrivia test site. Remote Sensing. 5:4961–4976. doi:10.3390/rs5104961

[30] Paloscia S., Santi E., Fontanelli G., Montomoli F., Brogioni M., Macelloni G., Pampaloni P., Pettinato S. 2014. The sensitivity of Cosmo-SkyMed backscatter to agricultural crop type and vegetation parameters. IEEE Journal of Selected Topics in Applied Earth Observations and Remote Sensing. 7(7):2856–2868.

[31] Pettinato S., Santi E., Brogioni M., Paloscia S., Palchetti E., Xiong C. 2013. The potential of COSMO-SkyMed SAR images in monitoring snow cover characteristics. IEEE Geoscience and Remote Sensing Letters. 10(1):9–13.

[32] Oh Y., Sarabandi K., Ulaby F. T. 1992. An empirical model and an inversion technique for radar scattering from bare surfaces. IEEE Transactions on Geoscience and Remote Sensing. 30:370–381.

[33] Attema E. P. W., Ulaby F. T. 1978. Vegetation modeled as a water cloud. Radio Science. 13:357–364.

[34] Brogioni M., Cagnati A., Crepaz A., Paloscia S., Pampaloni P., Pettinato S., Santi E., Xiong C., Shi J. C. 2014. Model investigations of backscatter for snow profiles related to avalanche risk. Proceedings of IEEE International Geoscience and Remote Sensing Symposium (IGARSS). pp. 2415–2418. doi:10.1109/IGARSS.2014.6946959

[35] Nagler T., Rott H. 2000. Retrieval of wet snow by means of multitemporal SAR data. IEEE Transactions on Geoscience and Remote Sensing. 38:754–765.

[36] Liang D., Xu X., Tsang L. 2008. The effects of layers in dry snow on its passive microwave emissions using dense media radiative transfer theory based on the quasicrystalline approximation (QCA/DMRT). IEEE Transactions on Geoscience and Remote Sensing. 46:3663–3671.

[37] Tsang L., Pan J., Liang D., Li Z. X., Cline D., Tan Y. H. 2007. Modeling active microwave remote sensing of snow using dense media radiative transfer (DMRT) theory with multiple scattering effects. IEEE Transactions on Geoscience and Remote Sensing. 45(4): 990–1004.

[38] Santoro M., Eriksson L., Askne J., Schmullius C. 2006. Assessment of stand-wise stem volume retrieval in boreal forest from JERS-1 L-band SAR backscatter. International Journal of Remote Sensing. 27:3425–3454.

[39] Fransson J. E. S., Israelsson H. 1999. Estimation of stem volume in boreal forests using ERS-1 C- and JERS-1 L-band SAR data. International Journal of Remote Sensing. 20:123–137.

Chapter 13

Advanced Methods in Neural Networks-Based Sensitivity Analysis with their Applications in Civil Engineering

Maosen Cao , Nizar F. Alkayem , Lixia Pan and Drahomír Novák

Additional information is available at the end of the chapter

http://dx.doi.org/10.5772/64026

Abstract

Artificial neural networks (ANNs) are powerful tools that are used in various engineering fields. Their characteristics enable them to solve prediction, regression, and classification problems. Nevertheless, the ANN is usually thought of as a black box, in which it is difficult to determine the effect of each explicative variable (input) on the dependent variables (outputs) in any problem. To investigate such effects, sensitivity analysis is usually applied on the optimal pre-trained ANN. Existing sensitivity analysis techniques suffer from drawbacks. Their basis on a single optimal pre-trained ANN model produces instability in parameter sensitivity analysis because of the uncertainty in neural network modeling. To overcome this deficiency, two successful sensitivity analysis paradigms, the neural network committee (NNC)-based sensitivity analysis and the neural network ensemble (NNE)-based parameter sensitivity analysis, are illustrated in this chapter. An NNC is applied in a case study of geotechnical engineering involving strata movement. An NNE is implemented for sensitivity analysis of two classic problems in civil engineering: (i) the fracture failure of notched concrete beams and (ii) the lateral deformation of deep-foundation pits. Results demonstrate good ability to analyze the sensitivity of the most influential parameters, illustrating the underlying mechanisms of such engineering systems.

Keywords: civil engineering, neural networks, sensitivity analysis, NNC-based sensitivity analysis, NNE-based sensitivity analysis

© 2016 The Author(s). Licensee InTech. This chapter is distributed under the terms of the Creative Commons Attribution License (http://creativecommons.org/licenses/by/3.0), which permits unrestricted use, distribution, and reproduction in any medium, provided the original work is properly cited.

1. Introduction

In solving complex civil engineering problems, conventional analytical and empirical methodologies suffer from many difficulties. This is mainly because of the limitations of such methods in handling large, complex structures that may require time-consuming and exhausting tasks. In such situations, soft-computing techniques come into the picture. They are effective estimation tools that reduce the cost and time of design and analysis. Neural networks are useful soft-computing tools that can be used for classification and prediction in complex civil engineering problems [1–3].

Sensitivity analysis is a necessary approach for understanding the relationship and the influence of each input parameter on the outputs of a problem. The key point behind sensitivity analysis is that by slightly varying each explicative input parameter and registering the response in the output, the explicative parameters with the highest sensitivity values gain the greatest importance. Sensitivity analysis of the most significant parameters can be very useful for analyzing complex engineering problems.

Neural network-based parameter sensitivity analysis in civil engineering systems is gaining more importance due to the remarkable ability of neural networks to explain the nonlinear relationships between the explicative and response variables of a problem [1, 4]. Commonly, a specific training technique is used to develop one optimal neural network to be a system model, and this model is then used for sensitivity analysis [5–10]. Yet, it is relatively difficult to determine the most optimal neural network model, for reasons such as random initialization of the underlying connection weights in the neural network model, different features of various learning techniques used to train the neural network, the absence of a reliable technique for defining the optimal structure in neural network modeling, etc. To overcome these difficulties, two potential techniques, namely neural network committee (NNC)-based sensitivity analysis [1] and neural network ensemble (NNE)-based sensitivity analysis [11], are illustrated. These two paradigms utilize a group of pre-trained optimal neural networks to handle the neural network modeling, thereafter implementing parameter sensitivity analysis individually and lastly defining the sensitivity of parameters. This chapter is organized as follows. A complete explanation is given of some traditional neural network-based sensitivity analysis. Thereafter, the NNC-based parameter sensitivity analysis method is presented, followed by a geotechnical engineering case study of strata movement and two case studies related to classical civil engineering. Then, the NNE-based sensitivity analysis paradigm is described, followed by two illustrative case studies. Finally, a complete summary of the chapter is presented.

2. Typical neural networks-based sensitivity analysis algorithms

Many studies have been concerned with improving existing neural network-based sensitivity analysis methods [9]. Among the different techniques, the partial derivative algorithm [5] and the input perturbation algorithm [10] have superior performance compared to other techniques based on the magnitude of weights [6, 7]. Therefore, these two algorithms are explored in detail in this chapter, along with some other techniques.

2.1. Partial derivative algorithm

The partial derivative algorithm is a famous neural network-based sensitivity analysis technique [5, 11]. Its characteristics enable it to deal with neural networks that apply first-derivative activation functions, such as back-propagation neural networks (BPNNs) and radial basis function neural networks (RBFNNs) [1, 8]. By implementing the partial derivative algorithm, it is possible to identify the variations of output parameters of neural networks with respect to small changes in each input parameter, thereby defining the contribution of each such input on the output parameters. This can be done by deriving the output parameters of the neural network with respect to input parameters, in other words, by calculating the Jacobian matrix that contains the partial derivatives of outputs with respect to inputs [5, 11].

For a successful BPNN model having input x_i with n_i as the total number of inputs and output y_k with n_k as the total number of outputs, the Jacobian matrix $\dfrac{\partial y_k}{\partial x_i}$ can be defined by using the chain rule as [1]

$$\frac{\partial y_k}{\partial x_i} = \frac{\partial y_k}{\partial O_k}\frac{\partial O_k}{\partial y_{h_n}}\cdots\cdots\frac{\partial y_{h_1}}{\partial O_{h_i}}\frac{\partial O_{h_i}}{\partial x_i} = \sum_{h_i}\sum_{h_{i-1}}\sum_{h_1}\begin{bmatrix} W_{h_n k}f'(O_k)W_{h_{n-1}h_n} \\ f'(O_{h_n})\cdots\cdots W_{ih_1}f'(O_{h_1}) \end{bmatrix} \tag{1}$$

where x_i is the ith input variable $h_n, h_{n-1}, \ldots,$ and h_i are the hidden neurons from the nth to the first hidden layer, respectively; $y_k, y_{h_n},$ and y_{h_1} are the output values for output neuron k, hidden neurons $h_n,$ and n_1 in the respective nth and the first hidden layer; $W_{h_n k}$ is the connection weight between the kth output neuron and the hidden neuron h_n; $W_{h_{n-1}h_n}$ is the connection weight between the hidden neurons h_{n-1} and h_n and W_{ih_1} is the connection weight between the ith input neuron and the hidden neuron h_1; $O_k, O_{h_n},$ and O_{h_1} are the weighted sums of kth output neuron, the hidden neuron $h_n,$ and h_1, respectively; f' denotes the derivative of the activation function f. $y_k, y_{h_n},$ and y_{h_1} can be given as

$$\left\{\begin{array}{l} y_k = f(O_k), O_k = \sum_{h_n} y_{h_n}W_{h_n,k} + b_k \\[2mm] y_{h_n} = f(O_{h_n}), O_{h_n} = \sum_{h_n} y_{h_{n-1}}W_{h_{n-1},k} + b_{h_n} \\[2mm] \vdots \\[2mm] y_{h_1} = f(O_{h_1}), O_{h_1} = \sum_{h_n} x_i W_{i,h_1} + b_{h_1} \end{array}\right. \tag{2}$$

where b_k, b_{h_n}, and b_{h_1} are the biases of the kth output neuron, the hidden neuron h_n, and, h_1, respectively.

For p training samples of each input x_i on the output y_k of the neural network, c_{ik} can be calculated as

$$c_{ik} = \sum_p \left| \left(\frac{\partial y_k}{\partial x_i} \right)_p \right| \tag{3}$$

For each input parameter, the value of c can be used as a factor for classification of the influence of total inputs on the outputs of the neural network model. The most important or crucial input parameter may have the highest c value [1].

2.2. Input perturbation algorithm

The input perturbation algorithm is another common method for neural-network-based sensitivity analysis [6, 9]. It implements a small perturbation on each input of the neural network model and measures the corresponding change in the outputs. This perturbation is applied on one input individually at a time while all other inputs are fixed, and the response for perturbation of each output is registered. Sensitivity analysis is performed by giving a rank for each response of the output generated by the same perturbation in every input parameter. The input that has the highest effect on the outputs after perturbation is considered the most influential or important [1].

In essence, when a larger amount of perturbation is added to the selected input parameter, the mean square error (MSE) of the neural network increases. The variance of the input parameter can be represented as $x_i = x_i + \Delta x_i$, where x_i is the current selected input variable and Δx_i is the perturbation. The perturbation can be varied from 0 to 50% by steps of 5% of the input value. Depending on the increasing value of the MSE corresponding to each perturbed input, outputs can be ranked and thus sensitivity analyses are performed [1, 8].

2.3. Weights method

This method was proposed by Garson [12] and Goh [13]. In this method, for each hidden neuron, the connection weights are divided into components related to each input neuron. This method was simplified by Gevrey et al. [8] to give the same results as the initial method. For the purpose of illustration, a multilayer neural network with a single hidden layer is considered; thereafter, for each hidden neuron the following calculations are used:

For $i = 1$ to n_i

    For $j = 1$ to n_j

$$D_{ij} = \frac{\left|W_{ij}\right|}{\sum_{i=1}^{n_i}\left|W_{ij}\right|} \tag{4}$$

End

End

where n_i and n_j are the number of input and hidden neurons, respectively; W_{ij} is the weight corresponding to input neuron i and hidden neuron j. The percentage relative contribution of all inputs RC_i is then calculated as

For $i = 1$ to n_i

$$RC_i = \frac{\sum_{j=1}^{n_j} D_{ij}}{\sum_{j=1}^{n_j}\sum_{i=1}^{n_i} D_{ij}} \tag{5}$$

End

2.4. Profile method

This method was proposed by Lek et al. [14–16], and further explained by Gevrey et al. [8]. The key point behind this method is to analyze one particular input at a time while fixing the values of all other inputs. The procedure starts by dividing the value of each input parameter into equal subintervals, whereas all other inputs are set prior to minimum, quarter, half, three quarters of the maximum and maximum, respectively. At the end of this task, patterns of five values corresponding to different input parameters result and the median value for each pattern is calculated. The median values are plotted with respect to the subintervals to form a profile that explains the contribution of the input parameter. Finally, for all inputs, a set of curves explaining the relative importance for all input parameters is obtained [8].

2.5. Stepwise method

In this method, one input parameter is blocked and the responses of the outputs are recorded. This process is performed step by step for all input parameters and the responses of the outputs are recorded by means of the MSE. Depending on the MSE, the relative importance of each input variable is ranked correspondingly. There are two main strategies for the stepwise method. The first is to construct a number of neural network models by evolving the input parameters one by one. This strategy is called forward stepwise, while the backward stepwise strategy can be implemented in the reverse way, that is, constructing neural network models by first using all input parameters and then blocking each input parameter [8, 17].

This method can be improved to reduce the difficulty of producing many neural network models by using a single model. In this model, one input parameter is blocked and the MSE is calculated. The parameter with the maximum MSE value is ranked as the most important and can then be either removed from the model or fixed at its mean value so that the contribution of other parameters can be found, and so on.

3. Neural network committee-based sensitivity analysis

Consider a neural network model with a sensitivity analysis-ranking vector $R = [r_1, r_2, ..., r_n]$ and the actual sensitivity analysis-ranking vector $R_0 = [a_1, a_2, ..., a_n]$, where r_i and a_i are the calculated and actual ranks of ith input parameter, respectively, and n is the number of input parameters. To reduce the difference between R and R_0 to minimum, it is not efficient to use single neural network model to perform sensitivity analysis. The reason is the absence of persistence in sensitivity analysis of one neural network model even when a major sensitivity analysis strategy is implemented. In recognition of this fact, it is more effective to utilize a set of good pre-trained neural network models instead of using a single optimal model for sensitivity analysis. This procedure is well used in neural network committee (NNC)-based sensitivity analysis [1].

The mathematical foundation of NNC-based sensitivity analysis starts from the weak law of large numbers in probability. Having $x_1, x_2, ...$ infinite set of random variables with no correlation between any two of them, each having the exact value of μ and variance σ^2, the sample average convergence in probability can be written as [18]

$$\overline{x}_n = \frac{\left(x_1 + x_2 + ... + x \right)}{n} \tag{6}$$

or, in other words, for a small number ε, the following can be expressed:

$$\lim_{n \to \infty} P\left(\left| \overline{x}_n \right| - \mu < \varepsilon \right) = 1 \tag{7}$$

By considering single neural network sensitivity analysis-ranking vector R, the elements $r_1, r_2, ...$ can be defined as random variables; in other words, R is composed of n random variables. In the case of neural network ensemble-based sensitivity analysis, a set of random variables $r_i^1, r_i^2, ..., r_i^m$ related to r_i are obtained. Depending on the weak law of large numbers, for a large number m, the mean of $r_i^1, r_i^2, ..., r_i^m$ can converge to the actual ranking values a_i in R_0. Therefore, in NNC-based sensitivity analysis, it is possible to find a ranking vector R that is close to the actual ranking vector R_0.

As the number of input variables is specified and the input variables are not completely random, due to the many specifications that appear during neural network model training, the condition of the weak law of large numbers that is applied on an infinite number of random variables is not satisfied. For this reason, optimization strategy can be an efficient tool to select a number of good pre-trained neural network models and skip those with weak performance. By electing the best neural network elements and eliminating the bad ones, optimization can generate good predictions of sensitivity analysis-ranking vectors [1].

Depending on the above principles, we can summarize NNC-based sensitivity analysis in three basic procedures. First, groups (seeds) of successful neural network models are prepared using neural network-training techniques such as back propagation (BP) or radial basis functions, etc. Then, a set of best-performance models are chosen to compose the optimal NNC that is used in performing ensemble neural network sensitivity analysis by individual applications of sensitivity analysis, giving large numbers of R. Finally, the mean of R is calculated to find the accurate approximation of R_0. A schematic diagram of NNC-based sensitivity analysis strategy is given in **Figure 1**.

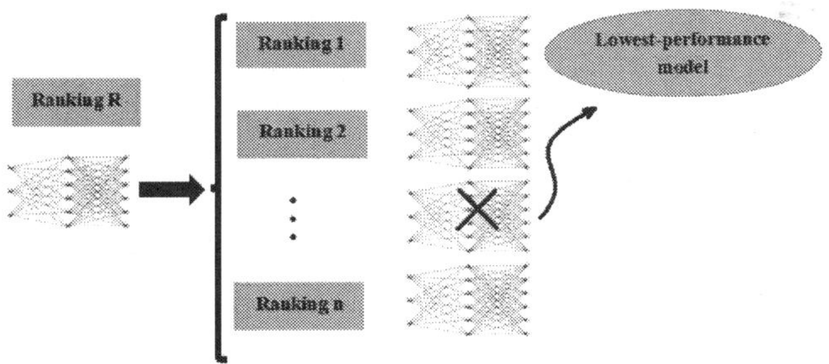

Figure 1. A schematic diagram of NNC-based sensitivity analysis strategy.

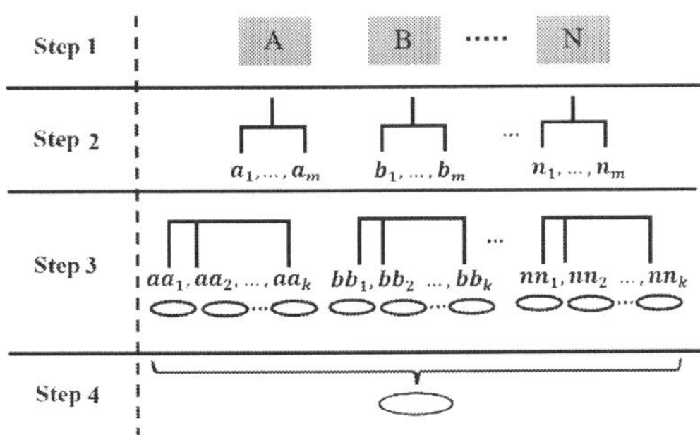

Figure 2. NNC-based sensitivity analysis strategy stepwise procedure: A–N, the neural network model seeds; $a_1 - a_m$, $b_1 - b_m$, and $n_1 - n_m$, the candidate groups of neural network models; $a_1 - aa_k$, $bb_1 - bb_k$, and $nn_1 - nn_k$, the superior neural network models; ellipse refers to a sensitivity analysis ranking of an input parameter.

The basic steps for the NNC-based sensitivity analysis algorithm are shown in **Figure 2** and can be explained as follows:

1. Select the best available types of neural network model empirically. These are called "seeds" for NNC-based sensitivity analysis.

2. Each seed involves a set of neural network models. These models are varied by means of a number of hidden neurons or hidden layers to produce a candidate group of neural network models.

3. Depending on the MSE, a subset k of superior neural network models is picked up, where $k = \frac{3}{10}m$ has been experimentally specified and m is the number of neural network models in the candidate group. Thereafter, sensitivity analysis is employed on each model to generate a group of sensitivity analysis-ranking vectors R.

4. For each input parameter, the mean of the related ranking number in the sensitivity analysis-ranking vector R is calculated to form a predicted ranking vector close to the actual ranking vector R_0, which is calculated as

$$a_i \approx \hat{a}_i = \frac{1}{NK}\sum\nolimits_{s=1}^{N}\sum\nolimits_{t=1}^{K} r_i^{st}, i = 1,2,\ldots,l \tag{8}$$

where $\hat{a}_i$ is the predicted value of a_i in R_0 for variable x_i in R, K is the number of elements in the candidate group of neural network models (committee), N is the number of neural network seeds, and l is the number of input parameters.

4. NNC-based sensitivity analysis of strata movement

Strata movement is a critical problem in geotechnical engineering because of the complex highly nonlinear properties involved. It is necessary to define the most significant factors involved in strata movement. Therefore, NNC-based sensitivity analysis strategy is used. The dataset of strata movement is composed of 168 samples taken from multiple typical observation stations of earth surface movement above underground metal mines. The dataset has six input parameters and three output parameters as shown in **Table 1**. These parameters characterize the working operation of strata movement of underground metal mines.

In NNC-based sensitivity analysis, four scenarios are chosen, depending on the output variables (**Table 1**): scenario (1) all output parameters, (2) only MAU, (3) only MAL, and (4) only AA. At the beginning, radial basis function and BP neural networks are selected as seeds, because of their proven ability to handle nonlinear features. Then, 50 neural network models are generated by each seed to construct two candidate sets of neural network models. Thereafter, 15 superior neural network models are chosen from each set to form a committee containing the best-performed neural network models. After that, sensitivity analysis is applied to each model by utilizing both a perturbation algorithm and a partial derivative algorithm to produce a group of ranking vectors R. Next, the sum of corresponding ranking numbers that is considered as a score for input parameters is calculated. The score is a reflection of the near actual ranking R_0. The sum is used instead of the mean to prevent the repetition of the identical values for different parameters, in order to have fewer neural network models from which to decide the final ranking. The best-performed neural networks and the input parameter ranking for scenario (1) are illustrated in **Table 2**.

Parameter	Characteristics	Parameter type
MCU	Mean consistency of upper wall rock	Input
LCL	Mean consistency of lower wall rock	Input
SAO	Slope angle of ore body	Input
TO	Thickness of ore body	Input
LO	Length of ore body	Input
DE	Depth of excavation	Input
MAU	Movement angle of upper wall rock	Output
MAL	Movement angle of lower wall rock	Output
AA	Avalanche angle	Output

Table 1. Measured parameters of strata movement [1].

Best-performed neural network model	MCU	LCL	SAO	TO	LO	DE
RBF1	5	6	1	4	3	2
RBF2	2	1	6	5	4	3
RBF3	3	6	5	2	4	1
RBF4	5	6	3	1	4	2
RBF5	4	6	3	2	5	1
RBF6	5	4	2	3	6	1
RBF7	4	6	5	2	3	1
RBF8	2	6	3	5	4	1
RBF9	4	6	5	2	3	1
RBF10	2	5	6	3	4	1
RBF11	3	4	1	6	5	2
RBF12	3	4	2	6	5	1
RBF13	2	4	3	6	5	1
RBF14	2	4	3	6	5	1
RBF15	4	2	3	5	6	1
BP1	1	4	3	6	5	2

Best-performed neural network model	MCU	LCL	SAO	TO	LO	DE
BP2	2	4	3	6	5	1
BP3	4	2	3	5	6	1
BP4	4	3	2	6	5	1
BP5	2	3	4	6	5	1
BP6	4	2	1	5	6	3
BP7	5	3	2	6	4	1
BP8	4	3	1	5	6	2
BP9	4	3	2	6	5	1
BP10	4	3	1	5	6	2
BP11	3	4	2	5	6	1
BP12	3	5	1	4	6	2
BP13	4	3	2	5	6	1
BP14	4	3	1	6	5	2
BP15	3	5	1	4	6	2

Table 2. Sensitivity analysis rankings produced by best-performed neural network model groups [1].

Scenarios	Score and ranking	MCU	LCL	SAO	TO	LO	DE
(1)	Score	101	120	80	138	148	43
	Ranking	3	4	2	5	6	1
(2)	Score	96	114	64	162	145	49
	Ranking	3	4	2	6	5	1
(3)	Score	96	81	87	75	155	136
	Ranking	4	2	3	1	6	5
(4)	Score	109	121	113	103	86	98
	Ranking	4	6	5	3	1	2

Table 3. NNC-based sensitivity analysis results for strata movement.

The outcome sensitivity analysis for the four scenarios is illustrated in **Table 3**. It is clear from the table that for scenario (1), *DE* has the highest importance, followed by *SAO, MCU, LCL, TO*, and *LO*, respectively. In scenario (2), the degree of importance is the same as in scenario (1), but *LO* is more significant than *TO*. Nevertheless, in scenario (3), *TO* has the highest significance, above that of *LCL, SAO*, and *MCU*, which have approximately similar significance, and then *DE* and *LO* have the least significance. Finally, in scenario (4) *LO* has the highest

contribution followed by *DE, TO, MCU, SAO*, and *LCL*, respectively. However, the contributions of *DE* and *TO* are very close to those of *MCU, SAO*, and *LCL*.

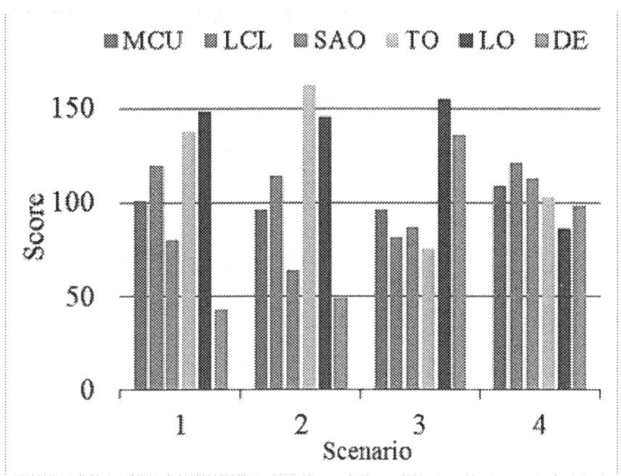

Figure 3. Activity analysis of dependent variables for strata movement based on NNC-based sensitivity analysis results [1].

The working condition of strata movement is defined by the predictability of response
parameter (output parameters). For this reason, the scores of the input variables after sensitivity analysis for three scenarios (*MAU, MAL,* and *AA*) that are related to the response
variables are plotted in **Figure 3**. The response variable with the highest sensitivity against
explicative variables has the highest predictability, and this can be calculated by finding the
variance of the score vector of the explicative variables. The result of that procedure is 1965.6,
1068.4, and 150, corresponding to the response variables *MAU, MAL,* and *AA*, respectively. It
is obvious that *MAU* has the highest predictability, followed by *MAL* and *AA*. Therefore, we
can consider the angles of the upper wall rocks as the most significant feature, ahead of the
lower wall rocks and the avalanche angle that are less important.

5. NNE-based parameter sensitivity analysis

The NNE-based parameter sensitivity analysis technique is a modified version of the NNC-
based sensitivity analysis. It reduces the time-consuming procedure of using different neural
network types as seeds by using just one preferred neural network type as the seed [4]. NNE-
based parameter sensitivity analysis incorporates the following steps: (1) one preferred type
of neural network is considered as the seed, (2) a set of k-neural network models that are varied
with regard to the number of hidden neurons and hidden layers is defined, (3) from k-neural
network models, a group of n best-performed models ($n < k$) is picked up and the other poorly
performed models are eliminated to form an NNE model, and (4) a sophisticated sensitivity

analysis algorithm is performed on the NNE model to obtain a sensitivity ranking of all input variables of the engineering problem under consideration. A schematic diagram of NNE-based parameter sensitivity analysis is shown in **Figure 4**.

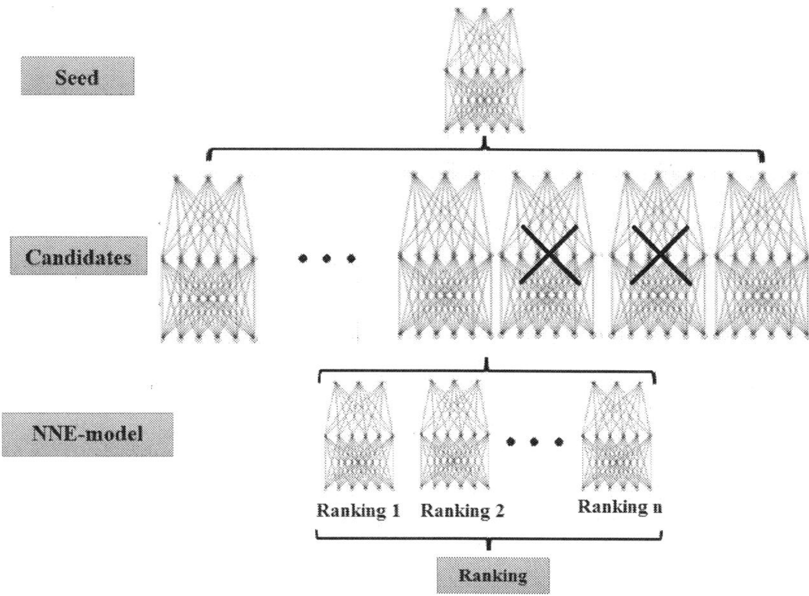

Figure 4. A schematic representation of NNE-based parameter sensitivity analysis.

6. Illustrative case studies

To highlight the application of NNE-based parameter sensitivity analysis technique, two civil engineering case studies are explained. The first is the determination of the importance of material properties in the fracture failure of a notched concrete beam and the second is the specification of significant parameters in the lateral deformation of a deep-foundation pit [4].

6.1. Fracture failure of notched concrete beam

Fracture failure is the most common problem facing engineers in the analysis and usage of concrete structures [19,20]. Good knowledge of appropriate material properties is necessary during modeling of the fracture behavior of concrete structures. Such material properties are defined by a three-point bending of a notched concrete specimen. Therefore, the NNE-based parameter sensitivity analysis strategy is used to find the most crucial material properties in the fracture failure of a notched concrete beam. The geometry of the notched concrete beam is shown in **Figure 5**, with experimentally determined mean values of material properties [21]: modulus of elasticity $E_c = 35$ GPa, tensile strength $f_t = 3$ MPa, compressive strength $f_c = 65$ MPa, fracture energy $G_f = 100$ N/m, and compressive strain at compressive strength in the uniaxial compressive test $e_c = 0.003$. A group of 20 notched concrete beam samples is prepared depending on a stratified Monte Carlo-type simulation called Latin hypercube sampling (LHS) [22], using FReET software [23] with a correlation control procedure [24].

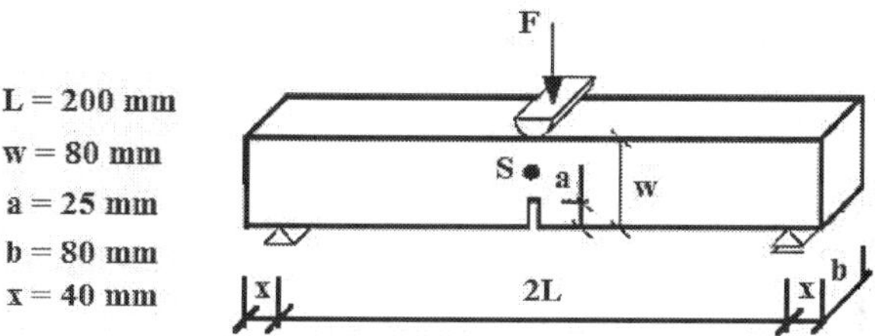

Figure 5. Notched concrete beam under three-point bending [4].

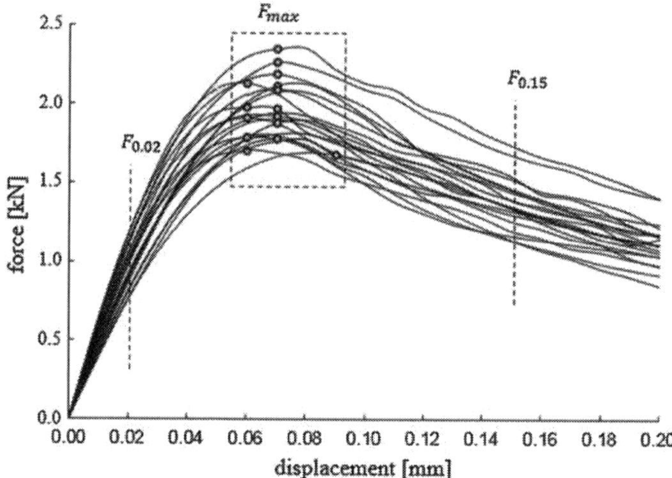

Figure 6. Force-displacement curves at the notch tip S from 20 simulated realizations of notched concrete beams [4].

The 20 notched concrete beam samples are determined by employing the following steps: (1) material properties are considered as random variables and mean values are obtained by experiments; (2) for each property, the LHS stochastic simulation is utilized to produce 20 random realizations of $\{E_c, f_t, f_c, G_f, e_c\}$ that feature variation of 0.15 and that obey a rectangular probability distribution, to impose variability for the creation of the training set. Each random realization determines a numerical nonlinear fracture mechanic calculation of a notched concrete beam; and (3) the finite element method (FEM) software ATENA [25] is applied to each realization to simulate the tensile fracture of the corresponding notched concrete beam. The fracture failure is described by a force-displacement curve at the notch tip S (**Figure 5**). A set of 20 force-displacement curves is illustrated in **Figure 6**. This set can be used as input data for the NNE-based sensitivity analysis. These curves describe the correlation between material fracture-mechanical properties and the nonlinear response of the beam. The sensitivity of the material properties to tensile fracture is studied depending on three forces: $F_{0.02}$, the force corresponding to 0.02-mm displacement; F_{max} the maximum force; and $F_{0.15}$ the force corresponding to 0.15-mm displacement. For each force, NNE-based parameter sensitivity analysis is applied to determine the significance of the material properties.

Parameter	Characteristics	Parameter type
E_c	Modulus of elasticity	Input
f_t	Tensile strength	Input
f_c	Compressive strength	Input
G_f	Fracture energy	Input
ε_c	Compressive strain	Input
$F_{0.02}$	Force at 0.02-mm displacement	Output
F_{max}	Maximum force	Output
$F_{0.15}$	Force at 0.15-mm displacement	Output

Table 4. Material properties in fracture failure of notched concrete beam [4].

Force	Ranking				
	E_c	f_t	f_c	G_f	ε_c
$F_{0.02}$	1	2	3	4	5
F_{max}	2	1	4	3	5
$F_{0.15}$	4	2	3	1	5

Table 5. Sensitivity analysis results of material parameters in fracture failure [4].

In NNE-based sensitivity analysis paradigm, a BP neural network with five input neurons and one output neuron (**Table 4**) is used as the seed to create a set of k-candidate neural network models. These models correlate the relationship between the material properties and the fracture failure. Depending on the performance of these models, the three best-performed neural network models are selected in the NNE model and the input perturbation algorithm is used for parameter sensitivity analysis. The result of the sensitivity analysis in this case is shown in **Table 5**. It is obvious from the table that f_t, followed by E_c and G_f, are the most important parameters in the fracture failure of the notched concrete beam.

6.2. Lateral deformation of deep-foundation pit

The construction of underground structures such as subway system tunnels, etc. requires deep-foundation pits. The working condition of a deep-foundation pit is usually defined by means of lateral deformation [26]. This lateral deformation usually involves a group of variables (**Table 6**), namely surface load q, deformation modulus of soil E, Poisson's ratio λ, soil cohesion C, and internal friction angle of soil φ. To analyze the working process of the deep-foundation pit, it is essential to study the sensitivity of these variables in order. Therefore, NNE-based parameter sensitivity analysis is applied to determine the importance of parameters in the lateral deformation of deep-foundation pits. For such analysis, a deep polygon-shaped foundation pit, as in [27], is utilized, having an excavation depth of 9.71 m, a width of earth-retaining wall of 8.7 m, and a length of reinforcement piles of 19.0 m, with the insertion ratio about 1.0. For testing cases, an orthogonal design of experiments is used to generate 25 testing cases, as shown in **Table 7** [27]. The testing cases are employed within the NNE-based sensitivity analysis paradigm to finally specify the contribution of each parameter to the lateral deformation y of the deep-foundation pits.

Parameter	Characteristics	Parameter type
q	Surface load	Input
E	Deformation modulus of soil	Input
ε	Poisson's ratio	Input
C	Soil cohesion	Input
φ	Internal friction angle of soil	Input
y	Lateral deformation of deep-foundation pit	Output

Table 6. Properties in lateral deformation of deep-foundation pit [4].

No.	q (kPa)	E (kPa)	ε	C (kPa)	φ (rad)	y (cm)
1	1 (5.0)	1 (3855)	1 (0.325)	1 (5.63)	1 (0.1386)	63.7
2	1	2 (6168)	2 (0.376)	2 (7.44)	2 (0.1834)	35.3
3	1	3 (7710)	3 (0.410)	3 (8.65)	3 (0.2133)	26.7
4	1	4 (9252)	4 (0.444)	4 (9.86)	4 (0.2432)	20.9
5	1	5 (11,565)	5 (0.478)	5 (11.68)	5 (0.2731)	12.5
6	2 (8.0)	1	2	3	4	55.8
7	2	2	3	4	5	32.1

No.	q (kPa)	E (kPa)	ε	C (kPa)	φ (rad)	y (cm)
8	2	3	4	5	1	21.9
9	2	4	5	1	2	16.3
10	2	5	1	2	3	25.2
11	3 (10.0)	1	3	5	2	47.8
12	3	2	4	1	3	26.1
13	3	3	5	2	4	16.2
14	3	4	1	3	5	30.4
15	3	5	2	4	1	22.1
16	4 (12.0)	1	4	2	5	37.1
17	4	2	5	3	1	18.0
18	4	3	1	4	2	34.9
19	4	4	2	5	3	25.8
20	4	5	3	1	4	18.9
21	5 (15.0)	1	5	4	3	25.2
22	5	2	1	5	4	42.4
23	5	3	2	1	5	30.1
24	5	4	3	2	1	22.4
25	5	5	4	3	2	15.6

Table 7. Orthogonal experimental design for producing testing samples [27].

Model	Ranking				
	q	E	λ	C	φ
NNM1	5	1	2	3	4
NNM2	5	1	2	3	4
NNM3	5	1	2	3	4

Table 8. Sensitivity analysis results in lateral deformation of deep-foundation pit [4].

As in the previous case study, a BP neural network is chosen as the seed in NNE-based sensitivity analysis to generate a set of k-candidate neural network models having five inputs and one output as listed in **Table 6**. By selecting three superior neural network models, namely NNM1, NNM2, and NNM3, and implementing input perturbation algorithm for sensitivity analysis, the ranking of each input parameter corresponding to each neural network model is shown in **Table 8**. It is clear that E is the most important parameter, followed by λ, C, ϕ, and q, respectively.

7. Summary

A short review of traditional neural network sensitivity analysis techniques was illustrated, followed by the presentation of two advanced techniques, NNC-based sensitivity analysis and NNE-based sensitivity analysis. These two techniques utilized selective superior neural network models along with some mathematical concepts to analyze the sensitivity of significant explicative variables. The efficiency of NNC-based sensitivity analysis paradigm was verified by studying the underlying influential parameters in strata movement. The effectiveness of NNE-based sensitivity analysis paradigm was proved by two case studies in civil engineering, the fracture failure of notched concrete beams and the lateral deformation of deep-foundation pits. These paradigms are essential for understanding the neural-network-based sensitivity analysis of critical engineering problems, due to their ability to determine the most and least important parameters, thereby reducing the inputs of neural network models to generate better predictability. They are good tools for analyzing the mechanism of engineering problems that black-box neural network models cannot explain.

Author details

Maosen Cao[1*], Nizar F. Alkayem[1], Lixia Pan[1] and Drahomír Novák[2]

*Address all correspondence to: cmszhy@hhu.edu.cn

1 Department of Engineering Mechanics, Hohai University, Nanjing, People's Republic of China

2 Faculty of Civil Engineering, Institute of Structural Mechanics, Brno University of Technology, Brno, Czech Republic

References

[1] Cao MS, Qiao P. Neural network committee-based sensitivity analysis strategy for geotechnical engineering problems. Neural Computing & Applications. 2008;17(5): 509–519. DOI: 10.1007/s00521-007-0143-5

[2] Cao M, Qiao P, Ren Q. Improved hybrid wavelet neural network methodology for time-varying behavior prediction of engineering structures. Neural Computing and Applications. 2009;18(7):821–832. DOI: 10.1007/s00521-009-0240-8

[3] Waszczyszyn Z, Ziemiański L. Neural networks in mechanics of structures and materials—new results and prospects of applications. Computers & Structures. 2001;79(22-25):2261–2276. DOI: 10.1016/S0045-7949(01)00083-9

[4] Cao MS, Pan LX, Gao YF, Novák D, Ding ZC, Lehký D, Li XL. Neural network ensemble-based parameter sensitivity analysis in civil engineering systems. Neural Computing & Applications. Forthcoming. DOI: 10.1007/s00521-015-2132-4

[5] Dimopoulos Y, Bourret P, Lek S. Use of some sensitivity criteria for choosing networks with good generalization ability. Neural Processing Letters. 1995;2(6):1–4. DOI: 10.1007/BF02309007

[6] Gedeon TD. Data mining of inputs: analysing magnitude and functional measures. International Journal of Neural Systems. 1997;8(2):209–218. DOI: 10.1142/S0129065797000227

[7] Wang W, Jones P, Partridge D. Assessing the impact of input features in a feedforward neural network. Neural Computing & Applications. 2000;9(2):101–112. DOI: 10.1007/PL00009895

[8] Gevrey M, Dimopoulos I, Lek S. Review and comparison of methods to study the contribution of variables in artificial neural network models. Ecological Modelling. 2003;160(3):249–264. DOI: 10.1016/S0304-3800(02)00257-0

[9] Montaño JJ, Palmer A. Numeric sensitivity analysis applied to feedforward neural networks. Neural Computing & Applications. 2003;12(2):119–125. DOI: 10.1007/s00521-003-0377-9

[10] Zeng X, Yeung DS. A quantified sensitivity measure for multilayer perceptron to input perturbation. Neural Computation. 2003;15(1):183–212. DOI: 10.1162/089976603321043757

[11] Yang Y, Zhang Q. A hierarchical analysis for rock engineering using artificial neural networks. Rock Mechanics and Rock Engineering. 1997;30(4):207–222. DOI: 10.1007/BF01045717

[12] Garson GD. Interpreting neural network connection weights. AI Expert. 1991;6(4):46–51.

[13] Goh ATC. Back-propagation neural networks for modelling complex systems. Artificial Intelligence in Engineering. 1995;9(3):143–151. DOI: 10.1016/0954-1810(94)00011-S

[14] Lek S, Belaud A, Baran P, Dimopoulos I, Delacoste M. Role of some environmental variables in trout abundance models using neural networks. Aquatic Living Resources. 1996;9(1):23–29.

[15] Lek S, Delacosteb M, Baranb P, Dimopoulosa I, Laugaa J, Aulagnierc S. Application of neural networks to modelling nonlinear relationships in ecology. Ecological Modelling. 1996;90(1):39–52. DOI: 10.1016/0304-3800(95)00142-5

[16] Lek S, Belaud A, Dimopoulos I, Lauga J, Moreau J. Improved estimation, using neural networks, of the food consumption of fish populations. Marine and Freshwater Research. 1995;46(8):1229–1236 . DOI: 10.1071/MF9951229

[17] Sung AH. Ranking importance of input parameters of neural networks. Expert Systems with Applications. 1998;15(3-4): 405–411. DOI: 10.1016/S0957-4174(98)00041-4

[18] Durrett R. Probability: Theory and Example, 3rd ed. Pacific Grove, CA: Duxbury; 2004. 521 p.

[19] Carpinteri A, Ferro G. Size effects on tensile fracture properties: a unified explanation based on disorder and fractality of concrete microstructure. Materials and Structures. 1994;27(10):563–571. DOI: 10.1007/BF02473124

[20] Rott JG. Computational modelling of concrete fracture [dissertation]. Delft: Technische Hogeschool Delft; 1988.

[21] Novák D, Lehký D. ANN inverse analysis based on stochastic small-sample training set simulation. Engineering Applications of Artificial Intelligence. 2006;19(7):731–740. DOI: 10.1016/j.engappai.2006.05.003

[22] Stein M. Large sample properties of simulations using Latin hypercube sampling. Technometrics. 1987;29(2):143–151 . DOI: 10.2307/1269769

[23] Novák D, Vořechovský M, Teplý B. FReET: software for the statistical and reliability analysis of engineering problems and FReET-D: degradation module. Advances in Engineering Software. 2014;72:179–192. DOI: 10.1016/j.advengsoft.2013.06.011

[24] Vořechovský M, Novák D. Correlation control in small-sample Monte Carlo type simulations I: a simulated annealing approach. Probabilistic Engineering Mechanics. 2009;24(3):452–462. DOI: 10.1016/j.probengmech.2009.01.004

[25] Červenka V, Jendele L, Červenka J. ATENA Program Documentation, Part 1: Theory. Prague: Červenka Consulting; 2009. 94 p.

[26] Feng S, Wu Y, Li J, Li P, Zhang Z, Wang D. The analysis of spatial effect of deep foundation pit in soft soil areas. Procedia Earth and Planetary Science. 2012;5:309–313. DOI: 10.1016/j.proeps.2012.01.052

[27] XU C, YE GB. Parameter sensitivity analysis of numerical model by cross test design technique. Hydrogeology and Engineering Geology. 2004;1:95–97.

Chapter 14

Artificial Neural Networks in Production Scheduling and Yield Prediction of Semiconductor Wafer Fabrication System

Jie Zhang, Junliang Wang and Wei Qin

Additional information is available at the end of the chapter

http://dx.doi.org/10.5772/63444

Abstract

With the development of artificial intelligence, the artificial neural networks (ANN) are widely used in the control, decision-making and prediction of complex discrete event manufacturing systems. Wafer fabrication is one of the most complicated and high competence manufacturing phases. The production scheduling and yield prediction are two critical issues in the operation of semiconductor wafer fabrication system (SWFS). This chapter proposed two fuzzy neural networks for the production rescheduling strategy decision and the die yield prediction. Firstly, a fuzzy neural network (FNN)-based rescheduling decision model is implemented, which can rapidly choose an optimized rescheduling strategy to schedule the semiconductor wafer fabrication lines according to the current system disturbances. The experimental results demonstrate the effectiveness of proposed FNN-based rescheduling decision mechanism approach over the alternatives (back-propagation neural network and Multivariate regression). Secondly, a novel fuzzy neural network-based yield prediction model is proposed to improve prediction accuracy of die yield in which the impact factors of yield and critical electrical test parameters are considered simultaneously and are taken as independent variables. The comparison experiment verifies the proposed yield prediction method improves on three traditional yield prediction methods with respect to prediction accuracy.

Keywords: semiconductor wafer fabrication system, rescheduling, fuzzy neural networks, yield prediction, decision mechanism

© 2016 The Author(s). Licensee InTech. This chapter is distributed under the terms of the Creative Commons Attribution License (http://creativecommons.org/licenses/by/3.0), which permits unrestricted use, distribution, and reproduction in any medium, provided the original work is properly cited.

1. The production scheduling and yield prediction of semiconductor wafer fabrication system (SWFS)

The semiconductor wafer fabrication system (SWFS) is one of the most sophisticated manufacturing systems. This kind of manufacture system is characterised by a different type of wafer process (batch and single process), hundreds of process steps, the large and expensive device, production unforeseen circumstances and re-entrant flow [1]. Semiconductor manufacturing orders are usually global, dynamic and customer driven since the 1990s. As a result, semiconductor manufacturers strive to achieve high-quality products using advance manufacturing technologies (such as process planning and scheduling and digitized indicators' prediction technologies) [2]. In recent years, production scheduling and yield prediction are always two issues above all in the complex SWFS.

An organization's competitive advantage is increasingly dependent on its response to market changes and opportunities, and in response to unforeseen circumstances (i.e. Machine breakdown, rush orders), so it is important to reduce inventory and cycle time, and improve resource utilization. Therefore, production scheduling is required to optimize the operation of SWFS and has been reviewed by Uzsoy and his colleagues [3]. SWFS operates in uncertain dynamic environments, facing with a lot of disturbances, such as machine failure, a lot of rework and rush orders [4]. Production rescheduling has been viewed as an efficient approach in responding to these uncertainties raised by the external environment and internal conditions of production [5]. In job shop and flow shop, heuristic algorithms and discrete event simulation methods are mainly applied in production scheduling problems [6–8]. However, the SWFS is large-scaled, complicated system with re-entrant flows, which is different from typical job and flow shop. Many rescheduling strategies improving traditional job shop rescheduling methods have been proposed and applied in SWFS in the recent decade [9, 10]. These methods using a single rescheduling strategy are not enough for the real-time dynamic manufacturing environment, which is more complex with disruptive events every day. For this reason, a layered rescheduling framework is needed to select rescheduling methodologies in SWFS according to the present system status.

Yield prediction plays an indispensable role in the semiconductor manufacturing factory for its powerful function of reducing cost, increasing production and maintaining a good relationship with customers. Before a malfunction is detected, the accurate prediction model of yield will serve as a warning role and help people take proactive measures to reduce the number of defect's wafers and increase the total yield of SWFS. An accurate prediction of yield plays a useful role in releasing the plan of production and optimizing the process of production, which will make the cycle time shorter and reduce fabrication cost of average units. To offer a reasonable and acceptable price and satisfy the customers, the prediction of manufacturing costs for products is necessary if they are still under development and the accurate prediction of yield can provide some advice for Ref. [11]. To maintain the good relationship with the customers, the order's due data should be guaranteed and the accurate prediction of yield is also useful in this aspect. Some organic problems located on the wafer such as microscopic particles, cluster defects, photo-resist, critical processing parameters would be the factors which affect the yield of the semiconductor wafer. With the statistic analysis models [12] and traditional artificial neural network (ANN) models [13], the prediction of semiconductor fabrication system's yield is difficult. A fuzzy neural network (FNN)-based yield model for yield prediction of semiconductor manufacturing systems is proposes in this chapter. In this system, the impacted factors, which are cluster defects, the defect's key attributed parameters, key electrical test parameters, should be considered in the same time. By this way, the precision of the wafer yield's prediction is improved.

2. The application of ANN in production scheduling and yield prediction of the SWFS

For selecting a scheduling strategy, the FNN approach is widely used. FNN is also an effective methodology for prediction of discrete event manufacturing systems, control and decision-making [14, 15]. For demonstrating the relationship between the monitoring features of a flexible manufacturing system and the conditions of tools, Li et al. [16] presented a fuzzy neural network approach. For controlling manufacturing process, Zhou et al. [17] used a fuzzy neural network approach. Chang et al. [18] created a FNN model of flow time estimation with data, which are generated from a foundry service company. The product design time was estimated with the FNN approach by Xu and Yan [19]. Chang et al. [20] used FNN approach to estimate the influence of the process on the results of the wafer fabrication in SWFS. However, the FNN approach has not been used to solve the problem of SWFS rescheduling problem. This chapter proposes the FNN-based rescheduling decision mechanism for SWFS. This methodology can solve the uncertainty problem and express the expert knowledge in weighted values. In the neural network, the evaluation of local weight values is the knowledge modelling of control rules. Rescheduling strategies, SWFS state parameters, disturbance parameters can be identified and analysed in this model. In this model, we can build the nonlinear relationship between these three components. With this approach, the layered rescheduling approach will be selected that make the yields rapid responsiveness and high productivity of the SWFS in an environment full of randomness.

To predict the wafer yield, Tong et al. [21] proposed a neural network-based approach through considering the clustering phenomenon of the defects in integrated circuit manufacturing. It was proved that the proposed approach was effective. For predicting wafer yield for integrated circuit with clustered defects, Tong and Chao [22] used a general regression neural network (GRNN) approach. Defect clustering patterns are simulated from three aspects: the size of chip, percentage of defects and the cluster pattern. A case study demonstrated the effectiveness of the approach of the model. For the lack of reliability and accuracy in the prediction of yield, an approach of a fuzzy set for yield learning was proposed by Chen and Wang [23]. A few of examples enhanced the reliability and precision of the forecasting of the yield. Chen and Lin [24] proposed a fuzzy-neural system with expert opinions, which can increase the precision of semiconductor yield prediction. The artificial intelligent-based yield forecasting models demonstrated above have some limitations that it only takes consideration of the physical parameters of wafer and the important attributed parameters of defects in wafer without considering the influence of variation of the key electrical test parameters. With the combining of neural network (NN) and memory-based reasoning (MBR), an integrated framework for a yield management system with techniques of hybrid machine learning was given by Chung and Sang [25]. In the forecasting model of the yield, some key electrical test parameters have been taken into consideration. With the use of wafer level electrical test data, a parametric neural forecasting model was constructed by Kim et al. [26] and Kim [27]. However, these yield forecasting models have not taken the attributed parameters of defects in wafer into consideration. This chapter proposes a yield forecasting model with the consideration of the wafer electrical test parameters and important attributed parameters of defects in wafer.

3. Artificial neural network for rescheduling decision mechanism in the SWFS

3.1. Layered rescheduling framework of SWFS

A layered rescheduling framework is proposed in order to reschedule the SWFS for the unstable environment which is shown in **Figure 1**. In the process of rescheduling framework, a three layers of rescheduling strategies are used. a three layers are machine group layer, machine layer and the system layer. The strategies of the rescheduling implement the dynamic scheduling, the global scheduling of SWFS and the machine scheduling. To choose the particular rescheduling strategy, the optimal rescheduling decision mechanism based on FNN approach. The layered rescheduling framework is described in detail in the following paragraph.

Global scheduling of SWFS. If there are some changes in the large-scale SWFS's condition or there are some disturbances, the rescheduling is needed and the global rescheduling of SWFS is managed for the adjustment of the global scheduling [28]. With the machine group layer's adjusted scheduling objectives, a local dynamic scheduling algorithm is applied for scheduling in the machine group layer [29]. In the end, with the machine group layer's adjusted scheduling objectives, machine scheduling is processed in real-time and the optimal machine real-time scheduling solutions are achieved.

Dynamic scheduling of SWFS. If there are some changes in the medium-scale SWFS's condition or there are some disturbances, the rescheduling in the machine group layer is needed and the local dynamic scheduling of SWFS is managed. In order to adjust the local scheduling of a machine group, a local dynamic scheduling algorithm is applied. With the adjusted scheduling objectives of the machine layer taken into consideration, machine scheduling of SWFS is processed.

Machine scheduling of SWFS. If there are some changes in the large-scale SWFS's condition or there are some disturbances, the rescheduling is just accomplished and in the same time, the machine scheduling is processed. Though they are same in the operation sequences of the lots, they are different in the operation start times of delayed lots.

FNN-based optimal rescheduling decision mechanism. With the consideration of the statuses and disturbances to SWFS, the rescheduling layer is chosen by optimal rescheduling decision mechanism. According to the fuzzy neural network, an algorithm for the system is stated in this paper.

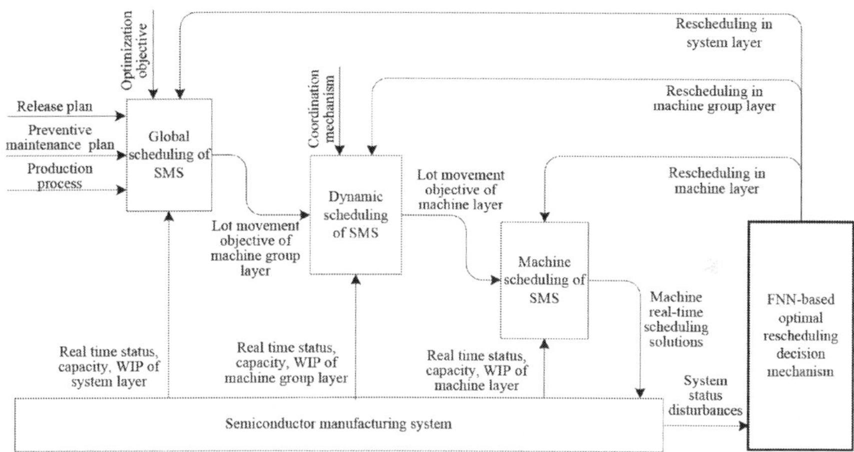

Figure 1. Layered rescheduling framework of SWFS.

3.2. FNN-based decision mechanism for rescheduling

Fuzzy neural network (FNN) is an ingenious combination of fuzzy logic and neural network, which inherits the advantages from both fuzzy system and neural network. The FNN has the characteristics of processing fuzzy information with fuzzy algorithms and learning with a high-speed parallel structure. The FNN approach is therefore adaptable and robust, and is well suited for the SMS rescheduling problem.

The FNN-based rescheduling decision model consists of an input layer, several hidden layers and an output layer. Input parameters connected with disturbances and state parameters are accepted in the input layer. The hidden layers calculate and transform the input parameters using fuzzy logic theory. The output layer produces the decision-making response of the rescheduling model. More details of this method are described.

3.2.1. Input factors in the proposed FNN model

The SMS's state and disturbance parameters are treated as input of the FNN, which can be detailed as: system disturbances parameter, average queue length, stability of SMS, average relative load and average slack time.

3.2.1.1. System disturbances parameter

Since the operating environments of SMS are uncertain and dynamic, disturbances mainly include: machine failures, lot reworks and rush orders. Once a disturbance has happened, an optimal rescheduling strategy must be selected and carried out to guarantee the stability and efficiency of SMS. Disturbances are converted into machine work times to quantify their effect. The mapping of disturbances to machine work times is defined as follows.

(1) Machine failures. The processing time in SMS increases if machine failures happen. Suppose that t^f refers to the increased process time caused by all machine failures, then,

$$t^f = \sum_{M_j^f \in F^f} \sum_{m_{ji} \in M_j^f} t^f_{ji} \tag{1}$$

where M_j^f is the failed machine group j, m_{ji} refers to the failed machine i of machine group j, t^f_{ji} represents the repair time of machine i of machine group j, and F^f is the set of failed machine group.

(2) Lot reworks. Lot reworks raise the output requirement of SMS. Suppose that t^r is the additional process time incurred by all lot reworks, then,

$$t^r = \sum_{M_j^r \in F^r} \sum_{p_{jk} \in R_j^r} t^r_{jk} \tag{2}$$

where M_j^r refers to the machine group j operating the rework lots, R_j^r refers to the set of the rework lots operated by the machine group j, p_{jk} refers to the rework lot k operated by the machine group j, t^r_{jk} refers to the process time of the rework lot k operated by the machine group j, F^r refers to the set of the machine group that operate rework lots.

(3) Rush orders. Rush orders also demand more of the production requirement of SMS. Suppose that t^o is the process time required by all rush orders, then,

$$t^o = \sum_{M_j^o \in F^o} \sum_{q_{jk} \in R_j^o} t^o_{jk} \tag{3}$$

where M_j^o represents the machine group j, that operates the rush orders in current plan time phase, R_j^o represents the set of the lots operated by machine group j in the rush orders; q_{jk} represents the lot k in the rush orders operated by machine group j, t^o_{jk} is the process time of the lot k operated by the machine group j in the rush orders, F^O represents the set of the machine group which are related with rush orders.

(4) System disturbances parameter. Suppose that td is the system disturbances parameter, denoting the total effect of disturbances on SMS scheduling. The formula to calculate td is shown as the (4).

$$td = t^f + t^r + t^o \tag{4}$$

3.2.1.2. Average queue length

Average queue length of machine groups reflecting the utility of the machine group is affected by disturbances. L is the average queue length of machine groups affected by disturbances; and the formula is shown in (5).

$$L = \frac{\sum_{M_j \in (F^r \cup F^f \cup F^o)} L_j}{N} \tag{5}$$

where M_j denotes the machine group j, L_j means queue length of machine group M_j, N refers to the number of machine group that affected by disturbances.

3.2.1.3. Stability of SMS

The stability of SMS is defined as the deviation in predicted average start time of a rescheduled strategy from the real start time. β denotes the stability of SMS, which is shown in (6).

$$\beta = \frac{\sum_{\substack{(i,s) \in S \\ tc_{is} \le tc}} \left| tc'_{is} - tc_{is} \right|}{\sum_{\substack{(i,s) \in S \\ tc_{is} \le tc}} q_{is}} \tag{6}$$

where tc'_{is} is practical start time of process stage s of product i, tc_{is} is computational start time of process stage s of product i which optimized with a global scheduling algorithm or re-scheduling strategy, q_{is} is the number of process stage s of product i, tc is the current time when disturbance happens, S is set of tasks of all machine group in SMS.

3.2.1.4. Average relative loads

Average relative loads denote the loads of machine groups measured from the current time to the end of the scheduling horizon which can be affected by disturbances. Let η represent the average relative loads, the formula for calculation is shown in (7).

$$\eta = \frac{\sum\limits_{\substack{(i,s)\in S_d \\ t_e \geq t_{is} \geq t_c}} tp_{is}}{\sum\limits_{M_j \in (F^r \cup F^f \cup F^o_3)} n_j (te - tc)} \qquad (7)$$

where tp_{is} denotes process time of process stage s of product i, te denotes the time point when scheduling is ended, n_j denotes the number of machine of machine group M_j, S_d represents set of tasks of machine group which affected by disturbances.

3.2.1.5. Average slack time

Average slack time represents the space that the machine groups can be adjusted when disturbances happen. Suppose ts is the average slack time, shown in (8).

$$ts = \frac{\sum\limits_{\substack{(i,s)\in S_d \\ t_e \geq t_{is} \geq t_c}} \left(t_{i(s+1)} - t_{is} - tp_{is} \right)}{\sum\limits_{\substack{(i,s)\in S_d \\ t_e \geq t_{is} \geq t_c}} q_{is}} \qquad (8)$$

3.2.2. Output variables

The output variables in the FNN output layer are related to the layered rescheduling strategies, which consists of the rescheduling in system layer, machine group layer, and machine layer. If a particular layered rescheduling strategy is selected, then the corresponding output variable is close to 1, otherwise it equals to 0. In FNN-based rescheduling decision model, suppose that y_1, y_2, y_3 are defined as output variables, then y_1, y_2, y_3 correspond to the rescheduling in system layer, rescheduling in machine group layer, and rescheduling in machine layer, respectively.

3.2.3. The structure of FNN

There are five layers in the rescheduling decision model based on FNN, as illustrated in **Figure 2**.

a.   The input vector is $X = [x1, x2, x3, x4, x5]T = [L, \beta, \eta, ts, td]T$. The function of node input-output is:

$$f_{i(1)} = x_{i(0)} = x_i; x_{i(1)} = g_{i(1)} = f_{i(1)}; i = 1, 2, \cdots 5 \qquad (9)$$

b.   In the second layer which is the fuzzifer layer, the function of the Gauss membership is adopted.

$$u_{ij} = e^{-\frac{(x_i - c_{ij})^2}{\sigma_{ij}^2}}, i = 1, 2, \cdots, 5,$$
$$j = 1, 2, \cdots, k_i \tag{10}$$

In this formula, cij is the centre and σ_{ij} is width. The node input–output function is:

$$f_{ij(2)} = -\frac{(x_i - c_{ij})^2}{\sigma_{ij}^2};$$

$$x_{ij(2)} = u_{ij} = g_{ij(2)} = e^{f_{ij(2)}} = e^{-\frac{(x_i - c_{ij})^2}{\sigma_{ij}^2}};$$
$$i = 1, 2, \cdots 5, j = 1, 2, \cdots, k_i \tag{11}$$

c. In the third layer as the rule layer, each node in the layer is a fuzzy rule which not only matches the front part of the fuzzy rule but also calculates the adaptive of the rule,

$$a_j = \prod_{l=1}^{5} u_{l_i}(x_{l_i}),$$
$$j = 1, 2, \cdots, n \tag{12}$$

In this layer, the input--output function is:

$$f_{j(3)} = \prod_{l=1}^{5} x_{l_i(2)} = \prod_{l=1}^{5} u_{l_i}(x_{l_i}); \, x_{j(3)} = g_{j(3)} = f_{j(3)};$$
$$j = 1, 2, \cdots, n x_{j(3)} = g_{j(3)} = f_{j(3)}; j = 1, 2, \cdots, n \tag{13}$$

d. In the fourth layer which is the normalized layer. In this layer, the node numbers are the same in the third layer. It normalized the adaptive values of these rules. And the input-output function is:

$$f_{j(4)} = \frac{x_{j(3)}}{\sum_{i=1}^{n} x_{i(3)}} = \frac{a_j}{\sum_{i=1}^{n} a_i};$$
$$x_{j(4)} = g_{j(4)} = f_{j(4)}; j = 1, 2, \cdots, n \tag{14}$$

e. The last layer is the output layer. It defuzzify the output variables. And each node describes a rescheduling strategy. While a rescheduling strategy is chose, the corresponding output is 1 or 0. The input-output function is:

$$f_{i(5)} = \sum_{j=1}^{n} w_{ij} x_{j(4)} = \sum_{j=1}^{n} w_{ij} b_j ; x_{j(5)} = g_{j(5)} = f_{j(5)} \; ; i = 1,2,3$$

$$x_{j(5)} = g_{j(5)} = f_{j(5)} \; ; i = 1,2,3$$

$$x_{j(5)} = g_{j(5)} = f_{j(5)} \; ; i = 1,2,3 \tag{15}$$

where w_{ij} is the connection weight parameter.

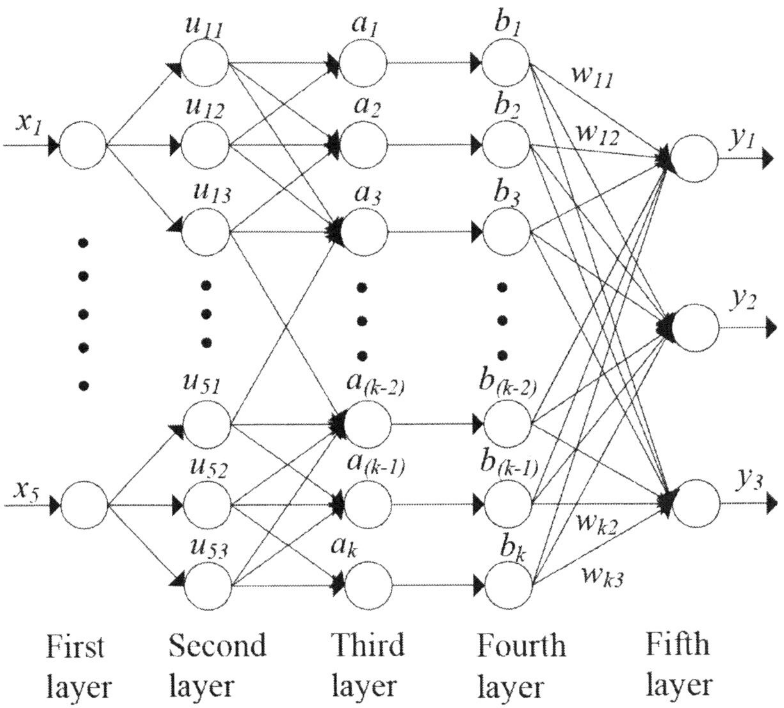

Figure 2. FNN structure.

3.2.4. The strategy of the fuzzy inference

The Mamdani-based fuzzy inference is applied in this FNN-based rescheduling decision model with a assumption that the fuzzy rule Ri describes the relationship between input and output. Then,

Ri:

IF x1 is A1i and x2 is A2i and … and xm is Ami,

THEN y1 is B1i and y2 is B2i and … and ym is Bki,

where

i = 1, 2, …, n.

n: number of rules.

m: number of input variables.

k: number of output variables.

A_{ji}: value of fuzzy linguistic variable xj.

B_{ji}: value of fuzzy linguistic variable yj.

3.3. Result and discussion

3.3.1. Experiment on the proposed FNN approach

In this section, the experiments are conducted to evaluate the effectiveness of the proposed FNN rescheduling decision mechanism. A discrete event simulation model is run to gather the experiment data, which is based on a 6-in. SWFS in Shanghai. This SWFS is composed by eleven machine groups, which add up to thirty-four machines in total. And three types of wafers are put into the SWFS. The processes of all three types of wafer lots are divided into dozes of stages, which is composed by a key step and several successive normal steps. One hundred and fifty records of rescheduling decision are collected from the simulation model, and shown in **Table 1**. Ninety records are used in model training, and 60 are taken to evaluate the model. The presented FNN approach is compared with the back propagation network (BPN) approach and the multivariate regression methodology, since the BPN and multivariate regression approaches are widely used in the rescheduling strategy decision and proven to be competitive [30, 31]. Furthermore, the detail numerical comparison of the FNN approach, BPNN approach and multivariate regression are demonstrated as follows.

Now, it's going to compare the experimental results which are made by these three methods. **Figure 3** shows the optimal rescheduling decision value and the model outputs. It shows that the FNN rescheduling method has the best convergence. We also contrast the RMSE and the decision coefficients R^2 of these three methodologies in **Table 2**. The FNN has the best performance for the RMSE which is 0.042 and has the largest of the R^2 values which is 0.9941. Hence, the rescheduling decision based on FNN has the best performance in these three methods.

Samples no	Average queue length of disturbed machine stations x_1 (lot)	Stability of scheduling x_2 (h)	Average load of disturbed machine stations x_3 (100%)	Average slack time of disturbed machine stations x_4 (h)	Disturbance x_5 (h)	Optimal rescheduling decision objective		
						Rescheduling in machine layer y_1	Rescheduling in machine group layer y_2	Rescheduling in system layer y_3
1	1	1.10	0.59	6.42	2.14	1	0	0
2	2	0.78	0.52	6.51	2.01	1	0	0
3	0	0.81	0.46	5.16	1.76	1	0	0
4	0	0.48	0.1	5.81	1.21	1	0	0
5	2	0.49	0.14	4.62	1.42	1	0	0
6	1	0.52	0.12	5.54	1.79	1	0	0
7	2	0.74	0.17	5.16	1.13	1	0	0
8	0	0.76	0.07	4.49	1.64	1	0	0
9	6	0.38	0.29	4.86	1.4	1	0	0
10	5	0.37	0.26	5.17	2.21	1	0	0
..	..	..	..	..	..	..	..	..
141	6	4.23	0.75	3.81	9.81	0	0	1
142	4	4.15	0.76	5.64	9.18	0	0	1
143	5	4.01	0.76	4.97	9.77	0	0	1
144	2	0.81	0.38	1.87	9.87	0	0	1
145	4	0.87	0.37	2.41	10.11	0	0	1
146	2	0.68	0.42	2.18	9.42	0	0	1
147	2	0.72	0.35	2.18	9.76	0	0	1
148	2	0.91	0.23	2.7	9.13	0	0	1
149	1	0.87	0.21	2.97	9.73	0	0	1
150	2	0.87	0.31	2.77	10.18	0	0	1

Table 1. One hundred and fifty records for numerical experiments.

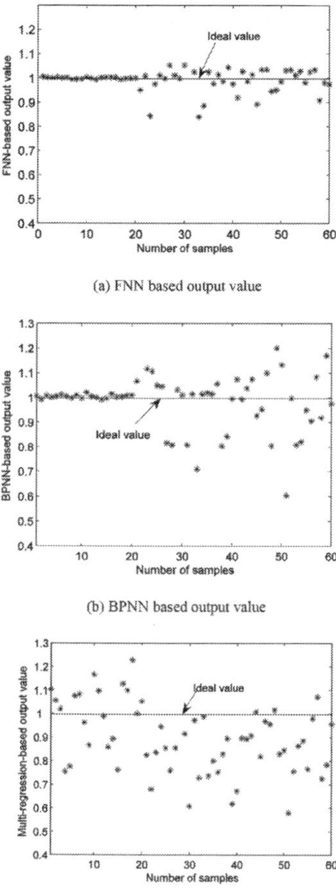

(a) FNN based output value

(b) BPNN based output value

(c) Multivariate regression based output value

Figure 3. The relationship between the rescheduling strategy output and ideal target output for the FNN, BPNN and multivariate regression methods. (a) FNN-based output value, (b) BPNN-based output value and (c) multivariate regression-based output value.

Rescheduling strategy model	RMSE	R^2		
		$R^2_{Y_1}$	$R^2_{Y_2}$	$R^2_{Y_3}$
FNN	0.0042	0.9880	0.9762	0.9941
BPNN	0.0132	0.9745	0.9178	0.9274
Multivariate regression	0.0897	0.85887	0.75566	0.70813

Table 2. Comparison of RMSE and decision coefficients among the FNN, BPNN and multivariate regression methods.

3.3.2. Experiment on the proposed rescheduling decision mechanism

The FNN rescheduling decision mechanism is used in our layered rescheduling method (Method 1). There are two other different rescheduling methods. One is the monolayer-based rescheduling approach (Method 2). Another one is the first come first served (FCFS) approach (Method 23). In our method, the FNN rescheduling decision mechanism figures out the optimal rescheduling approaches which include the global scheduling of SWFS, the dynamic scheduling and the machine scheduling. By contrast, the Method 2 only considers the rescheduling of the machine group layer. But in practice, the Method 3 is widely used in the Fab. In order to prove the efficiency of our approach, we also compared these three rescheduling methods in terms of the machine utilization and the daily movement, which are the important system targets for SWFS.

In the case study, the data are collected from a 6-in. SWFS in Shanghai. It products three kinds of lots which are renamed as A, B and C. The whole process is shown in **Table 4**. This SWFS has eleven key machine groups (shown in **Table 3**). which has 34 machines with MTTF and MTTR parameters. They are explained in Section 5. The SWFS simulation model is built by eM-plant 7.0 software. In the simulation, it took 12 days, including a 5-day warm-up. Ten times repeated trials of the same stimulation, in which the initiated loads of machines were different, were performed (3 rescheduling methods 10 replications). The results are shown in **Figures 4** and **5**, which illustrate:

1. Method 1 performs well in the rescheduling decision in the SWFS.

2. Method 1 outperforms method 2 and 3, which indicates the layered rescheduling method is more suitable than the conventional FCFS rescheduling approach and monolayer-based rescheduling approach in the complex SWFS.

Machine group number	Processing type	Number of machine	Batch size	MTBF	MTTR
1	Ion implant	3	1	70	1
2	Ion implant	4	1	70	1
3	Diffusion	3	5	100	2
4	Diffusion	4	5	110	2
5	Etching	2	1	90	1
6	Etching	4	1	80	1
7	Etching	3	1	60	1
8	Etching	2	1	70	1
9	Lithography	4	1	90	1
10	Lithography	3	1	80	1
11	Lithography	2	1	100	1

Table 3. Configuration of SWFS.

Stage number	Number of time period by product A	Machine group number of product A	Process time of product A by key machine t/hour	Number of time period by product B	Machine group number of product B	Process time of product B by key machine t/hour	Number of time period by product C	Machine group number of product C	Process time of product C by key machine t/hour
1	1	8	1	1	10	1	1	10	1
2	1	7	1	1	8	1	1	8	1
3	1	10	1	4	5	1	2	5	1
4	1	9	1	1	10	1	1	8	1
5	5	0	1	1	1	1	1	0	1
6	3	0	1	1	6	1	4	3	6
7	4	2	4	1	10	1	1	8	1
8	1	8	1	1	9	1	2	5	1
9	1	5	1	6	0	1	2	2	3
10	1	3	3	1	0	1	1	8	1
11	1	0	1	1	4	1	2	5	3
12	2	10	1	1	8	1	1	0	1
13	1	0	1	2	1	1	2	3	6
14	4	4	2	3	2	3	1	8	1
15	1	6	1	1	10	1	2	9	1
16	2	1	1	1	8	1	2	4	1
17	3	4	2	2	5	2	3	0	1
18	1	9	1	1	3	1	1	8	1
19	1	5	1	2	5	1	3	6	1
20	1	8	1	1	9	1	2	1	1
21	3	3	3	1	1	1	1	8	1
22	1	5	1	2	5	1	3	7	1
23	4	2	4	1	9	1	2	2	3
24	1	9	1	3	0	1	2	5	1
25	3	4	2	3	2	3	1	0	1
26	2	0	1	2	10	1	1	9	1
27	1	8	1	2	7	1	2	4	1
28	1	7	1	–	–	–	1	1	1
29	2	3	3	–	–	–	–	–	–
30	1	2	1	–	–	–	–	–	–

Table 4. Lot products whole process.

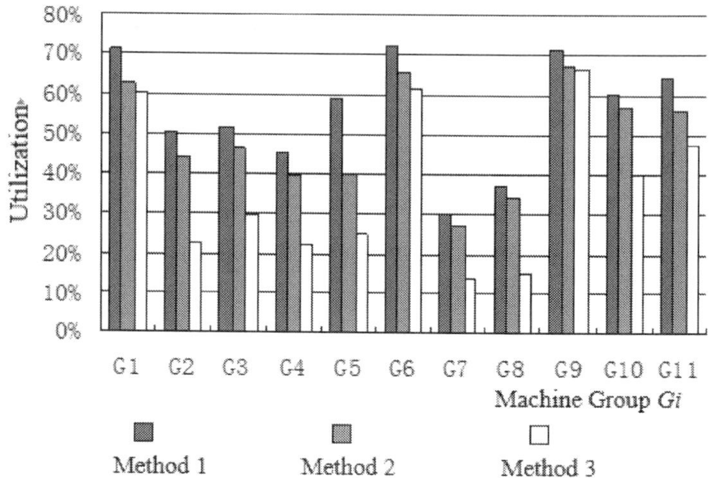

Figure 4. The utilization of machine group.

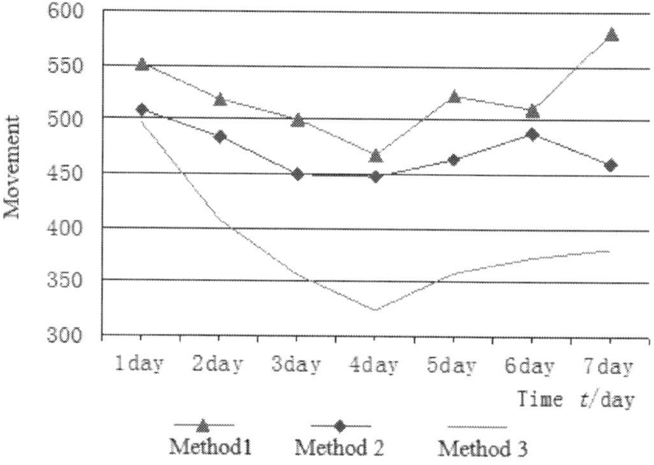

Figure 5. The utilization of machine group.

4. Artificial neural network approach for die yield prediction in the SWFS

4.1. FNN-based yield prediction model

The yield prediction model based on FNN is composed of three parts, which are an input layer, an output layer and several hidden layers. The three parts do the different jobs respectively. The input layer serves to accept input parameters connected with yield. The output layer does the job to get the yield response of the prediction model. The hidden layers are applied to compute and convert the input parameters which are on the basis of fuzzy logical theory. The following sections show a more detailed yield prediction model based on FNN.

4.1.1. Variables in FNN input layer

The input variables in the FNN prediction model include the following parameters: the critical electrical test parameters, wafer physical parameters and key parameters of defects in wafer. Critical process parameters refer to those electrical test parameters which are generally tested at the end of the wafer processing, and they have notable influences on the yield. Wafer physical parameters mainly refer to the size of the chip. Key parameters of defects in wafer Contain a number of defects, clustering parameter, mean number of defects in each chip and mean a number of defects in each unit area. Among these input variables, the critical electrical test parameters and clustering parameters are complex, and we will discuss them in the following sections.

4.1.1.1. Critical electrical test parameters

In the process of fabricating complex semiconductor wafer, there are more than one hundred electrical test parameters related to the probed wafer. This paper mainly does the research on establishing the exact relationship of a small number of critical electrical test parameters with yield. These critical electrical test parameters have significant influence on yield, and they have high correlating coefficients or exhibit a 'cliff' in the correlation graphs which means they can quickly improve the yield. Wong [32] proposed the hybrid statistical correlation analysis method, and the critical electrical test parameters are identified based on this method. Here, we remove some details of these electrical test parameters for confidentiality.

4.1.1.2. Clustering parameter

Clustering parameter displays cluster or clumps degrees of wafer defects in the defect map [33]. Suppose that the clustering parameter is expressed by c, shown in Eq. (1).

$$c = \min\left\{\frac{s_v^2}{\bar{v}^2}, \frac{s_w^2}{\bar{w}^2}\right\}$$

(22)

where the sample mean and variance of V_i is represented by $\bar{V}^2$ and S^2_v; and the sample mean and variance of W_i are represented by S^2_w. V_i and W_i are a series of defect intervals on the x and y axis defined as:

$$V_i = x_{(i)} - x_{(i-1)}, \ i = 1,2,...,n \tag{23}$$

$$W_i = y_{(i)} - y_{(i-1)}, \ i = 1,2,...,n \tag{24}$$

where $x_{(i)}$ refers to the ith smallest defect coordinates on x axis, and similarly, $y_{(i)}$ refers to the ith smallest defect coordinates on y axis, $x(0) = y(0) = 0$, and n refers to the quantity of defects on one wafer. If the defects are randomly scattered, the value of CI is close to 1, and when clustering of defects appears, the value of CI is likely to be greater than 1.

4.1.2. FNN structure

There are five layers in the rescheduling decision model based on FNN, as illustrated in **Figure 6**.

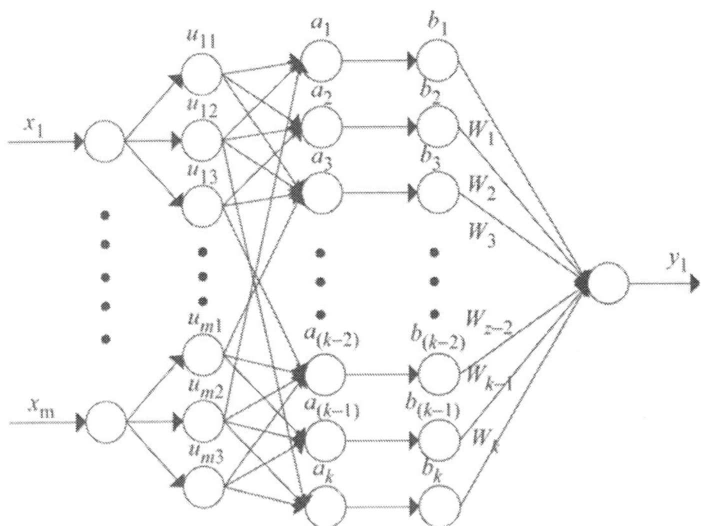

Figure 6. FNN model structure.

a.   The input vector is $X = [x_1, x_2, x_3, ..., x_m]$. The function of node input-output is:

$$f_i^{(1)} = x_i; \ x_i^{(1)} = g_i^{(1)} = f_i^{(1)}; i = 1, 2, \cdots m \tag{4-4}$$

b. In the second layer which is the fuzzifer layer, the function of the Gauss membership is adopted.

$$u_{ij}(x_i) = e^{-\frac{(x_i - c_{ij})^2}{\sigma_{ij}^2}} \tag{25}$$

In this formula, cij is the centre and σ_{ij} is width. The node input-output function is:

$$f_{ij}^{(2)} = -\frac{(x_i^{(1)} - c_{ij})^2}{\sigma_{ij}^2}; x_{ij}^{(2)} = u_{ij}(x_i^{(1)}) = g_{ij}^{(2)} = e^{f_{ij}^{(2)}} = e^{-\frac{(x_i - c_{ij})^2}{\sigma_{ij}^2}} \tag{26}$$

where $i = 1, 2, \cdots m$ and $j = 1, 2, \cdots, l_i$.

c. In the third layer as the rule layer, each node in the layer is a fuzzy rule which not only matches the front part of the fuzzy rule but also calculates the adaptive of the rule,

$$a_j = \prod_{i=1}^{m} u_{il_i}(x_i^{(1)}), j = 1, 2, \cdots, n \tag{27}$$

In this layer, the input-output function is:

$$f_j^{(3)} = \prod_{i=1}^{m} x_{il_i}^{(2)} = \prod_{i=1}^{m} u_{il_i}(x_i^{(1)}); \ x_j^{(3)} = a_j = g_j^{(3)} = f_j^{(3)}; j = 1, 2, \cdots, n \tag{28}$$

d. In the fourth layer which is the normalized layer. In this layer, the node numbers are the same in the third layer. It normalized the adaptive values of these rules. And the input-output function is:

$$b_j = \frac{a_j}{\sum_{i=1}^{n} a_i}, j = 1, 2, \cdots, n \tag{29}$$

Node input-output function in this layer is as follows.

$$f_j^{(4)} = \frac{x_j^{(3)}}{\sum_{i=1}^{n} x_i^{(3)}} = \frac{a_j}{\sum_{i=1}^{n} a_i}; \ x_j^{(4)} = b_j = g_j^{(4)} = f_j^{(4)}; j = 1,2,\cdots,n \tag{30}$$

e. The last layer is the output layer. It defuzzify the output variables. And each node describes a rescheduling strategy. While a rescheduling strategy is chose, the corresponding output is 1 or 0. The input-output function is:

$$f^{(5)} = \sum_{j=1}^{n} w_j x_j^{(4)} = \sum_{j=1}^{n} w_j b_j; \ O_{out} = x^{(5)} = g^{(5)} = f^{(5)} \tag{31}$$

where W_j is connection weight parameter of output layer, and O_{out} is the output of FNN model.

4.2. Case study

In this section, the experiments are conducted to evaluate the effectiveness of the proposed FNN method. This section presents a numerical experiment study to demonstrate the effectiveness of the approach proposed. Seven hundred and twenty wafer samples are obtained from a 6 in. SWFS in Shanghai, and each sample includes 360 records of wafer yield. Five hundred and fifty-two records are used in model training, and 168 are taken to evaluate the model. The attributes contained in each record are, in order, number of defects, clustering parameter, die yield, mean number of defects per unit area, chip size parameter, mean number of defects per chip, and 28 electrical test parameters, which is shown in **Table 5**. Each feature is acquired by test during the critical manufacturing process. The presented FNN approach is compared with the Poisson model, negative binomial model and BPNN approaches, since the three approaches are widely used in research on yield predicting and have been proved to be competitive [34–36]. Furthermore, the detail numerical comparison of the FNN approach, Poisson model, negative binomial model and BPNN approaches are demonstrated as follows.

Record	Number of defects	Mean number of defects/chip	...	Chip size parameter (cm²)	Clustering parameter	Process parameter 1	Process parameter 2	...	Process parameter 28	Yield (%)
1	21	0.14094	...	1	0.51836	322.7498	0.060865	...	1.169573	0.86577
2	45	0.30201	...	1	0.70814	324.4634	0.061573	...	1.172481	0.73826
3	16	0.10738	...	1	0.65597	322.1903	0.060648	...	1.176223	0.89262
4	21	0.14094	...	1	1.0277	313.9659	0.065036	...	1.162216	0.87248

Record	Number of defects	Mean number of defects/ chip	...	Chip size parameter (cm²)	Clustering parameter	Process parameter 1	Process parameter 2	...	Process parameter 28	Yield (%)
5	46	0.30872	...	1	0.59023	313.0953	0.068286	...	1.183461	0.73826
6	35	0.2349	...	1	0.73168	323.9832	0.061867	...	1.164384	0.81879
7	7	0.04698	...	1	0.73807	315.9001	0.059539	...	1.177436	0.95302
8	49	0.32886	...	1	0.75913	310.9356	0.060887	...	1.180799	0.72483
9	9	0.060403	...	1	0.57871	310.6571	0.06439	...	1.168414	0.9396
10	33	0.22148	...	1	0.83289	310.0921	0.068695	...	1.179983	0.80537
11	37	0.24832	...	1	0.69348	322.2567	0.068536	...	1.160716	0.77181
12	48	0.32215	...	1	0.9089	323.7277	0.069959	...	1.162259	0.73154
13	12	0.080537	...	1	0.6154	321.1246	0.067403	...	1.176334	0.91946
14	33	0.22148	...	1	0.85056	313.0574	0.068778	...	1.170839	0.78523
15	47	0.31544	...	1	1.0109	313.5133	0.063245	...	1.172714	0.72483
...	...	...	...	...	...	...	...	...	...	...
705	31	0.31959	...	1.44	1.0678	310.2484	0.065854	...	1.168734	0.82474
706	35	0.36082	...	1.44	0.67849	321.1613	0.06883	...	1.166041	0.83505
707	61	0.62887	...	1.44	1.00661	314.3752	0.066945	...	1.184936	0.75258
708	71	0.73196	...	1.44	0.95411	321.3472	0.061456	...	1.164627	0.7732
709	82	0.84536	...	1.44	1.5379	311.5562	0.060457	...	1.160369	0.73196
710	32	0.3299	...	1.44	1.2404	313.4114	0.067197	...	1.160229	0.80412
711	79	0.81443	...	1.44	1.5407	317.3192	0.067454	...	1.175912	0.7732
712	72	0.74227	...	1.44	2.4467	323.099	0.062285	...	1.171942	0.76289
713	58	0.59794	...	1.44	2.32601	318.6861	0.068344	...	1.174814	0.76289
714	57	0.58763	...	1.44	1.0014	316.3194	0.065981	...	1.173957	0.79381
715	73	0.75258	...	1.44	1.3139	322.1991	0.065962	...	1.180853	0.73196
716	46	0.47423	...	1.44	1.6882	320.4291	0.069517	...	1.166221	0.79381
717	80	0.82474	...	1.44	1.57021	316.6195	0.062461	...	1.16293	0.74227
718	38	0.39175	...	1.44	2.0034	317.0604	0.06606	...	1.171795	0.79381
719	18	0.18557	...	1.44	0.81646	323.2213	0.064985	...	1.167234	0.8866
720	72	0.74227	...	1.44	0.95479	319.6768	0.068621	...	1.175982	0.73196

Table 5. Partial wafer measurements parameters and yield.

4.2.1. Experiment on fuzzy neural network

The algorithm was programmed in Matlab 6.5, and ten factors were treated as input of the model, which are mean number of defects per chip, chip size, clustering parameter, mean number of defects per unit area, the number of defects per wafer and another five critical electrical test parameters.

Twenty-six rules for classification were identified the fuzzifier layer in the model. The 552 samples were utilized in the training of the FNN model with fivefold cross-validation. The learning process was explored in **Figure 7**. Afterward, the trained model was assessed by another 168 samples, which is demonstrated in **Table 6**. Furthermore, the linear regression analysis of the output of the FNN model is detailed in **Figure 8**.

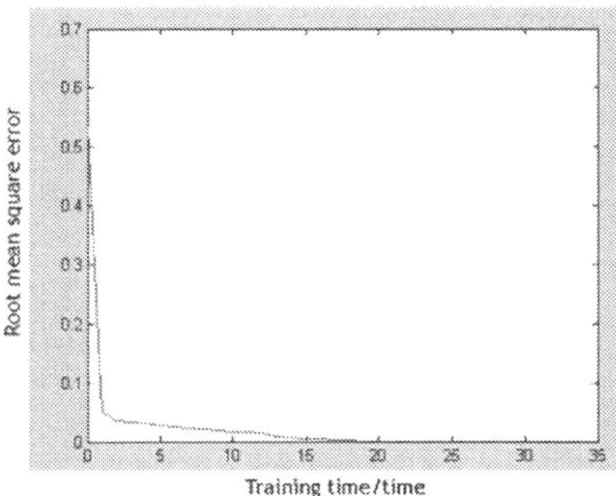

Figure 7. Fuzzy neural network learning curve.

Samples	The actual yield	The predicted yield	Relative error
1	0.72483	0.72514	0.000432
2	0.69128	0.69118	0.000146
3	0.8255	0.8337	0.009929
4	0.75168	0.74329	0.011168
5	0.75839	0.758	0.000513
6	0.73154	0.73031	0.001677
7	0.89933	0.89876	0.000632
8	0.75168	0.75211	0.000576
9	0.74497	0.74409	0.001179
10	0.75168	0.75002	0.002209
11	0.7651	0.7637	0.001824

Samples	The actual yield	The predicted yield	Relative error
12	0.85235	0.85658	0.004967
13	0.89933	0.90485	0.006143
14	0.9396	0.93918	0.000452
15	0.81208	0.81559	0.00432
...	...	...	...
160	0.75258	0.73323	0.025707
161	0.86598	0.84315	0.026365
162	0.74227	0.74376	0.002008
163	0.8866	0.88606	0.000609
164	0.73196	0.72817	0.005175
165	0.7732	0.76827	0.006381
166	0.75258	0.7456	0.009278
167	0.82474	0.83413	0.011391
168	0.83505	0.82249	0.01504

Table 6. The predicted yield based on FNN.

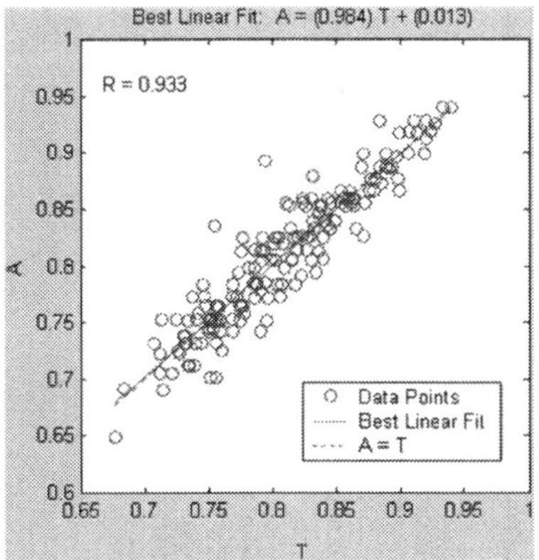

Figure 8. The linear regression analysis of the output of the FNN model.

4.2.2. Experiment of Poisson model

The Poisson model was built to predict wafer yield as follows.

$$Y = e^{-D_0 A}$$

(38)

In the model, Y means the wafer yield, D_0 denotes the defect density, and A is the chip size. The yield was forecasted by Poisson model, and the results of 168 samples can be found in **Table 7**. The lineal correlation analysis between the actual wafer yield and the prediction value is shown in **Figure 9**.

Samples	The actual yield	The predicted yield	Relative error
1	0.72483	0.57675	0.20429
2	0.69128	0.48117	0.30395
3	0.8255	0.79597	0.035769
4	0.75168	0.6552	0.12836
5	0.75839	0.66853	0.11849
6	0.73154	0.58064	0.20627
7	0.89933	0.89218	0.007953
8	0.75168	0.65081	0.13419
9	0.74497	0.61679	0.17206
10	0.75168	0.61267	0.18493
11	0.7651	0.59644	0.22044
12	0.85235	0.83988	0.014634
13	0.89933	0.87439	0.027733
14	0.9396	0.92883	0.011459
15	0.81208	0.74932	0.077284
...	...	...	...
160	0.75258	0.55222	0.26623
161	0.86598	0.75422	0.12905
162	0.74227	0.49038	0.33936
163	0.8866	0.84934	0.042026
164	0.73196	0.40431	0.44763
165	0.7732	0.48316	0.37512
166	0.75258	0.43547	0.42137
167	0.82474	0.75422	0.085502
168	0.83505	0.74311	0.1101

Table 7. The predicted yield based on the Poisson model.

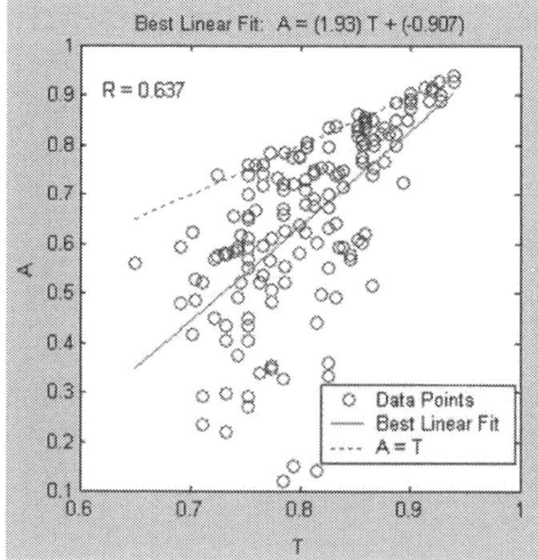

Figure 9. The linear regression analysis of the output of the Poisson model.

4.2.3. Experiment of negative binomial model

The negative binomial model is built to predict wafer yield as follows.

$$Y = \frac{1}{\left(1+D_0 A/a\right)^a} \tag{38}$$

In this model, Y means the defect-limited wafer yield, D_0 denotes the defect density, and A is the cluster coefficient. The yield was forecasted by negative binomial model and the results of 168 samples can be found in **Table 8**. The lineal correlation analysis between the actual wafer yield and the prediction value is shown in **Figure 10**.

Samples	The actual yield	The predicted yield	Relative error
1	0.72483	0.6395	0.11772
2	0.69128	0.57001	0.17543
3	0.8255	0.81257	0.015659
4	0.75168	0.69885	0.070289
5	0.75839	0.70919	0.064881
6	0.73154	0.64239	0.12187
7	0.89933	0.89708	0.002499
8	0.75168	0.69546	0.074787

Samples	The actual yield	The predicted yield	Relative error
9	0.74497	0.66949	0.10132
10	0.75168	0.66637	0.11349
11	0.7651	0.65417	0.14499
12	0.85235	0.85037	0.002326
13	0.89933	0.88098	0.020408
14	0.9396	0.93102	0.009135
15	0.81208	0.7737	0.047256
…	…	…	…
160	0.75258	0.61346	0.18486
161	0.86598	0.7748	0.10529
162	0.74227	0.5669	0.23626
163	0.8866	0.85746	0.032863
164	0.73196	0.50341	0.31225
165	0.7732	0.56152	0.27377
166	0.75258	0.52626	0.30072
167	0.82474	0.7748	0.06055
168	0.83505	0.76546	0.083336

Table 8. The predicted yield based on the negative binomial model.

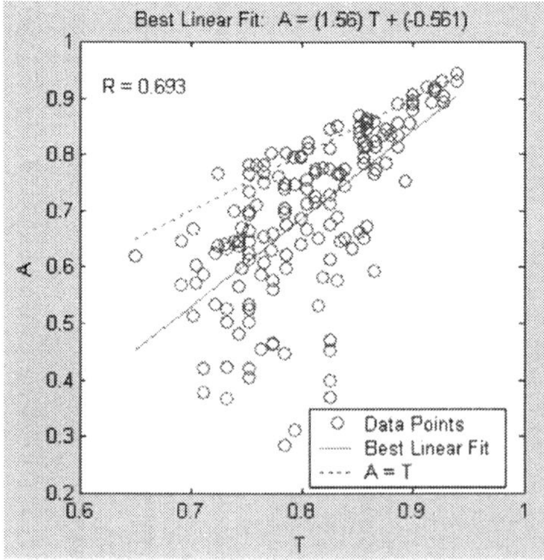

Figure 10. The linear regression analysis of the output of the negative binomial model.

4.2.4. Experiment of back-propagation neural network

A three layer BPNN is applied to predict wafer yield with ten input factors as same as the proposed FNN. The number of hidden neurons is determined by the empirical formula and selected to be 35. The yield was forecasted by BPNN and the results of 168 samples can be found in **Table 9**. The lineal correlation analysis between the actual wafer yield and the prediction value is shown in **Figure 11**.

Samples	The actual yield	The predicted yield	Relative error
1	0.72483	0.73495	0.013962
2	0.69128	0.7263	0.050661
3	0.8255	0.82385	0.001994
4	0.75168	0.76318	0.015293
5	0.75839	0.75985	0.001919
6	0.73154	0.75042	0.025807
7	0.89933	0.89876	0.000632
8	0.75168	0.76104	0.012456
9	0.74497	0.75932	0.019268
10	0.75168	0.73971	0.015921
11	0.7651	0.76666	0.002033
12	0.85235	0.83068	0.025423
13	0.89933	0.87383	0.028359
14	0.9396	0.93471	0.005204
15	0.81208	0.79469	0.021415
...	...	...	...
160	0.75258	0.72724	0.033671
161	0.86598	0.8581	0.009105
162	0.74227	0.7096	0.044007
163	0.8866	0.89151	0.005535
164	0.73196	0.68805	0.059996
165	0.7732	0.72722	0.059471
166	0.75258	0.71576	0.048929
167	0.82474	0.82683	0.00253
168	0.83505	0.82845	0.007907

Table 9. The predicted yield based on BPNN.

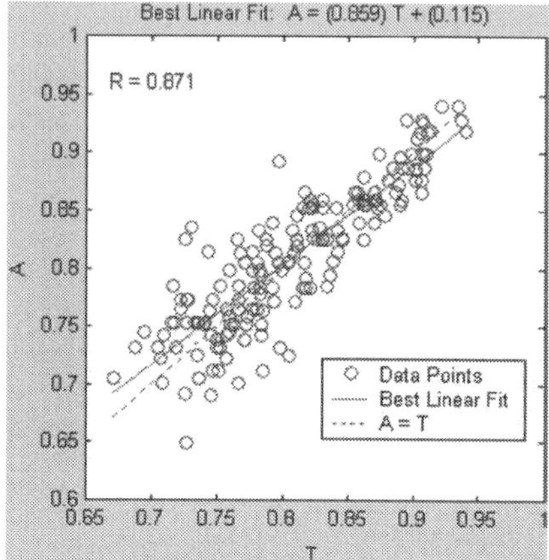

Figure 11. The linear regression analysis of the output of BPNN.

4.2.5. Results discussion

Aiming to assess the performance the proposed FNN methods, experiment with three contrast method was conducted for comparison. The lineal correlation analyses between the actual wafer yield and the prediction value of four methods are shown in **Figure 12**, which indicates that the FNN method outperforms other three methods from the view of convergence. The

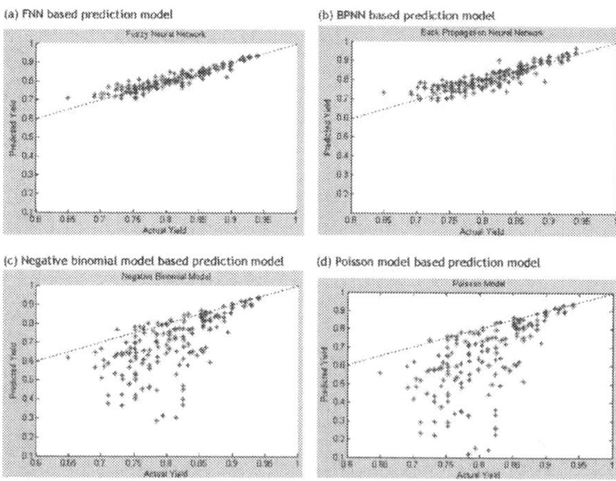

Figure 12. The relationship between the actual yields and predicted yields based on the FNN, BPNN and Poisson model and negative binomial model approach.

results of four methods in the RMSE and correlation coefficient R is presented in **Table 10**. The RMSE of the FNN method is 0.017, which is the smallest value above the four methods, and the R of the FNN-based model is 0.941, which is larger than other three methods. It indicates that the proposed FNN-based approach is more accurate and effective than other three methods, which are widely used in the yield predicting.

Yield prediction model	The actual yield		The predicted yield		RMSE	R
	Average	SD	Average	SD		
Poisson model	0.80864	0.06168	0.65394	0.18694	0.0169	0.637
Negative binomial model			0.70047	0.14789	0.0123	0.693
BPNN			0.80691	0.05736	0.0024	0.886
FNN			0.80838	0.05711	0.0017	0.941

Table 10. The comparisons of RMSE and correlation coefficients among the FNN, BPNN, Poisson model and negative binomial model.

5. Conclusion

The artificial neural networks (ANN) have a wide range of applications. For example, in complex discrete event manufacturing systems, they can be used to control, make decision and predict. SWFS is exactly such a complex manufacturing system. It has many characteristics, such as a mix of different process types, re-entrant flows, very expensive equipment and sequence dependent setup times and so on. In order to get more applications of ANN used in quality analysis and production scheduling in the semiconductor wafer fabrication system, this chapter implements two novel fuzzy neural networks that are used in the yield prediction of SWFS and rescheduling decision separately.

In the respect of rescheduling decision, this chapter puts forward a new method using a FNN model with which a system can make itself adapted to the current states and disturbances. In uncertain dynamic environments, current states and disturbances of the system are mathematically characterized. Rescheduling decision model, which assuming FNN builds the relationship between the inputs (i.e. disturbance, system state parameters) and the outputs (i.e. disturbance, system state parameters) of FNN. According to the current system disturbances, an optimal rescheduling method which can be used to schedule the semiconductor wafer fabrication lines is chosen by the make-decision model. We do experiment studies in Shanghai, which are based on 6-in. SWFS. The proposed rescheduling decision mechanism is proved to be effective by the linear regression between ideal targets and output of FNN. The rescheduling decision-making method which is proposed is demonstrated to be accurate by comparing with regression and traditional BPNN. We also do the comparison between the layered rescheduling method which is on the basis of FNN rescheduling decision mechanism and the two methods that are FCFS approach and the rescheduling approach based on the monolayer. The results indicate that, in respect of machine utilization and daily movement, layered rescheduling method, which is on the basis of FNN rescheduling decision mechanism, is superior to the other two approaches.

A yield prediction method for semiconductor manufacturing systems which is on the basis of new fuzzy neural networks is proposed for the yield prediction. This method builds the yield prediction model based on FNN by using the following parameters as input variables, which are the number of defects in each wafer, mean number of defects in each chip, mean number of defects in each unit area, clustering parameter, chip size and five critical electrical test parameters.

According to the data from the experiment studies in Shanghai which are based on 6-in. SWFS. The proposed rescheduling decision mechanism is proved to be effective by the linear regression between ideal targets and output of FNN. The rescheduling decision-making method which is proposed is demonstrated to be accurate by comparing with regression and traditional BPNN. The approach proposed in this paper has the advantage that it considers more variables' influences than other model such as negative binomial yield model, BPNN model and Poisson yield model. The variables here include physical parameters of wafer, key attributed parameters of defects and wafer electrical test parameters on wafer yield and so on. In a word, the model proposed in this paper is more accurate than the other traditional yield prediction approaches.

Acknowledgements

This work was supported by the State Key Program of the National Natural Science Foundation of China under Grant No. 51435009.

Author details

Jie Zhang*, Junliang Wang and Wei Qin

*Address all correspondence to: zhangjie_cims@hotmail.com

School of Mechanical Engineering, Shanghai Jiao Tong University, Shanghai, China

References

[1] Uzsoy, R., et al., A review of production planning and scheduling models in the semiconductor industry. Part II: shop-floor control IIE Transactions, 1994, 26(5): 44–55.

[2] Leachman, R.C., The competitive semiconductor manufacturing survey. IEEE international symposium on semiconductor manufacturing conference, 20–21 September 1993, Austin, Texas, USA. Piscataway, NJ: IEEE, 1993: 359–381.

[3] Uzsoy, R., et al., A review of production planning and scheduling models in the semiconductor industry. Part I: system characteristics, performance evaluation and production planning, IIE Transactions, 1992, 24(4): 47–60.

[4] Cheng, M., Sugi, M., Ota, J., Yamamoto, M., Ito, H., and Inoue, K., A fast rescheduling method in semiconductor manufacturing allowing for tardiness and scheduling stability. Proceeding of the 2006 IEEE, international conference on automation science and engineering, Shanghai, China, October, 2006: 7–10.

[5] Huang, H.P. and Chen, T.Y., A new approach to on-line rescheduling for a semiconductor foundry Fab. 2006 IEEE international conference on systems, man, and cybernetics, Taipei, China, October, 2006: 8–11.

[6] Kumar, R., Tiwari, M.K., and Allada, V., Modelling and rescheduling of a re-entrant wafer fabrication line involving machine unreliability, International Journal of Production Research, 2004, 42(21): 4431–4455.

[7] Maosn, S.J., Jin, S., and Wessels, M., Rescheduling strategies for minimizing total weighted tardiness in complex job shops, International Journal of Production Research, 2004, 42(3): 613–628.

[8] Toba, H., Segment-based approach for real-time reactive rescheduling for automatic manufacturing control, IEEE Transactions on Semiconductor Manufacturing, 2000, 13(3): 264–272.

[9] Tsai, C.J., and Huang, H.P., A real-time scheduling and rescheduling system based on RFID for semiconductor foundry fabs, Journal of the Chinese Institute of Industrial Engineers, 2007, 24(6): 437–444.

[10] Kumar, P.R., Scheduling semiconductor manufacturing plants, IEEE Control Systems Magazine, 1994, 14(6): 33–40.

[11] Kumar, N., et al., A review of yield modeling techniques for semiconductor manufacturing, International Journal of Production Research, 2006, 44(23): 5019–5036.

[12] Cunningham, S.P. and Spanos, C.J., Semiconductor yield improvement: results and best practices, IEEE Transactions on Semiconductor Manufacturing, 1995, 8(2): 103–109.

[13] Tong, L.-I. and Chao, L.-C., Novel yield model for integrated circuit with clustered defects, Expert Systems with Applications, 2008, 34: 2334–2341.

[14] Zhang, J., Qin, W., Wu, L.H., et al., Fuzzy neural network-based rescheduling decision mechanism for semiconductor manufacturing, Computers in Industry, 2014, 65(8): 1115–1125.

[15] Wu, L.H., Zhang, J., Fuzzy neural network based yield prediction model for semiconductor manufacturing system, International Journal of Production Research, 2010, 48(48): 3225–3243.

[16] Li, X.L., Yao, Y.X., and Yuan, Z.J., On-line tool condition monitoring system with wavelet fuzzy neural network, Journal of Intelligent Manufacturing, 1997, 8(4): 271–276.

[17] Zhou, Y.F., Li, S.J., Jin, R.C., A new fuzzy neural network with fast learning algorithm and guaranteed stability for manufacturing process control, Fuzzy Sets and Systems, 2002, 132(2): 201–216.

[18] Chang, P.C., Wang, Y.W., and Ting, C.J., A fuzzy neural network for the flow time estimation in a semiconductor manufacturing factory, International Journal of Production Research, 2008, 46(4): 1017–1029.

[19] Xu, D.M., and Yan, H.S., An intelligent estimation method for product design time, International Journal of Advanced Manufacturing Technology, 2006, 30(7–8): 601–613.

[20] Chang, Y.J., Kang, Y., Kang, Y., Hsu, C.L., Chang, C.T., and Chan, T.Y., Virtual metrology technique for semiconductor manufacturing. IEEE international conference on neural networks-conference proceedings, international joint conference on neural networks, Vancouver, BC, Canada, July, 2006: 5289–5293.

[21] Tong, L.-I., Lee, W.-I., and Su, C.-T., Using a neural network-based approach to predict the wafer yield in integrated circuit manufacturing, IEEE Transactions on Components, Packaging, and Manufacturing Technology – Part C, 1997, 20(4): 288–294.

[22] Tong, L.-I. and Chao, L.-C., Novel yield model for integrated circuit with clustered defects. Expert Systems with Applications, 2008, 34: 2334–2341.

[23] Chen, T. and Wang, M.J., A fuzzy set approach for yield learning modeling in wafer manufacturing, IEEE Transactions on Semiconductor Manufacturing, 1999, 12(2): 252–258.

[24] Chen, T. and Lin, Y.C., A fuzzy-neural system incorporating unequally important expert opinions for semiconductor yield forecasting, International Journal of Uncertainty, Fuzziness and Knowledge-Based Systems, 2008, 16(1): 35–58.

[25] Chung, K.S. and Sang, C.P., A machine learning approach to yield management in semiconductor manufacturing, International Journal of Production Research, 2000, 38(17): 4261–4271.

[26] Kim, T.S., et al., Yield prediction models for optimisation of high-speed micro-processor manufacturing processes. 26th IEEE/CPMT international electronics manufacturing technology symposium, 2–3 October 2000, Santa Clara, CA, USA. Piscataway, NJ: IEEE, 2000: 368–373.

[27] Kim, T.S., Intelligent yield and speed prediction models for high-speed microprocessors. IEEE electronic components and technology conference, 28–31 May 2002, San Diego, CA, USA. Piscataway, NJ: IEEE, 2002: 1158–1162.

[28] Zhai, W.B., Chu, X.N., Zhang, J., Ma, D., Jin, Y., and Yan, J.Q., Research of combination auction based short-term scheduling technology of semiconductor fabrication line, Journal of Mechanical Engineering, 2004, 40(9): 95–99.

[29] Zhai, W.B., Zhang, J., Yan, J.Q., and Ma, D., Research of ETAEMS/GPGP-CN based on dynamic scheduling technology of semiconductor fabrication, Journal of Mechanical Engineering, 2005, 46(3): 53–58.

[30] Wang, J., and Malakooti, B., Feed-forward neural network for multiple criteria decision making, Computer & Operations Research, 1992, 19(2): 151–167.

[31] Malhotra, M.K., Sharma, S., and Nair, S.S., Decision making using multiple models, European Journal of Operational Research, 1999, 114(1): 1–14.

[32] Wong, A.Y., A statistical parametric and probe yield analysis methodology. Proceedings of IEEE international symposium on defect and fault tolerance in VLSI systems, 6–8 November 1996, Boston, MA, USA. Los Alamitos, CA: IEEE Comput. Soc. Press, 1996, 131–139.

[33] Jun, C.-H., et al., A simulation-based semiconductor chip yield model incorporating a new defect cluster index, Microelectronics Reliability, 1999, 39: 451–456.

[34] Cunningham, J.A., The use and evaluation of yield models in integrated circuit manufacturing, IEEE Transactions on Semiconductor Manufacturing, 1990, 3(2): 60–71.

[35] Aakash, T. and Bayoumi, M.A., Defect clustering viewed through generalised Poisson distribution, IEEE Transactions on Semiconductor Manufacturing, 1992, 5(3): 196–206.

[36] Koren, I., Koren, Z., and Stepper, C.H., A unified negative binomial distribution for yield analysis of defect-tolerant circuits. IEEE Transactions on Computers, 1993, 42: 724–734.

Chapter 15

Neural Network Inverse Modeling for Optimization

Oscar May , Luis J. Ricalde , Bassam Ali ,

Eduardo Ordoñez López ,

Eduardo Venegas-Reyes and Oscar A. Jaramillo

Additional information is available at the end of the chapter

http://dx.doi.org/10.5772/63678

Abstract

In this chapter, artificial neural networks (ANNs) inverse model is applied for estimating the thermal performance (η) in parabolic trough concentrator (PTC). A recurrent neural network architecture is trained using the Kalman Filter learning from experimental database obtained from PTCs operations. Rim angle (ϕ_r), inlet (T_{in}), outlet (T_{out}) fluid temperatures, ambient temperature (T_a), water flow (F_w), direct solar radiation (Gb) and the wind velocity (V_w) were used as main input variables within the neural network model in order to estimate the thermal performance with an excellent agreement (R^2=0.999) between the experimental and simulated values. The optimal operation conditions of parabolic trough concentrator are established using artificial neural network inverse modeling. The results, using experimental data, showed that the recurrent neural network (RNN) is an excellent tool for modeling and optimization of PTCs.

Keywords: solar concentrating, thermal efficiency, neural networks, Kalman training optimization, solar energy

1. Introduction

About 80% of the energy consumed worldwide come from conventional energy sources, where more than 50% is used by the industry being a large part of this demand for the generation of heat industrial process [1, 2]. However, the use of fossil fuels to satisfy this demand has led to severe environmental impacts, which together with the decline of this resource has led to global energy policies focus on replacing fossil fuels with sustainable energy sources. The use of solar thermal systems could help to reduce CO_2 emissions and other pollutants in the atmosphere.

© 2016 The Author(s). Licensee InTech. This chapter is distributed under the terms of the Creative Commons Attribution License (http://creativecommons.org/licenses/by/3.0), which permits unrestricted use, distribution, and reproduction in any medium, provided the original work is properly cited.

Solar energy is one of the renewable energies that attract more attention due to its abundance, cleanliness, and the fact that it does not generate any pollution [3]. On the other hand, in the industries exist several processes that require thermal energy with temperature range between 60 and 250 °C for heat process generation; industries such as dairies, plastics, canned food, textile, paper, etc. employ this kind of energy to process such as drying, sterilizing, cleaning, evaporation, steam and conditioning warehouses space for both heating and cooling [4]. This energy could be easily supplied by solar collectors using photothermal conversion. The thermal storage process is used to supply the required power loading when there is no sunlight. Amongst the middle-temperature solar collectors are the parabolic trough, Fresnel, compound parabolic collectors (CPCs) and evacuated tubes. In this work, we consider parabolic trough solar concentrators (PTCs) that could yield the heat within the temperature between 90 and 400 °C. Parabolic trough solar concentrators (PTCs) are one of the most mature technologies developed in this area [5]. Nevertheless, the use of this technology entails certain difficulties because of a large number of operational and environmental parameters. This becomes an extremely complicated study on these systems, creating complex nonlinear equations for compression, which results in the employment of sophisticated control systems to operate and optimize the PTC performance, in order to maximize its cost-benefit during the operation. The modeling and simulation of these systems should take into account the collector, the thermal load, and the losses to the environment and the power auxiliary supply.

In the last decades, in the area of renewable energy, the employ of computational intelligence methods such as artificial neural networks (ANN) has been rising to perform modeling and optimization process [6] because all the information based on renewable energy systems is very volatile and it has too much noise and also the behavior does not present a linear trend. In recent years, one of the most promising approaches for modeling and control of the highly nonlinear processes is the use of recurrent neural network. For most applications on time series forecasting, recurrent neural network (RNN) using the back-propagation learning algorithm has presented good results. However, this learning law is based on the gradient descent method and its convergence speed could not meet the requirements when fast responses are needed. Another well-known training algorithm is the Levenberg-Marquardt whose main disadvantage is that it does not guarantee finding the global minimum and its learning speed could be slow since it depends on the initialization values. To overcome the learning speed and uncertainties issues, recently, the extended Kalman Filter (EKF)-based algorithms have been implemented to train neural networks. With the EKF-based algorithm, the learning convergence is improved [6]. Using the EKF training on recurrent neural networks drives to improve results mostly in control, identification and predictions applications where the critical variables are subject to uncertainties and unmodeled dynamics. However, the EKF training requires the heuristic selection of some design parameters, which is not always an easy task.

This chapter is focused on presenting the methodology used to conduct the process of modeling the thermal efficiency of an array of PTCs, in order to bring the system to optimal operating conditions through a desired efficiency by using ANN. The chapter is divided into five sections: Section 2 describes the experimental system composed by parabolic trough solar concentrations; Section 3 details the artificial neural network as modeling tool; Section 5 presents the development of the inverse modeling for optimization; and Section 6 describes the conclusions.

2. Experimental system: parabolic trough solar concentrations

2.1. Experiment description

The experimental system corresponds to a low enthalpy steam generation plant built according to the ASHRAE 93-1986 (RA 91) standard [7]; it is composed by:

- three PTCs (with 90° rim angle) with a length of 2.44 m and an aperture of 1.06 m;

- two storage thermic tanks of 120 L capacity which cover two functions: the first is to preheat the water for the characterization of PTC employing electrical resistances inside the tanks (the first with 3 kW and second with 6 kW) and the second is to store the energy produced by PTCs;

- a hydraulic circuit and two centrifugal water pumps of ½ HP is employed to recirculate the preheated water to PTCs and then return it to the tanks;

- a set of sensors consisting in a Hedland HB2800 flow meters, pressure and temperature meters at the storage thermic tanks outlet, such as pressure and temperature meters at the outlet of PTCs.

For the measurement of environmental conditions, a pyranometer, an anemometer and temperature sensors were employed. **Figure 1** shows the diagram of the experimental system.

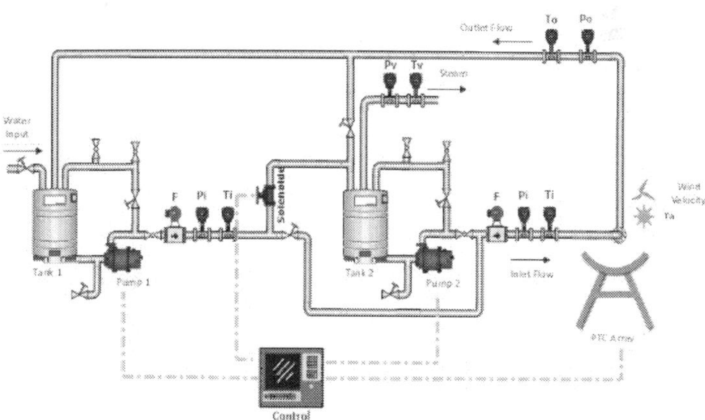

Figure 1. Operation diagram of parabolic solar concentration experimental system.

2.2. Performance of parabolic trough solar collector (PTC)

A parabolic trough solar concentrator consists of a shaped channel sheet with parabolic cross-section whose surface must have a high reflectance value (ρ); at the focus of parabola (f) is situated an absorber metal tube covered with a selective surface with high absorptivity (α) and low emissivity (ε). A glass tube with high transmissivity (τ) is placed concentric to the absorber to minimize the convective losses; in the same way, the space between both tubes must be evacuated to avoid the conduction losses. Inside the absorber tube, the working fluid gains energy due to the concentration of solar irradiation at the focal line resulting in the temperature increase of the working fluid [8]. **Figure 2** shows cross-section of a PTC.

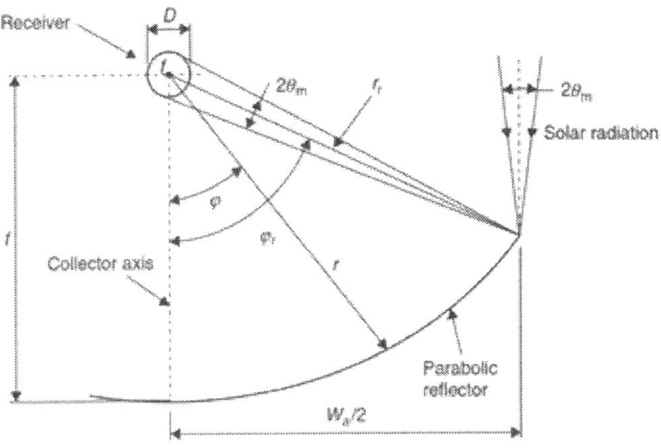

Figure 2. Parabolic trough solar concentrator.

Rim angle (ϕ_r)	a	B	c
40°	2	1.5795	1.4927
50°	2	1.7404	1.5199
60°	18	14.420	5.6055
70°	2	2.3000	1.5974
80°	2	2.7846	1.6485
90°	2	2.8284	2.4142

Table 1. Constant values respect the rim angle.

One of the most practical ways to calculate the dimensions of a PTC by considering the curve length S of the reflective surface is given by:

$$S = \frac{f}{a}\left(b - \frac{a}{2}\ln(f^2) + a\ln(cf)\right) \tag{1}$$

where the coefficients a, b and c are determinates by the angle that form the parabolic surface with respect to the focal line which is called rim angle (ϕ_r). **Table 1** shows the values of this these coefficients for different rim angles.

Another important parameter related to the rim angle (ϕ_r) is the aperture of the parabola (W_a). From **Figure 2** and simple trigonometry, it can be found [9] that:

$$W_a = 4f\tan\left(h_p/2\right) \tag{2}$$

where h_p is the latus rectum of the parabola.

2.2.1. Optical performance

The optical efficiency (η_0) of a PTC is defined as the ratio of solar energy that falls on the surface of the absorber tube and that which falls on the reflective surface of the collector. It is commonly given as [10]:

$$\eta_o = \rho\tau\alpha\gamma\left[\left(1 - A_f\tan(\theta)\right)\cos(\theta)\right] \tag{3}$$

where θ is the factor intersection receptor, θ is the sun rays incident angle and A_f is the ratio of the area of loss and opening area of the PTC (called geometric factor).

There are two types of errors associated with the parabolic surface: random and no random. The first type of errors is apparent changes in the sun width, scattering effects caused by random slope errors and associated with the reflective surface; these can be represented by normal probability distributions. The second class of errors depends on the manufacturing and operation of the collector. These errors are due to the reflector profile imperfections, misalignment and receiver location errors [11]. Random errors are modeled statistically to calculate the standard deviation of the distribution of the total energy reflected at normal incidence [12]:

$$\sigma_{Tot} = \sqrt{\sigma_{sol}^2 + 4\sigma_{pend}^2 + \sigma_{ref}^2} \tag{4}$$

where σ_{sol} is the standard deviation of the distribution of solar form, σ_{pend} is the standard deviation of the slope errors and σ_{ref} is the standard deviation of the distribution of the errors of the reflective surface.

2.2.2. Thermal performance

The experimental evaluation for thermal performing of PTC is realized according to the ASHRAE 93-1986 (RA 91) standard [7]. This standard provides a widely known method to obtain the thermal efficiency of solar energy collector that uses single phase fluids, in order to be compared with the similar solar collectors [13]. Therefore according to the standard, the thermal instantaneous efficiency (η_g) on a PTC is evaluated experimentally by considering:

$$\eta_g = \frac{m' C_p (T_o - T_i)}{(A_a G_b)} \tag{5}$$

where T_i and T_o are the inlet and outlet temperatures, respectively, m' is the mass flow rate, C_p is the specific heat, A_a is the aperture area of the collector and G_b is the direct solar irradiation component in the aperture plane of the collector. To avoid the phase change in the water that is used as thermal fluid, T_i is restricted between 20 and 90°C.

On the other hand, the PTC thermal efficiency (η_T) employing the first law of thermodynamic is given by [8]:

$$\eta_T = F_R \left[\eta_o - \frac{U_L}{C_o} \left(\frac{\Delta T}{G_b} \right) \right] \tag{6}$$

where ($\Delta T = T_i\ T_a$) is the temperature rise across the receiver, and T_a is the environmental temperature. As can be seen, Eq. (6) has the form of an equation of line, where $F_R U_L / C_O$ represents the pediment and $F_R \eta_o$ represents the interception. This relation can be applied to obtain experimentally the heat removal factor F_R and the overall heat loss coefficient U_L for a PTC.

3. Artificial neural network as modeling tool

3.1. Artificial recurrent neural networks

Artificial neural networks (ANN) are adaptive systems developed in the form of computational algorithms or electrics circuits, which are inspired in the biological neuron system operation. An ANN is composed of a large number of interconnected units called neurons that have a certain natural tendency for learning information from the outside world [14]. These structures are used to estimate or approximate functions that may depend on a lot of variables, which are generally unknown reason for why the ANN have been used in many practical applications such as pattern recognition, estimation of series time and modeling of nonlinear processes [15].

A model of ANN can be seen as a black box to which is entered a database composed of a series of input variables; each of these input variables is assigned an appropriate weighting factor called weight (W). The sum of the weighted inputs and the use of bias (b) for adjustment produce an input value applied to a transfer function to generate an output (**Figure 3**). The main feature of these models is that they do not require specific information on the physical behavior of the system or how they were obtained data [16].

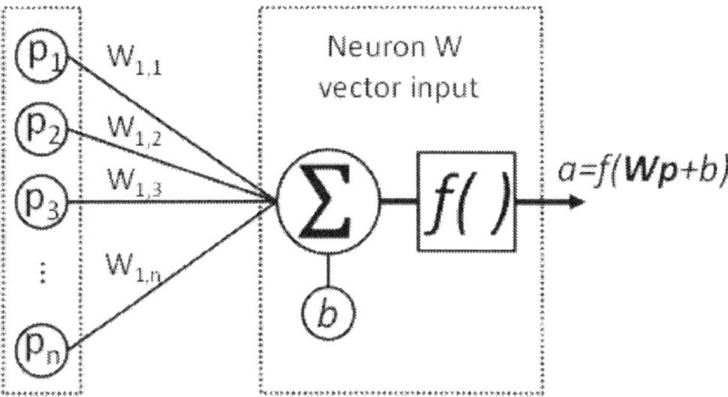

Figure 3. Artificial neuron with n inputs.

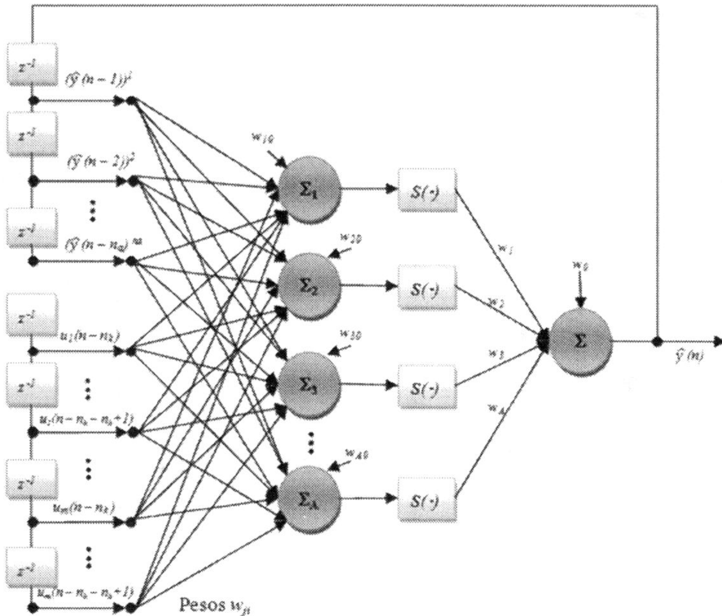

Figure 4. Recurrent neural network.

Among the many existing ANN models the most widely used is known as multi-layer perceptron (MLP) [17], which is used to solve multivariable problems by nonlinear equations using a process called training. The training process is performed through specific learning algorithms, where the most widely used is known as back-propagation through time [18]. The architecture of an MLP is usually divided into three parts known as: input layer, hidden layer and output layer. During the training process, the MLP learns from past errors to get a model that describes as closely as possible to the nonlinear phenomenon. To carry out this, during the training phase they adapt the weight and bias parameters until the approximation error is minimized [19].

A recurrent neural network responds temporally to an external input signal where the feedback allows the RNN to have a representation in state space; this versatility makes them convenient for diverse applications for modeling, optimization and control. The order in an RNN refers to the form in which the neuron activation potential is defined [20]. When the local activation potential is combined with products of signals coming from of the feedback or when products are made between the later and the external input signals to the network, a neural network of order emerges, where the order represents the number of signals that are multi-plied. In this work, in order to carry out modeling of the process, a high order recurrent neural network is designed. The structure is composed by an input vector, one hidden layer and an output layer composed of just one neuron with a linear activation function. In **Figure 4**, the designed recurrent neural network architecture is depicted.

According to **Figure 4**, $\rho_i(k)$ is the input i to the neural network, $v_j(k)$ is the neuron j activation potential, $y_j(k)$ represents the neuron j output, $v(k)$ is the output neuron activation potential, $\hat{y}(k)$ is the neuron output in the output layer (neural network output), $\phi(v_j(k))$ represents the neuron j activation function, $\phi(v(k))$ is the activation function of the output layer neuron, $w_{ji}(k)$ is the weight connecting the input i to the neuron j input, $w_j(k)$ is the weight connecting neuron j output to the neuron input in the output layer, and s and A are the inputs total number to the neurons in the hidden and output layers, respectively.

For the set of weights, we construct a weight vector that will be estimated by means of the Kalman Filtering. The Kalman Filtering (KF) algorithm was first designed as a method to estimate the state of a system under noise on the process and on the measurement. Consider a linear, discrete-time dynamical system described by

$$w(k+1) = F_{k+1,}w(k) + v_1(k) \tag{7}$$

$$y(k) = H(k)w(k) + v_2(k) \tag{8}$$

Eq. (7) is known as the process equation; $F_{k+1,k}$ is the transition matrix taking the state $w(k)$ from iteration k to iteration $k+1$ and $v_1(k)$ is the process noise. On the other hand, Eq. (8) is known as the output measurement, which represents $y(k)$ i.e. the observable part of the state at iteration k, $H(k)$ is the measurement matrix and $v_2(k)$ is the measurement noise. Both the process noise $v_1(k)$ and the measurement noise $v_2(k)$ are assumed as white noise with covariance matrices given by $E[v_1(l)v_1T(l)]=\delta_{k,l}Q(k)$ and $E[v_2(l)v_2T(l)]=\delta_{k,l}R(k)$. To deal with the nonlinear structure of the recurrent neural network mapping, an EKF algorithm is developed. The learning algorithm for the recurrent neural network based on the EKF is described as

$$K(k) = P(k)H^T(k)\left[R + H(k)P(k)H^T(k)\right], w(k+1) =$$
$$w(k) + K(k)\left[y(k) - \hat{y}(k)\right], P(k+1) = P(k) - K(k)H(k)P(k) + Q \tag{9}$$

where $P(k)$ and $P(k+1)$ are the prediction error covariance matrices, $w(k)$ is the neural weight vector, $y(k)$ is the measured output vector, $y(k)$ is the neural network output, $K(k)$ is the Kalman gain matrix, and Q and R are the state and measurement noise covariance matrices. The matrices P, Q and R are assumed to be diagonal and are initialized using random values P_0, Q_0 and R_0, respectively.

The $H(k)$ matrix is defined with each derivative of one of the neural network output, (y_i), with respect to one neural network weight, (w_j), as follows:

$$H_{ij}(k) = \left.\frac{\partial \hat{y}_i(k)}{\partial w_j(k)}\right|_{w(k)=\hat{w}(k+1)} \qquad i = 1,\ldots,o; \quad j = 1,\ldots,NW$$

where NW is the total number of neural network weights and o is the total number of outputs.

4. ANN inverse model

In order to solve the optimization problem proposed, a computational intelligence methodology is developed. The proposed approach is divided into two parts: first is the generation of a mathematical model by RNN and the second part is responsible for performing inverse neural network for the optimization process. **Figure 5** displays the methodology divided into three steps: (i) the first step consist in generate a database with the most important parameters

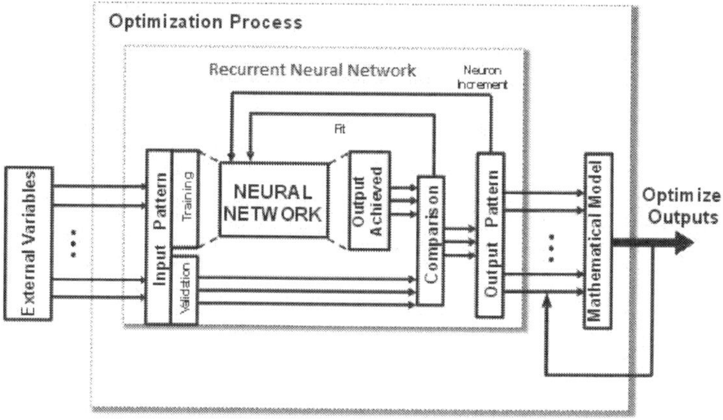

Figure 5. Optimization by neural network methodology.

that could affect the desired output, which is schematized in **Figure 6**, which in our case is the thermal efficiency, (ii) in the second step an RNN model is trained to obtain the best approximation error that relates the inputs with desirable outputs; (iii) in the last step one of the RNN inputs is selected to function as a control variable to perform the optimization process by an inverse neural network architecture.

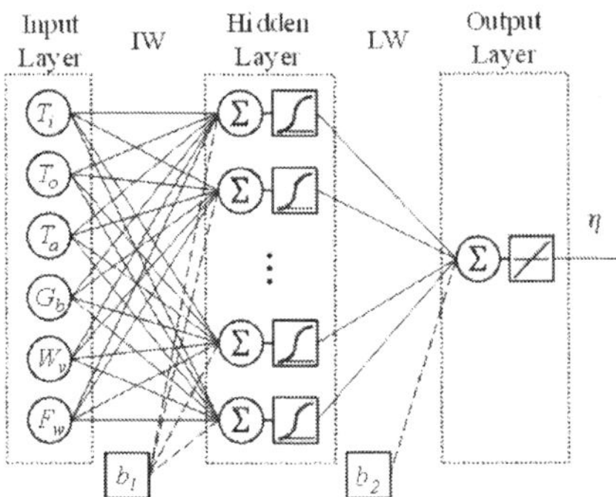

Figure 6. Neural network architecture for the mathematic model of thermal efficiency.

Parameters	Min	Max	Units
Input			
Operational variables			
Inlet flow temperature (T_{in})	27.75	86.30	[°C]
Outlet flow temperature (T_{out})	34.70	100.2	[°C]
Flow working fluid (F_w)	0.94	6.11	[L/min]
Environmental variables			
Ambient temperature (T_{amb})	24.26	33.99	[°C]
Direct solar radiation (G_b)	830.0	1014	[W/m²]
Wind velocity (V_w)	0.95	3.98	[m/s²]
Output			
Thermal efficiency (Eff)	0.16	0.63	[–]

Table 2. Parameters employed at the ANN prediction model.

Experimental database provided by Jaramillo et al. [13], consists of different η values calculated from the thermodynamic parabolic trough concentrator model (Eqs. (5) and (6)). The parameter measurements are divided into two categories: operational variables conformed by inlet temperature (T_i) and outlet temperature (T_o) working fluid, as well as flow working fluid (F_w); and environmental variables composed by ambient temperature (T_a), direct solar radiation (G_b) and wind velocity (V_w). **Table 2** shows the six parameters that form the database and the minimum and maximum ranges of each one.

The development of predictive mathematical model of the experimental database was divided into two processes; the main process (in these case 80%) was destined to RNN learning and testing process and the other part (20%) was employed for the validation of the results, in order to obtain a good representation of the data distribution.

At the training process, a normalized database was entered into a MLP architecture, where the number of neurons at the input and output layers was given by the number of input and output variables in the process, respectively. The Kalman Filter training algorithm in Eq. (9) was employed to obtain the optimum weights and bias for the RNN model as the one displayed in **Figure 4**.

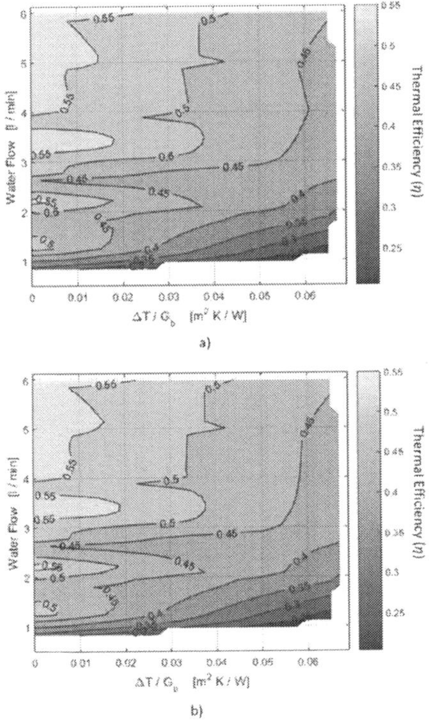

Figure 7. Thermal efficiency validation. (a) Experimental thermal efficiency not included at training and (b) simulate thermal efficiency from RNN model.

To validate the MLP model, a comparison was carried out employing the data not included in the training process. The output values comparison (thermal efficiency) was made in function of two variables, the heat loss parameter ($\Delta T/G_b$) and the working fluid flow. **Figure 7a** shows the real behavior of the thermal efficiency of the system in function of both parameters (heat loss parameter and fluid flow) and where can be seen a trend to decrease when ΔT increases [21]. Furthermore, **Figure 7b** represents the values of thermal efficiency obtained from the mathematical model generated with MLP where an appropriate reproduction of the real efficiency curves can be seen, demonstrating that the model is capable of adapting to the variations of flow and heat losses.

4.1. Optimization of the inverse artificial neural network

Once generated the desired mathematical model and proven effective, an optimization process is applied. To perform the optimization analysis, an input variable must be selected as control input. The selected variable in the present application was the water flow since it can be manipulated and quickly impact the system behavior. For the optimization process, the output generated by the ANN model (thermal efficiency) acts as input to a process modeled from experimental values, generating as output a control variable that minimizes the difference for the desired thermal efficiency. **Figure 8** displays the inverse ANN architecture.

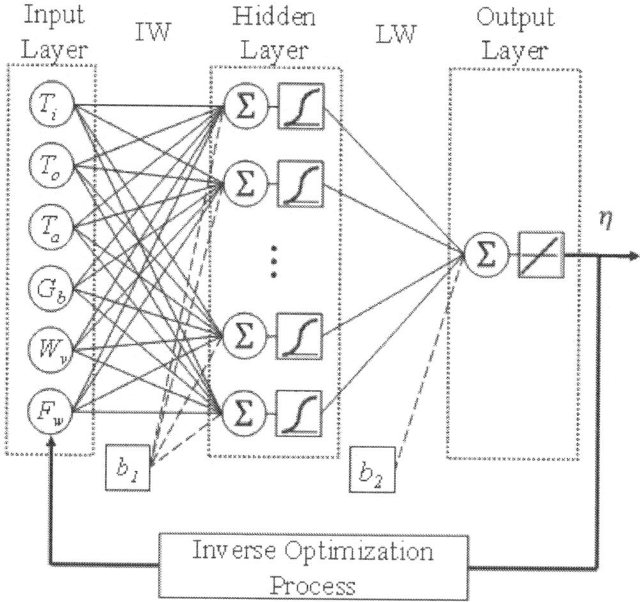

Figure 8. Inverse artificial neural network.

5. Conclusions

The aim of this chapter was to design an artificial neural network algorithm to predict the thermal performance of a parabolic trough concentrator, in order to develop a new approach for the estimation of the optimal operation condition of PTCs for a desired efficiency. A recurrent neural network was applied to model the nonlinear characteristics of the process with an excellent approximation of the thermal efficiency.

Author details

Oscar May[1], Luis J. Ricalde[1*], Bassam Ali[1], Eduardo Ordoñez López[1],
Eduardo Venegas-Reyes[2] and Oscar A. Jaramillo[3]

*Address all correspondence to: lricalde@correo.uady.mx

1 Universidad Autónoma de Yucatán, Facultad de Ingeniería, Av. Industrias no Contaminantes por Periférico Norte, Cordemex, Mérida, Yucatán, México

2 Investigador de Cátedras CONACYT, Centro de Investigación en Materiales Avanzados, Centro, Durango, México

3 Instituto de Energías Renovables, Universidad Nacional Autónoma de México, Privada Xochicalco s/n, Temixco, Morelos, México

References

[1] Zou B., Dong J., Yao Y., Jiang Y., An experimental investigation on a small-sized parabolic trough solar collector for water heating in cold areas, Applied Energy 163, 396–407, 2016.

[2] Fernández-García A., Rojas E., Pérez M., Silva R., Hernández-Escobedo Q., Manzano-Agugliaro F., A parabolic-trough collector for cleaner industrial process heat, Journal of Cleaner Production 89, 272–285, 2015.

[3] Mekhilef S., Saidur R., Safar A., A review of solar energy use in industries, Renewable and Sustainable Energy Reviews, 1777–1790, 2011.

[4] Venegas-Reyes E., Jaramillo O.A., Castrejón-García R., Aguilar J.O., Sosa-Montemayor F., Design, construction, and testing of a parabolic trough solar concentrator for hot water and low enthalpy steam generation. Journal of Renewable Sustainable Energy 4, 053103, 2012.

[5] Lamba D.K., A review on parabolic trough type solar collectors: innovation, applications and thermal energy storage. Proceedings of the National Conference on Trends and Advances in Mechanical Engineering; 2011. pp. 90–99.

[6] Sanchez E.N., Alanis A.Y., Rico J., Electric load demand prediction using neural networks trained by Kalman Filtering. IEEE International Joint Conference on Neural Networks, Budapest, Hungary; 2004. pp. 2771–2775.

[7] ANSI/ASHRAE 93-1986 (RA 91). Methods of testing to determine the thermal performance of solar collectors. American Society of Heating, Refrigerating and Air-Conditioning Engineers, Inc.; 1991.

[8] Kalogirou S., Solar Energy Engineering: Processes and Systems. USA: Academic Press; 2009. ISBN 978-0-12-374501-9.

[9] Duffie J., Beckman W., Solar Engineering of Thermal Processes. New Jersey: Elsevier; 2013.

[10] Valan-Arasu A, Sornakumar T., Design, manufacture and testing of fiberglass reinforced parabola trough for parabolic trough solar collectors. Solar Energy 81(10), 1273–1279, 2007.

[11] Güven H.M., Bannerot R.B., Determination of error tolerances for the optical design of parabolic troughs for developing countries. Solar Energy 36, 535–550, 1986.

[12] Rabl A., Active Solar Collectors and their Applications. New York, USA: Oxford University Press; 1984. ISBN 0-19-503546-1.

[13] Jaramillo O.A., Venegas-Reyes E., Aguilar J.O., Castrejón-García R., Sosa Montemayor F., Parabolic trough concentrators for low enthalpy processes. Renewable Energy 60, 529–539, 2013.

[14] Lippmann R.P., An introduction to computing with neural nets. IEEE ASSP Magazine 4(2), 4–22, 1987.

[15] Haykin S., Neural Networks. 2nd ed. Prentice Hall, New Jersey, USA, 1999.

[16] Bassam A., Conde-Gutierrez R. A., Castillo J., Laredo G., Direct neural network modeling for separation of linear and branched paraffins by adsorption process for gasoline octane number improvement. Fuel 124 (15) 158–167, 2014.

[17] Rumelhart D., Geoffrey E., Williams R.J., Learning internal representations by error propagation. Parallel distributed processing: explorations in the microstructure of cognition, Volume 1: Foundations. MIT Press; MA, USA, 1986.

[18] Demuth H., Beale M., Neural Network Toolbox for Use with MATLAB, User's Guide Version 4. The MathWorks, Natick, MA, USA, 2002.

[19] Wasserman P., Schwartz T., Neural networks. II. What are they and why is everybody so interested in them now?. IEEE Expert 3(1), 10–15, 1988.

[20] Sanchez E.N., Alanis A.Y., Loukianov A.G., Discrete-Time High Order Neural Control Trained with Kalman Filtering. Berlin, Germany: Springer-Verlag; 2008.

[21] May O., Ali B., Flota M., Ordoñez E.E., Ricalde L., Quijano R., Vega A.E., Thermal efficiency prediction of a solar low enthalpy steam generating plant employing artificial neural networks communications in computer and information science – Volume 597. In: Anabel Martin-Gonzalez, A., Uc-Cetina, V., editors. Intelligent Computing Systems – First International Symposium, ISICS 2016, Mérida, México, March 16–18, 2016, Proceedings; 2016.